Recent Progress in Mathematical Psychology

Psychophysics, Knowledge, Representation, Cognition, and Measurement

SCIENTIFIC PSYCHOLOGY SERIES

Stephen W. Link and James T. Townsend, Series Editors

MONOGRAPHS

William R. Uttal • Toward a New Behaviorism: The Case Against Perceptual Reductionism

Gordon M. Redding and Benjamin Wallace • Adaptive Spatial Alignment

John C. Baird • Sensation and Judgment: Complementarity Theory of Psychophysics

John A. Swets • Signal Detection Theory and ROC Analysis in Psychology and Diagnostics: Collected Papers

William R. Uttal • The Swimmer: An Integrated Computational Model of a Perceptual–Motor System

Stephen W. Link • The Wave Theory of Difference and Similarity

EDITED VOLUMES

Cornelia E. Dowling, Fred S. Roberts, and Peter Theuns • Recent Progress in Mathematical Psychology

Jonathan Grainger and Arthur Jacobs • Localist Connectionist Approaches to Human Cognition

F. Gregory Ashby • Multidimensional Models of Perception and Cognition

Hans-Georg Geissler, Stephen W. Link, and James T. Townsend • Cognition, Information Processing, and Psychophysics: Basic Issues

Recent Progress in Mathematical Psychology

Psychophysics, Knowledge, Representation, Cognition, and Measurement

Edited by

Cornelia E. Dowling
Technische Universität Carolo-Wilhelmina

Fred S. Roberts
Rutgers University

Peter Theuns
Vrije Universiteit Brussel

LEA LAWRENCE ERLBAUM ASSOCIATES, PUBLISHERS
1998 Mahwah, New Jersey   London

Lawrence Erlbaum Associates, Inc., Publishers
10 Industrial Avenue
Mahwah, NJ 07430

Cover design by Kathryn Houghtaling Lacey

Library of Congress Cataloging-in-Publication Data

Recent progress in mathematical psychology / edited
by Cornelia E. Dowling, Fred S. Roberts, Peter Theuns
      p.   cm.
    Chiefly papers originally presented at the July
1992 meeting of the European Psychology Group
in Brussels.
    Includes bibliographical references and index.
    ISBN 0-8058-1975-4 (hardcover : alk. paper)
    1.   Psychology—Mathematical models—Con-
gresses. 2. Psychometrics—Congresses. I. Dowling, Cornelia E. II. Roberts, Fred S. III. Theuns,
Peter
    BF39. R35 1998
    150'.1'51—dc21   97–31138
                                     CIP

Books published by Lawrence Erlbaum Associates are
printed on acid-free paper, and their bindings are
chosen for strength and durability.

Printed in the United States of America
10 9 8 7 6 5 4 3 2 1

Contents

Preface

Mathematical psychology is an interdisciplinary area of research in which we use methods of mathematics, operations research, and computer science in psychology. Now more than 30 years old, the field has continued to grow rapidly and has taken a life of its own. We have prepared a volume that summarizes recent progress in mathematical psychology as seen by some of the leading figures in the field, as well as some of its leading young researchers.

This volume received its impetus at the July 1992 meeting of the European Mathematical Psychology group in Brussels, a meeting at which many of the papers in the book were originally presented. The excitement about the field and its new directions led the participants at that meeting to suggest that a volume be prepared. However, the resulting book is not just conference proceedings; after the meeting in Brussels, the editors decided that a broader pool of contributions than could be taken from the meeting itself would enhance the volume, making it broader in scope, and of interest to a wider audience than simply a proceedings volume. Hence, we solicited papers from major figures in mathematical psychology, and were delighted at the response.

When, in 1971, a first meeting of the European "Mathematical Psychologists" was held in Paris, none of the participants may have realized that they would be the start of a long tradition. Nor may Eric Degreef and Jean Van Buggenhaut have realized that their book, *Trends in Mathematical Psychology* (Degreef & Van Buggenhaut, 1984) would only be the first in a sequence of which this present volume is the sixth. Other predecessor volumes arising from the meetings of the European Mathematical Psychology Group are by Roskam and Suck (1987), Roskam (1989), Doignon and Falmagne (1991) and Fisher and Laming (1994). We believe that this volume is a timely one because of growing interest in the field and the major developments that have taken place since the latter two volumes appeared.

Since the late 1950s, when several researchers in different fields, showing an interest in applying mathematical reasoning in psychology, began interacting through informal discussions, preprints, and seminars, a great deal has changed. Indeed, mathematical psychology has become a self-standing field, and one that, at least in the United States, has developed a thriving professional society (the Society for Mathematical Psychology) with a renowned journal. In Europe, interactions among mathematical psychologists remain informal, much like they were in the early 1970s. In 1971, the European Mathematical Psychology Group (EMPG) came into being as an informal group of scientists from various fields with common interests, methods, and approaches. Throughout the years, this group has grown, but never lost its informal nature. Now, every year a meeting of the group is organized, rotating from city to city in Europe. It was at the 23rd meeting of the EMPG in Brussels, organized by one of the editors of the volume, that the participants agreed that an edited volume should result and the editors were found among the participants. Subsequent meetings in Moscow in 1993, Madrid in 1994, Regensburg in 1995, Padua in 1996, and Nijmegen in 1997 have served to continue and spread the interest in both the field in general and this volume in particular.

In order to make sure that chapters in this volume were of high quality, we sent each submission to at least one referee. The referees were asked not only to judge if a chapter could be accepted, but also to help the author(s) make his or her contributions successful ones by making concrete suggestions. After revisions were made, the chapter was sent to the same or another referee, and sometimes several rounds of revisions were required. We are convinced that this interactive approach among authors, referees, and editors has resulted not only in a volume of extremely high quality, but also one with interesting contributions that, especially in the case of less experienced authors, might have failed to make it through the normal refereeing procedures employed by journals. Unhappily, it must be said that the editors succeeded only partly in developing all the submitted manuscripts into publishable chapters. In particular, we are sorry that this approach has not allowed us to include chapters from authors in Eastern Europe. Based on our experience in organizing an EMPG meeting and co-editing this volume, we feel that, in the future, more significant and systematic support of researchers from Eastern Europe will be needed if we are to share in the interesting research results from scientists from that part of the world.

Sixteen chapters made it through our refereeing process. These chapters naturally fell into a variety of areas that reflect many of the most important current directions of research in mathematical psychology. The chapters cover topics in measurement, decision and choice, psychophysics and psychometrics, knowledge representation, learning models, and cognitive modeling. Some of the major new ideas included in this volume are important new applications of concepts of measurement theory to social phenomena; surprising results in nonlinear utility theory; new directions in the theory of color discrimination; applications of boolean methods in the theory of knowledge spaces; applications of neural net ideas to concept learning; new results in inhibition theory; and new concepts about paired associate learning.

This volume has three chapters on measurement, decision, and choice. Much of psychology is concerned with decision and choice and the interest in this topic has turned out to be readily amenable to mathematical analysis using concepts such as lotteries, utility functions, subjective probabilities, and expected utilities. Peter Fishburn's chapter, "Utility of Wealth in Nonlinear Utility Theory," deals with a problem of great historical importance, the attempt to explain why some people make risky decisions and opt for choices with expected returns less than those of alternative choices. This problem is investigated through a widely studied notion in utility theory, that of a lottery on wealth w, and specifically a von Neumann–Morgenstern utility-of-wealth function $v(w)$. The author is concerned with the effect of special preference axioms for lotteries on the function $v(w)$. For instance, under the axiom that indifference between lotteries is preserved when a constant is added to all outcomes, $v(w)$ turns out to be either linear in w or a power function. In this chapter, related results are obtained for the weighted linear and the skew-symmetric bilinear generalizations of linear utility. Nonlinear utility representations are also considered, and two special axioms that are consistent with such representations are considered.

Traditionally, the theory of measurement has had many of its primary applications in the areas of decision making and psychophysics. In this volume, two of the chapters apply concepts of measurement in less traditional directions, by studying social phenomena such as modernism and social role. The contribution "Structuring Complex Concepts" by Rudi Janssens deals with the measurement of complex concepts that are used to describe a variety of such social phenomena. The author's approach adopts Boolean analysis of co-occurrence data in order to obtain a graphical representation that describes an order relation on the indicators utilized to measure the concept. The approach is compared to more classical deterministic and probabilistic methods, and is illustrated by an example dealing with data on the concept of "modernism" as observed in a migrant population. The author speculates about the use of similar methods to understand hard-to-measure concepts such as the attitude-related concepts of religiosity, traditionalism, and political participation.

In "Role Assignments and Indifference Graphs," Fred S. Roberts also studies the use of measurement-theoretical methods to understand social phenomena, in particular, the idea of social role. He studies a model of social role called the role assignment or role coloring that was introduced by Everett and Borgatti to formalize the idea that individuals with the same role will relate in the same way to other individuals playing counterpart roles. The chapter also studies the indifference graph model, which has a variety of applications in psychology, in particular in psychophysics, utility, matching experiments, and in developmental psychology. Indifference graphs give a model where the roles define more than a nominal scale and it makes sense to ask if two roles are close. This chapter explores the role assignment model and studies which situations satisfying the indifference graph model also satisfy the role assignment model. Motivated by the indifference graph model, the paper also introduces a modified role assignment model.

The origin of what we call mathematical psychology was closely tied to psychophysics. We include four chapters on psychophysics and psychometrics here. Tarow Indow's paper "Parallel Shift of Judgment-Characteristic Curve According to the Context in Cutaneous and Color Discriminations" is concerned with intensity discrimination in an experimental situation. The author develops a statistical model. Specifically, intensity discrimination thresholds of pressure were measured by the method of constant stimuli, using a standard stimulus s_0 applied to the right middle finger and a comparison stimulus s applied to the left middle finger. When sigmoid curves on $\log s$ and $P(\log s)$ were obtained for the judgments "$s > s_0$" and "$s < s_0$," these had the same slope, and when the distance between pressures was increased, $P(\log s)$ shifted, keeping the slope constant, with an increase in the interval of uncertainty. Just noticeable differences in various directions from s_0 in a color space form an ellipsoid, and the size of this ellipsoid changed according to the mode of appearance of the color, although its form and orientation remained the same. The statistical model proposed in the chapter postulates a latent variable and hypothesizes that the slope of the sigmoid is determined by the fluctuations of this variable, having its origin in the peripheral process. In contrast to some of the more abstract chapters in this volume, this chapter shows a direct practical application of the mathematical methods in psychology.

Gert Storms contributes a chapter on psychophysics entitled "A Maximum Likelihood Model for Psychophysical Data and Response Times." He introduces a model for the simultaneous scaling of repeated pairwise psychophysical or preference judgments. An algorithm for data analysis according to the model is presented. The model is validated with a psychophysical experiment and a simulation study. The model is found to provide good estimates of the psychophysical or preference data. This chapter provides an example of the use of mathematical modeling techniques to cast light on experimental results, and on the interplay between theory and experiment.

A great deal of research in psychophysics and psychometrics is concerned with reaction times. The chapter "Inhibition Theory and the Concept of Perseveration," by A.H.G.S. van der Ven, deals with this topic. According to inhibition theory, any mental act is considered as a continuous flow of alternating periods of attention and distraction. In this chapter, each individual reaction time is modeled as the sum of a series of alternating real working times and distraction times. The author is concerned with the perseveration hypothesis that assumes that reaction times, in overlearned prolonged work, show an increase at the beginning of the task due to an initially lower inhibition in subjects that is explained by the nonwork state previous to the task. The author describes an experiment designed to test the perseveration hypothesis by presenting both easy tasks (involving adding three single-digit numbers) and difficult tasks (involving adding six such numbers).

A fourth chapter on psychophysics is "A Formal Approach to Color Constancy: The Recovery of Surface and Light Source Spectral Properties Using Bilinear Models," by Michael D'Zmura and Geoffrey Iverson. This chapter is concerned with the longstanding problem of color-constancy in color vision. This is the problem of explaining the stability of surface color appearance under changing illumination. Specifically, the authors are concerned with determining the circumstances under which recovery of spectral properties is possible using bilinear models. They describe numerical and analytical methods for determining whether particular models relate visual data uniquely to light and surface spectral properties. The chapter is concerned with algorithms for recovering the spectral properties of both lights and surfaces. The authors discuss two-stage recovery algorithms in which the spectral properties of surfaces are recovered first and then used to recover these properties of light sources, or vice versa, and then one-stage recovery algorithms that recover the spectral properties of both light sources and surfaces simultaneously.

The set of all notions mastered by an individual about a specific topic is said to form the knowledge state of that individual. A knowledge state in turn is an element of a knowledge space, the set of knowledge states conceivable. Starting with the work of Doignon and Falmagne (1985), the theory of knowledge spaces has been developed to help us understand how students progress along their individual learning paths, and to develop methods for assessing the state of an individual's knowledge about a particular topic. We have four chapters in this volume on this subject. The paper by Cornelia Dowling and Cord Hockemeyer, "Computing the Intersection of Knowledge Spaces Using Only Their Bases," is concerned with the assessment of students' knowledge by using an adaptive procedure. Such a procedure uses a large pool of items from the field of knowledge being considered. Each student is presented some questions from the large item pool, and, using previous answers, questions are adapted to the student's individual knowledge. In using such a procedure, one makes heavy use of prerequisite relations between the items. These relationships are obtained by querying different experts. Because these experts' opinions differ, one approach is to use in a knowledge space only prerequisite relationships between items that a majority of experts feel should be included. The authors present an algorithm to compute these relationships. Specifically, given the bases of a number of knowledge spaces, the algorithm determines the basis of a knowledge space that is the intersection of these two spaces. The algorithm is then used in the problem of determining the knowledge space that represents the prerequisite relationships in which m out of n experts agree.

Jean-Claude Falmagne and Jean-Paul Doignon contribute to the theory of knowledge spaces in their chapter "Meshing Knowledge Structures." They are motivated by the need to design efficient procedures for the assessment of knowledge, that is, uncovering the actual knowledge state of an individual, while testing only a small subset of items. They define the knowledge structure for a given population and topic to be the collection of all knowledge states conceivable. Statistical methods for the assessment of knowledge are often useful only in situations where the number of items is much smaller than the actual size of the set of the items of interest. Hence, Falmagne and Doignon note that it is useful to consider how to build bigger, more comprehensive knowledge structures by combining such structures that only cover a limited part of a domain. In their technical chapter, they explore these kinds of combinations. In particular, they study the extent to which combinatorial properties are transferred from the parts to the whole.

Although much of the literature of knowledge spaces is deterministic in its approach, Kamakshi Lakshminarayan and Frank Gilson study a stochastic knowledge structure introduced by Falmagne (1989). In their chapter "An Application of a Stochastic Knowledge Structure Model," they study data previously analyzed using the normal ogive model, a model intended to model performance on items measuring complex, continuously distributed abilities along one latent ability dimension. The chapter examines both the model and its fit to the data. The authors show that the performance of the stochastic knowledge structure model is comparable to that of the normal ogive model.

Results in Boolean analysis can be applied in the field of knowledge spaces, and vice versa. Our final chapter on knowledge spaces, "Building a Knowledge Space Via Boolean Analysis of Co-Occurrence Data," by Peter Theuns, introduces a method for data analysis that results in a well-graded knowledge space. The introduced method is presented as a specific dichotomization method for Boolean analysis of co-occurrence data. The method is applicable to large data sets, and an example based on a large data set is used to illustrate the method.

Models of learning and information processing have been some of the central objects of study in mathematical psychology, and have a long history in the subject. In this volume, we have two chapters on learning models. Jeffrey N. Rouder and William H. Batchelder, in their chapter "Multinomial Models for Measuring Storage and Retrieval Processes in Paired Associate Learning," are concerned with memory research. They define and analyze a new family of multinomial processing tree models that deal with two aspects of paired associate learning, the storage and retrieval processes. The models are concerned with assessing the relative contributions of these two processes and are developed in the context of successive free recall tasks and cued recall tasks. The chapter places a major emphasis on issues of statistical inference and develops expressions for maximum likelihood estimators for several of the models. The authors discuss issues dealing with sparse categories and individual differences on correlated memory tests, analyze some well-known bizarre imagery data, and discuss the traditional practice of inferring storage and retrieval effects directly from performance data.

The chapter by Patrick Suppes and Lin Liang, "Concept Learning Rates and Transfer Performance of Several Multivariate Neural Network Models" is motivated partly by the desire to develop efficient and powerful methods of concept learning to use in the study of machine learning of natural language. The authors compare several learning models on six sets of data. They include data on species of Iris and species of beetles, on Swiss bank notes, on learning the "exclusive or" sentential connective, and learning identity and equipollence of sets. Six alternative learning models are presented and applied to the data sets. The models are all essentially neural network models for learning concepts, that is, they start with input vectors of feature data and end with classification responses as outputs. The discussion of so many models pinpoints the fact that the field is still not far enough along, but also the authors' view that there is no one model that will be "right" for all situations.

Processing of cognitive data is both a subject in the theory of learning and a subject in its own right that has been increasingly intriguing researchers in mathematical psychology. We present three chapters on cognitive modeling in this volume. When an observer sees a visual scene filled with a variety of perceptual objects, he or she makes a perceptual judgment and then some response. Certain judgments are carried out rather quickly and automatically, whereas others may require more or less attention. The chapter "Comparing Parallel and Sequential Multinomial Models of Letter Identification," by Vincent Brown, considers the concept of attention (also discussed in the chapter by van der Ven) and its role in the selection of a subset of sensory input for further processing. The chapter concentrates on multinomial models for such processing of sensory input. The author points out that the use of multinomial models has been widespread in such other fields as population biology, but that such models have not been as widely used in psychology. He studies an experimental situation in which observers are asked to identify the number and location of target letters in a two-item display in which display duration, luminance, and physical separation of the stimuli are varied. The chapter fits four multinomial models to the response data, two models of a parallel processing type and two of a sequential processing type, and concludes that a "Parallel Gestalt Model" is best fitting.

The chapter by Hubert Feger and Ulrich von Hecker, "Reciprocity as an Interaction Principle," deals with the effect of communication on the development of structure in a group. The idea is to understand the effect of the contact between two persons created by communication; the information content of the messages being communicated is not important. The starting point for the paper is a 1966 experiment of Flament and Apfelbaum, in which participants pass slips of paper with either a "0" or a "+" on them, and are evaluated at the end with the number of "+" messages in their possession. Flament and Apfelbaum claimed that the distribution (in terms of who gets what message) of "+" messages by a participant at any one round of the experiment varied proportionately with the distribution (in terms of who sent what message) of "+" messages received by them. Feger and von Hecker report on an attempt to replicate this experiment and to model the results. The model uses two principles, "immediate proportional reciprocity" (the Flament–Apfelbaum concept) and the "debtor principle," which additionally takes into account the resources provided by the sender to any position during the previous round or until the present. The authors test whether a group member uses one of these principles.

A fundamental theme in cognitive science is a comparison between the human brain and a computer. The paper "Additive Effects of Factors on Reaction Time and Evoked Potentials in Continuous Flow Models," by Richard Schweikert and Jeffrey Mounts, is motivated by the general goal of deciding which kind of computer, analog or digital, is the better model for the human mind. Specifically, it is motivated by the traditional models of Donders (1969) and Sternberg (1969), who conceive of the mental processing of a stimulus as a series of stages, each beginning with a discrete event such as the presentation of a stimulus. The alternative approach is a continuous flow model (such as in Eriksen & Schultz, 1977), in which we think of a stimulus as being presented, signals streaming through the system and the process continuing until the force in certain muscles overcomes an opposing force. The authors concentrate on the notion of additive effects, which arises in Sternberg's additive factor method and is based on the view that if two experimental factors selectively influence two different discrete serial stages, then their combined effect on response time will be the sum of their separate effects. This chapter concentrates on analyzing additive effects in continuous flow models, specifically emphasizing two dependent variables, response times, and evoked potentials. The authors discuss circumstances under which factors selectively influencing processes in such continuous flow models would have additive effects.

ACKNOWLEDGMENTS

We thank Sarah Roberts and Reuben Settergren for their extensive and extremely helpful editorial assistance. We gratefully thank all authors for their cooperation and support of this volume and the referees for their invaluable help in making the volume become what it is. We thank the series editors, Steve Link and Jim Townsend, for their help and support. We also thank Hervé Abdi, M. J. J. M. Candel, Hans Colonius, Mathieu Koppen, A. A. J. Marley, Alice O'Toole, Reinhard Suck, Jim Townsend, and Dominique Valentin for their help with earlier versions of this volume, and Hans Colonius and Hervé Moulin for their assistance in resolving problems of length. Fred Roberts thanks the U.S. National Science Foundation for its support under SES-9211492 and SBR-9709134 to Rutgers University. The editors wish to acknowledge the influence of the European Mathematical Psychology Group of Eddy Ruskam, editor of two predecessor volumes, who unfortunately passed away before the 1997 EMPG meeting was held, once more, at his home university in Nijmegen. We hope that this book will help mathematical psychology to continue its rapid development throughout the world.

Cornelia E. Dowling
Fred S. Roberts
Peter Theuns

REFERENCES

Degreef, E., & Van Buggenhaut, J. (1984). *Trends in mathematical psychology*. Amsterdam: Elsevier.

Doignon, J. -P., & Falmagne, J. -CL. (1985). Spaces for the assessment of knowledge. *International Journal of Man–Machine Studies, 23*, 175–196.

Doignon, J. -P., & Falmagne, J. -Cl. (1991). *Mathematical psychology: Current developments*. New York: Springer–Verlag.

Donders, F. C. (Trans.) (1969). On the speed of mental processes. In W. G. Koster (Ed.), *Attention and performance II* (pp. 412–431). Amsterdam: Elsevier. (Original work published 1868)

Eriksen, C. W., & Schultz, D. W. (1977). Information processing in visual search: A continuous flow conception and experimental results. *Perception & Psychophysics, 25*, 249–263.

Falmagne, J. -Cl. (1989). A latent trait theory via a stochastic learning theory for a knowledge space. *Psychometrika, 54*, 283–303.

Fischer, G. H., & Laming, D. (1994). *Contributions to mathematical psychology, psychometrics, and methodology*. New York: Springer–Verlag.

Roskam, E. E. (1989). *Mathematical psychology in progress*. Berlin: Springer–Verlag.

Roskam, E. E. & Suck, R. (1987). *Progress in mathematical psychology*. Amsterdam: North-Holland.

Sternberg, S. (1969). The discovery of processing stages: Extensions of Donders' method. In W. G. Koster (Ed.), *Attention and performance II* (pp. 276–315). Amsterdam: Elsevier.

Part I

Measurement, Decision, and Choice

Utility of Wealth in Nonlinear Utility Theory

Peter Fishburn
AT&T Labs–Research

More than 250 years ago, Daniel Bernoulli and Gabriel Cramer (Bernoulli, 1738/1954) proposed specific forms for a person's utility function U on wealth $x \geq 0$ to explain why prudent individuals often make risky decisions whose expected returns are less than the expected returns of other available choices. Bernoulli argued that the rate of increase in $U(x)$ is inversely proportional to the amount x, and hence, that U is a logarithmic function of wealth. Cramer chose $U(x) = \sqrt{x}$, which, like $U(x) = \log x$, says that utility of wealth increases at a decreasing rate. Since their era, and especially since the axiomatization of expected utility in von Neumann and Morgenstern (1944), a vast literature has evolved on the psychological measurement and economic implications of people's utility for wealth and of their utility for gains and losses from a current position. Various approaches and further references to the general topic are provided by Allais (1953/1979), Conlisk (1993), Edwards (1954), Fishburn (1988), Fishburn and Kochenberger (1979), Friedman and Savage (1948), Galanter (1962), Grayson (1960), Kahneman and Tversky (1979), MacCrimmon and Larsson (1979), Machina (1982), Mosteller and Nogee (1951), Robson (1992), Schoemaker (1980), Slovic and Lichtenstein (1983), and Swalm (1966). We concentrate here on the functional-forms theme initiated by Bernoulli and Cramer that gained new impetus from the theory of von Neumann and Morgenstern.

About 40 years ago, J. Pfanzagl (1959) proved that if a continuous and increasing von Neumann–Morgenstern utility function v on $\mathbb{R}^+ = [0, \infty)$

satisfies a certain consistency condition, then, up to positive affine rescaling, v has one of three forms:

$$v(x) = \begin{cases} x \\ k^x, & k > 1 \\ -k^x, & 0 < k < 1 \end{cases} \tag{1}$$

A few years earlier, Kemeny and Thompson (1957) derived the same linear and exponential forms from a similar condition for an individual's utility function in an n-person game, which says that optimal mixed strategies are unaffected by the addition of a constant sum to all payoffs. The forms in Equation 1 and other functional forms for a utility-of-wealth function v have subsequently been identified with special axioms for preference between lotteries, or with special conditions on risk attitudes, by Arrow (1974), Bell (1986, 1988, 1991), Brockett and Golden (1987), Farquhar and Nakamura (1987), Harvey (1981), Pratt (1964), Raiffa (1968), and Rothblum (1975), among others.

The present chapter extends their work into the realm of nonlinear utility. It focuses on two generalizations of the von Neumann–Morgenstern linear utility theory and two elementary axioms, one of which is Pfanzagl's consistency axiom. Special functional forms for other nonlinear generalizations of the von Neumann–Morgenstern theory are considered in an important companion paper by Miyamoto and Wakker (1993).

The generalizations examined in the present chapter are the weighted linear theory introduced in Chew and MacCrimmon (1979) and the skew-symmetric bilinear theory originally discussed in Kreweras (1961). We defer their definitions to the next section but note here that their differentiating feature involves transitive indifference. The skew-symmetric bilinear theory does not assume that the indifference relation ~ on the set of lotteries is transitive. Transitive indifference is assumed by the weighted linear theory. Otherwise, the two are identical (Fishburn, 1983, pp. 295, 300). Our two elementary axioms are preceded by a few definitions.

Let P denote the set of all finite-support probability distributions on R^+. Members of P are *lotteries*. We denote by (p, λ, q) the $\lambda/(1 - \lambda)$ convex combination of lotteries p and q: with $0 \leq \lambda \leq 1$,

$$(p, \lambda, q)(x) = \lambda p(x) + (1 - \lambda) q(x) \quad \text{for all } x \geq 0$$

When $p(x) = q(y) = 1$, we write (p, λ, q) as (x, λ, y). The convolution of p and the lottery that assigns probability 1 to x is denoted by $p * x$, so

$$(p * x)(y + x) = p(y) \quad \text{for all } y \geq 0$$

It is assumed throughout that $>$ is an asymmetric ($p > q \Rightarrow$ not $(q > p)$) binary relation on P. We view $>$ as an individual's strict preference relation on lotteries over wealth. The associated indifference relation $\sim$ on P is defined by

$$p \sim q \text{ if neither } p > q \text{ nor } q > p$$

It follows that $\sim$ is reflexive ($p \sim p$) and symmetric ($p \sim q \Rightarrow q \sim p$). When $x \geq 0$ appears on a side of $>$ or $\sim$, such as $x > q$ or $x > y$, it denotes the lottery that assigns probability 1 to itself. It will be assumed that more wealth is preferred to less:

$$x > y \Rightarrow x > y \text{ for all } x,y \geq 0$$

Our two elementary axioms are

A1. For all $x,y,z \geq 0$, $(x,\frac{1}{2},y + z) \sim (x + y,\frac{1}{2},z)$.

A2. For all $p \in P$ and $x,y \geq 0$, $p \sim y \Rightarrow p * x \sim y + x$.

A1 says that indifference holds between any two 50–50 lotteries with equal expected wealths. This axiom is very strong and would seem plausible only when x,y, and z are comparatively large. In the von Neumann–Morgenstern theory, A1 implies risk neutrality with $v(x) = ax + b$, $a > 0$. It implies neither of these things in our nonlinear theories and is even consistent with cyclic preferences, such as $p > q > r > p$, in the skew-symmetric bilinear theory.

A2 is Pfanzagl's consistency axiom. It says that indifference between a lottery and its certainty equivalent is preserved when x is added to all outcomes. This seems substantially more realistic than A1. As mentioned earlier, continuity and A2 imply Equation 1 in the von Neumann–Morgenstern linear theory. Their implications for our nonlinear theories are described in the next section.

We consider also the following special case of A1:

B1. For all $x,y \geq 0$, $\frac{x+y}{2} \sim (x,\frac{1}{2},y)$.

Although B1 is shown to be strictly weaker than A1, it implies A1 when $\sim$ is transitive.

Lemma 1. If $\sim$ is transitive then B1 $\Rightarrow$ A1.

Proof. By B1, $(x,\frac{1}{2},y + z) \sim (x+y+z)/2$ and $(x+y+z)/2 \sim (x + y,\frac{1}{2},z)$. If $\sim$ is transitive then $(x,\frac{1}{2},y + z) \sim (x + y,\frac{1}{2},z)$, as in A1.

The next section defines the utility representations for $(P,>)$ that we analyze under A1 and A2. It then notes the effects of our special axioms

TABLE 1.1
Functional Forms

Model	A1 (SSB) or B1	A2
Linear	$v(x) = x$	$v(x) = \begin{cases} x \\ \beta^x, \ \beta > 1 \\ -\beta^x, \ 0 < \beta < 1 \end{cases}$
Weighted linear	$\varphi(x,y) = u(x - y), \ x \geq y;$ $u(x) = \begin{cases} x \\ (t + \sqrt{t^2 - 1})^x - (t - \sqrt{t^2 - 1})^x : t > 1 \end{cases}$	$\varphi(x,y) = u(x - y)\beta^y, \ x \geq y;$ $u(x) = \begin{cases} x\beta^{\frac{x-1}{2}} \\ (t + \sqrt{t^2 - \beta})^x - (t - \sqrt{t^2 - \beta})^x : t > \sqrt{\beta} \end{cases}$
SSB	$\varphi(x,y) = \varphi(x - y,0), \ x \geq y$	$\varphi(x,y) = \varphi(x - y,0) \ \beta^y, \ x \geq y$

on the representations and summarizes the results in Table 1.1. The section concludes with the proof of a theorem that addresses the role of B1 in the skew-symmetric bilinear model. The following section proves our main theorem for A1 and A2 in that model, and the final section proves the special-effects theorem for the weighted linear case. Several of the sufficiency proofs use theorems for functional equations that are described in Aczél (1966).

This chapter is intended as an initial probe into the role of special axioms in nonlinear utility theories. Because its nonlinear representations and simplifying axioms cover only a fraction of the possibilities, it leaves a great deal of room for new research. The chapter focuses on technical results in representation theory and says little about the associated subject of risk attitudes. These are explored for nonlinear utility in Fishburn (1984b, 1988), Montesano (1988, 1991), Safra and Zilcha (1988), and Segal and Spivak (1990), among others, but deserve further treatment in the special-axioms setting.

NONLINEAR UTILITY AND SPECIAL FORMS

Our utility representations for $(P, >)$ are based on a function $\varphi \colon P \times P \to \mathbb{R}$ such that, for all $p, q \in P$, $\varphi(p,p) = 0$ and

$$p > q \Leftrightarrow \varphi(p,q) > 0 \tag{2}$$

We define φ on $\mathbb{R}^+ \times \mathbb{R}^+$ by $\varphi(x,y) = \varphi(p,q)$ when $p(x) = q(y) = 1$. The assumption that more wealth is preferred to less says that $\varphi(x,y) > 0$ whenever $x > y$. We say that φ is *continuous* if for all $(x_0, y_0) \in \mathbb{R}^+ \times \mathbb{R}^+$,

$$\lim_{(x,y) \to (x_0, y_0)} \varphi(x,y) = \varphi(x_0, y_0)$$

It will generally be assumed that φ is continuous, but we make no assumptions about differentiability.

The functional φ is *skew symmetric* if

$$\varphi(p,q) + \varphi(q,p) = 0 \quad \text{for all } p,q \in P$$

It is *linear* in its first argument if for all $p,q,r \in P$ and all $0 \leq \lambda \leq 1$,

$$\varphi[(p,\lambda,q),r] = \lambda\varphi(p,r) + (1 - \lambda)\varphi(q,r)$$

Linearity in the second argument is defined analogously and follows from skew symmetry and linearity in the first argument. We say that φ is *bilinear* when it is linear in each argument. By a straightforward induction, bilinearity implies that $\varphi(p,q)$ is the expected value of φ on $\mathbb{R}^+ \times \mathbb{R}^+$ with respect to the product measure $p \times q$:

$$\varphi(p,q) = \sum_x \sum_y p(x)q(y)\varphi(x,y) \tag{3}$$

We say that $(P,>)$ *has an SSB representation* if there exists a skew-symmetric and bilinear $\varphi: P \times P \to \mathbb{R}$ that satisfies Equation 2. Axioms for $(P,>)$ that are necessary and sufficient for an SSB representation are given in Fishburn (1982, 1988), and various features of the representation, including preference cycles, the existence of maximally preferred lotteries in finite sets, and connections to stochastic dominance, are discussed in Fishburn (1984a, 1984b, 1988). When $(P,>)$ has an SSB representation, its representing functional φ is unique up to proportionality transformations. That is, if φ_0 satisfies the representation, then so does φ_1 if and only if there is a constant $c > 0$ such that $\varphi_1(p,q) = c\varphi_0(p,q)$ for all $(p,q) \in P \times P$.

The more general of the nonlinear representations that we consider in connection with A1 and A2 uses an SSB representation. We incorporate the special features mentioned after Equation 2 by saying that $(P,>)$ *has an SSB model* φ if it has an SSB representation with functional φ such that φ is continuous and satisfies $\varphi(x,y) > 0$ whenever $x > y$.

Our other nonlinear representation uses two linear functionals defined on P, where $h: P \to \mathbb{R}$ is *linear* if for all $p,q \in P$ and all $0 \leq \lambda \leq 1$,

$$h(p,\lambda,q) = \lambda h(p) + (1 - \lambda)h(q)$$

We say that $(P,>)$ *has a weighted linear representation* if it has an SSB representation and $\sim$ on P is transitive. Suppose $(P,>)$ has a weighted linear representation with φ an SSB functional that satisfies Equation 2. Then, as shown in Fishburn (1983, 1988), $>$ also is transitive and there exist linear functionals u and ρ on P with $\rho \geq 0$ and ρ strictly positive on the preference interior of $(P,>)$ such that, for all $p,q \in P$,

$$\varphi(p,q) = u(p)\rho(q) - u(q)\rho(p) \tag{4}$$

If ρ is positive everywhere, then $p > q \Leftrightarrow u(p)/\rho(p) > u(q)/\rho(q)$. We define u and ρ on $\mathbb{R}^+$ by $u(x) = u(p)$ and $\rho(x) = \rho(p)$ when $p(x) = 1$. When Equations 2, 3, and 4 are combined for the weighted linear case, we have

$$p > q \Leftrightarrow \left[\sum_x p(x)u(x)\right]\left[\sum_y q(y)\rho(y)\right] > \left[\sum_x q(x)u(x)\right]\left[\sum_y p(y)\rho(y)\right]$$

One further assumption and two scaling conventions can be made for the weighted linear theory in our wealth setting. As shown in Fishburn (1983, appendix; 1988, pp. 124–125), ρ might vanish at an extreme point of $(P,\succ)$, that is, at $x = 0$. However, this is a rather anomalous possibility and we exclude it by assuming that ρ is positive everywhere. Then, without loss of generality, we fix $\rho(0) = 1$. The admissible transformations for the weighted linear representation (Fishburn, 1988, p. 132) allow the original u, say u_0, to be replaced by u_1 defined by $u_1(p) = u_0(p) - [u_0(0)/\rho(0)]\rho(p)$, so we do this to get $u = u_1$ with $u(0) = 0$. Thus, our scaling conventions are $\rho(0) = 1$ and $u(0) = 0$.

The preceding assumptions and conventions for the weighted linear case are summarized by saying that $(P,\succ)$ *has a weighted linear model* (u,ρ) if there are linear functionals u and ρ on P with $\rho > 0$, $(u(0),\rho(0)) = (0,1)$, $p > q \Leftrightarrow u(p)/\rho(p) > u(q)/\rho(q)$ for all $p,q \in P$, $u(x)/\rho(x) > u(y)/\rho(y)$ whenever $x > y$, and, for all $(x_0,y_0) \in \mathbb{R}^+ \times \mathbb{R}^+$,

$$\lim_{(x,y) \to (x_0,y_0)} [u(x)\rho(y) - u(y)\rho(x)] = u(x_0)\rho(y_0) - u(y_0)\rho(x_0)$$

The admissible transformations for u and ρ thus restricted are $u' = au$ and $\rho' = cu + \rho$ with $a > 0$ and $cu(x) + \rho(x) > 0$ for all $x \geq 0$. It is to be understood in this case that $\varphi(p,q) = u(p)\rho(q) - u(q)\rho(p)$, so the preceding continuity condition is the same as continuity for φ.

For completeness we say that $(P,\succ)$ *has a linear* (von Neumann–Morgenstern) *model* v if there is a linear functional v on P such that for all $p,q \in P$,

$$p > q \Leftrightarrow v(p) > v(q)$$

and, with $v(x) = v(p)$ when $p(x) = 1$, v on $\mathbb{R}^+$ is continuous and increasing. Traditional axioms for the linear representation appear in many places, including Herstein and Milnor (1953) and Fishburn (1970, 1988). It arises from the SSB representation when φ can be decomposed as $\varphi(p,q) = v(p) - v(q)$, which is possible if and only if $p \sim q \Rightarrow (p,\frac{1}{2},r) \sim (q,\frac{1}{2},r)$, for all $p,q,r \in P$, see Fishburn (1988, p. 16). It also is the special case of the weighted linear representation in which ρ can be defined as a positive constant. In the linear model, v is unique up to positive affine transformations of the form $v' = av + b$ with $a > 0$.

Table 1.1 summarizes the effects of our special axioms on the preceding three models. When $\varphi(x,y)$ is specified only for $x \geq y$, $\varphi(x,y)$ for $x < y$ is obtained from it by skew symmetry. In the weighted linear case we some-times omit the leading coefficient specified from our scaling, but it is made explicit in Theorem 2. In the weighted linear and SSB cases, $t = u(2)/[2u(1)]$ and $\beta = \varphi(2,1)/\varphi(1,0)$.

Formal statements of the results with interspersed commentary follow.

Theorem 1. Suppose $(P,\succ)$ has a linear model v. Then B1 holds if and only if $v(x) = ax + b$ for some $a,b \in \mathbb{R}$ with $a > 0$. A2 holds if and only if there exists $\beta > 0$ and $a,b \in \mathbb{R}$ with $a > 0$ such that, for all $x \geq 0$,

$$\begin{aligned}
v(x) &= ax + b & &\text{if } \beta = 1 \\
v(x) &= a\beta^x + b & &\text{if } \beta > 1 \\
v(x) &= -a\beta^x + b & &\text{if } 0 < \beta < 1
\end{aligned}$$

Part B1 follows easily from continuity, from the fact that v is increasing and the fact that B1 implies

$$v\left(\frac{x+y}{2}\right) = \frac{v(x) + v(y)}{2}$$

Part A2 is proved in Pfanzagl (1959). We show also how v for A2 in Theorem 1 follows from the next theorem, where

$$t = \frac{u(2)}{2u(1)} \qquad \beta = \frac{\varphi(2,1)}{\varphi(1,0)}$$

Theorem 2. Suppose $(P,\succ)$ has a weighted linear model (u,ρ). Then B1 holds if and only if

(a₁) $\varphi(x,y) = u(x - y)$ for all $x \geq y \geq 0$;
(b₁) either $t = 1$ and $u(x) = u(1)x$ for all $x \geq 0$, or $t > 1$ and

$$u(x) = \frac{u(1)}{2\sqrt{t^2 - 1}}[(t + \sqrt{t^2 - 1})^x - (t - \sqrt{t^2 - 1})^x] \text{ for all } x \geq 0$$

A2 holds if and only if

(a₂) $\varphi(x,y) = u(x - y)\beta^y$ for all $x \geq y \geq 0$;
(b₂) either $t = \sqrt{\beta}$ and $u(x) = u(1)x\beta^{(x-1)/2}$ for all $x \geq 0$, or $t > \sqrt{\beta}$ and

$$u(x) = \frac{u(1)}{2\sqrt{t^2 - \beta}} \left[(t + \sqrt{t^2 - \beta})^x - (t - \sqrt{t^2 - \beta})^x \right] \text{ for all } x \geq 0$$

The strengths of B1 and A2 in this case yield descriptions for φ in Theorem 2 that do not specify ρ explicitly. It can be recovered from $u(x)\rho(y) - u(y)\rho(x) = u(x - y)$ for B1 or $u(x)\rho(y) - u(y)\rho(x) = u(x - y)\beta^y$ for A2 with u extended negatively by $u(-x) = -u(x)$. With $y = 1$ we get $\rho(x) = [u(x)\rho(1) - u(x - 1)]/u(1)$ for B1 or $\rho(x) = [u(x)\rho(1) - u(x - 1)\beta]/u(1)$ for A2. In the first case, we take $\rho(1) = 1$, and in the second $\rho(1) = \beta$ to ensure that $\rho > 0$.

Pfanzagl's A2 result in Theorem 1 follows from the A2 result of Theorem 2 and the linear decomposition $\varphi(x,y) = v(x) - v(y)$. Suppose $u(x) = u(1)x\beta^{(x-1)/2}$ in b_2. Then

$$v(x) - v(y) = u(1)(x - y)\beta^{(x-y-1)/2}\,\beta^y = u(1)(x - y)\beta^{(x+y-1)/2}$$

Set $y = 0$ to obtain $v(x) = v(0) + u(1)x\beta^{(x-1)/2}$. Then

$$v(x) - v(y) = u(1)x\beta^{(x-1)/2} - u(1)y\beta^{(y-1)/2} = u(1)(x - y)\beta^{(x+y-1)/2}$$

This requires $2\sqrt{\beta} - 1 = \beta$ at $(x,y) = (2,1)$, or $(\sqrt{\beta} - 1)^2 = 0$, so $\beta = 1$ and $v(x) = ax + b$. Suppose next that $t > \sqrt{\beta}$ with $u(x)$ given by the last line of Theorem 2. Then, ignoring the leading coefficient of $u(x)$, we have

$$v(x) - v(y) = \beta^y[(t + \alpha)^{x-y} - (t - \alpha)^{x-y}], \qquad \alpha = \sqrt{t^2 - \beta}$$

Set $y = 0$ as before and then take $(x,y) = (2,1)$ to get $\beta = 2t - 1$. Since $\beta > 0$, this requires $t > \frac{1}{2}$. In addition, $\alpha = (t^2 - 2t + 1)^{1/2} = |t - 1|$. If $t > 1$ then $\beta > 1$ and

$$v(x) - v(y) = \beta^y[(2t - 1)^{x-y} - 1^{x-y}] = \beta^x - \beta^y$$

so we can take $v(x) = \beta^x$. If $\frac{1}{2} < t < 1$ then $0 < \beta < 1$ and

$$v(x) - v(y) = \beta^y[1^{x-y} - (2t - 1)^{x-y}] = -\beta^x + \beta^y$$

so here we can take $v(x) = -\beta^x$.

Our next theorem again takes $\beta = \varphi(2,1)/\varphi(1,0)$.

Theorem 3. Suppose $(P,>)$ has an SSB model φ. Then A1 holds if and only if

$$\varphi(x,y) = \varphi(x - y,0) \quad \text{for all } x \geq y \geq 0$$

A2 holds if and only if

$$\varphi(x,y) = \varphi(x - y,0)\beta^y \quad \text{for all } x \geq y \geq 0$$

The strength of A1 is reflected in the dependence of $\varphi(x,y)$ on only the difference between its arguments. When φ is twice differentiable, A1 is equivalent to $\partial^2\varphi(x,y)/(\partial y\partial x) = -\partial^2\varphi(x,y)/\partial x^2$; see Fishburn (1988, p. 156). An example is

$$\varphi(x,y) = 1 - e^{-(x-y)^2 - \sqrt{2}(x-y)} \quad x \geq y$$

This example, among others, shows that $>$ on P can by cyclic, say with $p > q > r > p$ via $\varphi(p,q) > 0$, $\varphi(q,r) > 0$ and $\varphi(r,p) > 0$. Hence, it is not true that $(P,>)$ has a weighted linear representation when it has an SSB representation and A1 holds.

Let

$$f(x) = \varphi(x,0)$$

The hypotheses of Theorem 3, including A1 and A2, do not imply that f is either increasing or nondecreasing. It could increase for small positive x and then oscillate or decrease asymptotically toward 0 as x gets large. Because it is natural to regard $\varphi(x,y)$ for $x > y$ as a surrogate measure of strength of preference for x over y in the lottery context, such behaviors seem anomalous. In fact, they are ruled out when we assume that $(P,>)$ satisfies first-degree stochastic dominance (Fishburn & Vickson, 1978; Levy, 1992). One requirement of first-degree stochastic dominance is

$$(x + \varepsilon,\lambda,y) > (x,\lambda,y) \quad \text{for all } 0 < \lambda \leq 1, \text{ all } x,y \geq 0, \text{ and all } \varepsilon > 0$$

If this holds then $[\lambda/(1 - \lambda)]\varphi(x + \varepsilon,x) + \varphi(x + \varepsilon,y) > \varphi(x,y)$, so $\lambda \downarrow 0$ gives $\varphi(x + \varepsilon,y) \geq \varphi(x,y)$, or $f(x + \varepsilon - y) \geq f(x - y)$ in Theorem 2 when $x \geq y$ and $\varepsilon > 0$.

To consider this further and to note the insufficiency of B1 for the first conclusion of Theorem 3, we define φ as *nondecreasing* if for all $x,y,z \geq 0$,

$$x > y \Rightarrow \varphi(x,z) \geq \varphi(y,z)$$

Suppose $(P,>)$ has an SSB representation and, for all $x,\Delta \geq 0$,

$$\varphi(x + \Delta,x) = \Delta + \min_n \ | \ x - n\Delta|$$

Then φ is continuous and $\varphi(x + \Delta,x) > 0$ when $\Delta > 0$. However, φ is *not* nondecreasing and, because it depends on x as well as Δ, $\varphi(x + \Delta,x) \neq \varphi(\Delta,0)$ for some x and Δ. The nondecreasing violation is crucial to the latter conclusion.

Theorem 4. Suppose $(P,>)$ has an SSB model φ and B1 holds. Then it might not be true that $\varphi(x,y) = \varphi(x - y,0)$ for all $x \geq y \geq 0$. However, if φ is nondecreasing, then $\varphi(x,y) = \varphi(x - y,0)$ for all $x \geq y \geq 0$.

Proof. The first conclusion was proved earlier. We prove the second by contradiction. Assume the hypotheses of the theorem along with φ nondecreasing, but suppose that $\varphi(x,y) = \varphi(x - y,0)$ is not always true. Assume without loss of generality that $\varphi(x + 1,x)$ is not constant in x. Let $g(x) = \varphi(x + 1,x)$. B1 implies that $g(x + 1) = g(x)$ for all $x \geq 0$. Using continuity, let g assume its minimum value on $(0,1)$ at δ_1 and its maximum value on $(0,1)$ at $\delta_0 \neq \delta_1$. Let $a = g(\delta_1)$ and $b = g(\delta_0)$ so $a < b$. By B1 and continuity we can choose $\varepsilon_0 > 0$ so that

$$g(x) > a + \frac{3}{4}(b - a) \qquad \text{for all } x \in \bigcup_{n=1}^{\infty} [n + \delta_0 - \varepsilon_0, n + \delta_0 + \varepsilon_0]$$

It also follows from continuity that there is an $\varepsilon^* > 0$ such that

$$\varphi(1 + \delta_1 + \varepsilon, \delta_1) \leq a + \frac{1}{4}(b - a) \qquad \text{for all } 0 \leq \varepsilon \leq \varepsilon^*$$

Then, by B1,

$$\varphi((n + 1)(1 + \varepsilon) + \delta_1, n(1 + \varepsilon) + \delta_1) \leq a + \frac{1}{4}(b - a)$$

for all $0 \leq \varepsilon \leq \varepsilon^*$ and all $n \in \{0,1,2, \ldots\}$. It follows that if there exist positive integers n and m along with $0 < \varepsilon \leq \varepsilon^*$ such that

$$m + \delta_0 - \varepsilon_0 \leq n(1 + \varepsilon) + \delta_1 \leq m + \delta_0 + \varepsilon_0 \tag{5}$$

then φ is not nondecreasing, because with $x = n(1 + \varepsilon) + \delta_1$ we have $\varphi(x + 1 + \varepsilon, x) \leq a + \frac{1}{4}(b - a) < a + \frac{3}{4}(b - a) \leq \varphi(x + 1,x)$. Take $n \geq 3/\varepsilon^*$. Then

$$\inf_{0<\varepsilon\leq\varepsilon^*} [n(1 + \varepsilon) + \delta_1] = n + \delta_1 < n + \delta_1 + 3 \leq \sup_{0<\varepsilon\leq\varepsilon^*} [n(1 + \varepsilon) + \delta_1]$$

so with $m = n + 1$ there is indeed an ε and n that satisfy Equation 5. Hence we contradict the hypothesis that φ is nondecreasing. It follows that $\varphi(x,y) = \varphi(x - y,0)$ for all $x \geq y \geq 0$.

PROOF OF THEOREM 3

We assume throughout this section that $(P,>)$ has an SSB model φ. Because it is easily seen that A1 is necessary for $\varphi(x,y) = f(x - y)$, and A2 is necessary for $\varphi(x,y) = f(x - y)\beta^y$, we turn to the sufficiency proofs.

Suppose A1 holds. By the B1 specialization of A1, $\varphi(x + 2\Delta, x + \Delta) = \varphi(x + \Delta, x)$ for all $x, \Delta \geq 0$. We apply this iteratively to get

$$\varphi(x + (n + 1)\Delta, x + n\Delta) = \varphi(x + \Delta, x) \quad \text{for all } x, \Delta = 0, \ n = 1, 2, \ldots$$

In the statement of A1 let $y = \Delta$ and $z = x + n\Delta$. Then, by bilinear expansion, $\varphi(x, x + \Delta) + \varphi(x, x + n\Delta) + \varphi(x + (n + 1)\Delta, x + \Delta) + \varphi(x + (n + 1)1, x + n\Delta) = 0$. We use skew symmetry and the preceding result to conclude that

$$\varphi(x + (n + 1)\Delta, x + \Delta) = \varphi(x + n\Delta, x)$$

Fix $\Delta_0 > 0$ and let $\Delta = \Delta_0/n$ in this equation. Then

$$\varphi(x + \Delta_0, x) = \varphi(x + (1 + \tfrac{1}{n})\, \Delta_0, x + \tfrac{1}{n}\Delta_0)$$

Take $x = 0$ here, then $x = \Delta_0/n$, $x = 2\Delta_0/n$, ... to obtain

$$\varphi(\Delta_0, 0) = \varphi(\Delta_0 + \tfrac{1}{n}\Delta_0, \tfrac{1}{n}\Delta_0)$$
$$= \varphi(\Delta_0 + \tfrac{2}{n}\Delta_0, \tfrac{2}{n}\Delta_0)$$
$$= \varphi(\Delta_0 + \tfrac{3}{n}\Delta_0, \tfrac{3}{n}\Delta_0) \ldots$$

It follows that for every $\Delta > 0$ and every positive rational number r, $\varphi(\Delta + r\Delta, r\Delta) = \varphi(\Delta, 0)$. Continuity then yields $\varphi(\Delta + a, a) = \varphi(\Delta, 0)$ for all $a > 0$, or

$$\varphi(x, y) = \varphi(x - y, 0) \quad \text{for all } x \geq y \geq 0$$

Suppose A2 holds. Take $x > y > z \geq 0$. By assumption, $\varphi(x, y) > 0$ and $\varphi(y, z) > 0$. Let $0 < \lambda < 1$ satisfy $\lambda\varphi(x, y) = (1 - \lambda)\varphi(y, z)$. Then $y \sim (x, \lambda, z)$. By A2, $y + \Delta \sim (x + \Delta, \lambda, z + \Delta)$, so $\lambda\varphi(x + \Delta, y + \Delta) = (1 - \lambda)\varphi(y + \Delta, z + \Delta)$. Therefore

$$\frac{\varphi(x, y)}{\varphi(y, z)} = \frac{\varphi(x + \Delta, y + \Delta)}{\varphi(y + \Delta, z + \Delta)} \quad \text{for } \Delta > 0 \qquad (6)$$

It follows from this that

$$\varphi(x, y) = \varphi(x + 1, x)\frac{\varphi(x - y, 0)}{\varphi(x - y + 1, x - y)} \quad x \geq y \geq 0$$

Let $g = \varphi(x + 1, x)$ and $F(\Delta) = \varphi(\Delta, 0)/\varphi(\Delta + 1, \Delta)$, $x, \Delta \geq 0$. Then

$$\varphi(x, y) = g(x)F(x - y) \quad x \geq y \geq 0$$

Substitution in Equation 6 gives $g(x)/g(y) = g(x + \Delta)/g(y + \Delta)$, $g > 0$. This implies $g(x)^2 = g(x + \Delta)g(x - \Delta)$, $\{x - \Delta \geq 0; x, \Delta \geq 0\}$, hence $2 \log g(x) =$

$\log g(x + \Delta) + \log g(x - \Delta)$. It follows (Aczél, 1966, p. 43) that $g(x) = ce^{ax}$, $c > 0$. Let $f(x - y) = cF(x - y)e^{a(x-y)}$ and $\beta = e^a$. Then

$$\varphi(x,y) = f(x - y)\beta^y \quad x \geq y \geq 0$$

This checks with $\varphi(2,1)/\varphi(1,0) = \beta$, and it implies that $\varphi(x - y, 0) = f(x - y)$.

PROOF OF THEOREM 2

We assume throughout this section that u and ρ are linear functionals on P with $\rho > 0$, $(u(0), \rho(0)) = (0,1)$,

$$p > q \Leftrightarrow \frac{u(p)}{\rho(p)} > \frac{u(q)}{\rho(q)} \quad \text{for all } p, q \in P$$

and $u(x)\rho(y) > u(y)\rho(x)$ when $x > y$, and that φ, defined by $\varphi(p,q) = u(p)\rho(q) - u(q)\rho(p)$, has a continuous restriction to $R^+ \times R^+$.

Suppose a_1 of Theorem 2 holds and $x \geq y \geq 0$. Then

$$\varphi\left(\frac{x+y}{2}, y\right) = u\left(\frac{x-y}{2}\right) = \varphi\left(x, \frac{x+y}{2}\right)$$

so $\varphi\left(\frac{x+y}{2}, (x, \frac{1}{2}, y)\right) = 0$ and therefore $\frac{x+y}{2} \sim (x, \frac{1}{2}, y)$. Hence B1 is necessary for the first part of the theorem.

Suppose a_2 holds and $p \sim y$. Then

$$0 = \varphi(p,y) = \sum_{z>y} u(z - y)\beta^y p(z) - \sum_{z<y} u(y - z)\beta^z p(z)$$

and therefore

$$0 = \sum_{z>y} u((z + x) - (y + x))\beta^{y+x} p(z) - \sum_{z<y} u((y + x) - (z + x))\beta^{z+x} p(z)$$

which is tantamount to $\varphi(p * x, y + x) = 0$ or $p * x \sim y + x$. Hence A2 is necessary for the second part of Theorem 2.

We now consider sufficiency. Suppose that B1 holds. By Lemma 1, A1 holds. By Theorem 3 and scaling,

$$u(x)\rho(y) - u(y)\rho(x) = \varphi(x,y) = \varphi(x - y, 0) = u(x - y) \quad x \geq y \geq 0$$

It follows that for $x \geq \Delta \geq 0$

$$u(x)\rho(\Delta) = \rho(x)u(\Delta) + u(x - \Delta)$$
$$u(x)\rho(x + \Delta) = \rho(x)u(x + \Delta) - u(\Delta)$$
$$u(x + \Delta)\rho(\Delta) - \rho(x + \Delta)u(\Delta) = u(x)$$

We substitute $\rho(\Delta)$ and $\rho(x + \Delta)$ from the first two equations into the third to get

$$u(x + \Delta)u(x - \Delta) + u(\Delta)^2 = u(x)^2 \quad x \geq \Delta \geq 0$$

The general continuous solutions for this functional equation (Aczél, 1966, pp. 136–137) are $u(x) = cx$, $u(x) = k \sin(cx)$, and $u(x) = k \sinh(cx)$. The second is infeasible in our context because it gives either $u \equiv 0$ or $u(x) < 0$ for some x.

Suppose $u(x) = cx$. Then $c = u(1)$ and $t = u(2)/[2u(1)] = 1$.
Suppose $u(x) = k \sinh(cx)$. Replacing $k/2$ by k, we have

$$u(x) = k(e^{cx} - e^{-cx}) \quad x \geq 0, c \neq 0$$

This gives $u(0) = 0$, $u(1) = k(e^c - e^{-c})$ and $u(2) = k(e^{2c} - e^{-2c})$, so

$$t = \frac{u(2)}{2u(1)} = \frac{e^c + e^{-c}}{2} > 1$$

Because $c \neq 0$, we can presume that k and c are positive. Given $t > 1$ it follows from $e^c + e^{-c} = 2t$ that c is unique and

$$c = \ln(t + \sqrt{t^2 - 1})$$

$$-c = -\ln(t + \sqrt{t^2 - 1}) = (\ln 1) - \ln(t + \sqrt{t^2 - 1}) = \ln\frac{1}{t + \sqrt{t^2 - 1}} = \ln(t - \sqrt{t^2 - 1})$$

Then $e^c + e^{-c} = (t + \sqrt{t^2 - 1}) + (t - \sqrt{t^2 - 1}) = 2t$. In addition,

$$k = \frac{u(1)}{e^c - e^{-c}} = \frac{u(1)}{2\sqrt{t^2 - 1}}$$

Hence $u(x)$ is as specified for $t > 1$ in the first part of Theorem 2.

For the latter half of Theorem 2, suppose that A2 holds. Then, by the latter half of Theorem 3,

$$u(x)\rho(y) - u(y)\rho(x) = \varphi(x,y) = \varphi(x - y, 0)\beta^y = u(x - y)\beta^y$$

A three-equations procedure similar to those for the A1 case gives

$$u(x + \Delta)u(x - \Delta)\beta^\Delta + u(\Delta)^2\beta^x = u(x)^2\beta^\Delta \quad x \geq \Delta \geq 0$$

Let

$$f(x) = \frac{u(x)}{\beta^{x/2}}$$

Then the preceding equation is

$$f(x + \Delta)f(x - \Delta) + f(\Delta)^2 = f(x)^2 \quad x \geq \Delta \geq 0$$

By the preceding result noted from Aczél (1966), either $f(x) = cx$ or $f(x) = k \sinh(cx)$.

Suppose $f(x) = cx$, so $u(x) = c\beta^{x/2}x$. Since $u(1) = c\beta^{1/2}$, $u(x) = u(1)\beta^{(x-1)/2}x$ and $t = u(2)/[2u(1)] = \sqrt{\beta}$.

Suppose $f(x) = k \sinh(cx)$. A procedure analogous to that for the sinh case for A1 yields the final conclusion of b_2 in Theorem 2.

REFERENCES

Aczél, J. (1966). *Lectures on functional equations and their applications.* New York: Academic Press.

Allais, M. (1979). Fondements d'une theorie positive des choix comportant un risque et critique des postulats et axiomes de l'école américaine [The foundations of a positive theory of choice involving risk and a criticism of the postulates and axioms of the American school]. In M. Allais & O. Hagen (Eds.), *Expected utility hypotheses and the Allais paradox* (pp. 27–145). Dordrecht, The Netherlands: Reidel. (Original work published 1953)

Arrow, K. J. (1974). *Essays in the theory of risk bearing.* Amsterdam: North-Holland.

Bell, D. E. (1986). Double-exponential utility functions. *Mathematics of Operations Research, 11,* 351–361.

Bell, D. E. (1988). One-switch utility functions and a measure of risk. *Management Science, 34,* 1416–1424.

Bell, D. E. (1991). *Contextual uncertainty conditions for utility functions.* Preprint, Harvard Business School, Cambridge, MA.

Bernoulli, D. (1954). Specimen theoriae novae de mensura sortis [Exposition of a new theory on the measurement of risk]. *Econometrica, 22,* 23–36. (Original work published 1738)

Brockett, P. L., & Golden, L. L. (1987). A class of utility functions containing all the common utility functions. *Management Science, 33,* 955–964.

Chew, S. H., & MacCrimmon, K. R. (1979). *Alpha-nu choice theory: A generalization of expected utility theory.* Working paper 669, University of British Columbia.

Conlisk, J. (1993). The utility of gambling. *Journal of Risk and Uncertainty, 6,* 255–275.

Edwards, W. (1954). The theory of decision making. *Psychological Bulletin, 51,* 380–417.

Farquhar, P. H., & Nakamura, Y. (1987). Constant exchange risk properties. *Operations Research, 35,* 206–214.

Fishburn, P. C. (1970). *Utility theory for decision making.* New York: Wiley.

Fishburn, P. C. (1982). Nontransitive measurable utility. *Journal of Mathematical Psychology, 26,* 31–67.

Fishburn, P. C. (1983). Transitive measurable utility. *Journal of Economic Theory, 31,* 293–317.

Fishburn, P. C. (1984a). SSB utility theory: An economic perspective. *Mathematical Social Sciences, 8,* 63–94.

Fishburn, P. C. (1984b). Elements of risk analysis in nonlinear utility theory. *INFOR, 22,* 81–97.

Fishburn, P. C. (1988). *Nonlinear preference and utility theory.* Baltimore, MD: Johns Hopkins University Press.

Fishburn, P. C., & Kochenberger, G. A. (1979). Two-piece von Neumann–Morgenstern utility functions. *Decision Sciences, 10,* 503–518.

Fishburn, P. C., & Vickson, R. G. (1978). Theoretical foundations of stochastic dominance. In G. A. Whitmore & M. C. Findlay (Eds.), *Stochastic dominance* (pp. 37–113). Lexington, MA: D. C. Heath.

Friedman, M., & Savage, L. J. (1948). The utility analysis of choices involving risk. *Journal of Political Economy, 56,* 279–304.

Galanter, E. (1962). The direct measurement of utility and subjective probability. *American Journal of Psychology, 75,* 208–220.

Grayson, C. J. (1960). *Decisions under uncertainty: Drilling decisions by oil and gas operators.* Cambridge, MA: Harvard University Press.

Harvey, C. M. (1981). Conditions on risk attitude for a single attribute. *Management Science, 27,* 190–203.

Herstein, I. N., & Milnor, J. (1953). An axiomatic approach to measurable utility. *Econometrica, 21,* 291–297.

Kahneman, D., & Tversky, A. (1979). Prospect theory: An analysis of decision under risk. *Econometrica, 47,* 263–291.

Kemeny, J. G., & Thompson, G. L. (1957). The effect of psychological attitudes on the outcomes of games. In M. Dresher, A. W. Tucker, & P. Wolfe (Eds.), *Contributions to the theory of games* (Vol. III, pp. 273–298). Princeton, NJ: Princeton University Press.

Kreweras, G. (1961). Sur une possibilité de rationaliser les intransitivités. *La Décision,* Colloques Internationaux CNRS, pp. 27–32.

Levy, H. (1992). Stochastic dominance and expected utility: Survey and analysis. *Management Science, 38,* 555–593.

MacCrimmon, K. R., & Larsson, S. (1979). Utility theory: Axioms versus "paradoxes." In M. Allais & O. Hagen (Eds.), *Expected utility hypotheses and the Allais paradox* (pp. 333–409). Dordrecht, The Netherlands: Reidel.

Machina, M. J. (1982). "Expected utility" analysis without the independence axiom. *Econometrica, 50,* 277–323.

Miyamoto, J. M., & Wakker, P. (1993). *Multiattribute utility theory without expected utility foundations.* Preprint, Department of Psychology, University of Washington, Seattle.

Montesano, A. (1988). The risk aversion measure without the independence axiom. *Theory and Decision, 24,* 269–288.

Montesano, A. (1991). Measures of risk aversion with expected and nonexpected utility. *Journal of Risk and Uncertainty, 4,* 271–283.

Mosteller, F., & Nogee, P. (1951). An experimental measure of utility. *Journal of Political Economy, 59,* 371–404.

Pfanzagl, J. (1959). A general theory of measurement: Applications to utility. *Naval Research Logistics Quarterly, 6,* 283–294.

Pratt, J. W. (1964). Risk aversion in the small and in the large. *Econometrica, 32,* 122–136.

Raiffa, H. (1968). *Decision analysis: Introductory lectures on choice under uncertainty.* Reading, MA: Addison-Wesley.

Robson, A. J. (1992). Status, the distribution of wealth, private and social attitudes to risk. *Econometrica, 60,* 837–857.

Rothblum, U. G. (1975). Multivariate constant risk posture. *Journal of Economic Theory, 10,* 309–332.

Safra, Z., & Zilcha, I. (1988). Efficient sets with and without the expected utility hypothesis. *Journal of Mathematical Economics, 17,* 369–384.

Segal, U., & Spivak, A. (1990). First order versus second order risk aversion. *Journal of Economic Theory, 51*, 111–125.

Schoemaker, P. J. H. (1980). *Experiments on decisions under risk*. Boston: Martinus Nijhoff.

Slovic, P., & Lichtenstein, S. (1983). Preference reversals: A broader perspective. *American Economic Review, 73*, 596–605.

Swalm, R. O. (1966, November–December). Utility theory—Insights into risk taking. *Harvard Business Review*, pp. 123–136.

von Neumann, J., & Morgenstern, O. (1944). *Theory of games and economic behavior*. Princeton, NJ: Princeton University Press.

Chapter 2

Structuring Complex Concepts

Rudi Janssens
Vrije Universiteit Brussel, Brussels, Belgium

One of the difficulties of analyzing social phenomena is dealing with the complex, hardly measurable concepts that are used to describe and explain them. One thinks in particular of attitude-related concepts like religiosity, traditionalism, political participation, and others that are time, space, and culture related, and thereby hard to define. Apart from the search for an applicable operationalization, usually resulting in a set of items of a questionnaire, one wants to convey the interrelation between the indicators as a clear structure by linking them to some mathematical language. This structure and its graphical representation, as a theoretical model, could be a subject of further research. In the literature, two data-analytic approaches are generally adopted to develop such a model: deterministic scaling and its probabilistic counterpart. Under certain circumstances, both can be highly unsatisfactory. In this chapter, an alternative model for dichotomous data is expounded and compared with deterministic and probabilistic scaling models, using data concerning modernism. Due to the mathematical setup, this chapter is restricted to the representation of the interrelations between the items, paying less attention to the search for a theoretical explanation of these interrelations.

COMPLEX CONCEPTS AND SCALING

In the social sciences, the term *concept* is frequently applied within several theories, resulting in an amalgam of descriptions and definitions. In his overview of the approach to the term *concept* from Plato to Geach, Weitz

(1988) could only admit failure in defining it. Most authors consider closed-ness as a central property of a concept. A concept is called *closed* if a clear distinction can be made between what is part of the concept and what is not. Ideally, it can be defined as the logical equivalent of a finite set in mathematics, which enables an enumeration or description of the elements that belong to it. Although most epistemological approaches to the social sciences consider their concepts as closed, applied research is often confronted with the lack of proper criteria for this demarcation problem. The kinds of concepts mentioned in the introduction are especially often operationalized into a set of items not monotonically related to the concept. These indicators only partly reflect the content of the concept, and moreover, are not exclusively related to one single concept. Because of these properties, such concepts are called *complex*.[1]

Apart from the fact that there does not exist a set of perfect indicators—so their choice is based on the state of the art of the field in question and the personal interests of the researcher—there is no sole means of dealing with these indicators in a research situation. One wants to consider the indicators as elements of an ordered set by assigning numbers to them that represent the position of each indicator in relation to the overall structure of the concept. For the analysis of complex concepts, this means that the numbers refer to the common content of the concept and the respective indicators. Exploratory applications of quantitative scaling methods offer this possibility. The use of a scaling method implies three fundamental choices: a unidimensional versus a multidimensional scaling method, a deterministic versus a probabilistic model, and the identification of the part of the data that is considered to be in error. When applied to the structuring of complex concepts, this traditional approach is less straightforward. The problems inherent in these choices are discussed briefly.

Dimensionality can be defined as the number of separate and interesting sources of variation for the object (Jacoby, 1991). Cultural concepts and attitudes are multidimensional by nature, because they are always subject to several sources of variation. If the individual, as a creative subject, is considered as the data source, a unidimensional approach is unrealistic. Also, because one has no control over the different sources of variability, a multidimensional approach is as problematic as a unidimensional one. In fact, dimensionality is a context- and individual-specific notion. What is judged unidimensional by some particular person or within a given setting may be multidimensional in other circumstances. According to Jacoby (1991), a researcher has to restrict himself or herself to "relevant" sources of information, according to the purpose of their use within the

---

[1]Similar concepts are also known as *latent*, but this term is not used here because of its close connection with the approach introduced by Lazarsfeld (1950).

measurement procedure. This suggests two different ways in which dimensionality can be interpreted, a theoretical and a mathematical one. *Theoretical dimensionality* comprises all relevant characteristics of a concept. It is the result of the definition or operationalization of the concept and is determined by the theory one starts from. *Mathematical dimensionality* arises from the obtained data and the applied measurement model. Multidimensional scaling assigns as many numbers to an object as the number of "relevant" dimensions that can be discerned. Such models assume that all sources of variability operate simultaneously in contributing to the observed differences. In social research, the number of dimensions, as an expression of variability, may easily exceed the number of selected indicators. One can take the 26 dimensions of modernity in the work of Inkeles and Smith (1974) as an example. To obtain an interpretable solution, however, the number of dimensions must be kept limited; each scaling technique uses its own definition of dimensionality to meet this criterion. The problems of a multidimensional approach can be illustrated by the attempts of Shye (1978, 1985) to construct an alterative for the unidimensional Guttman solution (Guttman, 1944). The shift from one to two or more dimensions led Shye into an area of technical and interpretative complexity. As a result, the only alternative to a Guttman scale he offered was a two-dimensional approach. Although he recognized the possibility of a structure with more than two dimensions, he offered no such structure. In fact, the difference between a unidimensional and multidimensional approach is artificial. When, for instance, analyzing a concept like *modernization,* many sources of variance may determine a process of modernization. Nevertheless, one wants to obtain a measure expressing the "degree of modernism" so that persons and groups can be compared. As a result, the set of theoretical dimensions is reduced to the number of dimensions allowed by the methodological approach. If one wants to construct a measurement model that fits the nature of complex concepts, one has to formulate an alternative for the idea of dimensionality.

The second choice to be made is between deterministic and probabilistic scaling. A deterministic approach may remind one of a positivistic view, represented by an axiomatic system with a set of rules offering no alternative action. In a scaling context, the term *deterministic* refers to a unique dominance relation between the indicators and their resulting position on the J-scale. Probabilistic scaling methods try to overcome this problem by relating probabilities to the individual indicators. The use of probabilities allows for deviations because the single dominance relation between the indicators is replaced by different relations that are each possible to some extent. One can select orders with high or low probability. The "most probable" model can be selected, from which deviations are possible. A probabilistic approach can also act as a self-imposed limitation. It is far from evident how to translate a cultural concept into probability theory. According to the model used and the assumptions made, different probabilities are tied to the indicators. Some models even assign probabilities to response patterns that are never observed. Probabilities are but an indication of the structure behind the concept, so this may result in a distortion of mathematical exactness. The aim of this contribution is to give structure to the concept in the first place. Therefore, the order between the indicators is more essential than the probabilities associated with them. Because this structure serves an explorative purpose, one is more interested in all possible orders than in the frequency of these possibilities. Therefore, it seems more important to concentrate on the possible orders than on the deterministic versus probabilistic discussion. This is a second problem that the measurement model for structuring complex concepts must deal with.

The concepts treated in this chapter are attitude related. No attitude, reflected by a combination of indicators, can be considered an error because no criteria are available to evaluate the validity of an attitude. Consequently, all combinations of indicators must be introduced into the obtained solution. If these attitudes are measured by a questionnaire, all responses must be considered as plausible.

BOOLEAN ANALYSIS: AN ALTERNATIVE APPROACH

In general, traditional scaling techniques are based on the assignment of real numbers to indicators, resulting in a specific order. Although the method of Boolean analysis, as introduced by Flament (1976), does not present itself as the ultimate answer to the questions posed here, it may have some practical worth. Boolean analysis translates the problem of structuring the indicators into a Boolean framework. Flament (1976) presented an alternative structuring method, resulting in a graphical representation built on the data set itself, and not evaluating a presupposed hierarchical model. The decision to render indicators of complex concepts into a Boolean framework is not surprising. The nature of these indicators excludes extensive measurement. One is not interested in the translation of individual indicators into a numerical relational system, but rather in the existence of combinations of present and absent indicators. The gathered data are considered as co-occurrence data (Feger, 1994), or a set of features occurring together. Basically, because Boolean analysis is restricted to the analysis of binary data, other types of data sets must be transformed to fit the method. In the following, some basic principles of Boolean analysis are explained. No detailed mathematical description of the method is given—only the information necessary for the practical application. For

TABLE 2.1
Imaginary Example of Response Patterns With Given Frequencies

Answer	Pattern	Frequency	Answer	Pattern	Frequency
abcd	1111	10	ab'c'd	1001	0
abcd'	1110	0	a'bc'd	0101	15
abc'd	1101	0	a'b'cd	0011	15
ab'cd	1011	0	a'b'c'd	0001	10
a'bcd	0111	25	a'b'cd'	0010	0
abc'd'	1100	0	a'bc'd'	0100	0
ab'cd'	1010	0	ab'c'd'	1000	0
a'bcd'	0110	0	a'b'c'd'	0000	5

a more detailed mathematical description of Boolean algebra and the link between this algebra and data analysis, the interested reader is referred to Flament (1976), Ragin (1987), and Theuns (1994, this volume).

The method of Boolean analysis, as applied here, is based on the work of Flament (1976), who used two basic Boolean techniques to obtain a structure within the indicators: Boolean minimization and Boolean implication. The first essential feature of Boolean analysis is the application of the principle of Boolean minimization. Using the laws of Boolean algebra and theorems derived from them, algorithms that uniquely decompose any set of Boolean expressions—for instance, a data set—as the Boolean sum of minimal subpatterns, called prime implicants, are built. Flament (1976) divided the set of all possible response patterns (R) into a set of observed patterns (R^*) and a set of nonobserved patterns (R^0). The prime implicants of R^0 he called PCUs. Because $R^* \cup R^0 = R$ and $R^* \cap R^0 = \emptyset$, the original data set is completely characterized by the Boolean sum of its PCUs. Several algorithms to obtain this expression were presented in Flament (1976) and Ragin (1987). Second, Flament (1976) built a structure on this unique expression based on the application of Boolean implication to the set of nonobserved patterns. This structure he called an *implication scheme*. This implication scheme reflects the hierarchical structure of the concept.[2]

A hypothetical example illustrates the method. Suppose an imaginary questionnaire consisting of four binary questions yielding 16 possible response patterns has observed response patterns with the frequencies in Table 2.1.

The theoretical set of all possible responses (R) can be divided into two sets: R^0, the set of nonobserved patterns, with frequencies equal to 0; and R^*, the set of actual or observed patterns, with nonzero frequencies:

---

[2]A more detailed description of Boolean analysis as described by Flament (1976) is also found in the chapter by Theuns in this volume.

$$R^0 = \{\text{patterns with frequency } f_i = 0\}$$
$$R^* = \{\text{patterns with frequency } f_i > 0 \}$$

In this example, R^0 and R^* can be written as:

$R^0 = \{abcd', ab\acute{c}d, ab'cd, abc'd', ab'cd', a'bcd', ab'\acute{c}d, a'b'cd', a'b\acute{c}d', ab'\acute{c}d'\}$

$R^* = \{abcd, a'bcd, a'bc'd, a'b'cd, a'b'\acute{c}d, a'b'\acute{c}d'\}$

From R^0 the set P of PCUs can be derived. This example yields the following set of subpatterns: $P = \{ab', a\acute{c}, ad', cd', bd'\}$. These subpatterns only occur in response patterns of R^0 and not in any pattern of R^*, and are minimal in the sense that a further Boolean minimization is impossible. As a result of the minimization process, R^0 can be summarized by the following disjunctive canonical form:

$$ab' \oplus a\acute{c} \oplus cd' \oplus bd'$$

The obtained set of PCUs results in the implication scheme given in Fig. 2.1.

According to Fig. 2.1, if a person answers a, the person will answer b, c, and d as well. Thus, if the person answers a, the rest of the responses are known. If the person answers a', more possibilities occur. Because the relation between b and c cannot be specified by answering a', a respondent has four possibilities to answer those two questions, but he or she will always answer d if the person responds positively toward b or c. A positive response on d, while getting a', b', and $\acute{c}$ as answers, is also possible. As a last possibility included in the implication scheme, somebody can answer all the questions negatively. This means that R^*, the set of possible response patterns, equals the enumeration: $\{abcd, a'bcd, a'bc'd, a'b'cd, a'b'\acute{c}d, a'b'\acute{c}d'\}$. One may conclude that the implication scheme (Fig. 2.1) reflects the hierarchical structure within the selected indicators.

In contrast to probabilistic models, Boolean analysis treats all patterns as having an equal weight. Each pattern has importance as a demonstration

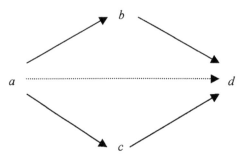

FIG. 2.1.   Implication scheme for example in Table 2.1.

of the possibility of that particular combination of responses. An advantage of this approach is that the information contained in low-frequency patterns, which might be interesting from a theoretical point of view, is not discarded. When two features that theoretically cannot appear together do, and no error is assumed, this can be a justification to reexamine the present theory. This illustrates that theoretical and methodological concerns cannot be separated when measuring complex concepts. On the other hand, so-called error patterns, which are due to inaccuracy on the part of the respondent, are judged with the same weight as patterns with a high frequency. Boolean analysis imposes no restrictions on the response patterns that do appear in the dataset. In practice, R^* will contain many patterns, especially when the number of items increases. In spite of the strong theoretical base of the method, the structuring of real-life data requires more flexibility. For Boolean analysis, the criterion to select a response pattern is its existence. To obtain an interpretable representation that avoids the shortcomings mentioned earlier and results in a solution that is not too complicated for analytic purposes, it is desirable to attach conditions to this selection. The selection condition, called α, may refer to the following decisions: One may distinguish the accepted from the rejected patterns according to their frequencies, or one may reject specific combinations of answers because they contain inconsistencies within the theoretical framework on which the research is based. A procedure that differentiates between the response patterns is called a dichotomization method (Flament, 1976; Van Buggenhaut & Degreef, 1987). Dichotomization can be based on mathematical criteria (e.g., Van Buggenhaut, 1987), on theoretical considerations (e.g., Theuns, this volume), or, on a combination of both. As a result, instead of dividing R into R^0 and R^*, one may divide it into R_α^0 and R_α^* with:

$$R_\alpha^0 = \{\text{patterns rejected according to condition } \alpha\}$$
$$R_\alpha^* = \{\text{patterns accepted according to condition } \alpha\}$$

Whatever criterion is used, it is essential to obtain a unique solution to enable the comparison of different subgroups or data sets.

SCALING REAL-LIFE DATA

In this section[3] Boolean analysis and a deterministic and a probabilistic scaling method are compared. Considering the restricted applicability of

---

[3]This section is based on the data from the project "Family Formation and Value Patterns of Turkish Women in Flanders and Brussels," a joint research project of the Centrum voor Sociologie (VUB), Centrum voor Statistiek en Operationeel Onderzoek (VUB), and Semenarie voor Demografie (UG).

dimensionality, only unidimensional methods, such as a projection of several theoretical dimensions into one mathematical dimension, are selected. This comparison has two purposes: It offers an opportunity to test the abilities of Boolean analysis "in the field," and, if compared with two other traditional approaches in the human sciences, it illustrates the advantages of the method. As a deterministic scaling method, Guttman analysis is applied (Guttman, 1944); the probabilistic alternative is represented by the Mokken scale analysis for polychotomous items, or MSP (Mokken, 1971; Debets & Brouwer, 1989). Only a brief outline of the methods is given in this chapter. Boolean analysis is applied such that a solution with PCUs of length ≤2 is preferred (see Van Buggenhaut, 1987).

By analogy with the cohesion threshold method (Van Buggenhaut, 1987), the degree of cohesion is defined as the proportion of the population that fits the obtained implication scheme, irrespective of the number of response patterns. The *grade of cohesion*[4] is used as a fit parameter, which enables one to decide whether the representation, obtained by reducing the complexity of the implication scheme, still holds for a considerable part of the population. It has the advantage that it can easily be calculated for all kinds of scaling methods.

The measurement of "modernism" is a typical example used to illustrate complex concepts. A considerable list of publications on this topic shows that an operationalization of modernism is not obvious. Moreover, an additional problem is posed because in this case the respondents are female Turkish migrants registered in Belgium. Although as a group they share a common tradition, the concept of modernism is situated within the framework of a society characterized by a different tradition. In this chapter, only the data about the husband–wife relationship are used. The selection of these items is based on previous research on modernism in Turkey (Fox, 1973), but only those that make sense in a migration environment and refer to the field of interest of the researchers are selected (see also Janssens, 1993a, 1993b). Yet, one is not solely interested in the frequency tabulation of the indicators but rather in their mutual interrelations. Because little systematic research on similar concepts of modernism has been accomplished, Boolean analysis, as an exploratory technique, is applied. Considering the aim of this chapter, no background variables are included in the analysis.

To measure the husband–wife relationship, the following items were selected:

a. Women do not always have to do what their husbands say.

---

[4]The grade of cohesion is defined as the percentage of the research population for which the obtained result holds.

   b. Women can talk to strange men, even if their husband does not know them.
   c. If the husband has visitors, the wife should not retreat into another room.
   d. Women can show themselves in public without wearing a head scarf.
   e. Women have to play a role in social, political, and religious life.
   f. Women have the right to work outside the house.
   g. Important decisions should be made together.

The response categories were reduced to a modern (egalitarian relationship between husband and wife) versus traditional (dominance of husband) alternative. In the following figures the characters all refer to a modern attitude.

Guttman Scaling

Scalogram analysis or Guttman scaling (Guttman, 1944), as a basic technique in research on attitudes, is applied as a first approach. The unidimensional and cumulative property of this method enables one to order the items by degree of modernism. The basic idea is that the higher the degree of modernism included in the item, the less often a respondent chooses the modern alternative. As a result of the analysis, a scale is obtained, ranking the items from high to low degrees of modernism, so that the researcher can recover the response pattern of a person from the number of items to which a positive response is given. All patterns deviating from this solution are defined as error.

The two basic properties mentioned earlier both illustrate the weaknesses of the method. A unique dominance relation between the selected items is seldom found, and for an increasing number of items n, the discrepancy between the arithmetic series of the accepted patterns and the geometric series of possible response patterns may result in a considerable set of response patterns defined as error patterns. If n dichotomous items are presented, $n + 1$ out of the 2^n possible patterns will be included in the analysis. For the presented data set, 8 patterns out of the possible 128 are selected. This results in the scale presented in Fig. 2.2.

Guttman analysis results in a scale with a coefficient of reproducibility[5] of 0.8535. This statistic, introduced by Guttman (1944), is a measure of the probability of reproducing the response pattern from the number of

---

[5]This coefficient is defined as 1 minus the ratio between the total number of errors and the total number of respondents times the number of items, with error defined as the number of corrections one has to make to obtain an accepted pattern from a rejected response pattern.

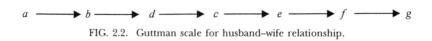

FIG. 2.2. Guttman scale for husband–wife relationship.

items positively responded to. Guttman (1944) stated that a coefficient of reproducibility higher than 0.9 is required to obtain a valid scale. As a consequence, the obtained scale is rejected. To compare the representation obtained by Guttman analysis with the representations of the other scaling techniques, the degree of cohesion is calculated. The scale in Fig. 2.2 holds true for 56.6% of the respondents.

Mokken Scaling

The Mokken scale analysis for polychotomous items (MSP) is a probabilistic version of scalogram analysis for both dichotomous and polychotomous items. This means that the responses are given according to a probability distribution that does not exclude the possibility that, within a certain range, a subject gives a positive response to a more difficult item even if the subject responds negatively to an easier one. For a description of the method, see Debets and Brouwer (1989).

Scalability coefficients, based on the error definition of Guttman, are calculated and permit ranking of the items. From a given pool of items, MSP allows the stepwise construction of one or more scales. Mokken (1971) defined a scale as a set of items that are positively correlated, with the property that every item's coefficient of scalability is larger than or equal to a given positive constant c. If the scalability coefficient H[6] of a set of items drops below c, the variable that most recently entered the stepwise construction of the scale will be dropped. Three scale types can be constructed: a strong scale (with $0.50 \leq H$), an average scale (with $0.40 \leq H < 0.50$), and a weak scale (with $0.30 \leq H < 0.40$). The stronger the scale, the better is its representation of the data set.

MSP, applied to the data concerning the husband–wife relationship of Turkish migrants, results in two scales: a 6-item weak scale, and, a 4-item strong scale. The first solution fits 14 patterns and has a degree of cohesion of 58.6%. The strong scale selects 31 patterns and results in a grade of cohesion of 83.8%. To obtain a weak scale, item g is dropped from the original Guttman scale. The strong scale drops items b and e as well. This results are presented in Figs. 2.3 and 2.4.

---

[6]The scalability coefficient is defined as 1 minus the sum of the observed number of errors according to the Guttman scale model over the sum of the expected number of errors, assuming the responses to the items are independent across persons and the marginals are fixed (Debets & Brouwer, 1989).

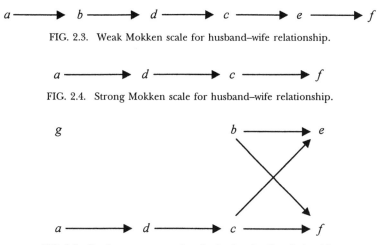

FIG. 2.3. Weak Mokken scale for husband–wife relationship.

FIG. 2.4. Strong Mokken scale for husband–wife relationship.

FIG. 2.5. Boolean representation for husband–wife relationship.

Boolean Analysis

Finally, the method of Boolean analysis is applied. The dichotomization is based on a mathematical criterion. To maintain the interpretability of the implication scheme, only PCUs with a maximum length of 2 are allowed. The lowest dichotomization threshold for which all PCUs have length ≤ 2 is 19, which gives an implication scheme in which 11 response patterns are restrained. This results in a grade of cohesion of 73.8%. Figure 2.5 presents the obtained implication scheme.

A BRIEF COMPARISON OF THE RESULTING REPRESENTATIONS

Table 2.2 presents a brief overview of the applied methods. In total, R^* contained 67 out of the 128 possible response patterns (see Appendix), with 747 respondents questioned. Three measures are selected to compare the methods: the number of items selected for the representation of the data (restrained items), the number of accepted patterns according to the representation (restrained patterns), and the percentage of the research population for which the obtained result holds (grade of cohesion). Although they are highly interrelated, each contains specific information about how the representations are built, which helps to explain the differences between the methods.

From the number of restrained items, a first conspicuous difference between Guttman scaling and Boolean analysis, on the one hand, and

TABLE 2.2
Comparison of Scaling Models

Scale Type	Restrained Items	Restrained Patterns	Grade of Cohesion
Guttman	7	8	56.6
Mokken weak	6	14	58.6
Mokken strong	4	31	83.8
Boolean analysis	7	11	73.8

Mokken scaling, on the other, can be derived. Although MSP establishes a representation on the scalability of a specific item, Guttman scaling and Boolean analysis offer a pattern-based approach. The advantage of MSP is that it nearly always results in a scale, whereas Guttman scaling selects a fixed set of patterns that are evaluated afterward. In this particular example, the Guttman solution would be rejected, where MSP offers a 4- and a 6-item solution. By allowing a partial order, Boolean analysis increases the number of restrained patterns within a 7-item solution. Because scaling is used for exploratory purposes, only Boolean analysis results in an acceptable solution. Guttman scaling fails to give an appropriate hierarchical structure, and MSP fails to structure the complete set of items. The problem with Guttman scaling and MSP is that for both methods, unidimensionality is used as a synonym for a unique order. Going back to the definition of Jacoby (1991), the fact that a specific source of variation can be identified does not imply that its effect is monotone. As a consequence, a single dimension, defined according to Jacoby (1991), may result in different orders. Referring to the example about gender relations, the Boolean solution illustrates that all indicators are interrelated, except for item g. One may conclude that the sample of respondents is selected so that no variation is found in the responses to item g. This is no reason to drop the item (MSP) or to force a relation with the other items (Guttman scaling), because it provides important information about the gender relations and a similar result is not guaranteed when compared with a different sample.

If one concentrates on the restrained patterns, the Guttman solution always results in $n + 1$ patterns if n items are selected. The relaxation of the strict dominance relation between the items allows more patterns to be restrained when Boolean analysis is used. By dropping more items, the number of patterns in the Mokken solution increases even further. The relation between the number of items and the number of patterns in MSP is obvious. In general, if n dichotomous items are selected, 2^n possible response patterns may be found, so:

$$|R^0| + |R*| = 2^n$$

If out of the n items, k are selected by the MSP method to form a unidimensional scale, introducing a total order relation on those items, $k + 1$ subpatterns of length k are accepted, and the responses on $n - k$ items are of no importance for the determination of the order between these k indicators. For dichotomous items, $2^{(n-k)}$ possible subpatterns of length $(n - k)$ can be counted for each of the $k + 1$ subpatterns selected by the Mokken scale. This results in $(k + 1)2^{(n-k)}$ possible response patterns. If k decreases, the number of possible response patterns increases. This does not automatically imply that the number of restrained patterns increases with the same number, because not all patterns belong to R^*. According to the strong Mokken solution, 40 possible response patterns out of the 128 are selected, and in this particular case 31 out of 67 observed patterns correspond to the obtained solution. Because only 4 items are scaled and no information about the others is given, some patterns of R^* do not belong to the set of corresponding patterns whereas some of R^0 do. Only Boolean analysis, as it is applied here, guarantees that $R_\alpha^* \subseteq R^*$.

A last comparison is based on the grade of cohesion. This measure has a double advantage: it can easily be calculated, so that representations resulting from different methods can be compared, and its interpretation is straightforward. The strong Mokken solution has a high fit, but because three items are dropped, only relations among four items are expressed, so some patterns of R^0 are included in the set of patterns corresponding to the representation. If all indicators are included, Boolean analysis results in the highest grade of cohesion. The disadvantage of this measure is that it is only appropriate if all items are included into the obtained solution.

DISCUSSION

The method of Boolean analysis is presented as an alternative to the traditional scaling techniques applied in social research. That it is alternative is illustrated by its position in relation to uni- versus multidimensional and deterministic versus probabilistic approaches. The most salient feature, compared to other methods, is its translation of the idea of dimensionality. When Boolean analysis is applied, it does not make much sense to derive the number of dimensions from the obtained graphical representation. As an alternative, the different orders obtained from the Boolean analysis can be used, so that dimensionality only refers to the theoretical dimensionality of the concept under investigation. The application of graph theory and the methodology used within artificial intelligence research may shed more light on the dimensionality problem of the obtained solution.

Another important feature of Boolean analysis is that all response patterns are judged possible and that none of them are defined as error patterns. Nevertheless, because the number of patterns may increase, a smaller set of accepted patterns is used as a base for the analysis of the concept. To obtain some general conclusions about the concept or to compare different data sets based on the result of Boolean analysis, it is important to define a condition that results in a unique solution. This condition determines a fixed set of patterns for which the interrelations between the indicators are derived. Boolean analysis can be considered a deterministic approach in the sense that a unique solution is obtained, but not if deterministic refers to a unique order within the indicators.

This chapter is but an introduction to the use of Boolean analysis as a scaling method. Undoubtedly, the method offers some advantages: A partial order between the indicators is allowed, a high correspondence between the obtained graphical representation and the set of observed patterns is found, a positive correlation between the indicators is not assumed, and, all observed patterns are judged to have the same weight, so the solution does not depend too heavily on the selection of the sample. Apart from these advantages, some remarks need to be made. One of the most important problems is to understand the relation between the complex concept under study and the criterion that determines the set of accepted response patterns. The formulation of a dichotomization criterion depends on the state of the art of the existing theories of the concept under study. If no theoretical criterion is available, one has to go back to a more arbitrary mathematical solution. Additionally, it is necessary to develop a distance measure, linked to this criterion, with the property that all respondents whose response patterns are observed but neglected by the dichotomization criterion can be situated in relation to the obtained solution. Another aspect that asks for further research is the development of fit parameters based on the number of patterns included in the obtained solution. Nevertheless, Boolean analysis presents itself as a valuable scaling approach within the behavioral sciences.

REFERENCES

Debets, P., & Brouwer, E. (1989). *MSP, a program for Mokken scale analysis for polychotomous items.* Groningen, The Netherlands: iec ProGAMMA.

Feger, H. (1994). *Structure analysis of co-occurence data.* Aachen, Germany: Verlag Shaker.

Flament, C. (1976). *L' analyse booléenne de questionnaire.* Paris: Mouton.

Fox, G. L. (1973, November). Some determinants of modernism among women in Ankara, Turkey. *Journal of Marriage and the Family,* pp. 718–730.

Guttman, L. (1944). A basis for scaling qualitative data. *American Sociological Review, 9,* 139–150.

Inkeles, A., & Smith, D. H. (1974). *Becoming modern. Individual change in six developing countries.* Cambridge, MA: Harvard University Press.

Jacoby, G. L. (1991). *Data theory and dimensional analysis.* Newbury Park, CA: Sage.

Janssens, R. (1993a). *De islam als normerend kader voor de Turkse migrantenvrouw. Een literatuurstudie.* Working papers on Etnische minderheden in België, Centrum voor Sociologie, Vrije Universiteit Brussel, en Seminarie voor Demografie, Universiteit Gent, WP 1993–2.

Janssens, R. (1993b). *Migratie, religiositeit en modernisme. Een onderzoek naar de religiositeit van Turkse migrantenvrouwen en de invloed ervan op een aantal waarden, normen en opinies.* Working papers on Etnische minderheden in België, Centrum voor Sociologie, Vrije Universiteit Brussel, en Seminarie voor Demografie, Universiteit Gent, WP 1993–2.

Lazarsfeld, P. F. (1950). The logical and mathematical foundation of latent structure analysis. In S. A. Stouffer, L. Guttman, E. A. Suchman, P. F. Lazarsfeld, S. A. Star, & J. A. Clausen *Measurement and prediction, Studies in social psychology in World War II* (Vol. 4, pp. 362–413). New York: Wiley.

Mokken, R. J. (1971). *A theory and procedure of scale analysis with applications in political research.* The Hague: Mouton.

Ragin, C. C. (1987). *The comparative method. Moving beyond qualitative and quantitative strategies.* Berkley: University of California Press.

Shye, S. (1978). Partial order scalogram analysis. In S. Shye (Ed.), *Theory construction and data analysis in the behavioral sciences* (pp. 265–279). San Francisco: Jossey-Bass.

Shye, S. (1985). *Multiple scaling.* Amsterdam: Elsevier.

Theuns, P. (1994). A dichotomization method for Boolean analysis of quantifiable co-occurence data. In G. H. Fisher & D. Laming (Eds.), *Contributions to mathematical psychology, psychometrics, and methodology* (pp. 389–402). New York: Springer-Verlag.

Van Buggenhaut, J. (1987). Questionnaires booléens: schémas d'implications et degrés de cohesion. *Mathématiques et Sciences Humaines, 98,* 9–20.

Van Buggenhaut, J., & Degreef, E. (1987). On dichotomisation methods in Boolean analysis of questionnaires. In E. E. Roskam & R. Suck (Eds.), *Progress in mathematical psychology—1* (pp. 447–453). Amsterdam: Elsevier.

Weitz, M. (1988). *Theories of concepts. A history of the major philosophical tradition.* London: Routledge & Kegan Paul.

APPENDIX
Actual Patterns for Husband–Wife Relation

Pattern	Frequency	Representation
1111111	96	ΓΩΣ
1111110	1	ΩΣ
1111101	3	
1111011	3	Σ
1110111	9	
1110011	2	
1110001	1	
1101111	3	
1101011	1	
1101101	1	
1101000	2	
1100111	6	
1100101	1	
1100011	2	
1100001	1	
1011111	33	ΣB
1011100	2	
1011011	6	Σ
1010111	8	
1010110	1	
1010101	1	
1010011	1	
1010001	1	
1001111	5	
1001011	1	

Pattern	Frequency	Representation
1000111	9	
1000101	3	
1000011	2	
0111111	39	ΓΩΣ
0111110	1	ΩΣ
0111101	2	
0111100	1	
0111011	1	Σ
0111010	1	Σ
0111000	1	
0110111	29	ΣB
0110101	1	
0110011	3	Σ
0110001	1	
0101111	4	
0101011	1	
0100111	35	ΣB
0100110	1	Σ
0100101	7	Σ
0100011	5	Σ
0100001	5	Σ
0011111	71	ΓΩΣ
0011110	1	ΩΣ

Pattern	Frequency	Representation
0011101	5	
0011100	1	
0011011	13	Σ
0011010	1	Σ
0010111	59	ΓΩΣ
0010110	2	ΩΣ
0010101	3	
0010011	9	
0010001	7	
0001111	19	Σ
0001101	3	
0001011	6	
0001000	2	
0000111	109	ΓΩΣ
0000110	7	ΩΣ
0000101	35	ΣB
0000100	1	Σ
0000011	28	ΓΩΣ
0000010	3	ΩΣ
0000001	17	ΓΩΣ
0000000	4	ΓΩΣ

Note. The following indications are used to mark the actual patterns (ordered from A to F) accepted by the respective representations: Γ for a Guttman scale, Ω for the weak Mokken scale, Σ for the strong Mokken scale, and B for the representation used by Boolean analysis.

Chapter 3

Role Assignments and Indifference Graphs

Fred S. Roberts
Rutgers University

In this chapter, we explore the relationships between two models of social relationships that are formulated using graph theory. One is a model known as role assignment or role coloring. The other is called an indifference graph, and also has applications in decision and choice theory, psychophysics, perceptual geometry, developmental psychology, and many other areas.

Role assignments were introduced by Everett and Borgatti (1991) to model social role. Everett and Borgatti called them *role colorings*. They arise from the idea that if social role is defined properly, then individuals with the same role will relate in the same way to other individuals playing counterpart roles. This idea was formalized first in the language of graph homomorphisms and vertex partitions by White and Reitz (1983). The recent literature on role assignments is summarized in the articles by Everett and Borgatti (1994) and Roberts and Sheng (in press). Specifically, let $G = (V,E)$ be a graph consisting of a set of V of vertices and a set of E of unordered pairs of vertices called edges. (For all graph-theoretical terminology that is not defined here, see Roberts, 1984). The vertices can be used to stand for individuals in some social groups, and an edge between x and y means that x and y are related in some way (such as being friends). If v is a vertex of graph G, the (*open*) *neighborhood* $N(v)$ of v in G consists of all vertices w *adjacent* to v in G, that is, so that $\{v, w\} \in E(G)$. Now, think of assigning a role to each vertex in G. For simplicity, we can use one of the "colors" 1, 2, . . . , k, although any k numbers or other symbols would suffice. Let $r(x)$ denote the role assigned to vertex x. [We do not require, as is common in vertex coloring, that $r(x)$ be different from $r(y)$ if x is adjacent to y.] Let $r(N(v)) = \{r(x): x \in N(v)\}$. Then, following Everett and Borgatti (1991), we say that r defines a *role assignment* if

$$r(x) = r(y) \rightarrow r(N(x)) = r(N(y)) \tag{1}$$

In a role assignment, if two individuals have the same role, they are related (in G) to individuals with the same sets of roles. We say that r is a k-*role assignment* if it is a role assignment and it uses exactly the integers 1, 2, . . . , k as values $r(x)$. To give an example, for the graph of Fig. 3.1, we can define a role assignment by taking $r(a) = r(e) = r(h) = 1$, $r(b) = r(d) = r(f) = r(i) = 2$, $r(c) = r(g) = 3$. This is a role assignment because $r(N(a)) = r(N(e)) = r(N(h)) = \{2,3\}$, $r(N(b)) = r(N(d)) = r(N(f)) = r(N(i)) = \{1,2,3\}$, and $r(N(c)) = r(N(g)) = \{1,2\}$.

Almost every graph has two *trivial* role assignments: Let $r(x)$ be 1 for all x; and let all $r(x)$ be different. The former does not work if there are some isolated vertices but not all vertices are isolated. The question is to determine if there is a k-role assignment for different values of k.

In the role assignment model, we place no significance in the number defining a role in the sense that we don't ask whether the role assigned to x is smaller than that assigned to y, or close to that assigned to y, and so forth. The numbers define a nominal scale, and any one-to-one transformation of numbers gives a comparable definition of roles. A different kind of model arises if the numbers defining roles do carry some significance. We can then, for example, try to assign numbers to individuals so that individuals who are related are exactly those whose corresponding role-defining numbers are close. If $f(x)$ is the number assigned to x, we than have the well-known model

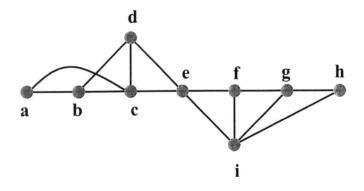

FIG. 3.1. A graph having a role assignment with three roles.

$$\{x,y\} \in E(G) \leftrightarrow |f(x) - f(y)| \leq \delta \tag{2}$$

where δ is some fixed positive number (thought of as a threshold or just noticeable difference). The graphs for which we can find a function f were called *indifference graphs* by Roberts (1969) and have been widely studied as models in psychology and other areas. (See Roberts, 1978, for some references.) To give an example, note first that we may as well take δ to be 1, as we do throughout this chapter, for if there is an f satisfying Equation 2 with δ, then f/δ satisfies Equation 2 with 1. The graph of Fig. 3.2 is an indifference graph. For example, we can take $f(x_1) = 0$, $f(x_2) = 0.7$, $f(x_3) = 1.5$, $f(x_4) = 2.2$, $f(x_5) = 2.6$, $f(x_6) = 2.8$, $f(x_7) = 3.7$, $f(x_8) = 4.2$, $f(x_9) = 5.0$.

In this chapter, we investigate the relation between the role assignment model and the indifference graph model and, in particular, seek to understand the extent to which the fact that a graph satisfies one model implies that it satisfies the other.

The idea of closeness also suggests the following variant on the role assignment model. Given two sets S and T of numbers, let us define the *distance* $d(S,T)$ to be min $\{|s - t|: s \in S, t \in T\}$. Of course, d is not necessarily a metric in the standard sense, because the triangle inequality can fail. We investigate an alternative notion of distance later. If $T = \phi$, we shall use the convention that $d(S,T) = 0$ if $S = \phi$ and $d(S,T) = \infty$ otherwise. We say that a function r on $V(G)$ defines a *threshold role assignment* if

$$r(x) = r(y) \rightarrow d[r(N(x)),r(N(y))] \leq 1 \tag{3}$$

We say that r is a *k-threshold role assignment* if it is a threshold role assignment and the "colors" 1, 2, . . . , k are used as values of $r(x)$.

In the next section, we discuss the question: What indifference graphs have k-role assignments? In the section that follows, we study graphs that have only the two trivial role assignments mentioned earlier, the so-called role-primitive graphs, and, in particular, we ask if there are indifference graphs that are role-primitive. A third section studies threshold role as-

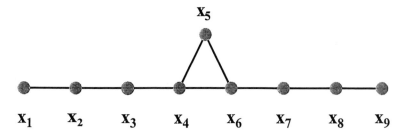

FIG. 3.2. A connected indifference graph that is not 2-role assignable.

signments. The final section is a discussion section, concentrating on topics for further investigation.

ROLE ASSIGNMENTS AND INDIFFERENCE GRAPHS

As we have already observed, almost every graph is 1-role assignable. Simply let $r(x) = 1$ for all x. We begin by investigating 2-role assignability.

It is not hard to show that many graphs that are 2-role assignable are not indifference graphs. For example, Everett and Borgatti (1991) noted that every connected bipartite graph with an edge is 2-role assignable. (Simply assign role 1 to all vertices in one of the bipartite classes and 2 to all vertices in the other class.) There are many bipartite graphs that are not indifference graphs. In fact, all trees except paths are examples of such graphs, because it is well known (Roberts, 1969) that an indifference graph cannot have a generated subgraph $K(1,3)$ (four vertices u, a, b, c with edges $\{u,a\}$, $\{u,b\}$, and $\{u,c\}$). The first theorem will help us to show that, to a large extent, indifference graphs are 2-role assignable.

Theorem 1. Suppose a connected graph G consists of a connected graph H and a collection of independent vertices K with every vertex of H adjacent to some vertex of K. Then G is 2-role assignable.

Proof. Let the vertices of H get role 1 and those of K get role 2. Then given x in K, by connectedness of G, there is a vertex in H adjacent to x, and by independence of K, there is no vertex of K adjacent to x. Hence, $r(N(x)) = \{1\}$. Given x in H, there is by hypothesis a vertex in K adjacent to x. Hence, $r(N(x))$ includes the number 2. If H has just one vertex, then $r(N(x)) = \{2\}$. If H has at least one other vertex, then connectedness of H implies that x is adjacent to some vertex of H, and so $r(N(x)) = \{1,2\}$. In any case, all vertices x assigned role 2 have the same $r(N(x))$, that is, $\{1\}$, and all vertices assigned role 1 have the same $r(N(x))$, either $\{2\}$ if H has one vertex or $\{1,2\}$ if H has at least two vertices.

$$\text{Q.E.D.}$$

To state and prove the next theorem, we need a few definitions. A *cut vertex* in a connected graph is a vertex whose removal disconnects the graph. Roberts (1971) showed that if G is an indifference graph, there is a vertex ordering

$$x_1, x_2, \ldots, x_n \qquad (4)$$

that is *compatible* in the sense that if $i \leq j < k \leq l$ and if $\{x_i, x_l\} \in E(G)$, then $\{x_j, x_k\} \in E(G)$.

Theorem 2. Every connected indifference graph without cut vertices and at least two vertices is 2-role assignable.

Proof. We define H and K as in Theorem 1. Given a compatible vertex ordering as in Equation 4, let $x_1 = x_{j_1}$ belong to K. Follow the compatible ordering, including all vertices in H until we come to the first vertex x_{j_2} not adjacent to x_{j_1}. Include x_{j_2} in K. Continue along the compatible ordering, including all vertices in H until we come to the first vertex x_{j_3} not adjacent to x_{j_2}. Include x_{j_3} in K. And so on. Now, K is an independent set. For, if $j_u < j_v$ and there is an edge between x_{j_u} and x_{j_v}, then u and v differ by more than 1. Hence, there is w so that $j_u < j_w < j_v$. Applying the definition of compatibility to $j_u \leq j_{w-1} < j_w \leq j_v$, we conclude that $x_{j_{w-1}}$ and x_{j_w} are adjacent, contrary to the way we defined these vertices. Next, note that H is connected. For, because G is connected, compatibility implies that x_i is adjacent in G to x_{i+1} for all i. Moreover, again by compatibility, x_{j_u-1} is adjacent to x_{j_u+1}, for otherwise there could be no edge x_i to x_j for $i < j_u < j$ and x_{j_u} is a cut vertex. This shows that following vertices in H in their order in the compatible order gives a chain in graph H, and so H is connected. Finally, given x in H, we can find v in K adjacent to x. For, by definition of H, x is adjacent to the preceding x_{j_u} chosen for K.

Q.E.D.

Remark. The idea of compatible ordering gives an alternative proof of Theorem 2, which is perhaps simpler. If $x_1, x_2, \ldots, x_n$ is a compatible vertex ordering, let $r(x_i)$ be 1 if i is odd and 2 if i is even. Because there are no cut vertices, it is not hard to see from compatibility that unless G consists of exactly two or exactly three vertices, then every vertex is adjacent to its two following or two preceding vertices. Hence, $r(N(x)) = \{1,2\}$ for all vertices x. If G has exactly two vertices, the coloring is a trivial 2-role assignment. If G has three vertices, then because G is connected and there is no cut vertex, G has to be a triangle and we conclude that $r(N(x_1)) = r(N(x_3)) = \{1,2\}$ and so, again, we have a 2-role assignment.

Theorem 3. There are connected indifference graphs that are not 2-role assignable.

Proof. Consider the graph of Fig. 3.2. If r is a 2-role assignment, then without loss of generality $r(x_1) = 1$. If $r(x_2) = 1$, then $r(x_j) = 1$ for all j. Thus, $r(x_2) = 2$. If $r(x_3) = 1$, then $r(x_4) = 2$ because we must have $r(N(x_3)) = r(N(x_1)) = \{2\}$. Also, by similar reasoning from $r(x_4)$, we conclude that

$r(x_5) = 1$ and $r(x_6) = 1$. But now $r(N(x_1)) \neq r(N(x_5))$, and $r(x_1) = r(x_5)$, a contradiction. Hence, we conclude that $r(x_3) = 2$. Because we must have $r(N(x_3)) = r(N(x_2)) = \{1,2\}$, it follows that $r(x_4) = 1$. Similarly, we conclude that $r(x_5) = 2$ and $r(x_6) = 2$. Because x_9 has only one neighbor, we must have $r(x_9) = 1$, for otherwise $r(N(x_9))$ would have to equal $r(N(x_2)) = \{1,2\}$. Then, we must have $r(x_8) = 2$ and, because $r(N(x_8)) = r(N(x_2)) = \{1,2\}$, we must have $r(x_7) = 2$. But then $r(N(x_7)) = \{2\}$, which is a contradiction.

Q.E.D.

Remark.   It turns out that the graph of Fig. 3.2 is not 3-role assignable or 4-role assignable, but it is 5-role assignable. To see the latter, simply define $r(x_1) = r(x_9) = 1$, $r(x_2) = r(x_8) = 2$, $r(x_3) = r(x_7) = 3$, $r(x_4) = r(x_6) = 4$, $r(x_5) = 5$.

We turn next to k-role assignments.

Remark.   For every $k > 1$, there is a connected indifference graph with more than k vertices that is not k-role assignable. For $k = 2$, Theorem 3 gives an example. For $k > 2$, the chain of $k + 1$ vertices provides an example. To see why it is not k-role assignable, note that two vertices x and y must get the same roles while all vertices other than x have distinct roles, and similarly for all vertices other than y. Hence, because $k > 2$, $r(N(x)) \neq r(N(y))$.

We next note that Theorem 2 generalizes to k-role assignments.

Theorem 4.   Suppose G is a connected indifference graph and $x_1, x_2, \ldots , x_n$ is a compatible order. Suppose that $2 \leq k \leq |V(G)|$ and that for every i, x_i is adjacent either to at least the k following vertices or to all following vertices. Then G is k-role assignable.

Proof.   Given a compatible order as in Equation 4, assign the roles 1, 2, 3, ... , k, 1, 2, 3, ... , k, ... to the vertices in this order. Suppose $r(x_i) = r(x_j)$ with $j > i$. Then $j - i = tk$ for some $t \geq 1$. Thus, x_i has at least k following vertices and so is adjacent to at least the k following vertices. It follows that $r(N(x_i)) = \{1,2, \ldots , k\}$. Similarly, $x_{i+(t-1)k}$ is adjacent to at least the k following vertices and hence to x_j. It follows by compatibility that x_j is adjacent to at least the k preceding vertices, and so $r(N(x_j)) = \{1,2, \ldots , k\}$. Therefore, $r(N(x_i)) = r(N(x_j))$.

Q.E.D.

It is natural to ask whether or not every connected indifference graph G without cut vertices has a k-role assignment for all $k \leq |V(G)|$.

ROLE-PRIMITIVE INDIFFERENCE GRAPHS

Following Everett and Borgatti (1991), we say that a graph is *role-primitive* if the only role assignments it has are the two trivial ones where either all vertices get the same role or all vertices get different roles. We also say that a graph is *almost role-primitive of order $h > 2$* if it has $h + 1$ vertices, it has a 2-role assignment, but it has no k-role assignment for any $2 < k \leq h$.

Theorem 5 (Everett & Borgatti, 1991). There is a role-primitive graph.

Proof. Everett and Borgatti (1991) showed that the graph of Fig. 3.3 is role-primitive.

Remark. Everett and Borgatti (1994) gave a smaller role-primitive graph, one of eight vertices, and attributed the example to Erik Jacobson. It is an open question to determine the size of the smallest role-primitive graph. Everett and Borgatti (1991) showed that every role-primitive graph has the identity as its automorphism group.

The graph of Fig. 3.3 is not an indifference graph. This follows because vertices x_2, x_3, x_4, x_5, x_9, x_{10} generate a subgraph that is a forbidden subgraph for indifference graphs in the characterization by Roberts (1969). In this section, we ask if there is a role-primitive connected indifference graph. We have not been able to settle this question. However, we have the following result.

Theorem 6. For arbitrarily large h, there is a connected indifference graph that is almost role-primitive of order h.

Proof. In the proof, we use the notation iFj to mean that every vertex of role i is forced to be adjacent to a vertex of role j (because some vertex of role i is adjacent to a vertex of role j) and iNj to mean that no vertex of role i is adjacent to a vertex of role j (because some vertex of role i is not adjacent to a vertex of role j). Consider the graph of Fig. 3.4, with h

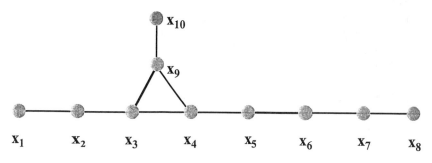

FIG. 3.3. A role-primitive graph.

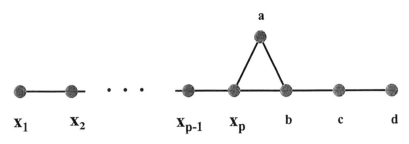

FIG. 3.4.   For arbitrarily large p, this graph is almost role-primitive of order $h = p + 3$.

$= p + 3$, $p \geq 5$. We show that there are arbitrarily large values of p for which this graph is almost role-primitive of order h. Suppose there is a role assignment r using k roles, $2 < k \leq h$. Without loss of generality suppose that $r(x_1) = 1$. If $r(x_2) = 1$, then $r(x_i) = 1$ for all i, which is a contradiction. Thus, without loss of generality, assume $r(x_2) = 2$. If $r(x_3)$ is 1 or 2, then $r(x_i)$ is 1 or 2 for all i, which again is a contradiction. Continuing with this argument, we conclude that if $k \leq p$, we may assume that $r(x_i) = i$, $i = 1$, $2, \ldots, k$, and if $k > p$, we may assume that $r(x_i) = i$ for $i = 1, 2, \ldots, p$. We now consider three cases.

Case 1: $k > p$. If $r(a)$ and $r(b)$ are both in $\{1,2 \ldots, p\}$, then we conclude that $r(v) \in \{1,2, \ldots, p\}$ for all vertices v, which is impossible because r uses $k > p$ roles. Hence, without loss of generality, we assume that $r(a) = p + 1$ or $r(b) = p + 1$.

Subcase 1.1: $r(a) = r(b) = p + 1$. Then $(p + 1)\text{N}i$ for $i \neq p$, $p + 1$ and so $r(c) = p$ or $p + 1$. If $r(c) = p$, then $r(d) = p - 1$, because $p\text{F}(p - 1)$ (because x_p is adjacent to x_{p-1}). However, $(p - 1)\text{F}(p - 2)$ (because x_{p-1} is adjacent to x_{p-2}), and this is violated for vertex d. If $r(c) = p + 1$, then $(p + 1)\text{F}p$ implies that $r(d) = p$, and we again have a contradiction because $p\text{F}(p - 1)$.

Subcase 1.2: $r(a) = p + 1$, $r(b) \neq p + 1$. If $r(b) < p + 1$, then $q\text{N}(p + 1)$ for $q = 1, 2, \ldots, p - 1$ implies that $r(b) = p$. Now $p\text{F}(p - 1)$ implies that $r(c) = p - 1$ and $(p - 1)\text{F}(p - 2)$ implies that $r(d) = p - 2$. But then we contradict $(p - 2)\text{F}(p - 3)$, which applies because $p \geq 5$. Thus, suppose $r(b) > p + 1$. Without loss of generality, $r(b) = p + 2$. Then $r(c) \geq p$ because $q\text{N}(p + 2)$ for $q < p$. If $r(c) \leq p + 2$, then because $j\text{F}(j - 1)$ for $2 \leq j \leq p + 2$, we have $r(d) = r(c) - 1 \geq p - 1 > 2$. But $r(d)\text{F}(r(d) - 1)$, which we cannot satisfy. Thus, $r(c) > p + 2$ and without loss of generality, we assume $r(c) = p + 3$. Now $r(d)$ can only be $\geq p + 2$ because $(p + 3)\text{N}q$ for $q \leq p + 1$. If $r(d)$ is $p + 2$ or $p + 3$, we violate $r(d)\text{F}(r(d) - 1))$. If it is greater than $p + 3$, then every vertex gets a different role and we use $h + 1$ roles, contrary to the assumption that $k \leq h$.

Subcase 1.3: $r(a) \neq p + 1$, $r(b) = p + 1$. If $r(a) < p + 1$, then $r(a) > 1$ because $1Np$. Hence, $r(a)F(r(a) - 1)$, which is impossible because $r(a) \neq p + 1$. Hence, we suppose $r(a) > p + 1$, and without loss of generality $r(a) = p + 2$. Then because $qN(p + 1)$ for $q < p$, we have $r(c) = p$, $p + 1$, or $p + 2$ or $r(c) > p + 2$. If $r(c) = p$ or $p + 1$, then because $qF(q - 1)$ for $q = p$, $p + 1$, we have $r(d) = r(c) - 1$. However, this violates $(r(c) - 1)F(r(c) - 2)$. If $r(c) = p + 2$, then by $(p + 2)Fp$, we have $r(d) = p$. Because $p \geq 5$, this is contrary to $pF(p - 1)$. If $r(c) > p + 2$, we may assume without loss of generality that it equals $p + 3$. Now $qN(p + 3)$ for $q \leq p$ or $q = p + 2$. Hence, $r(d) = p + 1$ or $r(d) \geq p + 3$. If $r(d) = p + 1$, we violate $(p + 1)F(p + 2)$ with d. If $r(d) = p + 3$, we violate $(p + 3)F(p + 1)$ with d. If $r(d) > p + 3$, then every vertex gets a different role and we use $h + 1$ roles, contrary to assumption.

Case 2: $k = p$. Now qNp for $q < p - 1$ implies that $r(a)$ and $r(b)$ are each $p - 1$ or p. They cannot both be $p - 1$ because $(p - 1)N(p - 1)$. They cannot both be p because $pF(p - 1)$ and a would not be adjacent to a vertex of role $p - 1$. If $r(a) = p - 1$ and $r(b) = p$, then we violate $(p - 1)F(p - 2)$ with vertex a. If $r(a) = p$ and $r(b) = p - 1$, then $(p - 1)F(p - 2)$ and $(p - 2)F(p - 3)$ give us $r(c) = p - 2$, $r(d) = p - 3$. The latter violates $(p - 3)F(p - 4)$, which holds because $p \geq 5$.

Case 3: $k < p$. Note that $r(N(x_i)) = \{i - 1, i + 1\}$ for $i = 2, \ldots, k - 1$ and $r(N(x_1)) = \{2\}$. It follows that $r(x_{k+1})$ could only be $k - 1$ or k. We now consider two subcases.

Subcase 3.1: $r(x_{k+1}) = k - 1$. It follows that iNi for all i and that role i can only be adjacent to roles $i - 1$ or $i + 1$. Hence, $r(a)$ is either $r(x_p) + 1$ or $r(x_p) - 1$, and similarly for $r(b)$. However, because $[r(x_p) + 1]N[r(x_p) + 1]$ and $[r(x_p) - 1]N[r(x_p) - 1]$ and $[r(x_p) - 1]N[r(x_p) + 1]$, we could not have a adjacent to b.

Subcase 3.2: $r(x_{k+1}) = k$. We first note that we can choose p arbitrarily large so that $r(x_p) \neq k$ if $k = 3$ and if $k = 4$ and $r(x_p) \neq k - 1$ if $k = 3$. This is because if $k = 3$, the sequence $(r(x_1), r(x_2), \ldots, r(x_p))$ is $(1, 2, 3, 3, 2, 1, 2, 3, 3, 2, 1, \ldots)$ and if $k = 4$, the sequence is $(1, 2, 3, 4, 4, 3, 2, 1, 2, 3, 4, 4, 3, 2, 1, \ldots)$. Thus, if $k = 3$, $r(x_p) \neq k$ and $r(x_p) \neq k - 1$ hold for $p = 6, 11, 16, 21, 26, 31, \ldots$ and if $k = 4$, $r(x_p) \neq k$ holds for $p = 6, 7, 8, 9, 10, 13, 14, 15, 16, 17, 20, 21, 22, 23, 24, 27, 28, 29, 30, 31, \ldots$ and there are arbitrarily large values of p falling in both of these sets of numbers, in particular $p = 6, 16, 21, 31, \ldots$. Thus, we assume for the rest of the proof that $r(x_p) = k - 1$ implies that $k > 3$ and $r(x_p) = k$ implies that $k > 4$.

In this subcase, it follows that iNi for all $i \neq k$ and that for $i \neq k$, role i can only be adjacent to roles $i - 1$ or $i + 1$. If $r(x_p) \neq k$, then we know that $r(a)$ is either $r(x_p) + 1$ or $r(x_p) - 1$, and similarly for $r(b)$. However, because $[r(x_p) + 1]N[r(x_p) + 1]$ unless $r(x_p) = k - 1$, because $[r(x_p) - 1]N[r(x_p) - 1]$, and because $[r(x_p) - 1]N[r(x_p) + 1]$, we could not have a adjacent to b unless $r(x_p) = k - 1$, $r(a) = r(b) = k$. In this case, $r(c) = k$, $r(d) = k - 1$ or $r(c) = k - 1$, $r(d) = k$ or $r(c) = k - 1$, $r(d) = k - 2$ follow because kNj for $j \neq k - 1$, k and because $kF(k - 1)$, $(k - 1)Fk$, $(k - 1)F(k - 2)$, the latter because $k > 2$. If $r(d) = k - 1$, $(k - 1)F(k - 2)$ is violated. If $r(d) = k$, kFk is violated. If $r(d) = k - 2$, then we violate $(k - 2)F(k - 3)$, which holds because, by choice of p, we have $k > 3$ when $r(x_p) = k - 1$. We conclude that $r(x_p) = k$. By choice of p, $k > 4$ in this case. Because $r(x_p) = k$, $r(a)$ and $r(b)$ are each either k or $k - 1$. They cannot both be $k - 1$ because $(k - 1)N(k - 1)$. They cannot both be k because $kF(k - 1)$ and a would not be adjacent to a vertex of role $k - 1$. We cannot have $r(a) = k - 1$ and $r(b) = k$, because $(k - 1)F(k - 2)$, which holds because $k > 4$. If $r(a) = k$ and $r(b) = k - 1$, then $r(c) = k$, $r(d) = k - 1$ or $r(c) = k$, $r(d) = k$ or $r(c) = k - 2$, $r(d) = k - 3$ or $r(c) = k - 2$, $r(d) = k - 1$. In the first, second, and third cases, $r(d)F(r(d) - 1))$, which holds because $k > 4$, is violated by d. In the fourth case, $(k - 1)Fk$ is violated by d.

Q.E.D.

Remark. It should be noted that for $k = 2$, there is always a k-role assignment for the graph of Fig. 3.4: namely, we can take $(r(x_1), r(x_2), \ldots, r(x_p))$ to be the sequence $(1, 2, 2, 1, 2, 2, 1, \ldots)$. If $r(x_p) = 1$, then take $r(a) = r(b) = r(c) = 2$, $r(d) = 1$. If $r(x_p) = 2$, then take $r(a) = 1$, $r(b) = r(c) = 2$, $r(d) = 1$.

THRESHOLD ROLE ASSIGNMENTS

It turns out that the notion of threshold role assignment as we have defined it is too broad. In fact, we have the following theorem.

Theorem 7. Every graph G is k-threshold role assignable for all k such that $2 \leq k \leq |V(G)|$.

Proof. Let I be the set of isolated vertices in G. Suppose first that I has at least $k - 2$ vertices. If G has only isolated vertices, any assignment r using k different roles will be a k-role assignment, because $r(N(x)) = r(N(y)) = \phi$ for all x, y, so $d[r(N(x)), r(N(y))] = 0$. If G has some nonisolated vertices, note that each connected component of $G - I$ has a spanning tree. Let H be the union of these spanning trees. Then H is a bipartite graph with vertices in classes A and B and all edges going between a vertex of A and a vertex of B. Let r be defined arbitrarily on I using roles, $1, 2, \ldots, k -$

2 (with some repetitions if needed), and take $r(a) = k - 1$ for all $a \in A$ and $r(b) = k$ for all $b \in B$. If $r(x) = r(y)$, then $x,y \in I$, or $x,y \in A$, or $x,y \in B$. If $x,y \in I$, then $r(N(x)) = r(N(y)) = \phi$, so $d[r(N(x)),r(N(y))] \leq 0$. If $x,y \in A$, then, since neither is in I, each is adjacent to a vertex of B and so $k \in r(N(x)) \cap r(N(y))$ and we have $d[r(N(x)),r(N(y))] = 0$. Similarly, if $x,y \in B$, $k - 1 \in r(N(x)) \cap r(N(y))$, again giving us $d[r(N(x)),r(N(y))] = 0$.

Suppose next that I has at most $k - 3$ vertices. Let x_1 be a vertex in I, if there is any. Let x_2 be a different vertex in I. Continue until we run out of vertices in I. Let x_j be the last vertex chosen; hence $j \leq k - 3$. Let G' be the graph obtained by removing vertices $x_1, x_2, \ldots, x_j$ from G. Let H be the subgraph of G' defined by taking a spanning tree in each connected component of G'. Then H is a forest and, because H has no isolated vertices, every tree in H has at least two vertices. Every tree of more than one vertex has a pendant vertex, a vertex adjacent to exactly one other vertex. Let x_{j+1} be a pendant vertex of some tree making up H. Note that $H - x_{j+1}$ is still a forest. Let x_{j+2} be an isolated vertex of $H - x_{j+1}$ if there is one, and otherwise a pendant vertex of one of the trees of $H - x_{j+1}$. Let x_{j+3} be an isolated vertex of $H - x_{j+1} - x_{j+2}$ if there is one, and otherwise a pendant vertex of one of the trees of $H - x_{j+1} - x_{j+2}$. Continue in this way until we have chosen vertices $x_1, x_2, \ldots, x_{k-2}$. The remaining graph H' is a forest and is therefore bipartite. Let A and B be two classes of vertices of H' so that all edges go between classes. Because we always use up an isolated vertex if possible, note that H' has at most one isolated vertex. We may assume that this vertex, if it exists, is in class B. Now define r on G by letting $r(x_i) = i$, $i = 1, 2, \ldots k - 2$, $r(a) = k - 1$ if $a \in A$, and $r(b) = k$ if $b \in B$. To see that r defines a k-threshold role assignment, suppose that $r(x) = r(y)$. Then x and y both belong to A or both belong to B. If x and y both belong to A, then neither is isolated in H' and so each is adjacent to some vertex of B. Hence, $r(N(x))$ and $r(N(y))$ both contain k and we conclude that $d[r(N(x)),r(N(y))] = 0$. Suppose that x and y both belong to B. At most one of these is isolated in H'. Say y is not. Then y is adjacent to some vertex of A, and so $r(N(y))$ contains $k - 1$. If x is not isolated in H', then x is also adjacent to some vertex of A and $r(N(x))$ also contains $k - 1$, giving us $d[r(N(x)),r(N(y))] = 0$. If x is isolated in H', then x_{k-2} is adjacent to x, for otherwise we would have chosen x before x_{k-2}. Hence, we conclude that $k - 2$ is in $r(N(x))$, giving us $d[r(N(x)),r(N(y))] \leq 1$.

Remark. If $k = 1$, the theorem fails with our convention about $d(S,\phi)$. This issue arises if G has both an isolated vertex and a nonisolated vertex.

Because threshold role assignments are so easily attainable as we have defined them, it is tempting to consider alternative definitions. One natural one is to modify the definition of distance $d[r(N(x)),r(N(y))]$ that underlies the concept. A natural way to do that is to define the distance between sets S and T of numbers, $d(S,T)$, to be the smallest integer p so that for every $s \in S$, there is $t \in T$ with $|s - t| \le p$, and for every $t \in T$ there is $s \in S$ with $|s - t| \le p$. This distance is sometimes called the Hausdorff distance. We say that r is a k-*threshold/close role assignment* if Equation 3 holds with this definition of distance. We again use the convention that $d(S,\phi)$ is 0 for $S = \phi$ and ∞ for $S \ne \phi$.

Trivially, every graph of at least two vertices is 2-threshold/close role assignable. Simply use the role 1 on all isolated vertices and the role 2 on all other vertices. If there are no isolated vertices, use the role 1 on one vertex, chosen arbitrarily, and the role 2 otherwise. Because the only roles used are 1 and 2 and because $|1 - 2| \le 1$, 2-threshold/close role assignability follows.

Theorem 8. Every graph G of at least three vertices is 3-threshold/close role assignable.

Proof. If all vertices of G are isolated, then we can use roles 1, 2, and 3 arbitrarily on vertices.

If there are some isolated vertices, then we use role 1 on all isolated vertices and roles 2 and 3 arbitrarily on the rest of the vertices. Then if $r(x) = r(y) = 1$, we have $r(N(x)) = r(N(y)) = \phi$ and $d[r(N(x)),r(N(y))] = 0$. If $r(x) = r(y) = 2$ or 3, we have $r(N(x))$ and $r(N(y))$ each either equal to $\{2\}$, $\{3\}$, or $\{2,3\}$, so $d[r(N(x)),r(N(y))] \le 1$.

If G has no isolated vertices but at least two connected components, then use role 1 on one component and roles 2 and 3 arbitrarily on the rest of the vertices. If $r(x) = r(y) = 1$, then $r(N(x)) = r(N(y)) = \{1\}$, so $d[r(N(x)),r(N(y))] = 0$. If $r(x) = r(y) = 2$ or 3, the situation is the same as in the previous case.

Suppose G is connected. If G has no vertices of degree of 1, assign one vertex role 1, one vertex role 3, and all others role 2. If G has one vertex of degree 1, assign it role 1, assign one other vertex role 3, and assign all remaining vertices role 2. If G has at least two vertices of degree 1, assign one of them role 1 and the other role 3 and assign all remaining vertices role 2. If x is assigned role 2 and is adjacent only to the vertex assigned role 1 or to the vertex assigned role 3, then x has degree 1. Because the vertex assigned roles 1 or 3 to which it is adjacent also has degree 1, it follows by connectedness that G consists of just these two vertices, which contradicts our hypothesis that G has at least three vertices. We conclude that if $r(x) = r(y) = 2$, then $r(N(x))$ and $r(N(y))$ can never be $\{1\}$ or $\{3\}$ and can only be $\{2\}$, $\{1,2\}$, $\{1,3\}$, $\{2,3\}$ or $\{1,2,3\}$. Hence, $d[r(N(x)),r(N(y))] \le 1$.

Q.E.D.

Theorem 9. Every connected indifference graph without cut vertices and having $n \ge 4$ vertices is 4-threshold/close role assignable.

Proof. If $n = 4$, it is 4-threshold/close role assignable by giving all vertices a different role. So, assume $n \geq 5$. Let $x_1, x_2, \ldots, x_n$ be a compatible ordering of vertices. Let $r(x_1) = 1$ and $r(x_2) = 2$. If all remaining vertices are adjacent to x_2, let $r(x_n) = 4$ and $r(x_i) = 3$ for all remaining vertices. Then $r(x_i) = 3$ and $n \geq 5$ implies that $r(N(x_i)) = \{1,2,3,4\}$ or $\{2,3,4\}$ and the distance between these two sets is 1. If there is a remaining vertex not adjacent to x_2, find the smallest m so that x_m is not adjacent to x_2. Because x_3 is not a cut vertex, we must have x_2 adjacent to x_4, so $m \geq 5$. Let $r(x_i) = 3$ for $i = 3, 4, \ldots, m - 1$ and $r(x_i) = 4$ for $i = m, m + 1, \ldots, n$. Note that because $m \geq 5$, every vertex of role 3 is adjacent to another vertex of role 3. Thus, if $r(x_i) = r(x_j) = 3$, then $r(N(x_i))$ and $r(N(x_j))$ both contain $\{2,3\}$. It follows that $d[r(N(x_i)), r(N(x_j))] \leq 1$. If $r(x_i) = r(x_j) = 4$, then $r(N(x_i))$ and $r(N(x_j))$ are each either $\{3,4\}$ or $\{4\}$, and again we conclude that $d[r(N(x_i)), r(N(x_j))] \leq 1$.

Q.E.D.

DISCUSSION

We have only begun the exploration of the relationship between the two models of role assignment and indifference graph. In the process, we have left open a number of questions. First, we can ask whether or not every connected indifference graph G without cut vertices has a k-role assignment for all $k \leq |V(G)|$. Second, we do not know if there is a role-primitive indifference graph. Finally, our results about threshold/close role assignments (Theorems 8 and 9) leave open several questions. One is whether every graph of four or more vertices is 4-threshold/close role assignable, and, more generally, whether every graph of k or more vertices is k-threshold/close role assignable, $k \geq 4$. A second question is whether every connected indifference graph without cut vertices and with at least five vertices is 5-threshold/close role assignable or, more generally, whether every such graph with at least k vertices is k-threshold/close role assignable, $k \geq 5$.

ACKNOWLEDGMENTS

I gratefully acknowledge the support of National Science Foundation grant SES-9211492 to Rutgers University. I would also like to thank Li Sheng for her helpful comments and in particular for her suggestions of improved proofs of Theorems 4 and 6.

REFERENCES

Everett, M. G., & Borgatti, S. (1991). Role colouring a graph. *Mathematical Social Sciences, 21,* 183–188.

Everett, M. G., & Borgatti, S. (1994). Regular equivalence: General theory. *Journal of Mathematical Sociology, 19,* 29–52.

Roberts, F. S. (1969). Indifference graphs. In F. Harary (Ed.), *Proof techniques in graph theory* (pp. 139–146). New York: Academic Press.

Roberts, F. S. (1971). On the compatibility between a graph and a simple order. *Journal of Combinatorial Theory, 11,* 28–38.

Roberts, F. S. (1978). *Graph theory and its applications to problems of society.* NSF-CBMS Monograph No. 29. Philadelphia, PA: SIAM.

Roberts, F. S. (1984). *Applied combinatorics.* Englewood Cliffs, NJ: Prentice-Hall.

Roberts, F. S., & Sheng, L. (in press). Role assignments. In Y. Alavi (Ed.), *Graph theory, combinatorics, algorithms, and applications.*

White, D. R., & Reitz, K. P. (1983). Graph and semigroup homomorphisms on networks of relations. *Social Networks, 5,* 193–234.

Part II

Psychophysics and Psychometrics

Parallel Shift of Judgment-Characteristic Curve According to the Context in Cutaneous and Color Discriminations

Tarow Indow
University of California, Irvine

The method of constant stimuli is one of the early accomplishments of the quantitative approach in psychology. Pairs of stimuli (s_j, s_0), j = 1, 2, . . . ,n, are presented and, in three-category judgment, two series of rates, $p_U(s_j)$ for the judgment "$s_j > s_0$" (U), and $p_L(s_j)$ for the judgment "$s_j < s_0$" (L), are observed. Then, by fitting curves $P_U(s)$ and $P_L(s)$ to these data, we can determine the difference thresholds, $e_U(s_0)$ and $e_L(s_0)$, of the standard stimulus s_0. The difference, $e_U(s_0) - e_L(s_0)$, is called the *interval of uncertainty* (IU) and its midpoint is called the *subjective equality* with s_0. Elaborate fitting methods were proposed in the early 20th century (see Brown & Thomson, 1925; Guilford, 1936). When the author was a student in Tokyo, his professor, a PhD of E. G. Boring, said that studying these methods had been a nightmare for students. However, the method of constant stimuli was not used in obtaining fundamental quantitative information in psychophysics, such as contours of equal loudness or brightness, so not many solid results were gained from its applications. This is an unfortunate example of a mismatch in interest between mathematically minded methodologists and active researchers. Traditionally, the trend in change of $P(s_j)$ is called a *psychometric curve*. However, because the current connotation of *psychometrics* is psychological testing rather than psychophysics, *judgment characteristic curve* seems to be a more appropriate name for $P(s)$. This name is used in this chapter.

Two cases are presented in which the same peripheral stimulation leads to different perceptions in different contexts, and the judgment characteristic curves are parallel on the continuum of s or log s across these contexts. The first case is the discrimination of pressures, s_j on the tip of the middle finger of the left hand and s_0 on that of the right hand. The context is the distance between the two fingers, which can be altered by changing the position of the arms. When the subject perceives a larger distance between the two pressures, $P_U(s)$ and $P_L(s)$ respectively shift to the right and to the left with no change in slope, and IU $= e_U(s_0) - e_L(s_0)$ becomes larger. The second case is the region of color stimuli s in a three-dimensional (3-D) color space, which are indiscriminable from a standard color stimulus s_0. This region can be defined through an extended form of the method of constant stimuli over multiple directions from s_0. When the mode of appearance (context) of s_0 was changed, it was found that the size of the indiscriminable region changed but that its form and orientation remained the same, which implies the same parallel shift of $P(s)$ in each direction from s_0 through the change of mode.

The parallel shift of curves similar to that of $P(s)$ was discussed first by Levine (1970, 1972), and then by Falmagne (Chapter 6, 1985). In these articles, curves are of various forms. In the present chapter, the discussion is limited to the standard form that appears in the method of constant stimuli. This curve is given by the same equation as the Gaussian distribution function (sigmoid) $\Phi(s)$, although the stimulus s is not a random variable. In this article, this is denoted as $P(s) = \Phi(s|e(s_0), \sigma^2)$ where $e(s_0)$ and σ are the location and slope parameters of the curve. Whenever possible, the parameters are omitted.

PROCESS UNDERLYING COMPARISON JUDGMENTS
AND THE IMPLICATION OF PARALLEL SHIFT OF $\Phi(s)$

The fact that $P(s) = \Phi(s)$ holds under a fixed context leads to the following model of the underlying latent process. Greek letters are used to denote latent variables. It suffices to describe the model only for $P_U(s)$.

1.   When a pair (s,s_0) is presented, two random variables ξ and ξ_0 are generated "within the subject" such that the judgment U, "$s > s_0$," occurs if and only if (iff) $\zeta = (\xi - \xi_0) > \varepsilon$, where ε is a positive constant. For any $s = s$, assume that ξ and ξ_0 respectively follow Gaussian distributions around means $\bar{\xi}_s$ and $\bar{\xi}_0$, with the same variance σ_ξ^2. Assume that the correlation between ξ and ξ_0 is a constant ρ for all s of s. Then the distribution of ζ for (s,s_0) is also Gaussian, with mean $\zeta_s = (-\bar{\xi}_0)$ and variance $\sigma_\zeta^2 = k\sigma_\xi^2$ where $k = [2(1 - \rho)]$. This density function is denoted by $\phi(\zeta; \zeta_s, \sigma_\zeta^2)$, where the term before the semicolon is the random variable and the last two are its parameters. Then,

$$P_U(s) = \Pr\{\zeta > \varepsilon\} = \int_{\varepsilon}^{\infty}\phi(\zeta;\ \tilde{\zeta}_s,\sigma_\zeta^2)\ d\zeta = \int_{-\infty}^{t_s(\varepsilon)}\phi(t;\ 0,1)\ dt \qquad (1)$$

where $t = (\zeta - \tilde{\zeta}_s)/\sigma_\zeta$ and $t_s(\varepsilon) = -(\varepsilon - \tilde{\zeta}_s)/\sigma_\zeta$.

2. The mean $\tilde{\xi}_s$ of the distribution of ξ caused by s is a function of s. Depending on whether $P(s)$ or $P(\log s)$ is at issue, we have to assume that the relation between $\tilde{\xi}_s$ and s is linear or logarithmic. When linear, $\tilde{\xi}_s = \alpha s - \beta$ and, for $P_U(s)$, $\alpha > 0$,

$$P_U(s) = \Phi(s|e_U(s_0),\ \sigma_U^2) = \int_{-\infty}^{s}\phi(s;\ e_U(s_0),\sigma_U^2)\ ds \qquad (2)$$

and

$$\sigma_\zeta = \alpha\sigma \qquad \tilde{\zeta}_s = \alpha(s - s_0) \qquad \varepsilon = \alpha(e_U(s_0) - s_0) \qquad (3)$$

When $s = e_U(s_0)$, then $\Phi[e(s_0)] = 0.5$. When $s = s_0$, then $\tilde{\zeta} = 0$, and

$$P(s_0) = \Phi(-t_0(\varepsilon)|0,1) \qquad t_0(\varepsilon) = \varepsilon/\sigma_\zeta \qquad 0 \le P(s_0) < 0.5 \qquad (4)$$

3. The shift of $\Phi_U(s)$ on s keeping its slope constant through different contexts implies that the context affects $e_U(s_0)$ and hence ε only, whereas σ_ξ, k, and σ are independent of the context. For the judgment L, "$s < s_0$," $P_L(s) = 1 - \Phi(s|e_L(s_0),\sigma_L^2)$. For $\Phi(\log s)$, s in Equation 2 is to be replaced by $S = \log s$.

DISCRIMINATION OF PRESSURES TO THE TIPS
OF MIDDLE FINGERS OF LEFT AND RIGHT HANDS

When we compare two objects, it is natural to place the two close together. With regard to discrimination of intensity, Köhler (1933) and Lauenstein (1933) proposed the following hypothesis to account for this fact: The discrimination is not determined by the difference in intensity of two excitations in the brain per se, but by the *gradient* between the two. Jacobs (1933) showed that the brightness difference threshold of two lights simultaneously presented increases as a function of the distance between the two retinal images, provided the two images are always on retinal positions with the same sensitivity. According to the experiment of Kleinbub cited in Köhler (1933), however, if two lights at different locations are successively fixated so that the two images fall on the fovea one by one, then the threshold remains the same when the spatial separation of the two lights is changed.

Amano (1944) performed an experiment on intensity discrimination of pressures, which corresponds to Jacobs's experiment on light. Two pressure stimuli (s, s_0) were simultaneously given to the tips of index fingers of the left and right hands, respectively. Depending on the position of the arm, the distance between the two fingers was either 2, 42, or 82 cm. Then the difference threshold increased according to the distance. Indow (1959) tried to see whether the same phenomenon reported by Kleinbub occurred when two pressure stimuli were successively given to the same finger tip. The position of the finger was changed by the movement of the arm during the time interval.

The experiment consists of two parts. Part I is a replication of Amano's experiment on simultaneous pressure comparison to successive comparison. The standard stimulus s_0 was given to the right middle finger, and then, after an interval of 4 sec, a comparison stimulus s_j was given to the left middle finger. Depending on the position of the arms, the distance between s_0 and s_j was set at either 10 or 100 cm. During the interval, the subject was asked to move his or her left arm as shown in A and B in I of Fig. 4.1, to make the condition comparable to that in Part II. In Part II, s_0 and s_j were successively given to the middle finger of the left hand. During the 4-sec interval, the left arm was moved as shown in A and B in II of Fig. 4.1. The subject perceived the pressures at the tip of the same finger but at different positions, that is, with a separation of 10 cm in A and 100 cm in B. Notice that, during the 4-sec interval, about the same amount of arm movement was involved in I and II. For the same subject, the same set of nine appropriately chosen comparison stimuli, $\{s_j\}$ in which $s_5 = s_0$, was used throughout all the four conditions. The blindfolded subject judged each pair (s_j, s_0) 40 times, with the three categories, U, L, and "indiscriminable." Hence, data $p_U(s_j)$ and $p_L(s_j)$ were independent. Several sessions were necessary to complete each experiment, and sessions for 10

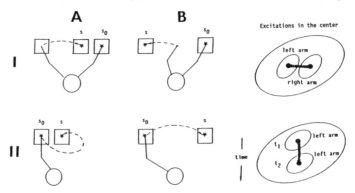

FIG. 4.1. Condition of arms in experiment on intensity discrimination of pressures on tips of fingers.

and 100 cm were evenly distributed in the order of experimentation to make the results comparable.

Because Weber's ratio is large in cutaneous sensation, it was more appropriate to use $\Phi(\log s)$ rather than $\Phi(s)$. Denote $S = \log_{10} s$. First, four curves, $\Phi_{XD}(S)$, $X = U$ or L, and $D = 10$ or 100 cm, were fitted separately by the algorithm of Finney (1952) (more detail in Bock & Jones, 1968). Then, it became clear that the four curves had almost the same slope on S. Hence, the four $\Phi_{XC}(S)$ were refitted under the constraint to have a common slope. The maximum likelihood estimates of five parameter values, $e_{XC}(S_0)$ and one slope parameter (σ in terms of S), as well as the goodness of fit, are given in Table 4.1. Even under this strong constraint, none of the seven curves was rejected. In the arm condition I, the interval of uncertainty, $IU_D = e_{UD}(S_0) - e_{LD}(S_0)$, increased when D was changed from 10 to 100 cm, and the difference $\Delta IU = IU_{100} - IU_{10}$ (>0) was significant in each subject. In the arm condition II, however, the null hypothesis of ΔIU being 0 was not rejected. This is analogous to the result of Kleinbub's experiment on brightness discrimination. The maximum likelihood estimation of $e_X(S_0)$ provided the necessary information for these statistical tests.

In A and B of Fig. 4.1, the pressure impressions stem from the same peripheral stimulations. However, the subject perceived different distances between the pressures in A and B. This perceptual difference is due to some proprioceptive stimulations from both arms (I) and from the left arm (II). If the discrimination is determined by the gradient between two excitations in the brain, they must be separated by a larger distance in B than in A in condition I. Then there are two possibilities for the effect of context (arm position). One is that the excitations occur in different positions of the brain according to the context, and hence the distance between ξ and ξ_0 is changed. The other is that the positions of ξ and ξ_0 are not affected by the context, but the same topographical distance between the two (thick horizontal line in Fig. 4.1) changes its functional meaning. A naive analogue to this situation would be the change of conductance of the medium in between. According to the second possibility, two excitations under arm condition II occur at the same position in the brain, but are separated by an intervening process corresponding to the time interval (thick vertical line in Fig. 4.1). The result suggests that no change in this vertical distance is induced by the change of the arm position.

It is not the purpose of this chapter to discuss the gradient hypothesis or positions of excitations in the brain. What should be emphasized here is that $\Phi_{XD}(S)$, for $X = U$ or L, and $D = 10$ or 100 cm, have a common slope. This implies that the random fluctuation of the latent variable ξ is determined by the peripheral excitation and is independent of the context, whereas the judgment on $\zeta = (\xi - \xi_0)$, which is based on the central process, is sensitive to the context. The separation of σ_ζ and $\tilde{\xi}_S$, similar to

TABLE 4.1

Results of Experiment on Intensity Discrimination of Pressures on Tips of Fingers

Subjects		Goodness of Fit of $\Phi(S,\ S = \log_{10} s$ (gram), With a Common Slope $(1/\sigma)$ and Difference Thresholds, $e_U(s_0)$ and $e_L(s_0)$						Changes of $IU = e_U(s_0) - e_L(s_0)$ Between 10 cm and 100 cm Intervals (Fig. 4.1) and Tests of Significance of $\Delta IU = IU_{100} - IU_{10}$					
		$e_{10}(s_0)$	$e_{100}(s_0)$	σ	x_0^2	df	P	IU_{10}	IU_{100}	ΔIU	$\sigma(\Delta IU)$	t	P^a
Part I													
Sa	U :	1.692	1.707	0.0781	20.71	24	II	0.118	0.163	0.045	0.0153	2.94	0.002
	L :	1.574	1.544										
Ta	U :	1.810	1.818	0.0862	24.45	27	II	0.121	0.146	0.025	0.0146	1.71	0.03
	L :	1.689	1.672										
Sn	U :	1.744	1.784	0.0814	11.44	14	II	0.073	0.096	0.023	0.0148	1.55	0.06
	L :	1.671	1.688										
Sk	U :	1.692	1.731	0.0695	35.00	30	IV	0.098	0.140	0.042	0.0168	2.50	0.006
	L :	1.594	1.591										
Part II													
M	U :	1.746	1.749	0.0802	29.40	25	IV	0.158	0.133	−0.025	0.0152	1.64	0.10
	L :	1.588	1.616										
Sn	U :	1.714	1.723	0.0923	17.31	16	III	0.079	0.084	0.005	0.0137	0.04	0.96
	L :	1.635	1.639										
I	U :	1.671	1.661	0.0723	22.37	18	IV	0.034	0.025	−0.009	0.0150	0.60	0.54
	L :	1.637	1.636										

Note. Goodness of fit, $P = \Pr(x^2 > x_0^2)$: I, 0.90–1.00; II, 0.75–0.90; III, 0.50–0.75; IV, 0.25–0.50.
[a]For Part I, P is by one-tailed test; for Part II, P is by two-tailed test.

that between noise and signal in signal detection theory, is obtained by the use of the almost obsolete method of constant stimuli.

DISCRIMINATION ELLIPSOIDS FOR TWO MODES OF APPEARANCE: APERTURE AND (SIMULATED) SURFACE COLORS

When a color target with a homogeneous surround is presented on a monitor, its mode of appearance changes according to the luminance of the surround. When the surround is dark or its luminance is sufficiently lower than that of target, the target appears to be filled by light of the color corresponding to its spectral pattern $\{P_\lambda\}$, where P and λ are radiant flux and wavelength, respectively. The target's appearance is called *aperture color* (A-mode). The colors of objects we see under natural conditions are of a different mode. It is called *surface color* (S-mode). We can touch a surface color, but we feel as if our finger will go through an aperture color. When the sky is clear, its appearance is of aperture color mode. When the intensity of light is changed, a color of S-mode changes from blackish to whitish whereas a color of A-mode changes from dim to bright. When a brown surface is observed through a reduction tube with black inside, the A-mode color filling the tube is not brown, but rather dark reddish color. In order for a target to appear brown, blackness has to be induced from its surround. When a target is in a sufficiently brighter surround, it appears like a patch of colored paper placed on the background. Depending on its $\{P_\lambda\}$, the target appears black, white, or brown, and so on. Because it is textureless, this mode of appearance is called *simulated surface color* (S'-mode).

Most basic data on colorimetry and color vision were obtained with A-mode colors. The number of colors we can discriminate is on the order of seven million, and there are infinitely many spectral patterns $\{P_\lambda\}$ that yield the same color. Hence, the best way to specify the chromatic properties of light is to represent all these spectral patterns by a point in a space of a small number of dimensions. This is called a *color space* (Wyszecki & Stiles, 1982). The Commission Internationale de l'Eclairage (CIE) established a color space having three coordinates (x, y, Y), for a 2° target in 1936 and for a 10° target in 1964. The light coming from a TV display tube and the light sent to the camera from an original object are entirely different in $\{P_\lambda\}$, but the two are represented by points close in the space (x, y, Y). This system has been defined solely on the basis of color matching experiments with A-mode colors. The three variables per se are not intended to represent visual processes, except that Y is related to brightness and (x, y) to hue and saturation. A plane (x, y) with a fixed level of luminance Y is called a *chromaticity diagram*. The distance between two points P_j and P_k in the space (x, y, Y) is not a metric for the difference we perceive between the two colors. When just-noticeable differences (jnd's) in various directions from a point P_0 are plotted, they form an ellipsoid around P_0 in the space. This is called a *discrimination ellipsoid*. If the region around a point P_0 is isotropic, jnd's should form a sphere around s_0, and if the entire color space is homogeneous with regard to jnd, we should expect that all discrimination spheres for various P_0 should have be the same size.

Most discrimination ellipsoids of A-mode colors are obtained by the following *matching* procedure in (x,y,Y). In a small bipartite target, a color stimulus $s_0 = (x_0,y_0,Y_0)$ is fixed in one side and the subject adjusts the stimulus s on the other side until the whole target is filled with the same color. Essentially, this is the procedure by which the (x,y,Y) system has been defined. When the matching with s_0 is repeated, we have a distribution of matched results $s_m = (x_m,y_m,Y_m)$. The region in which s_m falls with probabilities larger than a given value is ellipsoidal around P_0 (Brown & MacAdam, 1949, and others). Its size depends on the specified value of probability. When Y is kept constant in the adjustment of s, we have a discrimination ellipse in the chromaticity diagram (x,y) corresponding to that luminance Y (MacAdam, 1942, and others).

To determine jnd's for a color of S-mode, this matching by adjustments cannot be employed, because a painted surface s cannot be adjusted while being observed. We can prepare a set $\{s_j\}$ of comparison surface colors differing from s_0 in various directions, and present each (s_j,s_0) to define the percentage $p(s_j)$ for judgment "the two are discriminable." If s_j differs from s_0 along a continuum s with a direction Λ only, we can expect that, using the same notations as in Equation 2,

$$P_\Lambda(s) = \Phi(s|e(s_0)_\Lambda, \sigma_\Lambda{}^2) \tag{5}$$

This judgment characteristic curve changes, according to direction Λ, not only its location, $e(s_0)_\Lambda$, but also its slope, which is related to $\sigma_\Lambda{}^{-1}$. Using the data $p(s_j)$ in which s_j are varied in various directions, we can test directly whether $e(s_0)_\Lambda$ form an ellipsoid $E(s_0)$. If this is the case, each distance s_Λ from s_0 should have the same meaning when measured by the radius $e(s_0)_\Lambda$ of $E(s_0)$ in each of the directions Λ. Namely, for all $\bar{s}_j = (s_j - s_0)/e(s_0)_\Lambda$, the same judgment characteristic curve $P(\bar{s})$ should hold. Indow and Morrison (1991) developed an algorithm to define such an ellipsoid $E(s_0)$ that gives the best fit to the data $p(\bar{s}_j)$ thus converted. Then, this direction-independent judgment characteristic curve has only one parameter, t_0 (>0):

$$P(\bar{s}) = \Phi(u|0,1)$$
$$u = t_0(\bar{s} - 1) \qquad t_0 = -\Phi^{-1}(p(s_0)|0,1) \tag{6}$$

where $p(s_0)$ is the observed rate of "discriminable" judgment for the pair of identical stimuli (s_0,s_0). This judgment is called *false discrimination*. Irrespective of Λ, when s is at the boundary of $E(s_0)$, that is, $(s - s_0) = e(s_0)_\Lambda$, then $u = 0$, and $P(0) = 0.5$. For (s_0, s_0), $\bar{s} = 0$ and $u = -t_0$. That is, the slope of Equation 6 is determined by t_0 and hence by $p(s_0)$.

The obtained $E(s_0)$ values of S-mode colors are reported in Indow and Morrison (1991) and those of S'-mode colors in Indow, Robertson, von Grunau, and Fielder (1992). In all cases, $P(\bar{s})$ of Equation 6 based on these estimated $E(s_0)$ gave acceptable fits to the data. The experiment by Indow et al. was performed with the purpose of comparing two $E(s_0)$ values of the same subject under the same condition, one by the traditional method, matching (*M-method*), and the other by the paired comparison method just stated (*C-method*). Two squares (each $1.62° \times 1.62°$, separated by $0.32°$ from side to side) were presented for 0.5 sec on a Textronix display, and their mode of appearance (context), $C = A$ or S', was controlled by the luminance of the surround, and $E_C(s_0)$ were obtained for the same two subjects by the M- and C-methods. A pair was presented for 0.5 sec, with s_0 on the right and a comparison s_j on the left. The latter could be varied along seven directions, Λ, each passing through s_0. The standard stimulus s_0 was of six kinds, red (R), yellow (Y), green (G), blue (B), achromatic (A), and brown (Br). The luminance Y_0 of each s_0 was set at the level that gives the highest saturation of the color.

In the M-method with s_0, during the presentation intervals, the subject adjusted s for the next presentation along s_Λ (one of the seven directions). Presentations of (s_0, s) were repeated until s and s_0 appeared to be the same. The final position of s on s_Λ was a matched result $s_m = (x_m, y_m, Y_m)$ for s_0. The continuum s_Λ in the next adjustment was randomly chosen from the seven directions. In each direction, matching was repeated 16 times. Hence, for each s_0, the number of matched results s_m was 7×16 for a subject.

In the C-method with s_0, s on the left was chosen randomly from the set $\{s_j\}$ for s_0, $j = 1, 2, \ldots, n$, where $n = (7 \times 10 + 1)$, 10 comparison stimuli s_j in each of the seven directions plus one identical pair. The judgment was of two categories, discriminable or not. Each pair (s_j, s_0) was judged 30 times by each subject. The experiment to define an $E(s_0)$ by the M- or C-method was distributed over several sessions, and the order of sessions of different s_0, modes, and methods was randomized.

Results relevant to this article are given in Fig. 4.2 and Table 4.2. Fig. 4.2 shows the averaged results of $E(s_0)$, separately estimated with two subjects: ellipses in the chromaticity diagram (x, y) and the third radius in the direction of luminance Y. Except for $s_0 = Y$ (yellow), the M-method gave almost the same ellipsoids for colors of A- and S'-modes, whereas the C-method gave larger, but similar in shape and orientation, ellipsoids for colors of A-mode. Table 4.2 shows individually observed rates of false discrimination, $p(s_0)$. Clearly, there is a tendency for $p(s_0)$ to be larger in S'-mode than in A-mode.

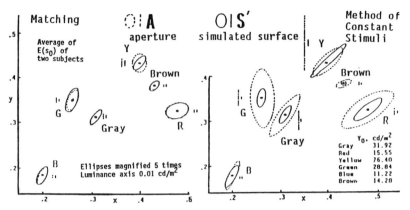

FIG. 4.2. Discrimination ellipses on the chromaticity diagram (magnified five times) and the length of luminance axis (bars) by two methods for two modes of appearance. From "Metrics in Color Spaces: Im Kleinen und im Grossen," by T. Indow, 1994, in G. H. Fisher and D. Leming (Eds.), *Contributions to Mathematical Psychology, Psychometrics, and Methodology* (p. 8). New York: Springer-Verlag. Copyright © 1994 by Springer-Verlag. Adapted with permission.

TABLE 4.2
False Discrimination Rates $p(s_0)$ for the Color Stimuli (s_0, s_0)

Color s_0		(Subject)	A-Mode	S'-Mode
A:	Achromatic	(T.I.)	.069	.444
		(M.I.)	.129	.484
R:	Red	(T.I.)	.089	.421
		(M.I.)	.107	.480
Y:	Yellow	(T.I.)	.200	.413
		(M.I.)	.448	.456
G:	Green	(T.I.)	.209	.206
		(M.I.)	.117	.468
B:	Blue	(T.I.)	.331	.420
		(M.I.)	.119	.395
Br:	Brown	(G.F.)	.344	.472
		(M.v.G.)	.385	.416

THE PROCESS UNDERLYING DISCRIMINATION ELLIPSOIDS $E(s_0)$

Fluctuation in the Latent Process for a Color Stimulus

For a color stimulus s, we have to think of a 3-D random variable $\{\xi_I\}$, $I = 1,2,3$, in the latent process. Suppose that $\{\xi_I\}$ for s_0 follows a Gaussian distribution, $\phi_3(\{\xi_I\}; \{\bar{\xi}_I(s_0)\}, \Sigma)$, with the 3×3 variance-covariance matrix Σ. Then $\{\xi_I\}$ for which ϕ_3 is larger than a value of density L forms an ellipsoidal area around $\{\xi_I(s_0)\}$. Its shape and orientation depend on Σ, and its size depends on L. The situation is the same for any 3-D Gaussian random variable if it is obtained from $\{\xi_I\}$ through an affine transformation, because the transformation only changes Σ to a new variance–covariance matrix. Denote by $\{\xi_x,\xi_y,\xi_Y\}$ such $\{\xi_I\}$ that are related to the CIE (x,y,Y) in the following way: $\xi_x = \alpha_x x$, $\xi_y = \alpha_y y$, $\xi_Y = \alpha_Y Y$. Then, when s_0 is repeatedly presented, (x,y,Y) as counterparts of $\{\xi_x,\xi_y,\xi_Y\}$ are 3-D Gaussian random variables with the means (x_0,y_0,Y_0) and a variance–covariance matrix. Hence, we can understand why s_m matched with s_0 is embraced with a given probability in an ellipsoid around (x_0,y_0,Y_0). Notice, however, that ϕ_3 of $\{\xi_I\}$ given earlier is not the density function of matched results s_m.

Ellipsoids by the C-method

When (s,s_0) is presented, we can imagine a line connecting the two latent 3-D random points, ξ for s and ξ_0 for s_0. Denote the distance between the two endpoints of this line by $\zeta = (\xi - \xi_0)$. For the same pair (s,s_0), the line from ξ_0 to ξ can vary in its direction and length from presentation to presentation. Its length ζ is a scalar random variable, which is positive or negative according to whether ξ is on the right or left of ξ_0. We can think of a unidimensional distribution of ζ for repeated presentations of (s,s_0). Let us assume that it is Gaussian, $\phi(\zeta;\ \bar{\zeta}_s,\sigma_\zeta^2)$, and the parameters are functions of s. Consider s differing from s_0 in a fixed direction Λ, and suppose that the "discriminable" judgment occurs iff $|\zeta| > \varepsilon$, where ε is a positive constant independent of the value of s and of the direction Λ. Then Equation 1 holds for $P_\Lambda(s)$. If $\bar{\zeta}_s = \alpha_\Lambda |s - s_0|$, then $P_\Lambda(s)$ is given by Equation 2, which is identical to Equation 5. From Equation 3,

$$\sigma_\Lambda = \sigma_\zeta/\alpha_\Lambda \qquad |e_\Lambda(s_0) - s_0| = \varepsilon/\alpha_\Lambda \tag{7}$$

When Equation 6 holds,

$$t_0 = -\Phi^{-1}(p(s_0)|0,1) = \varepsilon \tag{8}$$

In this model, the ellipsoidal form $(e(s_0)_\Lambda - s_0)$ in the space of s is solely due to the local anisotropy around s_0, that is, α_Λ^{-1}. If the space is isotropic, the indiscriminable region is a sphere with radius ε/α. Thus far, s_0 is fixed. If σ_ζ, ε, and α_Λ are independent of s_0, ellipsoids $E(s_0)$ should be identical in form, size, and orientation for all s_0. Clearly, this is the case neither in the (x,y,Y) space nor in the Munsell space (Indow, 1993). Hence, the parameters σ_ζ, ε, and α_Λ are treated as functions of s_0.

As to the effect of mode of appearance, the C-method gives a paradoxical result. In A-mode presentation, the ellipsoids are larger (the right-hand plot in Fig. 4.2) and the rates of false discrimination, $p(s_0)$, are smaller (Table 4.2). The former implies that the discrimination is more difficult, whereas the latter implies that the discrimination is more accurate. Equations 7 and 8 shed light on this result. If $\sigma_\zeta(s_0)$ and α_A were not affected by mode, $\sigma(s_0)_A$, which determines the slope $P_A(s)$ of Equation 5, would be constant through the change of mode. If $\varepsilon_A(s_0) > \varepsilon_{S'}(s_0)$, $e(s_0)_A$ shifts in A proportionally to the left and right of s_0 according to Equation 7, which would yield $E_A(s_0)$ that is larger in size but the same in form and orientation as $E_{S'}(s_0)$. According to Equation 8, however, $\Phi^{-1}(p(s_0)|0,1)$ shifts toward the negative direction and $p(s_0)$ is smaller in A-mode presentation. Furthermore, for the same s_0, ratio$(E) = E_A(s_0)/E_{S'}(s_0)$ and ratio(t_0) = $(t_0(s_0)$ in A$)/(t_0(s_0)$ in $S')$ must be the same, because both are equal to $\varepsilon_A(s_0)/\varepsilon_{S'}(s_0)$. Figure 4.3 part I shows this relationship. Values of $t_0(s_0)$ were obtained through Equation 6 from $p(s_0)$ in Table 4.2. The scatter of points is not too far from the equality line. The large scatter is understandable because the data $p(s_j)$ were based on only 30 judgments from each subject and the sizes of $E(s)$ were defined in terms of the three directions only. It was problematic to define ratio(E) for $s_0 = Y$ (yellow). This problem will be discussed later. The basic trend does not change even when Y is excluded from the plot, however.

Ellipsoids by the M-Method

The left plot in Fig. 4.2 shows that $E_A(s_0)$ and $E_{S'}(s_0)$ are identical when defined by the M-method. Again, the result for $s_0 = Y$ (yellow) is an exception. In most studies, a matched result $s_m = (x_m, y_m, Y_m)$ was obtained through simultaneous adjustments in various directions from s_0 (e.g., Brown & MacAdam, 1949; Wyszecki & Fielder, 1971). In this case, we can think of 3-D random variables $\{\zeta_I\}$, $I = x, y, Y$, for (s_m, s_0). As explained in the first part of this section, if this follows a Gaussian distribution $\phi_3\{\{\zeta_I\};$ $(0, 0, 0), \Sigma_m\}$, and $\zeta_x = \alpha_x(x_m - x_0)$, $\zeta_y = \alpha_y(y_m - y_0)$, $\zeta_Y = (Y_m - Y_0)$, then we have a color discrimination ellipsoid around (x_0, y_0, Y_0). Then, for $E_A(s_0) = E_{S'}(s_0)$ to hold, it is necessary that the variance-covariance matrix Σ_m, and the mapping parameters α_x, α_y, α_Y, remain the same through the change of mode. This is the condition assumed before for the result of the C-method: $E_A(s_0)$ and $E_{S'}(s_0)$ are similar.

The M-method constructed $E_M(s_0)$ in the following way from the data $\{s_m\}$, consisting of 91 values (13 in each of the seven directions). The distribution of s_m in a fixed direction Λ was assumed to be given by $\phi(s_m; s_0, \sigma^2(s_0)_\Lambda)$, a slice of a 3-D Gaussian distribution through s_0 in that direction. As in most other studies, the size of $E_M(s_0)$ was defined so that the radius $e(s_0)_\Lambda$ in the direction Λ is equal to $\sigma(s_0)_\Lambda$. Under this condition, the ellipses in the chromaticity diagram and the third radius along the luminance Y

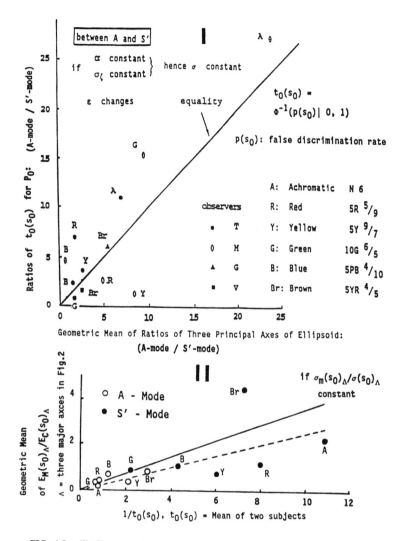

FIG. 4.3. (I) Change of size of discrimination ellipsoids and change of t_0 [from $p(s_0)$ in Table 4.2] from A to S′ mode. (II) Change of size of ellipsoids from M- to C-method and $1/t_0$ [from $p(s_0)$ in C-method].

were estimated. The observed distribution of $s_m = (x_m, y_m, Y_m)$ was well fitted by $E_M(s_0)$ thus obtained.

In each step of adjustment of s of (s, s_0) in direction Λ, we can assume the same latent process as in the C-method, $\phi(\zeta; \tilde{\zeta}_s, \sigma_\zeta^2)$. Because the direction of adjustment is fixed, the subscript Λ is omitted in this paragraph. The adjustment is terminated whenever such a pair (s_m, s_0) is reached that yields ζ close enough to 0, that is, $|\zeta| < \varepsilon$. The probability of having such a ζ for a value s_m on s_Λ is

$$f(s_m) = \int_{-\varepsilon}^{\varepsilon} \phi(\zeta;\ \tilde{\zeta}(s_m),\sigma_{m\zeta}{}^2)\ d\zeta$$

This is a rectangular-like area having a base of 2ε and a top slightly tilted to the left or right depending on whether $\tilde{\zeta}(s_m)$ is greater than or less than 0. Putting both cases together, we have a rectangle and its area is proportional to the density at the center of the base,

$$f(s_m) \propto \phi(0;\ \tilde{\zeta}(s_m),\sigma_{m\zeta}{}^2) \tag{9}$$

In the M-method, $\tilde{\zeta}(s_m)$ is a random variable. If the right side of Equation 9 is replaced by its conjugate density function $\phi(\tilde{\zeta}(s_m);0,\sigma_{m\zeta}{}^2)$, which is always equal in value to $\phi(0;\ \tilde{\zeta}(s_m),\sigma_{m\zeta}{}^2)$, and under the assumption of $\tilde{\zeta}(s_m) = \alpha_\Lambda(s_m - s_0)$ as in the C-method, we have $\phi(s_m;\ s_0,\sigma^2(s_0)_\Lambda)$, and

$$\sigma_m(s_0)_\Lambda = \sigma_{m\zeta}/\alpha_\Lambda \tag{10}$$

This is defined to be the radius of $E_M(s_0)$ in the direction Λ. Hence, if $\sigma_{m\zeta}$ is assumed to be constant for Λ, the ellipsoidal form of the indiscriminable region around s_0 in this space is solely due to the local anisotropy, $1/\alpha_\Lambda(s_0)$, as was the case in $E_C(s_0)$.

The finding that $E_A(s_0) = E_{S'}(s_0)$ in the A-method implies that, as in the C-method, $\sigma_{m\zeta}(s_0)$ and α_Λ are not affected by mode. However, these may be functions of the color s_0 and the method, M or C. The other parameter, ε, which is assumed in the C-method to change according to mode, is not involved in this model for the M-method. Denote the radius of $E(s_0)$ in the direction Λ from s_0 by $E(s_0)_\Lambda$. Then, in the M-method, $E_M(s_0)_\Lambda/\sigma_m(s_0)_\Lambda = 1$. In the C-method, $E_C(s_0)_\Lambda/\sigma(s_0)_\Lambda = t_0(s_0)$ according to Equation 6. Hence,

$$E_M(s_0)_\Lambda/E_C(s_0)_\Lambda = C(s_0)/t_0(s_0) \qquad C(s_0) = \sigma_m(s_0)_\Lambda/\sigma(s_0)_\Lambda \tag{11}$$

Figure 4.3 part II shows this relationship. The ordinate is the geometric mean of the left-side ratios, where Λ represents the directions of the three major axes of the ellipsoids in Fig. 4.2, and the abscissa is $1/t_0(s_0)$, where $t_0(s_0)$ is the mean of two values used in the upper plot I. Roughly speaking, points are scattered around a straight line passing through the origin. If we accept this proportionality between the two variables, $C(s_0)$ in Equation 11 can be regarded as a constant and its value is given by the slope. The slope of the solid line for all colors is about 0.3. If $s_0 = Br$ is regarded as an outlier, the slope of the dotted line is about 0.22. From Equation 7 and 10,

$$C(s_0) = [\sigma_{m\zeta}(s_0)/\sigma_\zeta(s_0)]/[(\alpha_\Lambda(s_0) \text{ in } M)/(\alpha_\Lambda(s_0) \text{ in } C)] \qquad (12)$$

If the same mapping $\alpha_\Lambda(s_0)$ holds around s_0 for the C- and M-methods, the denominator of Equation 12 is unity, which means that $C(s_0) = \sigma_{m\zeta}(s_0)/\sigma_\zeta(s_0)$ must be a constant over all the colors. This situation is in accordance with the fact that $E_M(s_0)$ in the left side of Fig. 4.2 are similar in size and orientation to $E_{S'}(s_0)$ in the right side. That the slope is less than unity, that is, $\sigma_{m\zeta}(s_0) < \sigma_\zeta(s_0)$, is understandable because s_m is the final result of repeated adjustments.

The model discussed here does not take into account the dynamic aspect of the process of adjusting s before each s_m is obtained. Robbins and Monro (1951, p. 405) discussed a matching process in which s_i is changed to $s_{i+1} = s_i \pm 0.5c_i$ according to whether s_i is perceived as smaller (<) or larger (>) than s_0, where $\{c_i\}$ is any sequence of positive constants of type $1/n$. Then the distribution of s_n is asymptotically Gaussian with mean s_0 and a vanishing variance (Falmagne, 1985; Wasan, 1969).

GENERAL COMMENTS

The judgment characteristic curves, $P_U(S)$ and $P_L(S)$, for simultaneous comparison of pressures in the first experiment are sigmoids of the same slope on $S = \log s$, where U and L respectively mean the judgments "$s > s_0$" and "$s < s_0$." When the distance D between the pressures is increased from 10 cm to 100 cm by changing the arm position as shown in part I of Fig. 4.1, $P_U(S)$ shifts to the right and $P_L(S)$ to the left, each keeping its slope constant. This result was well supported by a strict statistical test. A hypothesis was proposed that the change of the arm position affects the judgmental process on $\zeta = (\xi - \xi_0)$ but not the fluctuation of each latent random variable, ξ or ξ_0. The fluctuation may have its origins in the peripheral process. To obtain a judgmental characteristic curve is time-consuming, especially in cutaneous sensation in which (s_j, s_0) cannot be presented in quick succession. Hence, D was varied only in two ways in the author's experiment, and many questions were left open. The most important one is the relation between ε and the distance D. According to the gradient hypothesis, this will tell how the thick horizontal line in part I of Fig. 4.1 changes its functional distance according to D. In Amano's experiment in which $D = 2$, 42, and 82 cm, the interval of uncertainty $IU(D)$ shows a trend slightly concave downward when plotted against D.

Color discrimination ellipsoids $E(s_0)$ measured by the C-method become larger when the appearance mode of s_0 is changed from S' to A. However, except for $s_0 = Y$ (yellow), their form and orientation remain the same, which implies the parallel and proportional shift of $\Phi(s|e(s_0)_\Lambda, \sigma^2(s_0)_\Lambda)$ in all directions Λ, according to the change of mode. Ellipsoids $E(s_0)$ obtained by the M-method are not affected by the change of mode. Again, $E(s_0)$ for $s_0 = Y$ exhibits a slightly different behavior. In this analysis of $E(s_0)$, the discussion was limited to the oversimplified general trend observed with six colors s_0, and no statistical tests were made. It is again laborious to obtain an ellipsoid $E(s_0)$, and hence many questions are left open. It would not even be surprising if each color were to manifest its own idiosyncracy. In the right plot of Fig. 4.2, $E_{S'}(s_0)$ and $E_A(s_0)$ for $s_0 = G$ seem to differ slightly in orientation. In general, $E(s_0)$ for $s_0 = Y$ behaves very differently from others. When the mode is changed from S' to A, $E_A(Y)$ is extended a great deal along the luminance Y-axis. However, on the chromaticity diagram (x,y), in which hue and saturation are represented, $E_A(Y)$ is extended only in the direction of hue change but not in the direction of saturation change. The extension in the direction of hue only is noticeable in $E_M(Y)$ obtained by the M-method as well. The marked idiosyncracy of yellow has been observed in other respects as well (Indow & Stevens, 1966; Indow, 1987). When $s_0 = Br$, $E_A(Br)$ is larger than $E_{S'}(Br)$ but similar in the C-method, and $E_A(Br)$ is identical with $E_{S'}(Br)$ in the M-method. The fact that the same trend as for other colors (except for Y) was observed for this s_0 is particularly interesting because this stimulus yields drastically different colors according to its mode: brown in S'-mode and dark reddish color in A-mode. In general, why is ε larger in A-mode than in S'-mode? It may be related to the perceptual impression that A-mode colors are less "tangible" or "palpable." The mode of appearance must be determined by the process in the brain, not in the periphery.

All the findings stated so far suggest the following hypothesis as to the latent variable ξ. Its fluctuation and its correspondence with the stimulus s have their origin in the peripheral process and are independent of the context. The perceptual effect of context (the perceived position of the arms, or the mode of appearance of color) and judgment concerning ξ are processes in the brain. Hence, the critical value ε for $\zeta = (\xi - \xi_0)$ is sensitive to context. In the experiment on pressures to the fingers, ε is affected by the context in condition I, but not in condition II. In the C-method in the experiment on color, ε is independent of direction Λ of ξ from ξ_0, but changes according to the context.

REFERENCES

Amano, T. (1944). *Study of comparison process.* Tokyo: Sanseido Press. (in Japanese)

Bock, R. D., & Jones, L. V. (1968). *The measurement and prediction of judgment and choice.* San Francisco: Holden-Day.

Brown, W., & Thomson, G. H. (1925). *The essentials of measurement.* Cambridge, England: Cambridge University Press.

Brown, W. R. J., & MacAdam, D. L. (1949). Visual sensitivities of combined chromaticity and luminance differences. *Journal of Optical Society of America, 39*, 808–834.

Falmagne, J.-C. (1985). *Elements of psychophysical theory.* New York: Oxford University Press.

Finney, D. J. (1952). *Probit analysis: A statistical treatment of the sigmoid response curve.* Cambridge, England: Cambridge University Press.

Guilford, J. P. (1936). *Psychometric methods.* New York: McGraw-Hill.

Indow, T. (1959). *Analysis of impression: Methods and applications.* Unpublished doctoral dissertation, Keio University, Tokyo. (in Japanese)

Indow, T. (1987). Psychologically unique hues in aperture and surface colors. *Die Farbe, 34,* 253–260.

Indow, T. (1993). Indiscriminable regions, color differences, and principal hue vectors in Munsell space. *Die Farbe, 39,* 15–23.

Indow, T. (1994). Metrics in color spaces: Im kleinen und im grossen. In G. H. Fisher & D. Laming (Eds.), *Contributions to mathematical psychology, psychometrics, and methodology* (pp. 3–17). New York: Springer.

Indow, T., & Morrison, M. L. (1991). Construction of discrimination ellipsoids for surface colors by the method of constant stimuli. *Color Research and Application, 16,* 42–56.

Indow, T., Robertson, A. R., von Grunau, M. & Fielder, G. H. (1992). Discrimination ellipsoids of aperture and simulated surface colors by matching and paired comparison. *Color Research Application, 17,* 6–23.

Indow, T., & Stevens, S. S. (1966). Scaling of saturation and hue. *Perception and Psychophysics, 1,* 253–271.

Jacobs, M. H. (1933). Uber den Einfluss des phanomenalen Abstandes auf die Unterschiedungsschwelle fur Helligkeit [On the influence of perceptual distance upon differential threshold for brightness]. *Psychologische Forschung, 17,* 98–142.

Köhler, W. (1933). Zur Psychophysik der Vergleichs und Raums [On psychophysics of comparison and space]. *Psychologische Forschung, 17,* 343–360.

Lauenstein, O. (1933). Ansatz zur einer Physiologischen Theorie des Vergleich und Zeirfehler [A physiological theory of comparison and time-error]. *Psychologische Forschung, 17,* 130–177.

Levine, M. V. (1970). Transformations that render curves parallel. *Journal of Mathematical Psychology, 7,* 130–177.

Levine, M. V. (1972). Transforming curves into curves with the same shape. *Journal of Mathematical Psychology, 9,* 1–16.

MacAdam, D. L. (1942). Visual sensitivities to color differences in daylight. *Journal of Optical Society of America, 32,* 247–274.

Robbins, H., & Monro, S. (1951). A stochastic approximation method. *Annals of Mathematical Statistics, 22,* 400–407.

Wasan, M. T. (1969). *Stochastic approximation.* Cambridge Tracts in Mathematics and Mathematical Physics 58. Cambridge, England: Cambridge University Press.

Wyszecki, G., & Fielder, G. H. (1971). New color-matching ellipse. *Journal of Optical Society of America, 61,* 1501–1513.

Wyszecki, G., & Stiles, W. S. (1982). *Color science: Concepts and methods, quantitative data and formulae* (2nd ed.). New York: Wiley.

Chapter 5

A Maximum Likelihood Model for Psychophysical Data and Response Times

Gert Storms
Katholieke Universiteit Leuven

A model for the simultaneous scaling of repeated pairwise judgments and response times is introduced. The model is presented as a model for psychophysical choices, but it can also be used for analyzing repeated pairwise preference data.

In the first section, the assumptions of the model are outlined. Next, the estimation procedure is presented, and in the third section, experimental data are reviewed that validate the model. Finally, the results of a simulation study are presented that justify the assumptions made for the distribution of the response time variable.

THE MODEL

Assumptions Regarding the Choice Process

The model supposes that a person p repeatedly compares the different stimulus pairs (i,j) by situating the two stimuli on a (personal) psychophysical continuum, and that the choices are influenced by the *comparability* of the stimulus pair: the dispersion of the pair-specific choice process.

The pairwise judgments can be thought of as a random variable, with a preassumed distribution. Suppose that U_{ip} indicates the random variable that situates the stimulus i on the psychophysical continuum of a person p, and that

$$U_{ip} \sim N(X_{ip}, \sigma_{ip}^2) \tag{1}$$

for every stimulus $i = 1, \ldots, N$ and for every person $p = 1, \ldots, M$. If we assume that a pairwise judgment is made, at the presentation of a stimulus pair (i,j), by comparing the values U_{ip} and U_{jp}, then this comparison is a Thurstonian choice process (Thurstone, 1927, 1959). It follows that

$$U_{ip} - U_{jp} \sim N(X_{ip} - X_{jp}; \sigma_{ij}^2) \tag{2}$$

where

$$\begin{aligned}
\sigma_{ijp}^2 &= \mathrm{VAR}(U_{ip} - U_{jp}) \\
&= \sigma_{ip}^2 + \sigma_{jp}^2 - 2\,\mathrm{COV}(U_{ip}, U_{jp})
\end{aligned} \tag{3}$$

The probability that stimulus i is chosen above j in replication r can then be described as

$$\begin{aligned}
P(y_{ijpr} = 1) &= P(U_{ip} > U_{jp}) \\
&= P(U_{ip} - U_{jp} > 0) = Q_{ijp} \\
&= \int_{-\infty}^{q_{ijp}} \phi(z)\, dz = \Phi(q_{ijp})
\end{aligned} \tag{4}$$

$$P(y_{ijpr} = 0) = P(U_{ip} < U_{jp}) = 1 - Q_{ijp}$$

where $q_{ijp} = (x_{ip} - x_{jp})/\sigma_{ijp}$, and where ϕ and Φ are the density and the cumulative distribution function of the standard normal distribution. The parameter σ_{ijp} is a measure of comparability, or a measure of uncertainty of the judgment. (A smaller uncertainty allows for more extreme choice proportions, even for small differences between u_{ip} and u_{jp}. A larger uncertainty results in less extreme choice proportions.) In what follows we call σ_{ijp} the uncertainty parameter.

The overparameterization problem of the Thurstonian choice process (De Soete, 1983; Heiser & De Leeuw, 1981; Takane, 1980, 1987; Thurstone, 1927) can be overcome in different ways. We later relate the response times (RTs) to the uncertainty parameters, and we further assume that these parameters are not person specific (resulting in parameters σ_{ij} instead of σ_{ijp}). This assumption enables us to rewrite Equation 4 as

$$U_{ip} - U_{jp} \sim N(x_{ip} - x_{jp}; \sigma_{ij}^2) \tag{5}$$

Consequently, we change Equation 4 to $q_{ijp} = (x_{ip} - x_{jp})/\sigma_{ij}$. (This assumption is not necessary to make the model identifiable, but without this assumption the model results in totally separate scaling for each of the subjects.)

Assumptions Concerning the RTs

As in Takane and Sergent's (1983) MAXRT model, we assume that the RTs are distributed lognormally (Storms & Delbeke, 1992). We further assume that the mean logarithmic RTs for the stimulus pairs are, for every person, linearly related to the uncertainty parameter σ_{ij}:

$$\ln T_{ijpr} \sim N(p_p \sigma_{ij} + a_p; \gamma_p^2) \tag{6}$$

So the model incorporates the following parameters: the scale values x_{ip} ($m \times n$ in number), the $[n \times (n-1)/2]$ uncertainty parameters σ_{ij}, and the response parameters, by which we mean the linear coefficients (p_p), the additive constants (a_p), and the standard deviations of the RTs γ_p (m parameters each).

ESTIMATION PROCEDURE: MAXIMIZING THE LIKELIHOOD

Formulating the Probabilities

The joint density $g(t_{ijpr}, y_{ijpr})$ of a response Y_{ijpr} and an RT T_{ijpr} can be written as

$$
\begin{aligned}
g(t_{ijpr}, y_{ijpr}) &= P(y_{ijpr}) \, P(t_{ijpr}/y_{ijpr}) \\
&= P(y_{ijpr}) \, P(t_{ijpr}) \\
&= g(t_{ijpr}) Q_{ijp}^{y_{ijpr}} (1 - Q_{ijp})^{(1 - y_{ijpr})}
\end{aligned} \tag{7}
$$

where $g(t_{ijpr})$ is the lognormal density function expressed in Equation 6. The joint likelihood for the total set of observations is:

$$L = \prod_p \prod_{i,j} \prod_r g(t_{ijpr}, y_{ijpr}) \tag{8}$$

where the products are taken over m persons (index p), $n(n-1)/2$ stimulus pairs (indices i and j), and s replications (index r). The model thereby assumes independence of the observations (T_{ijpr}, Y_{ijpr}) over p, i, j, and r. Because the logarithm of L is maximal for the same parameter values as the function L, the parameters are estimated by maximizing $\ln L$, where

$$
\begin{aligned}
\ln L &= \sum_p \sum_{i,j} \sum_r \ln[g(t_{ijpr}, y_{ijpr})] \\
&= \sum_p \sum_{i,j} \sum_r \ln[g(t_{ijpr}) Q_{ijp}^{y_{ijpr}} (1 - Q_{ijp})^{(1 - y_{ijpr})}]
\end{aligned} \tag{9}
$$

which amounts to

$$\ln L = \sum_p \sum_{i,j} \sum_r \ln(g(t_{ijpr})) + \sum_p \sum_{i,j} \{n_{ijp} \ln Q_{ijp} + (s - n_{ijp})\ln(1 - Q_{ijp})\}$$
$$= \Psi_1 + \Psi_2 \tag{10}$$

where $n_{ijp} \sum_r y_{ijpr}.$

Breaking Down the Likelihood Function

In order to facilitate the derivation, the log-likelihood function can be further broken down, in a way similar to Takane and Sergent's (1983) technique in the MAXRT model. If we define h_{ijp} as

$$h_{ijp} = p_p \, \sigma_{ij} + a_p \tag{11}$$

then we can derive from Equation 6 that, for some constant c,

$$\ln g(t_{ijpr}) = c - \frac{1}{2}\left[\ln \gamma_p^2 + \frac{\ln(t_{ijpr}) - h_{ijp}}{\gamma_p^2} \right] \tag{12}$$

We can rewrite Ψ_1 as

$$\Psi_1 = c - \frac{1}{2}\sum_p N_p \ln \gamma_p^2 - \frac{1}{2}\sum_p \sum_{i,j} \sum_r \frac{(\ln t_{ijpr} - h_{ijp})^2}{\gamma_p^2} \tag{13}$$

where N_p is the total number of observations of person p [here $N_p = sn(n - 1)/2$]. We can further break Ψ_1 down into

$$\Psi_1 = c - \frac{1}{2}\sum_p N_p \ln \gamma_p^2 - \Psi_1^* - \Psi_1^{**} \tag{14}$$

where

$$\Psi_1^* = \frac{1}{2}\sum_p \sum_{i,j} \frac{s(\bar{g}_{ijp} - h_{ijp})^2}{\gamma_p^2} \tag{15}$$

and

$$\Psi_1^{**} = \frac{1}{2} \sum_p \sum_{i,j} \sum_r \frac{(\ln t_{ijpr} - \bar{g}_{ijp})^2}{\gamma_p^2}$$

with $\bar{g}_{ijp} = [\sum_r \ln(t_{ijpr})]/s$.
The function to be maximized becomes then

$$\ln L = -\frac{1}{2} \sum_p N_p \ln \gamma_p^2 - \Psi_1^* - \Psi_1^{**} + \Psi_2 \tag{16}$$

The Estimation Algorithm

As in Takane and Sergent (1983), Fisher's scoring algorithm was used to maximize the log-likelihood described in Equation 16. Due to the large number of parameters to be estimated, the parameter set was divided into smaller subsets that were adjusted successively in every iteration. The order of optimization of the parameters was: scale values (x_{ip}), uncertainty parameters (σ_{ij}), linear coefficients (p_p), additive constants (a_p), and finally, the standard deviations of the response times (γ_p).

Because the additive constants (a_p) only appear in Ψ_1^*, which is quadratic in a_p, their conditional values can be estimated directly:

$$a_p = \frac{\sum_{i,j} s\bar{g}_{ijp} - p_p \sum_{i,j} sM^*}{N_p} \tag{17}$$

where M^* equals σ_{ij}.

The Gradient Vectors gθ

The derivatives of the log-likelihood function for the remaining four sorts of parameters are presented next.

For the scaling values, we find

$$\frac{\partial \ln L}{\partial x_{ip}} = \frac{\partial(\Psi_2)}{\partial x_{ip}} \tag{18}$$

where

$$\frac{\partial(\Psi_2)}{\partial x_{ip}} = \sum_{i,j} \left(\frac{n_{ijp}}{Q_{ijp}} - \frac{s - n_{ijp}}{1 - Q_{ijp}} \right) \left(\frac{\partial Q_{ijp}}{\partial x_{ip}} \right) \tag{19}$$

with

$$\left(\frac{\partial Q_{ijp}}{\partial x_{ip}}\right) = \phi(q_{ijp})\left(\frac{1}{\sigma_{ij}}\right) \qquad \text{for } ip$$

$$= \phi(q_{ijp})\left(\frac{-1}{\sigma_{ij}}\right) \qquad \text{for } jp$$

Deriving the log-likelihood function for the σ_{ij} terms gives

$$\frac{\partial \ln L}{\partial \sigma_{ij}} = \frac{\partial(-\Psi_1^*)}{\partial \sigma_{ij}} + \frac{\partial(\Psi_2)}{\partial \sigma_{ij}} \tag{20}$$

where

$$d\frac{\partial(-\Psi_1^*)}{\partial \sigma_{ij}} = \sum_p \frac{s(\bar{g}_{ijp} - h_{ijp})}{\gamma_p^2}\left(\frac{\partial h_{ijp}}{\partial \sigma_{ij}}\right) \tag{21}$$

with $(\partial h_{ijp}/\partial \sigma_{ij}) = p_p$, and where

$$\frac{\partial(\Psi_2)}{\partial \sigma_{ij}} = \sum_p \sum_{i,j}\left(\frac{n_{ijp}}{Q_{ijp}} - \frac{s - n_{ijp}}{1 - Q_{ijp}}\right)\left(\frac{\partial Q_{ijp}}{\partial \sigma_{ij}}\right) \tag{22}$$

with

$$\left(\frac{\partial Q_{ijp}}{\partial \sigma_{ij}}\right) = -\phi(q_{ijp})\left(\frac{1}{\sigma_{ij}}\right)$$

The linear coefficients only appear in Ψ_1. Differentiating with respect to p_p results in

$$\frac{\partial \ln L}{\partial p_p} = \frac{\partial(-\Psi_1^*)}{\partial p_p}$$
$$= \sum_{ij} \frac{s(\bar{g}_{ijp} - h_{ijp})}{\gamma_p^2}\left(\frac{\partial h_{ijp}}{\partial p_p}\right) \tag{23}$$

where $(\partial h_{ijp}/\partial p_p) = \sigma_{ij}$.
Finally, the derivatives for the standard deviates γ_p are

$$\frac{\partial \ln L}{\partial \gamma_p} = \frac{-N_p}{\gamma_p} + \frac{\partial(-\Psi_1^*)}{\partial \gamma_p} + \frac{\partial(-\Psi_1^{**})}{\partial \gamma_p} \tag{24}$$

where

$$\frac{\partial(-\Psi_1^*)}{\partial\gamma_p} = \sum_{i,j} \frac{s(\bar{g}_{ijp} - h_{ijp})^2}{\partial\gamma_p^3} \tag{25}$$

and

$$\frac{\partial(-\Psi_1^*)}{\partial\gamma_p} = \sum_{i,j}\sum_{p} \frac{(\ln t_{ijpr} - \bar{g}_{ijp})^2}{\partial\gamma_p^3} \tag{26}$$

The Formation Matrices H(θ)

All the formation matrices, except $H(x_{ip})$ for the scale values, are diagonal matrices. For calculating the inverse of $H(x_{ip})$ the Moore–Penrose method for the generalized inverse was used.

The formation matrix for the scale values is

$$-E\left(\frac{\partial^2 \ln L}{\partial x_{ip}\, \partial x_{jp}}\right) = \sum_{i,j}\left(\frac{s}{Q_{ijp}} - \frac{s}{1 - Q_{ijp}}\right)\left(\frac{\partial Q_{ijp}}{\partial x_{ip}}\right)\left(\frac{\partial Q_{ijp}}{\partial x_{jp}}\right) \tag{27}$$

where

$$\frac{\partial Q_{ijp}}{\partial x_{ip}} = \frac{\phi(q_{ijp})}{d_{ij}} \quad \text{and} \quad \frac{\partial Q_{ijp}}{\partial x_{jp}} = \frac{-\phi(q_{ijp})}{d_{ij}}$$

The information matrix $H(d_{ij})$ for the uncertainty parameters is

$$-E\left(\frac{\partial^2 \ln L}{\partial d_{ij}\, \partial d_{kl}}\right) = \sum_{p}\left(\frac{s}{\sigma_p^2}\right)\left(\frac{\partial h_{ijp}}{\partial d_{ij}}\right)^2 + \sum_{p}\left(\frac{s}{Q_{ijp}} - \frac{s}{1 - Q_{ijp}}\right)\left(\frac{\partial Q_{ijp}}{\partial d_{ij}}\right)^2 \tag{28}$$

where

$$\frac{\partial h_{ijp}}{\partial d_{ij}} = p_p$$

and where

$$\frac{\partial Q_{ijp}}{\partial d_{ij}} = -\phi(q_{ijp})\frac{(x_{ip} - x_{jp})}{d_{ij}^2}$$

The information matrix for the linear coefficients p_p is

$$-E\left(\frac{\partial^2 \ln L}{\partial p_p \, \partial p_p}\right) = \sum_{i,j}\left(\frac{s}{\sigma_p^2}\right)\left(\frac{\partial h_{ijp}}{\partial p_p}\right)^2 \qquad (29)$$

where

$$\frac{\partial h_{ijp}}{\partial p_p} = d_{ij}$$

Finally, for $H(\sigma_p)$ a simple structure is obtained:

$$-E\left(\frac{\partial^2 \ln L}{\partial p_p \, \partial p_p}\right) = \frac{2N_p}{\sigma_p^2} \quad \text{if } \sigma_p = \sigma_q$$
$$= 0 \qquad \text{otherwise} \qquad (30)$$

Initial Parameter Values

For the initial σ_p values, the mean standard deviation of the response times per person was calculated. For the scale values, an arbitrary starting value was chosen, and the stimuli were scaled according to a linearly increasing relation between the physical values of the stimuli and their psychophysical scale values. The values x_{ip} and x_{iq} (for the different subjects) were set equal. The initial values for the comparability indices d_{ij} were inversely proportional to the choice proportions of each of the stimulus pairs. For the initial parameter values of the p_p terms and the a_p, least squares estimates were calculated, based on

$$\bar{g}_{ijp} = p_p h_{ijp} + a_p \qquad (31)$$

for all stimulus pairs (i,j) and for all subjects p.

A PSYCHOPHYSICAL EXPERIMENT

To validate the model, a psychophysical experiment was conducted, where pairs of random dot patterns were presented in the form of differently sized and shaped rectangles. Subjects were asked to choose the rectangle with the highest density of dots. We will outline the procedure of the experiment briefly next.

Subjects. Eight subjects volunteered in this experiment. All subjects were employed in the psychology Department of the Leuven University (five research assistants and three secretaries).

Stimuli. All possible pairs of the nine differently shaped and sized rectangles in Fig. 5.1, filled with random dot patterns, were used as stimuli. The density of the dot pattern of each rectangle remained fixed during the experiment. The density varied from 10.1571 dots/cm² for rectangle 1, to 13.4075 dots/cm² for rectangle 9, with increasing steps of equal size (0.4063).

Apparatus. The stimuli were presented on an NEC Multisync II color monitor (with a graphical resolution of 640 × 350 pixels) and a LASER 286/2 PC. The presentation order of the stimuli was computer-based and random. Responses were given on a device with two response buttons that were connected to the "game I/O connector" of the computer. After every trial, the identification number of the stimulus pair, the response of the subject, and the reaction time were filed.

Procedure. In their instructions, subjects were told that they would be presented with pairs of rectangles, each filled with a random dot pattern, and that they would be asked to choose the rectangle with the more dense dot pattern, regardless of its size or shape. Subjects were to respond by

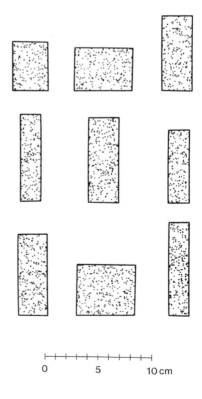

FIG. 5.1. Stimuli from the psycho-physical experiment.

0   5   10 cm

pushing the response button that corresponded to the rectangle chosen. They were told to take as much time as they needed to perform the task, but to answer immediately, as soon as they reached a decision.

Subjects were acquainted with the stimuli and the task in a training session, which was identical in nature to the six experimental sessions that followed later on. The data from the training session were excluded from the final data set. Every session consisted of 72 presentations [each pair was presented in both orders (i,j) and (j,i)]. Subjects chose the time of their sessions, with the restrictions that no two consecutive sessions were held on the same day, and that the whole experiment did not last longer than 2 weeks. The duration of a single session varied between 5 and 10 min. Subjects performed the task individually, in a half-darkened room. The rectangles disappeared from the screen as soon as one of the response buttons was pushed.

RESULTS

Goodness of Fit

The data from the experiment were analyzed with the model already described. The likelihood value for the final parameter estimates was −56.2792. The correlations between the observed and the predicted choice proportions per stimulus pair were calculated for each subject individually, as well as aggregated over the eight subjects. The correlation on the aggregated data set (288 data points) was 0.86. The values for separate subjects (based on 36 data points) were 0.94, 0.76, 0.92, 0.90, 0.83, 0.77, 0.63, and 0.86.

We also calculated the correlations between the observed and the predicted mean response times per stimulus pair. The correlation for the data set aggregated over all subjects was 0.94. This high value is somewhat misleading, because intersubjective differences were much higher than intrasubjective differences, leading to a long, small scatter plot, consisting of eight separate groupings, one for every subject. The separate correlations per subject were 0.85, 0.12, 0.94, 0.74, 0.46, 0.05, 0.69, and 0.63. The model completely fails for the prediction of the response times of three subjects, whereas it gives good results for three, and acceptable results for the remaining two subjects, taking into account the large variance due to error that usually characterizes response times (Takane & Sergent, 1983). It can be concluded that the model predicts the choice responses very well, but that the goodness of fit for the response times differs widely between subjects.

The Estimated Parameters

The psychophysical functions of the 8 subjects are given in Fig. 5.2. The model always finds a nonmonotone increasing function, indicating that the shape and the size of the rectangles has a large influence on the perception of the dot density. The estimated values for the response parameters and uncertainty parameters are given in Table 5.1.

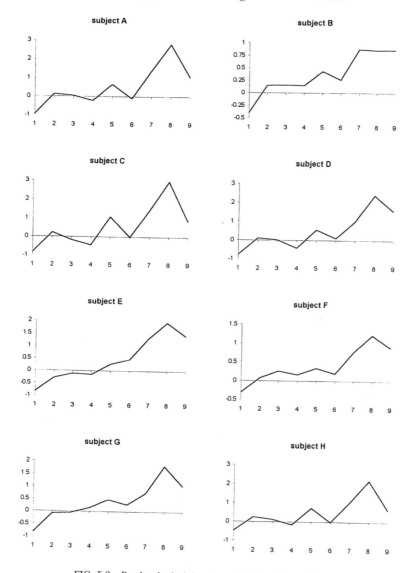

FIG. 5.2. Psychophysical functions for the eight subjects.

TABLE 5.1
Estimated Parameter Values

Subject	Response Parameters		
	p_p	a_p	σ_p^2
1	−0.429	8.144	0.371
2	−0.036	8.291	0.405
3	−0.751	9.111	0.402
4	−0.400	8.454	0.395
5	−0.121	8.248	0.336
6	0.013	7.627	0.378
7	−0.372	8.527	0.407
8	−0.221	8.115	0.319

	Uncertainty Parameters σ_{ij}								
	1	2	3	4	5	6	7	8	9
2	2.007								
3	1.691	1.495							
4	1.321	1.834	1.529						
5	1.784	1.623	1.712	1.879					
6	1.678	1.738	1.456	1.674	1.432				
7	1.882	1.962	1.929	2.049	1.626	2.192			
8	2.634	2.292	2.656	2.254	2.201	2.267	2.228		
9	2.065	1.835	1.705	2.030	1.427	1.824	1.546	1.897	

Can the Uncertainty Parameters Be Interpreted in Terms of Dissimilarity?

Tversky and Russo (1969) showed in a psychophysical experiment that, for a fixed difference on a psychological scale, a pairwise discrimination becomes easier if the presented stimuli are more similar. In line with these findings, we tried to interpret the uncertainty parameters that were estimated for every stimulus pair as a measure of dissimilarity between the two stimuli in the pair. A KYST analysis (Kruskal, Young, & Seery, 1978; Shiffman, Reynolds, & Young, 1981) of the estimated d_{ij} terms resulted in solutions with "stress" values of 0.163, 0.078, and 0.033, in one, two, and three dimensions, respectively. Only the stress for the three-dimensional solution provided an acceptable goodness of fit, but no interpretations that relate the resulting configuration to characteristics of the rectangles were found.[1]

---

[1]Klahr (1969) reported, for solutions in three dimensions with randomly generated d_{ij} of eight stimuli, that there is more than 0.10 chance to obtain stress values of 0.033 or smaller. Therefore, it does not seem unlikely that no real three-dimensional structure underlies the data.

FOUR SIMULATIONS

Takane and Sergent's (1983) multidimensional scaling model (MAXRT) for response times and same/different judgments assumed that response times were distributed lognormally. In a simulation study Storms and Delbeke (1992) showed that the model was quite robust with respect to violations of the assumed underlying distribution of response times. They showed that data generated with normal, exponential, and Pareto distributions resulted in virtually indistinguishable parameter estimates. Storms (1995) gave further evidence that this robustness is likely a general feature of maximum likelihood multidimensional scaling (MDS) models. The generalizability of these findings for the model proposed in this paper was investigated in a similar simulation study, which was described in Storms and Delbeke (1992). The parameter estimates from the experiment reported here were used to generate data according to four different methods. A first method generated the data completely according to the model (i.e., the choice data were generated based on Equation 5 and the RTs were generated based on Equation 6). Next, a second set of data was generated, where the response (the psychophysical judgment) was, as in the first generated data set, based on the model (Equation 5), but the response times were exponentially distributed, with the same mean and variance as the lognormally generated RTs from the first data set. The third and fourth generated data sets only differed from the second set in the distribution of the RTs: Again the response was based on the model, but the RTs were distributed normally and as a Pareto distribution, respectively, again with the same means and variances as the data from the first set.

The data from the four generated data sets were analyzed with the model, that is, with the assumption of lognormally distributed RTs. The results from these analyses are summarized in Table 5.2. It can be seen that the log-likelihood for the lognormally generated RT data set is substantially higher than the corresponding value for the Pareto and exponentially distributed RT data, and that the (symmetric) normally generated

TABLE 5.2
Goodness-of-Fit and Goodness-of-Recovery
Indices for the Simulated Data

		Goodness-of-Fit		Goodness-of-Recovery	
	$\ln L$	T_{ijpr}	Y_{ijpr}	x_{ip}	σ_{ij}
Lognormal RT	3385.58	0.98	0.96	0.98	0.35
Exponential RT	1355.75	0.97	0.97	0.97	0.56
Normal RT	−581.80	0.93	0.98	0.97	0.42
Pareto RT	1888.60	0.98	0.97	0.97	0.25

RT data resulted in a far worse value. Yet the goodness-of-fit correlations (between predicted and observed values), for the RTs as well as for the psychophysical judgments are all very good (with a slightly lower coefficient for the RT data that were generated exponentially). The goodness of recovery was evaluated by correlating the estimated parameters with the true underlying parameters (used to generate the data). As can be seen in the column second from the right of Table 5.2, the scale values x_{ip} found by the model were very close to the actual underlying scale values. The estimates of the uncertainty parameters, however, turned out to be rather weak. Yet, when comparing the results from the data set based on different underlying RT distributions, almost no difference could be detected between the four data sets, indicating that the results from Storm and Delbeke (1992) can be generalized to the model presented in this chapter.

CONCLUSION AND SUGGESTIONS FOR FURTHER RESEARCH

This chapter introduced a maximum likelihood model for psychophysical judgments and response times. The model was applied to the data from a psychophysical experiment where subjects compared the density of randomly distributed dot patterns presented in differently shaped and sized rectangles. The results showed that subjects' perception of the density was quite strongly influenced by the shape and the size of the rectangles. The simulation study showed that the model does a good job in recovering the underlying scale values x_{ip}, but that the uncertainty parameters that characterize every stimulus pair were not estimated accurately by the model. It was also shown that, as predicted from the studies by Storms (1995; Storms & Delbeke, 1992), the model is robust with respect to violations of the assumed underlying RT distributions, at least when comparing predicted and observed responses (psychophysical judgments) and RTs. Also, when comparing the estimated scale values of the stimuli, the model seems quite robust to violations of the assumed RT distribution. This robustness occurs despite the instability of the estimates of the uncertainty parameters. Variations of the model, where these uncertainty parameters can be modeled differently, may perhaps render the estimates of the uncertainty parameters more stable, and may explore the possibility of interpreting these parameters as a dissimilarity index. A variation, where the d_{ij} terms are constrained according to the factorial model (Heiser & De Leeuw, 1981; Takane, 1980), and where

$$d_{ij}^2 = (\mathbf{y}_i - \mathbf{y}_j)'(\mathbf{y}_i - \mathbf{y}_j) \tag{32}$$

may be worth further investigation. In this model $\mathbf{y}_i$ and $\mathbf{y}_j$ are vectors of dimension b, so that d_{ij} amounts to the Euclidean distance between stimuli

i and j in a b-dimensional space. The model then becomes a moderate stochastic transitivity model (Halff, 1976).

A second possible variation is suggested by the large differences in the goodness-of-fit correlations between the observed and predicted mean RTs. This finding may be the result of differences in stimulus perception, differences that may be caused by interindividual variations in the importance that subjects give to the dimensions that underlie the stimulus space. In line with this hypothesis, the model can be changed according to the INDSCAL model, proposed by Carroll and Chang (1970). In this variation, the subject index p must be restored in the definition of the uncertainty parameters d_{ijp}, and it must be further assumed that

$$d_{ijp} = \sqrt{\sum_{t=1}^{b} w_p(y_{it} - y_{jt})^2} \tag{33}$$

where y_{it} and y_{jt} are the coordinated of stimuli i and j in dimension t, and where w_{pt} is a weight, representing the saliency of dimension t for person p. Whether the proposed variations render the estimates of the uncertainty parameters more stable or not is a question that needs further research.

ACKNOWLEDGMENTS

The author thanks Luc Delbeke, Geert De Soete, and Paul De Boeck for their useful comments on an earlier version of this manuscript, and Dominiek Christiaens and Noël Bovens for their help in programming the experiment.

REFERENCES

Carroll, J. D., & Chang, J. J. (1970). Analysis of individual differences in multidimensional scaling via an n-way generalization of "Eckard-Young" decomposition. *Psychometrika, 35*, 283–319.

De Soete, G. (1983). On the relation between two generalized cases of Thurstone's Law of Comparative Judgments. *Mathématiques et Sciences Humaines, 21*, 45–57.

Halff, H. M. (1976). Choice theories for differentially comparable alternatives. *Journal of Mathematical Psychology, 14*, 244–246.

Heiser, W., & De Leeuw, J. (1981). Multidimensional mapping of preference data. *Mathématiques et Sciences Humaines, 19*, 39–96.

Klahr, D. (1969). A Monte Carlo investigation of the statistical significance of Kruskal's nonmetric scaling procedure. *Psychometrika, 34*, 319–330.

Kruskal, J. B., Young, F. W., & Seery, J. B. (1978). *How to use KYST-2A, a very flexible program to do multidimensional scaling and unfolding.* Internal Report, Bell Telephone Laboratories, Murray Hill, NJ.

Shiffman, S. S., Reynolds, M. L., & Young, F. W. (1981). *Introduction to multidimensional scaling: Theory, methods, and applications.* New York: Academic Press.

Storms, G. (1995). On the robustness of maximum likelihood scaling for violations of the error model. *Psychometrika, 60,* 247–258.

Storms, G., & Delbeke, L. (1992). The irrelevance of distributional assumptions on reaction times in multidimensional scaling of Same/Different judgment tasks. *Psychometrika, 57,* 599–614.

Takane, Y. (1980). Maximum likelihood estimation in the generalized case of Thurstone's model of comparative judgment. *Japanese Psychological Research, 22,* 188–196.

Takane, Y. (1987). Analysis of contingency tables by ideal point discriminant analysis. *Psychometrika, 52,* 493–513.

Takane, Y., & Sergent, J. (1983). Multidimensional scaling models for reaction times and same-different judgments. *Psychometrika, 48,* 393–423.

Thurstone, L. L. (1927). A law of comparative judgment. *Psychological Review, 34,* 273–286.

Thurstone, L. L. (1959). *The measurement of values.* Chicago: University of Chicago Press.

Tversky, A., & Russo, E. (1969). Substitutability and similarity in binary choices. *Journal of Mathematical Psychology, 6,* 1–12.

Chapter 6

Inhibition Theory and the Concept of Perseveration

A. H. G. S. van der Ven
University of Nijmegen, Nijmegen, The Netherlands

All inhibition models that have been developed thus far (van der Ven & Smit, 1982; van der Ven, Smit, & Jansen, 1989; Smit & van der Ven, 1995), are based on the general assumption that any mental act that requires a minimum amount of mental effort actually consists of a continuous sequence of alternating periods of attention (or work) and distraction (or nonwork). In periods of attention the person is actually working at the task, whereas in periods of distraction the person is not working on the task. Distractions are unconscious, involuntary periods of nonwork. Distractions should not be confused with periods of nonwork in which subjects consciously take time out. These inhibition models have been developed to account for the reaction-time fluctuations in prolonged work tasks. In prolonged work tasks subjects are required to engage in simple, repetitive activities, such as letter cancellation, detecting differences in simple shapes, adding three digits, and so on. Performance is recorded as a series of response (or reaction) times. Subjects are instructed to work as quickly and as accurately as possible. The items should be answered in a self-paced continuous manner, in which the subject cannot afford to take intermediate rest pauses between responses. In this way one is able to study "the fluctuations which always occur in any person's continuous output of mental work, even when this is so devised as to remain of approximately constant difficulty" (Spearman, 1927, p. 320). Prolonged work tasks are used especially in concentration tests, which were already in use by the beginning of this century (see, among others, Binet, 1900).

In the past few years several models (van der Ven & Smit, 1982; van der Ven et al., 1989) have been proposed in order to account for oscillation in reaction times. These models are all based on the assumption that distractions are periods of recovery from accumulated inhibition. The notion of recovery has been suggested before in the literature by several authors (Bills, 1935, p. 571; Hull, 1951, p. 74, postulate X.A; Spearman, 1927, p. 327). In this article a new model is used as the frame of reference because it is psychologically more plausible. The model is known as the beta inhibition model, and it is described in more detail in Smit and van der Ven (1995).

THE BETA INHIBITION MODEL

Previous models, as well as the model presented here, the beta inhibition model, were developed to account for the sequence of RTs that can be observed when a single repetitive task is administered to a single subject. They are all based on the same general process of alternating latent periods of work and distraction. The individual working times are denoted by W_{jk} and the individual distraction times by D_{jk}, where j denotes a period and k a response. Each period j consists of a working time and a distraction time, except the last period $N+1$, which only consists of a working time. The response (or reaction) time T_k that the subject needs for response k is modeled as the sum of the working and distraction times:

$$T_k = W_{1,k} + D_{1,k} + W_{2,k} + D_{2,k} + \ldots + W_{N,k} + D_{N,k} + W_{N+1,k}$$

where N is the number of distractions. N is a random variable, which may be dependent on k. Only the time T_k is *observed*. The individual working times W_{jk} and the resting or distraction times D_{jk} are *latent*. It is assumed that the period occupied in producing a response always begins with a real working time, $W_{1,k}$, and also ends with a real working time, $W_{N+1,k}$. A similar formula has been proposed by Berger (1982, p. 22). Instead of D_{jk}, he used B_{jk}, where $B_{1,k}$, $B_{2,k}$, and so on represent the interrupt times or blocks. As soon as the total working time $\Sigma_j W_{jk}$, reaches some fixed limit A, the response will be uttered, and the observed response time T_k is equal to A plus the sum of the intervening distractions. In other words:

$$T_k = A + D_{1,k} + D_{2,k} + \ldots + D_{N,k}$$

The person alternates between two states: state 1, working, and state 0, distraction. The transitions from one state to the other are random and are described by the transition rates (or hazard rates) λ_0 and λ_1, where λ_0 is the rate of transition from distraction to working and λ_1 the rate of transition from working to distraction. When in state i ($i = 1,0$) at time t, the probability of a transition to the other state occurring in the infinitesimal time interval $(t, t + dt)$ is given by $\lambda_i \, dt$. This idea of switching between mental states with Poisson infinities was already explored by Donio (1964).

Assumptions of the Model

In the beta inhibition model used in this chapter, the transition rates λ_0 and λ_1 are assumed to be dependent on a latent variable: *inhibition*, which increases during work and decreases during distraction. Inhibition is a function of time, and is denoted $Y(t)$. Y will increase during work and decrease during rest (or distraction). The model has the following more specific assumptions.

1. Inhibition increases linearly with rate a_1 during work. If the person is in state 1 from time t_0 to time $t_0 + t$ then $Y(t_0 + t) = Y(t_0) + a_1 t$.
2. Inhibition decreases linearly with rate a_0 during rest. If the person is in state 0 from time t_0 to time $t_0 + t$ then $Y(t_0 + t) = Y(t_0) - a_0 t$.

There are no special reasons for making inhibition change linearly, except that linear change is a common and simple assumption. One might also define inhibition to change exponentially with time. In that case assumption 2 agrees entirely with Hull's postulate X.B (Hull, 1951, p. 74), which states that with the passage of time since its formation, $I(R)$ spontaneously dissipates approximately as a simple decay function of time t, that is, $I(R) = I(0)[10 \exp(-at)]$. Assumption 1 is a natural consequence of postulate X.B for the case where $I(R)$ increases.

The assumptions of the beta inhibition model regarding the functional dependence of λ are as follows.

3. During work the transition rate $\lambda_1(t)$, which represents the inclination to stop working, depends on the inhibition by $\lambda_1(t) = c_1 M/(M - Y(t))$.

Note that as $Y(t)$ approaches the upper limit M (during a work interval) the transition rate $\lambda_1(t)$ approaches infinity and this forces a transition to state 0 (rest) before the inhibition can reach M.

4. During rest the transition rate $\lambda_0(t)$ is given by $\lambda_0(t) = c_0/Y(t)$.

Note that as $Y(t)$ approaches zero (during a distraction), the transition rate $\lambda_0(t)$ goes to infinity, and this forces a transition to state 1 (work) before the inhibition can reach zero. The probability distribution function

$F_1(t) = P(W \leq t)$ for an individual work interval W starting at time t_0 may be obtained as follows:

$$P(W > t) = \exp[-\int_{t_0}^{t_0+t} \lambda_1(t_0 + s) \, ds]$$

$$= \exp[-\int_{t_0}^{t_0+t} c_1 M /(M - Y(t_0) - a_1 s) \, ds]$$

$$= \exp[(c_1 M / a_1)\ln\{[M - Y(t_0) - a_1 t]/[M - Y(t_0)]\}]$$

$$= [(M - Y(t_0) - a_1 t)/(M - Y(t_0))]^{(c_1 M/a_1)}$$

Finally, $F_1(t) = P(W \leq t) = 1 - P(W > t)$. Analogously for a distraction interval D, beginning at time t_0, the distribution function $F_0(t) = P(D \leq t)$ is obtained as follows:

$$P(D > t) = \exp[-\int_{t_0}^{t_0+t} \lambda_0(t_0 + s) \, ds]$$

$$= \exp[-\int_{t_0}^{t_0+t} c_0/(Y(t_0) - a_0 s) \, ds]$$

$$= \exp[(c_0/a_0)\ln\{[Y(t_0) - a_0 t]/Y(t_0)\}]$$

$$= \{[Y(t_0) - a_0 t]/Y(t_0)\}^{c_0/a_0}$$

Then $F_0(t) = P(D \leq t) = 1 - P(D > t) = 1 - [(Y(t_0)-a_0 t)/Y(t_0)]^{c_0/a_0}$. Assumptions 1–4 and the assumption that the total real working time, A, is constant over responses specify the model completely.

Even without specifying the functional dependence of λ_1 and λ_0 the stabilizing influence of inhibition on the process may still be appreciated. Because λ_1, the inclination to stop working, increases during work, and the inclination to start work, λ_0, increases while resting, extremely long intervals (of work as well as distraction) are less likely than they would be with constant transition rates. In the long term this will cause $Y(t)$ to oscillate around a certain equilibrium in a stationary way. Smit and van der Ven (1995) have shown that in the beta inhibition model $Y(t)/M$ has a beta distribution. This was the reason for the "beta" in the name of the model.

THE POISSON INHIBITION MODEL

In the case of the beta inhibition model it is very difficult to derive exact expressions for the moments and the correlation function of the $Y(t)$ process and the reaction time sequence. Therefore, it was decided to resort to a mathematically more convenient model, which is a special case of the beta inhibition model. The model has the same assumptions as the beta inhibition model, except for assumption 3, which is now replaced by assumption 5:

5. During work the transition rate $\lambda_1(t)$, which represents the inclination to stop working, is independent of the inhibition: $\lambda_1(t) = c_1$ (positive constant).

Because a task requires for its completion an amount of working time A, and during this time interruptions occur with rate c_1, it follows that the number of distractions is Poisson distributed with mean $c_1 A$. This was the reason for the "Poisson" in the name of the model. Smit and van der Ven (1995) proved that the stationary distribution of $Y(t)$ has a gamma distribution. This is why this model is also referred to as the gamma inhibition model. For $M \rightarrow \infty$ the beta inhibition model converges to the Poisson inhibition model.

Statistical Measures to Be Used in the Experiment

Smit and van der Ven (1995) showed that, in the beta inhibition model as well as in the gamma inhibition model, the expectation of the reaction time T in the stationary case is as follows:

$$E[T] = A + (a_1/a_0)A$$

This shows that when the process $\{T_k\}$ has reached the stationary state, the expectation of T is independent of c_0 and c_1.

In the long term (when k increases) the inhibition $Y(t)$ will oscillate around a stable equilibrium, $E[Y]$. If the initial value of $Y(0)$ at the beginning of the experiment or test deviates from the equilibrium value, then the process $\{T_k\}$ is not stationary. Depending on the value of $Y(0)$, one will see a more or less gradually increasing or decreasing curve. It has been shown by Smit and van der Ven (1995) that in the case of the gamma inhibition model, the long-term trend of the time series can be described by the following exponential function:

$$E[T_k] = \alpha + \beta \gamma^{k-1} \qquad 0 \le \gamma \le 1$$

The parameters α, β, and γ are functions of the parameters a_0, a_1, c_0, c_1, and A. When β is negative the curve is increasing, and when β is positive it is decreasing. For large k the expectation of the reaction time, $E[T_k]$, reaches its asymptote α, where $\alpha = E[T]$. The trend parameters α, β, and γ are estimated by a two-step least-square procedure in which, for each value of γ

in the range $[0,1]$, α and β are estimated by minimizing the residual sum of squares (SS error). Subsequently, the γ with the smallest SS error is taken as the final solution. The estimated values of α, β, and γ are denoted by $\hat{\alpha}$, $\hat{\beta}$, and $\hat{\gamma}$, respectively. For the predictions to be tested, the parameters α and β are important. No predictions are made regarding the parameter γ. In the case when $\hat{\gamma}$ equals 1, α cannot be computed. In these cases, the parameter α was estimated by taking the mean of the reaction times in the last part of the time series, and the value of β by taking for $\alpha + \beta$ the mean of the reaction times at the very beginning of the series. In the experiment that follows, α was estimated in these cases by taking the mean of reaction times 10–15 (the last six reaction times) and β by taking reaction times 2–4 (three reaction times, the first being excluded because it served as a dummy variable). The estimates obtained in this way are conservative in comparison with the true values of α and β. The minimum reaction time was taken as an estimate of the parameter A. This is necessarily an overestimate as, according to the model, the minimum reaction time is always larger than or equal to A. Let $a = a_1/a_0$. The formula for $E[T]$ can now be rewritten as follows: $a = (E[T] - A)/A$, where $a = a_1/a_0$. Substituting $\hat{\alpha}$ for $E[T]$, and the shortest reaction time for A, gives an estimate for a. Because the minimum reaction time is an overestimate of A, the estimated value of a is an underestimate of the true value of a.

THE PERSEVERATION HYPOTHESIS

Reaction-time curves obtained in overlearned prolonged work tasks usually show an increase at the beginning of the test and, after some time, reach a stationary state (see Jansen & Roskam, 1989; van Breukelen, Jansen, Roskam, van der Ven, & Smit, 1987; van der Ven et al., 1989). These increasing curves should not be interpreted in terms of fatigue, but in terms of *perseveration*. Perseveration is a technical term, coined by Spearman (1927, chapter 17), denoting a gradual change in performance depending on the mental state of the subjects before starting with the task. If fatigue was the underlying cause, one should expect marginally increasing curves, but the actual reaction-time curves are marginally decreasing. A hypothesis is now introduced to account for the phenomenon of increasing reaction-time curves. The hypothesis is referred to as the perseveration hypothesis.

According to the Poisson inhibition model, if the inhibition at the beginning of the task is different from its stationary value, then it will take some time for the stationary state to be reached. One may expect that, generally, the inhibition at the beginning of a task will be lower, because in a state of nonwork it will fluctuate at a lower level than in a state of work. This expectation is based on the following hypothesis:

The parameter a_1 for the pretask (or no-task) condition will be lower than for the actual task condition and, as a result, the stationary mean of the pretask (or no-task) condition will be lower than the stationary mean of the actual task condition.

The initial inhibition at the beginning of the task will be equal to the final inhibition in the pretask (= no-task) condition. In the time preceding the actual task (the pretask condition) the inhibition fluctuates at a lower level in comparison to the level of fluctuation that will be reached in the stationary state at the end of the actual task. The inhibition at the beginning of the actual task will therefore generally be lower than the stationary mean of the inhibition in the actual task, and this will cause the emergence of an increasing reaction-time curve.

In order to make it possible to test the hypothesis with real data, it is necessary to make an additional assumption, which as such is not tested, but taken for granted. The assumption reads as follows:

The parameter a_0, which represents the rate of decrease of inhibition during rest, is only dependent on the subject and not on the task.

This assumption implies that all changes in a_1 as a result of task change are equivalent to changes in a, where a is equal to the ratio a_1/a_0.

PREVIOUS EXPERIMENTS

The perseveration hypothesis was previously tested in two experiments, one by van Breukelen and another by Jansen (see van Breukelen et al., 1987). The experiments by van Breukelen and Jansen[1] were originally reported in van Breukelen (1989) and Jansen (1990), and, in condensed form in van Breukelen et al. (1987). The experiment in van Breukelen et al. (1987) is referred to as the Bourdon experiment and the experiment by Jansen as the Pauli experiment. In both experiments the same experimental design was used.

Description of the Experiments

In the experiment by van Breukelen the experimental task consisted of a computerized version of the Bourdon cancellation test. There are two versions available for this test: the Bourdon–Wiersma test (see Huiskam & de Mare, 1947, and Kamphuis, 1962) for adults and the Bourdon–Vos test

---

[1]The author thanks Gerard J. van Breukelen and Ronald W. Jansen for providing the data of the original experiments.

(Vos, 1988) for children. A similar test was mentioned by Spearman (1927), who called it "Fours" (crossing out groups of four dots from among groups of three, four, and five dots). In the experimental version of the test, patterns of three, four, or five dots were presented to the subject, who had to respond by pressing one of two buttons: the right button with the right index finger for a group of four dots, or the left button with the left index finger for a group of three or five dots. The dot pattern of size 3 × 3 cm were presented in the center of a 30 × 30 cm TV screen at a distance of about 80 cm. The dot patterns were presented successively in blocks of seven. Within blocks each response triggered the next stimulus (pattern); that is, no rest pauses were given between stimuli. The stimuli in each block were arranged in such a way that repetition effects and difficulty effects were about the same in each block. Each experimental condition consisted of 224 trials resulting in 32 block reaction times (RTs). Several experimental conditions were run, among them a continuous work condition and a discontinuous work condition. In the continuous work condition, no rest pauses were given between blocks. All dot patterns (stimuli) were presented in a continuous sequence. In the discontinuous work condition, rest pauses of 3 sec were interposed between blocks of stimuli. After these 3 sec the subject could prolong this pause until the subject chose to resume the task by pressing a button. In van Breukelen et al. (1987), van Breukelen (1989), and Jansen (1990) the continuous work condition is referred to as the *massed condition*, and the discontinuous work condition as the *spaced condition*. Subjects were 20 male and 20 female student volunteers from the University of Nijmegen. In the original study (van Breukelen, 1989), the first trial in a block of seven was used as a dummy trial. These dummy trials were excluded from the analysis and served mainly to absorb undesirable postrest effects in the discontinuous work conditions. Therefore, in the statistical analysis reported by van Breukelen (1989) block RTs actually consisted of summations of six stimulus RTs (RTs 2–7) instead of summations of seven stimulus RTs (RTs 1–7).

In the experiment by Jansen, the experimental task consisted of a computerized modification of the Pauli test (Arnold, 1975), which is a digit addition task. It was administered in a two-choice reaction-time format. The sum of each individual addition was less than 10. An example of an item as it was displayed is: 3 + 4 = 7. Subjects were asked to decide whether the addition was correct or incorrect by pressing the "YES" or "NO" button. For each addition used in the experiment there was a correct and an incorrect answer. An example of an incorrect addition is: 3 + 4 = 6. The stimuli were also presented on a 30 × 30 cm display at a distance of about 80 cm. In order to avoid repetition and difficulty effects in the experiment by Jansen the additions (trials) were presented in blocks of eight. Similar to the experiment by van Breukelen, the experiment by Jansen also had a continuous work condition and a discontinuous work condition. However, in contrast to the experiment by van Breukelen, in the discontinuous work condition rest pauses of 3 sec were not only given between blocks but also within blocks, that is, after the fourth trial. In the continuous work condition no rest pauses were provided, neither between stimuli nor between blocks. Each experimental condition consisted of 256 trials resulting in 32 block RTs. Subjects were 16 male and 16 female student volunteers, aged between 18 and 30 years, from the University of Nijmegen. In the original study (van Breukelen, 1989), two trials were used as dummy trials: the first trial and the fifth trial of a block. These dummy trials were excluded from the analysis for the same reason as given earlier. Therefore, in the statistical analysis of the experiment by Jansen that is reported in van Breukelen (1989), block RTs actually consisted of summations of six stimulus RTs (RTs 2–4 and 6–8).

In both experiments, subjects were instructed to work quickly, but without making errors. It was emphasized that errors could not be corrected. No feedback was given on either RTs or errors. In both experiments, each experimental condition resulted in a series consisting of 32 block RTs, and the statistical analysis was based on block RTs summed over six responses.

Explanation of the Results

The deliberately interposed resting periods of 3 sec, which were given in the discontinuous form of the task (not to be confused with the latent rest intervals during work), can be considered as no-task periods. So, in fact, one alternates between periods of tasks and no tasks. The no-task condition is assumed to be easier than the task condition. Then, according to the perseveration hypothesis, a_1 for the no-task period will be lower than a_1 for the task period. Within each of these periods the parameter a_1 is constant. Therefore, one may represent a_1 (as well as a) as a step function in time where a_1 has a constant lower value during the interposed rest periods (no-task periods) and a constant higher value during the periods of work (task periods). According to the perseveration hypothesis, this implies that, during the interposed rest periods, the inhibition will gradually oscillate to a lower value (the stationary value that belongs to the no-task period), and it will again oscillate to a higher value during the periods of repeating the task. When the interposed rest periods are sufficiently large, this will result in a flat (no trend) reaction-time curve. Moreover, the mean and the variance will both be lower than the stationary mean and variance of the curve in which no interposed resting periods are given (the continuous condition in the experiments by van Breukelen and Jansen). These predictions were borne out in both experiments.

THE EXPERIMENT

In the experiment described next the perseveration hypothesis was tested by using two different tasks varying only in difficulty. In one condition the easier task was given first. In the second condition the more difficult task was given first. The first task was immediately followed by the second without any interposed resting period.

Predictions

The perseveration hypothesis implies that if the subject at the end of an easier task is asked to turn to a more difficult task, the initial inhibition at the beginning of the more difficult task will be equal to the inhibition at the end of the easier task. If the subject has reached the stationary state in the easier task, then the inhibition fluctuates at a lower level in comparison to the level of fluctuation that will be reached in the stationary state at the end of the more difficult task. The inhibition at the beginning of the more difficult task will therefore generally be lower than the stationary mean of the inhibition, and this will cause the emergence of an increasing reaction-time curve in the more difficult task.

A similar reasoning holds when a subject is asked to turn from a difficult task to an easier task. The initial inhibition at the beginning of the easier task will be equal to the inhibition at the end of the more difficult task. If the subject has reached the stationary state in the more difficult task, then the inhibition fluctuates at a higher level in comparison to the level of fluctuation that will be reached in the stationary state at the end of the easier task. The inhibition at the beginning of the easier task will therefore generally be higher than the stationary mean of the inhibition, and this will cause the emergence of a decreasing reaction-time curve in the easier task. According to the perseveration hypothesis, the following predictions can be made:

1. When an easy task is followed by a more difficult task, the reaction-time curve in the easy task will be increasing as well as the reaction-time curve in the more difficult task. In both cases $\beta < 0$.
2. When a difficult task is followed by an easier task, the reaction-time curve of the difficult task will be increasing ($\beta < 0$) but the reaction-time curve of the easier task will be decreasing ($\beta > 0$).

For the prediction to be tested, only the parameters α and β are of importance. No predictions are made regarding the parameter γ.

Tasks

The easy task was the addition of three single digits and the difficult task six single digits. In order to obtain binary responses, the following procedure was followed: First the digits (three or six of them) were added together. Next, the digits occurring in the result were themselves added together. Lastly, the subject indicated whether the final result was even or odd. For example, given the three digits, 3, 5, and 8, the subject has first to calculate the sum, which is 16; then calculate the sum of the digits in this result, $1 + 6$, which equals 7; and finally, indicate whether this result is even or odd by pressing a button. The actual digits presented in each addition problem were randomly selected without replacement from the set {1,2,3,4,5,6,7,8,9}. In pilot experiments it was found that when the result of an addition was 10 or a multiple of 10, subjects became confused and often made mistakes in adding the digits in the result. For this reason, problems giving 10 as a result were excluded.

Design

Before the experiment subjects were allowed to practice as much as they wished in order to get used to the task. In the actual experiment, two conditions were set up. In the first condition a sequence of 30 three-digit problems was immediately followed by a series of 15 six-digit problems. No rest pauses were given, either between the individual problems or between the two series. This procedure was administered five times (five trials). In the second condition, a series of 15 six-digit problems was immediately followed by a series of 30 three-digit problems. Again, no rest pauses were given, either between problems or between series. This order was also administered five times. In the case of three-digit problems, the reaction times used in the analysis that follows correspond to the time taken for two consecutive problems. This made these reaction times comparable to the reaction times for the six-digit problems, because the work in solving two three-digit problems is approximately the same as the work in solving one six-digit problem. The problems were presented on a computer screen, and when an answer was given, the next problem was displayed immediately. The first condition, in which three-digit problems were followed by six-digit ones, was always given first (five trials). The second condition, in which six-digit problems were followed by three-digit ones, was administered the next day (five further trials).

In reaction-time experiments the dependent variable is usually a single reaction time. In this experiment, however, the dependent variable is a vector, consisting of the consecutive reaction times in the series. The variables of interest are the statistical measures described already, such as the long-term trend coefficients $\hat{\alpha}$ and $\hat{\beta}$, the inhibition ratio $\hat{a}$, and the minimum reaction time in the series, which is denoted by $\hat{A}$, because it is an estimate for the total real working time A.

Subjects

Five female psychology students, aged from 21 to 23 years, volunteered as subjects. They received special credit points for their participation.

Controlling the Manipulation

According to Runkel and McGrath (1972, p. 209) the investigator must somehow observe (and check) any variable that he or she manipulates in order to verify the success of the manipulation, that is, to make sure that the variable assumes its intended value(s). Now, the predictions already mentioned apply only when a_1 in the easier task is smaller than in the more difficult task. It could, for example, be the case that the use of six-digit problems, in comparison to the three-digit problems, has an effect only on the total working time, A, and not on a_1. Because the parameter a_1 cannot be estimated, it was assumed that the parameter a_0 does not change from one series to the next. This implies that all changes in a_1 are equivalent to changes in a. Now, the intended effect of the manipulation (three-digits vs. six-digits) can be checked. If the experimental manipulation has been successful, then one would expect that in the first condition of the experiment, in which a series of three-digit problems is followed by a series of six-digit problems, the estimated value of a will be lower in the first series than in the second. Similarly, one would expect that in the second condition of the experiment, in which a series of six-digit problems is followed by a series of three-digit problems, the estimated value of a in the first series will be higher than in the second. The mean values of $\hat{a}$ are given in Table 6.1 along with the mean values of the shortest reaction time. The reaction times are measured in seconds.

With respect to the shortest reaction time, no interaction should be expected according to the theory. The experiment is a two-factor experiment with repeated measurements over only one factor. The within-subjects factor is series with two levels, and the between-subjects factor is conditions, also with two levels. With respect to the mean estimated values of a the results in Table 6.1 are in accordance with the prediction. The interaction between series and conditions with the estimated value of a as the dependent variable is significant at the 5% level ($p = .046$) and the mean values are according to expectation. The interaction between series and conditions with the minimum reaction time as the dependent variable is, as

TABLE 6.1
Means and Standard Deviations of Individually
Estimated a and Minimum Reaction Time $\hat{A}$

	$\hat{a}$				
	Series 1		Series 2		
Condition	Mean	SD	Mean	SD	N
1	0.647	0.398	0.752	0.398	25
2	0.744	0.293	0.590	0.305	25
	$\hat{A}$				
	Series 1		Series 2		
Condition	Mean	SD	Mean	SD	N
1	4.500	1.100	4.522	1.202	25
2	4.035	0.826	3.762	0.703	25

expected, not significant ($p = .236$). These results imply that the manipulation has been successful.

Results

Average reaction-time curves across subjects and trials per series are displayed in Fig. 6.1. The best fitting exponential regression curves are also given in Fig. 6.1. These curves were computed on the basis of the RTs 2–15. The first reaction times were excluded because in the experiments by van Breukelen and Jansen (see van Breukelen et al., 1987) it was observed that during the test, in the case of a change of task, the first reaction time was usually larger than the subsequent ones, probably due to the extra time needed to adapt to the new situation. For this reason first reaction times were treated as dummy variables and disregarded in the estimation of the parameters such as α, β, and γ, and A and a.

The best fitting exponential curves in Fig. 6.1 are clearly in accordance with the predictions. The six-digit problems in the first condition show an increase of the reaction times, whereas the three-digit problems in the second condition show a decrease. Statistical tests are given later. Note that the six-digit problems in the second condition generally have lower reaction times in comparison to the three-digit problems in the first condition. The same holds for the three-digit problems in the second condition, which have considerably lower reaction times in comparison to the three-digit problems in the first condition. This may be explained by as-

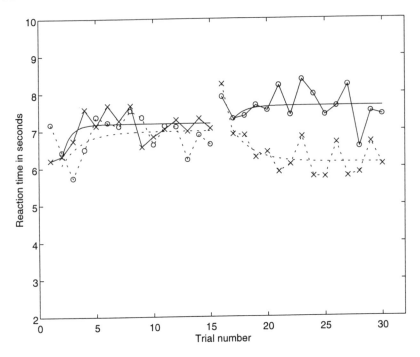

FIG. 6.1. Averaged observed (sawtooth) and theoretical (smooth) curves. *Note.* Solid line: first condition (three-digit problems followed by six-digit problems); dashed line: second condition (six-digit problems followed by three-digit problems); crosses: three-digit problems; circles: six-digit problems.

suming a reminiscence effect between conditions (see Discussion). The second condition was always given after the first condition. The presentation order of conditions was not counterbalanced across subjects.

Estimated values of α, β, and γ based on reaction times 2–15 are given in Table 6.2. The coefficients $\hat{\alpha}$ and $\hat{\beta}$ in Table 6.2 are entirely according to predictions. Moreover, it is interesting to observe that in the first condition the $\hat{\alpha}$ (7.191) of the first series (the three-digit problems) has about the same values as $\hat{\alpha} + \hat{\beta}$ (7.282) in the second series (six-digit problems). A similar conclusion holds in the second condition. The $\hat{\alpha}$ (6.992) of the first series (six-digit problems) has even exactly the same value as $\hat{\alpha} + \hat{\beta}$ (6.992) in the second series (three-digit problems).

The previous analysis related to the mean reaction-time curve averaged over subjects, and individual differences in trend were not taken into account. To examine trend in more detail, one could perform an analysis of variance with the individual coefficients $\hat{\alpha}$ and $\hat{\beta}$ as dependent variables. However, when $\hat{\gamma}$ equals 1, $\hat{\alpha}$ and $\hat{\beta}$ cannot be computed. Estimates of $\hat{\gamma}$ with $0 < \hat{\gamma} < 1$ were obtained in 58 cases. In 18 cases $\hat{\gamma}$ was equal to zero

TABLE 6.2
Estimated Values of α, β, and γ (RT 2–15)

Condition	Series	$\hat{\alpha}$	$\hat{\beta}$	$\hat{\gamma}$	Residual SS
1	1	7.195	−0.905	0.246	1.331
1	2	7.653	−0.371	0.368	2.647
2	1	6.992	−0.903	0.557	2.523
2	2	6.128	+0.865	0.586	1.797

TABLE 6.3
Means and Standard Deviations of Individually
Estimated $\hat{\alpha}$ and $\hat{\beta}$ With Adapted Estimates When $\hat{\gamma} = 0$ or 1

| | $\hat{\alpha}$ | | | | |
| | Series 1 | | Series 2 | | |
Condition	Mean	SD	Mean	SD	N
1	7.303	2.165	7.809	2.262	25
2	7.004	1.690	5.971	1.456	25

| | $\hat{\beta}$ | | | | |
| | Series 1 | | Series 2 | | |
Condition	Mean	SD	Mean	SD	N
1	−0.714	2.024	−0.615	2.951	25
2	−1.179	1.951	1.093	1.589	25

and in 24 cases unity. For these 24 cases $\hat{\alpha}$ and $\hat{\beta}$ were estimated according to the procedure described in the previous section. The parameter α was estimated in these cases by taking the mean of reaction times 10–15 (the last six reaction times) and the value of β by taking for $\hat{\alpha} + \hat{\beta}$ the mean of reaction times 2–4. Cell means and standard deviations are given in Table 6.3. The results in Table 6.3 are also in accordance with predictions. The sign of $\hat{\beta}$ is again as predicted. The interaction between series and conditions with $\hat{\alpha}$ as the dependent variable is significant at the 1% level ($p = .003$), as is also the interaction between series and conditions with $\hat{\beta}$ as the dependent variable ($p = .013$).

DISCUSSION

In controlling for the success of the experimental manipulation, there appeared to be a significant main effect of conditions ($p = .017$) on the minimum reaction time as the dependent variable (see Table 6.1). The average minimum reaction time is lower in condition 2. However, condition

2 was administered subsequent to condition 1. This phenomenon could be explained by assuming that the total real working time is reduced due to reminiscence. According to Eysenck and Frith, "Reminiscence is a technical term, coined by Ballard (1913) in 1913, denoting improvement in the performance of a partially learned act that occurs while the subject is non-working, i.e., not performing the act in question" (Eysenck & Frith, 1977, p. 3). Usually, the longer the period of nonwork, the larger the improvement. The period of nonwork between condition 1 and condition 2 was 1 day. Before the actual experiment was started, subjects could practice as much as they wanted to in order to get used to the task, and, indeed, no evidence was found for any learning effect within each test administration. However, this does not imply that learning could not still play a role with respect to the general level of the reaction-time curve, influencing a parameter such as the minimum reaction time. In this experiment the sequence of the conditions was not balanced across subjects. This is probably the main reason for the decrease in the average minimum reaction time between conditions.

Now that learning seems to take place between conditions, one might also ask whether it can take place between trials. A separate analysis was undertaken for each condition and each series with trials as the main experimental factor. For each trial, the mean values (over subjects) of $\hat{\alpha}$, $\hat{\beta}$, $\hat{A}$, the minimum reaction time, and $\hat{a}$, were computed. A trend analysis was performed on the means using orthogonal polynomials. No significant effects were found except for the minimum reaction time $\hat{A}$, in condition 1 (series 1) and condition 2 (series 2). Accordingly, only the results of these cases are displayed. The respective means and standard deviations are given in Table 6.4. In condition 1 and series 1, the first-degree polynomial coefficient was significant at the 5% level ($p = .022$), and in condition 2 and series 2 at the 10% level ($p = .083$). No significant effects were found in condition 1 and series 2, and in condition 2 and series 1. The results show that there is a between-trials learning effect for the easy—that is, the three-digit—problems, but not for the difficult—six-digit—problems. No explanation has been found for this differential effect.

TABLE 6.4
Means and Standard Deviations of the Minimum Reaction Time

| Trial | Condition 1, Series 1 | | Condition 2, Series 2 | | N |
	Mean	SD	Mean	SD	
1	5.396	1.405	4.078	0.684	5
2	4.946	1.096	4.088	1.045	5
3	4.269	0.930	3.852	0.401	5
4	3.758	0.449	3.494	0.692	5
5	4.130	0.916	3.296	0.376	5

TABLE 6.5
Means and Standard Deviations of the Regression
Coefficient b Computed Across Trials

Condition	Series 1		Series 2		
	Mean	SD	Mean	SD	N
1	-0.372	0.227	-0.190	0.372	5
2	-0.099	0.163	-0.216	0.210	5

The method of orthogonal polynomials assumes a constant linear polynomial coefficient across subjects. It is possible that the linear coefficient is subject dependent. Therefore, an additional test was performed with a subject-dependent linear coefficient as the dependent variable. For each subject, and for each condition and each series, a regression weight b was computed across the five trials. This was done separately for $\hat{\alpha}$, $\hat{\beta}$, minimum reaction time, and $\hat{a}$. Subsequently, for each of these parameters, a separate analysis of variance was performed with b as the dependent variable. This analysis involves two factors with repeated measures. Each factor (conditions and series) has two levels and all (five) subjects received all the four treatments. Again, the linear coefficient b showed a significant effect only with respect to the minimum reaction time, which, as was to be expected, concerned the interaction between conditions and series. The results are displayed in Table 6.5. According to the previous results, the mean value of the regression weight b should be lower for the three-digit problems, that is, in the case of treatments: condition 1 and series 1, and condition 2 and series 2. The interaction is significant at the 5% level ($p = .052$). Both results clearly indicate that a between-trials learning or reminiscence effect affected only the shortest reaction time and only in the case of the three-digit problems. This leads to the following conclusion: When a task is overlearned, reminiscence may still take place. However, it only affects the total real working time.

ACKNOWLEDGMENTS

The author thanks J. C. Smit, F. M. Gremmen and Dr. D. R. J. Laming for their helpful suggestions.

REFERENCES

Arnold, W. (1975). *Der Pauli-Test.* New York: Springer-Verlag.
Ballard, P. B. (1913). Obliviscence and reminiscence. *British Journal of Psychology, Monographical Supplement, 1*(2).

Berger, M. (1982). The "scientific approach" to intelligence: An overview of its history with special reference to mental speed. In H. J. Eysenck (Ed.), *A model of intelligence* (pp. 23–43). New York: Springer.

Bills, A. G. (1935). Fatigue, oscillations and blocks. *Journal of Experimental Psychology, 18,* 562–573.

Binet, A. (1900). Attention et adaptation [Attention and adaptation]. *L'Annee Psychologique, 6,* 248–404.

Donio, J. (1964). *Some stochastic learning models with time as a continuous parameter.* Doctoral thesis, Stanford University, Stanford, CA.

Eysenck, H. J., & Frith, C. D. (1977). *Reminiscence, motivation and personality.* London: Plenum Press.

Huiskamp, J., & de Mare, H. (1947). Enige opmerkingen over de WiersmaBourdon test [Some remarks about the Wiersma–Bourdon test]. *Nederlands Tijdschrift voor de Psychologie* [Dutch Journal of Psychology], *2,* 75–78.

Hull, C. L. (1951). *Essentials of behavior.* Westport, CT: Greenwood Press.

Jansen, R. W. T. L. (1990). *Mental speed and concentration.* Unpublished doctoral dissertation, University of Nijmegen, The Netherlands.

Jansen, R. W., & Roskam, E. E. (1989). Mental processing and distraction. In E. E. Roskam (Ed.), *Mathematical psychology in progress* (pp.   ). Berlin: Springer-Verlag.

Kamphuis, G. H. (1962). Een bijdrage tot de geschiedenis van de Bourdon-test [A contribution to the history of the Bourdon test]. *Nederlands Tijdschrift voor de Psychologie* [Dutch Journal of Psychology], *17,* 247–268.

Runkel, P. J., & McGrath, J. E. (1972). *Research on human behavior.* New York: Holt, Rinehart & Winston.

Smit, J. C., & van der Ven, A. H. G. S. (1995). Inhibition in speed and concentration tests: The Poisson inhibition model. *Journal of Mathematical Psychology, 39,* 265–273.

Spearman, C. (1927). *The abilities of man.* London: Macmillan.

van Breukelen, G. J. P. (1989). *Concentration, speed and precision in mental tests.* Unpublished doctoral dissertation, University of Nijmegen, The Netherlands.

van Breukelen, G. J. P., Jansen, R. W. T. L., Roskam, E. E. C. I., van der Ven, A. H. G. S., & Smit, J. C. (1987). Concentration, speed and precision in simple mental tasks. In E. E. Roskam & R. Suck (Eds.), *Progress in mathematical psychology* (pp. 175–193). Amsterdam: Elsevier.

van der Ven, A. H. G. S., & Smit, J. G. (1982). *Serial reaction times in concentration tests and Hull's concept of reactive inhibition.* In H. C. Micko & U. Schulz (Eds.), *Formalization of psychological theories* (pp. 203–256). Proceedings of the 13th European Mathematical Psychology Group Meeting, Bielefeld. Report of the Universität Bielefeld, Schwerpunkt Mathematisierung, Bielefeld, Federal Republic of Germany.

van der Ven, A. H. G. S., Smit, J. C., & Jansen, R. W. T. L. (1989). Inhibition in prolonged work tasks. *Applied Psychological Measurement, 13,* 177–191.

Chapter 7

A Formal Approach to Color Constancy: The Recovery of Surface and Light Source Spectral Properties Using Bilinear Models[1]

Michael D'Zmura
Geoffrey Iverson
University of California, Irvine

This chapter describes our recent work on the problem of color constancy (D'Zmura, 1992; D'Zmura & Iverson, 1993a, 1993b, 1994; Iverson & D'Zmura, 1994). Our formal approach to the problem emphasizes the recovery of the spectral properties of light sources and surfaces that combine to produce the reflected light that reaches the eye. We rely on bilinear models of the visual response to reflected light, and our first aim, after a brief review of color constancy, is to describe such bilinear models.

The recovery of surface and light source spectral properties using bilinear models had been studied primarily in the case in which a single light shines on a collection of surfaces (Brill, 1978, 1979; Buchsbaum, 1980; Maloney & Wandell, 1986; Sällström, 1973). Yet lights and surfaces play symmetric roles in bilinear models, and the general case is one in which multiple lights shine sequentially on multiple surfaces (D'Zmura, 1992). Each illuminant provides a different *view* of the surfaces, in analogy to work on structure from motion (Ullman, 1979a, 1979b).

Our aim was to determine the circumstances under which recovery of spectral properties using bilinear models is possible. An important issue is uniqueness, which involves problems of identifiability similar to those encountered in other disciplines. We describe numerical and analytical methods for determining whether particular bilinear models, when pre-

---

[1]This chapter is based on an invited address presented by D'Zmura at the 1994 Annual Meeting of the Society for Mathetmatical Psychology, held at the University of Washington, Seattle.

sented with a certain number of views of a certain number of surfaces, relate visual data uniquely to light and surface spectral properties. For the recovery of spectra to be possible, the relation between data and scenes must be unique. We discuss uniqueness in the context of two-stage recovery algorithms, in which the spectral properties of one of either surfaces or light sources are recovered first and then used in a second stage to recover the spectral properties of the other. Results support the intuition that information provided by additional views of surfaces lets a visual system determine a higher dimensional, more accurate description of surface spectral properties (D'Zmura, 1992; D'Zmura & Iverson, 1993a, 1993b; Iverson & D'Zmura, 1994).

We then turn to a general recovery algorithm that uses bilinear models to recover the spectral properties of lights and surfaces simultaneously (D'Zmura & Iverson, 1994). The algorithm is applicable to all problems handled by two-stage recovery algorithms but has a wider scope. In particular, for a p-chromatic visual system (for a trichromatic visual system $p = 3$), there is only a finite number of situations in which two-stage linear recovery algorithms may be applied, while there is an infinite number of situations in which general linear recovery may be applied. The chapter concludes with a discussion of how a visual system can use bilinear models to determine spectral descriptions of arbitrarily high dimension for lights and surfaces, when provided adequate information.

WHAT IS COLOR CONSTANCY?

Color constancy concerns the representation of surface colors in such a way that surface color appearance does not depend on the spectral properties of the light source. People with normal color vision exhibit approximate color constancy (Beck, 1972; Burnham, Evans, & Newhall, 1957; Gelb, 1929; Helson, 1938; Helson, Judd, & Warren, 1952; Judd, 1940; Katz, 1935). Normal color vision is trichromatic: A light with any spectral properties can always be matched in appearance by an appropriate linear combination of three primary lights (Lennie & D'Zmura, 1988; Wyszecki & Stiles, 1982). This trichromacy is evident in the design of color televisions: The three phosphors on a television screen, revealed by close inspection to be present in small colored picture elements, are red, green, and blue primaries that are excited to appropriate levels to match a desired color stimulus.

Trichromacy is due to the presence of three classes of cone photoreceptors in the eye. Each class has a characteristic spectral sensitivity that can be described by a function of wavelength λ. The wavelengths in the electromagnetic spectrum to which we are visually sensitive fall in the range 400–700 nm. Standard names for the three functions of wavelength that correspond to the three types of photoreceptors are $R(\lambda)$, $G(\lambda)$, and $B(\lambda)$.

These are sometimes called the red, green and blue functions, even though the corresponding photoreceptors most definitely do not produce red, green, and blue percepts (the discredited Young–Helmholtz theory). The function $R(\lambda)$ has its peak spectral sensitivity in the longer wavelength region of the spectrum (toward 700 nm) where lights appear orange and red. The function $G(\lambda)$ is most sensitive to intermediate wavelengths, and the function $B(\lambda)$ is most sensitive to short wavelengths that appear blue or violet (toward 400 nm).

The initial response of a trichromatic visual system to a light is described by three numbers r, g, and b, which are the responses of the photoreceptors with sensitivities $R(\lambda)$, $G(\lambda)$, and $B(\lambda)$, respectively. These responses are determined by the number of light quanta absorbed by the photoreceptors, and are obtained by integrating the product of the light and photoreceptoral spectral functions across the visible spectrum:

$$r = \int R(\lambda)L(\lambda)\, d\lambda$$
$$g = \int G(\lambda)L(\lambda)\, d\lambda \qquad (1)$$
$$b = \int B(\lambda)L(\lambda)\, d\lambda$$

The cone photoreceptors in each eye's retina are small and numerous (Curcio, Sloan, Kalina, & Hendrickson, 1990; Curcio, Sloan, Packer, Hendrickson, & Kalina, 1987; Østerberg, 1935; Williams, 1985, 1988), leading to the idealization of the visual response to a spatial pattern of lights as a vector field, namely, a triple $[r\ g\ b]$ of quantum catches at each location on the retina.

Consider now the response of the visual system to lights reflected from surfaces. Figure 7.1 illustrates how the response to a set of surfaces changes when the light shining on the surfaces changes. At the top are shown the spectral power distributions of two sources, the neutral daylight illuminant D_{65} and the yellowish tungsten lightbulb type illuminant A, both of which are standards of the Commission Internationale d'Eclairage (CIE). The spectral function for D_{65} is approximately flat across the visible spectrum, lending it a neutral white appearance, while the function for illuminant A is biased toward longer wavelengths, which lends it a colored, yellow appearance. In the center of Fig. 7.1 is depicted a placard formed of flat pieces of Munsell chip paper. Munsell chips are standard colored papers with well-studied properties (Indow, 1988; Newhall, Nickerson, & Judd, 1943). The figure provides the designations for each Munsell chip in the (imaginary) placard; the designation 10G 3/4, for instance (middle left), refers to a particular green piece of paper. The visual response to the reflected lights is shown at the bottom in terms of chromaticities. These

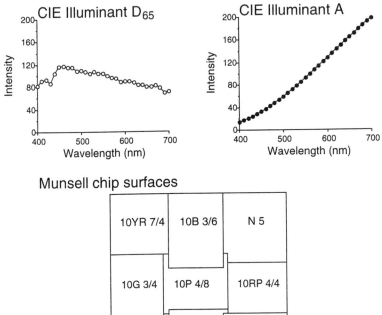

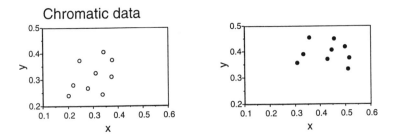

FIG. 7.1. Visual data from reflected lights. CIE standard illuminants D_{65} and A, with spectral power distributions shown at top, shine on Munsell chip surfaces (middle) to produce chromatic data (bottom) that differ. The chromatic data are plotted as (x,y) chromaticities for the CIE 1931 standard observer (Wyszecki & Stiles, 1982).

chromaticities are projections of three-dimensional visual responses onto a two-dimensional color space with coordinates termed (x,y), in which variations in intensity are immaterial. Figure 7.1 shows that the chromatic responses to the reflected lights from the surfaces viewed under D_{65} differ substantially from the responses to the surfaces when viewed under illuminant A.

The basic fact of color constancy is that although lights from surfaces and their corresponding visual responses change when the spectral properties of illumination change, surface color appearance does not change. Land provided the best known demonstrations of color constancy (Land, 1983, 1986). As diagrammed in Fig. 7.2, two placards with colored papers are presented side by side. Land called his placards Mondrians, because individual papers in the placards are arranged in a way reminiscent of paintings by Piet Mondrian. The Mondrian on the left is lit by a sum of three primary light sources of adjustable intensity, while the Mondrian on the right is lit by a steady, white light. Land would adjust the primaries to set the light source on the left to a neutral white and then ask the audience to look at the two papers marked by asterisks. The paper on the left might appear yellow, for instance, while the one on the right might appear red. Physical measurements of the lights from the two surfaces would show that the reflected lights are, not surprisingly, different. Land would then set the light on the left so that physical measurements of the lights reflected from the two surfaces match. Despite the physical match, the surface on the left would retain its yellow appearance, thus demonstrating color constancy.

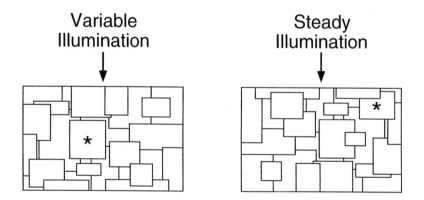

FIG. 7.2.   Land's demonstration of color constancy. Two surfaces of different color, marked by the asterisks, produce different reflected lights when viewed under white light. When these surfaces are made to produce identical reflected lights by changing the illumination at left, the surface at left retains its color appearance, so demonstrating color constancy (Land, 1983, 1986).

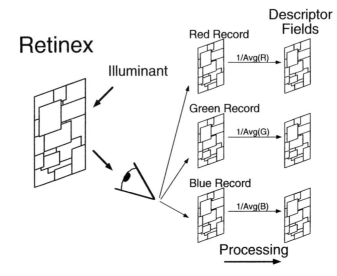

FIG. 7.3. Retinex and response normalization. Brainard and Wandell (1986) showed that Land's Retinex algorithm is equivalent asymptotically to a form of von Kries adaptation (von Kries, 1905): The space-varying responses of R, G, and B photoreceptors (the "Records") are scaled by the space-averaged R, G, and B response, respectively.

The basic idea behind Land's account of color constancy, which he called Retinex, is an old one (Brainard & Wandell, 1986; Judd, 1940; von Kries, 1905). It is illustrated in Fig. 7.3. The vector field of trichromatic responses is split into its three scalar field components, termed the red, green, and blue records. Each record is normalized appropriately to provide a descriptor field. The normalization is equivalent to having knobs on the red, green, and blue records that are used to adjust color balance in response to changing illumination. For instance, if the light source is too red, then the red knob is used to turn down the red record to provide appropriately normalized descriptors. The three descriptors that result for each location in the visual field are then used to describe surface color. One problem with this sort of color constancy scheme is that if it works, one does not know why. If it does not work, one does not know why not.

BILINEAR MODELS

Researchers in the 1970s sought to analyze the problem of color constancy formally (Brill, 1978, 1979; Buchsbaum, 1980; Sällström, 1973). In a simple physical situation, a reflected light $L(\lambda)$ is given by the product of an illuminant spectral power distribution $A(\lambda)$ (like those at the top of Fig. 7.1) and a surface reflectance function $R(\lambda)$:

$$L(\lambda) = A(\lambda)R(\lambda) \qquad (2)$$

A surface reflectance function describes what fraction of incident light is reflected at each wavelength and so takes on values between 0 (no reflection, viz., complete absorption) and 1 (total reflection). Because the notation $R(\lambda)$ for a reflectance function conflicts with the notation for the photoreceptoral sensitivity $R(\lambda)$, we change $R(\lambda)$, $G(\lambda)$, and $B(\lambda)$ to $Q_1(\lambda)$, $Q_2(\lambda)$, and $Q_3(\lambda)$. The quantum catches q_k, for $k = 1, 2, 3$, of a trichromatic visual system with photoreceptoral spectral sensitivities $Q_k(\lambda)$, $k = 1, 2, 3$, are then given by the integrals:

$$q_k = \int Q_k(\lambda)L(\lambda) \, d\lambda \qquad \text{for } k = 1, 2, 3 \qquad (3)$$

The key to the formal analysis of color constancy is the following argument. Surface reflectance functions describe the intrinsic propensities of surfaces to reflect light. They do not depend on the spectral properties of an illuminant. A piece of green grass will reflect light in the same way whether it is viewed outdoors under D_{65} or indoors under illuminant A. A visual system that recovers a surface's reflectance function and uses it to represent surface color appearance would exhibit color constancy, because its representation of surface color does not depend on illumination.

How can one recover reflectance functions from three quantum-catch data per surface? A brief glance at Equations 2 and 3 shows that this is generally impossible. Three data per surface will not suffice to recover two functions that each may vary in infinitely many ways, particularly when these two functions are confounded in a product.

The solution to the conundrum is illustrated in Fig. 7.4. One assumes that illuminant and reflectance functions do not vary in infinitely many ways; rather, they vary along a finite number of dimensions, a number that is more closely matched to the (trichromatic) capabilities of the visual system. This assumption is actually valid in a variety of physical situations. At the top of Fig. 7.4 are shown the basis functions for a three-dimensional model of daylight illumination. Judd, MacAdam, and Wyszecki (1964) performed a principal components analysis of 622 measurements of different phases of daylight and found that over 99% of the variance could be accounted for using a three-dimensional model with the basis functions pictured. One of these functions (the flat one) corresponds to intensity variations; a second is a "yellow–blue" variation that corresponds to the presence or absence of the solar disk (yellow) or the sky (blue); the third

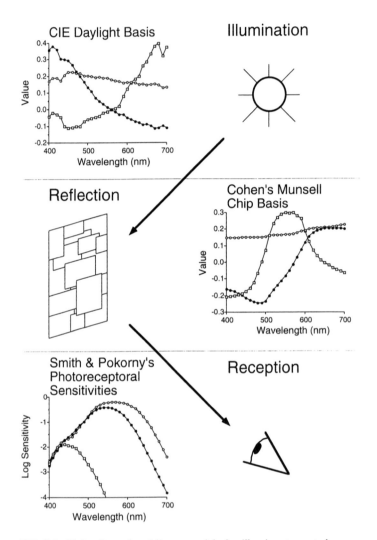

FIG. 7.4. Finite-dimensional linear models for illuminant spectral power distributions and surface reflectance functions. At top are pictured the three CIE standard daylight basis functions (Judd, MacAdam, & Wyszecki, 1964; Wyszecki & Stiles, 1982); appropriate linear combinations of these reproduce the spectral power distributions of the various phases of daylight. In the middle are pictured three basis functions for a linear model of Munsell chip reflectance functions determined by Cohen (1964). At bottom are the three spectral sensitivity curves determined by Smith and Pokorny (1975) for human color vision (on a logarithmic scale).

is a "red–green" variation that corresponds to the presence or absence of various particles in the atmosphere. An illuminant $A(\lambda)$ that falls within the span of m such basis functions can be described as an appropriate linear combination:

$$A(\lambda) = \sum_{i=1}^{m} a_i A_i(\lambda) \qquad (4)$$

The m coefficients a_i in the expansion are illuminant descriptors that correspond to the spectral power distribution $A(\lambda)$.

In the middle of Fig. 7.4 are shown three basis functions for a linear model of the surface reflectance functions of Munsell chips. Cohen (1964) showed that over 99% of the variance in the set of Munsell chip reflectance functions could be accounted for using just the three basis functions shown. These functions again correspond roughly to intensity, "red–green," and "yellow–blue" variations. More recent work by Parkkinen, Hallikainen, and Jaaskelainen (1989) suggests that a visual system may need a model with as many as eight dimensions to describe precisely the reflectance functions that are met in natural viewing situations. Speaking generally, a linear model for reflectance of n dimensions can be used to describe a particular reflectance function $R(\lambda)$ as follows:

$$R(\lambda) = \sum_{j=1}^{n} r_j R_j(\lambda) \qquad (5)$$

Provided that the n-dimensional model accurately describes variation among reflectances in a particular environment, then recovering the n model descriptors r_j for each surface is tantamount to color constancy.

Using the two linear models (Equations 4 and 5), a reflected light $L(\lambda) = A(\lambda)R(\lambda)$ can be expressed as

$$L(\lambda) = \left[\sum_{i=1}^{m} a_i A_i(\lambda) \right] \left[\sum_{j=1}^{n} r_j R_j(\lambda) \right]$$

$$= \sum_{i=1}^{m} \sum_{j=1}^{n} a_i r_j A_i(\lambda) R_j(\lambda) \qquad (6)$$

We wish to determine the visual response to such lights. The bottom of Fig. 7.4 shows the three photoreceptoral spectral sensitivities of Smith and Pokorny (1975), which are thought to correspond closely to the sensitivities of human cone photoreceptors. Although we are most interested in trichromatic visual systems, we also consider dichromatic, tetrachromatic, and higher order visual systems. In general, we work with a p-chromatic visual system with spectral sensitivities $Q_k(\lambda)$ and quantum catches q_k, for $k = 1, \ldots, p$. The quantum catches are then (Equations 3 and 6)

$$q_k = \int Q_k(\lambda) \left[\sum_{i=1}^{m} \sum_{j=1}^{n} a_i r_j A_i(\lambda) R_j(\lambda) \right] d\lambda$$

$$= \sum_{i=1}^{m} \sum_{j=1}^{n} a_i r_j \left[\int Q_k(\lambda) A_i(\lambda) R_j(\lambda)\ d\lambda \right] \text{ for } k = 1, \ldots, p \qquad (8)$$

In applications, the basis functions for illumination $A_i(\lambda)$, $i = 1, \ldots, m$, are known, as are the basis functions for reflectance $R_j(\lambda)$, $j = 1, \ldots, n$, and the photoreceptoral spectral sensitivities $Q_k(\lambda)$, $k = 1, \ldots, p$. Thus the integrals at the bottom of Equation 8 are known values that relate unknown descriptors a_i and r_j to known quantum-catch data q_k. We use these known integrals to define bilinear model matrices $\mathbf{B}_j$, $j = 1, \ldots, n$:

$$(\mathbf{B}_j)_{ki} = \int Q_k(\lambda) A_i(\lambda) R_j(\lambda)\ d\lambda \qquad k = 1, \ldots, p,\ i = 1, \ldots, m \qquad (9)$$

The bilinear model matrices that correspond to the situation illustrated in Fig. 7.4 are three in number ($j = 1, \ldots, n = 3$). Each of the three matrices has size 3×3 for a total of 27 model parameters. For the model illustrated in Fig. 7.4, each row corresponds to a particular photoreceptoral spectral sensitivity $k = 1, \ldots, p = 3$, and each column corresponds to a particular basis function for illumination $i = 1, \ldots, m = 3$. In general, the bilinear model matrices are n in number and have matrix size $p \times m$.

Rewriting Equation 8 using the bilinear model matrices, we arrive at the following compact expression:

$$q_k = \sum_{i=1}^{m} \sum_{j=1}^{n} r_j (\mathbf{B}_j)_{ki} a_i \qquad k = 1, \ldots, p \qquad (10)$$

This equation expresses a bilinear model for quantum catch data from reflected lights. Holding the reflectance descriptors constant, one sees that the quantum catches vary linearly with the illuminant descriptors. Likewise, holding the illuminant descriptors constant shows that the quantum catches vary linearly with the reflectance descriptors.

Spectral recovery schemes use the known quantum catch data and the known bilinear model matrix entries to determine the unknown descriptors for reflectance and illumination. Note that because the quantum-catch data are related bilinearly to the descriptors, the latter may only be recovered up to a single unknown scale factor. For instance, a light of intensity 10 shining on a surface of reflectance 0.1 produces the same reflected light as a light of intensity 5 shining on a surface of reflectance 0.2. This trade-off between the intensities of lights and surfaces results in a single unknown scale factor for spectral recovery schemes.

COLOR STRUCTURE FROM CHROMATIC MOTION

There are a host of color constancy schemes that use bilinear models to help recover the spectral properties of lights and surfaces. These include (a) gray-world schemes (Buchsbaum, 1980; D'Zmura & Lennie, 1986), in which one assumes that the average reflectance function presented to the viewer is a spectrally flat gray, so that the space-averaged light that reaches the eye bears the chromatic properties of the illuminant. Knowledge of the illuminant is then used to recover reflectance functions. There are also (b) two-stage linear recovery schemes (D'Zmura, 1992; D'Zmura & Iverson, 1993a, 1993b; Iverson & D'Zmura, 1994; Maloney, 1985; Maloney & Wandell, 1986) and (c) a general linear recovery scheme with a single stage (D'Zmura & Iverson, 1994), review of which occupies us in this chapter. There are also (d) nonlinear recovery schemes (D'Zmura & Iverson, 1993c; Tsukada & Ohta, 1990), (e) schemes that use information from specular highlights (D'Zmura & Lennie, 1986; Lee, 1986), and (f) schemes that use information from interreflections (Drew & Funt, 1992). Finally, there are probabilistic color constancy algorithms (Brainard & Freeman, 1994; D'Zmura, Iverson, & Singer, 1995; Trussell & Vrhel, 1991) that use stochastic, finite-dimensional linear models for reflectance and illumination to estimate light and surface spectral properties.

Our present concern is with two-stage linear recovery algorithms. These were introduced by Maloney and Wandell (1986) to handle cases in which a single light provides uniform illumination of a set of surfaces. Their trichromatic algorithm uses quantum-catch data from each surface to recover reflectance and light source descriptors. Maloney and Wandell found that a trichromatic visual system can recover spectral descriptors if reflectances are described by a two-dimensional linear model. Their recovery of two descriptors per surface reflectance is illustrated in Fig. 7.5. If surface reflectances vary in only two dimensions, then reflected lights will span a plane in the space of quantum catches. The position of the plane in the space of quantum catches corresponds to the three-dimensional spectral properties of the illuminant, up to the unknown scaling factor that corresponds to an intensity trade-off. In the first stage of the recovery algorithm, one uses the position of the plane to estimate the illuminant; in the second stage, the

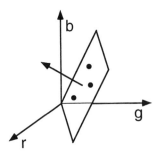

FIG. 7.5. Quantum-catch data in the situation studied by Maloney and Wandell (1986). The quantum-catch triples from surfaces with reflectance functions that vary in two dimensions, when viewed under uniform illumination, describe a plane in the space of quantum-catch data. The position of the plane corresponds to the chromatic properties of the illuminant, indicated by the normal vector, while the position of a surface's triple within the data plane corresponds to the reflectance.

estimate of the illuminant is used to recover the two-dimensional reflectances.

As mentioned earlier, we would like to recover at least three and possibly as many as eight descriptors per surface. Our starting point was the idea that color constancy is first a problem if illumination changes, and that a change in illumination provides more information about spectral properties (D'Zmura, 1992). Figure 7.6 illustrates this idea. As in Land's demonstrations, the illumination of a set of surfaces changes in time, say, from D_{65} to illuminant A (top). Each illuminant provides a different *view* of a set of surfaces (middle), with reflectance properties that are *rigid* or unchanging. Provided that the visual system can identify the surface of origin for quantum-catch data collected before and after the illuminant change (an assumption of *surface correspondence*), the visual system can attempt to use the change or *motion* in the chromatic data (bottom) to help recover color descriptors.

There is evidently a strong analogy between color constancy and what is termed "structure from motion" (Ullman, 1979a, 1979b). Suppose that points with fixed positions on a rigid body such as a cube are projected onto a flat display as points of light. A single view of these points does not provide the information that is needed to determine three-dimensional structure. If one now provides further views of the points by rotating the rigid body, then the three-dimensional configuration of the points can be determined and three-dimensional structure is perceived: One determines structure from motion (Bennett, Hoffman, Nicola, & Prakash, 1989; Grzywacz & Hildreth, 1987; Hoffman & Flinchbaugh, 1982; Ullman, 1979a, 1979b). In analogy, suppose that surfaces in a Mondrian display are lit by a single light. A trichromatic visual system recovers, at best, two descriptors per surface reflectance; this is the result of Maloney and Wandell (1986). Our first result was to show that if the light is changed to provide a second view of the Mondrian, then a three-dimensional description of each surface can be determined (D'Zmura, 1992). Land's demonstrations of color constancy, in which a Mondrian is illuminated by several lights in sequence, suggest that the visual system interprets such chromatic motion (change

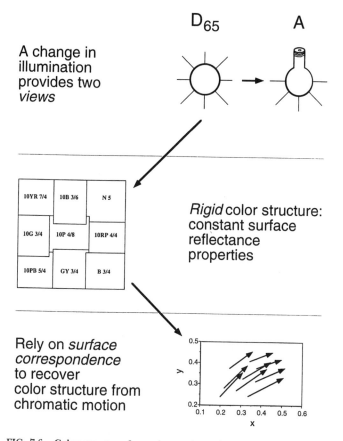

FIG. 7.6. Color structure from chromatic motion. See text for details.

in chromatic data) readily. This position is buttressed by our own experimental work on the detection of nonrigid chromatic motion (D'Zmura & Mangalick, 1994) and by that of Foster, Craven, and Sale (1992) and Craven and Foster (1992). This latter group independently conceived and developed the analogy between color constancy and structure from motion in experiments involving judgments of appearance and visual search.

We realized that the question of whether particular bilinear models can be used to recover spectral properties from multiple views (provided by spectrally independent illuminants) of multiple surfaces was a quite general one that could be investigated systematically and rigorously. We wanted to know whether spectral recovery from quantum-catch data is possible for a p-chromatic visual system that is presented with v views of s surfaces and that uses m- and n-dimensional models for illumination and reflectance, respectively.

Each choice of the five parameters corresponds to a different color constancy problem that can be identified by its quintuple $(p\ m\ n\ v\ s)$. The

TABLE 7.1
List of Symbols

Bilinear model parameters	
p	Number of photoreceptoral types
m	Illuminant model dimension
n	Reflectance model dimension
v	Number of views
s	Number of surfaces
Functions of wavelength	
$A(\lambda)$	An illuminant spectral power distribution
$A_i(\lambda)$	The ith illuminant model basis function, $i = 1, \ldots, m$
$L(\lambda)$	A reflected light's spectral power distribution
$Q_k(\lambda)$	The kth photoreceptoral spectral sensitivity function, $k = 1, \ldots, p$
$R(\lambda)$	A reflectance function
$R_j(\lambda)$	The jth reflectance model basis function, $j = 1, \ldots, n$
Scalars, descriptors, vectors and matrices	
$a_i, a_{wi}, \mathbf{a}_w, \mathbf{a}$	Illuminant descriptors
$\beta_k, \mathbf{B}_j$	Bilinear model matrices
$r, g, b; q_k, q_{tuk}$	Quantum-catch data
$r_j, r_{ij}, \mathbf{r}_i, \mathbf{r}$	Reflectance descriptors
Miscellany	
E, U	Numbers of equations and monomial unknowns, respectively, provided by the model check algorithm
Q, D	Number svp of quantum-catch data and number $sn + vm$ of unknown descriptors to be recovered, respectively

meanings of the five parameters are listed in Table 7.1, which contains a complete list of symbols. As an example, the Maloney and Wandell trichromatic algorithm (1986) corresponds to the problem $(p\ m\ n\ v\ s) = (3\ 3\ 2\ 1\ 2)$. In English, a trichromatic visual system, using a three-dimensional model for illumination and a two-dimensional model for reflectance, uses a single view of two or more surfaces to recover the corresponding numbers of spectral descriptors. As another example, our first result was to show that recovery is possible for the problem $(p\ m\ n\ v\ s) = (3\ 3\ 3\ 2\ 3)$: There are bilinear models that a trichromatic visual system can use to recover, from two views of three or more surfaces, three descriptors per light and per surface (D'Zmura, 1992). We naturally wanted to classify all color constancy problems $(p\ m\ n\ v\ s)$ as to whether spectral recovery is possible and, if so, under what circumstances.

UNIQUE RECOVERY

To determine conditions that must hold if recovery is to be unique, let us first generalize Equation 10 to handle v views of s surfaces. The quantum-catch response of the kth photoreceptoral mechanism to the view provided by the wth illuminant of the tth surface, for $k = 1, \ldots, p$, for $w = 1, \ldots,$ v, and for $t = 1, \ldots, s$, is given by

$$q_{twk} = \sum_{i=1}^{m} \sum_{j=1}^{n} r_{tj}(\mathbf{B}_j)_{ki} a_{wi} \qquad (11)$$

The total number Q of quantum-catch data is svp, which is the product of the number s of surfaces, the number v of views (illuminants), and the number p of photoreceptoral classes. The number D of descriptors is $sn + vm$, which is the number s of surfaces multiplied by n descriptors per surface, plus the number v of illuminants multiplied by m descriptors per illuminant. Unique recovery is possible only if the number of data equals or exceeds the number of descriptors. One must take into account the single unknown scaling factor, revealing $Q \geq D - 1$ or

$$svp \geq sn + vm - 1 \qquad (12)$$

to be a necessary condition for unique recovery.

Two further necessary conditions for unique recovery follow from the use of two-stage linear recovery algorithms. Referring to Equation 11, these work by:

1. Applying the inverse of the $s \times n$ matrix of reflectance descriptors formed by r_{tj} on the left to separate reflectance from illuminant descriptors.

2. Isolating the illuminant descriptors by applying the inverses of the $p \times m$ bilinear model matrices $\mathbf{B}_j$, for $j = 1, \ldots, n$, to the quantum-catch data.

3. Using a singular value decomposition to solve the resulting linear homogeneous system that involves only the (inverse) unknown reflectance descriptors.

4. Finally, using the estimates of the reflectance descriptors to determine illuminant descriptors (D'Zmura, 1992; D'Zmura & Iverson, 1993a).

The inversions in steps 1 and 2 generate two further necessary conditions for unique two-stage linear recovery: $s \geq n$ and $p \geq m$.[2] Substituting these

---

[2] We assume that the s surfaces differ from one another, namely, that their vectors of descriptors span the n-dimensional space ($s \geq n$) and that the v illuminants differ from each other, namely, that their descriptor vectors span a v-dimensional subspace ($v \leq m$).

two inequalities into the inequality of Equation 12 leads, after manipulation, to the condition for two-stage recovery,

$$pv > n \qquad (13)$$

namely, the product of the number p of photoreceptoral types and the number v of views must exceed the number n of descriptors to be recovered per surface reflectance.

Note that although these conditions on the five parameters of a color constancy problem are certainly necessary for unique recovery, they are far from being sufficient, as they do not speak to the structure of a model's matrices.

Spectral recovery is only possible if the bilinear model relates quantum-catch data to physical scenes in a unique, one-to-one fashion. This argument leads to necessary and sufficient conditions for unique recovery and is illustrated in Fig. 7.7. Suppose (on the left) that two illuminants with descriptor vectors $\mathbf{a}_1$ and $\mathbf{a}_2$ shine sequentially on the three surfaces with descriptor vectors $\mathbf{r}_1$, $\mathbf{r}_2$, and $\mathbf{r}_3$ to provide quantum-catch data vectors $\mathbf{d}_1$, $\mathbf{d}_2$, and $\mathbf{d}_3$, indexed according to surface. Suppose further (on the right) that two illuminants $\mathbf{a}_1'$ and $\mathbf{a}_2'$ provide two views of the surfaces $\mathbf{r}_1'$, $\mathbf{r}_2'$, and $\mathbf{r}_3'$ to produce the quantum-catch data $\mathbf{d}_1'$, $\mathbf{d}_2'$, and $\mathbf{d}_3'$. If the two sets of quantum catch data are identical, it had better be the case that the lights and surfaces on the left are identical to the lights and surfaces on the right—up to an unknown scale factor—because otherwise unique recovery of spectral data is impossible. Thus for the example in Fig. 7.7, $\mathbf{a}_w = \sigma \mathbf{a}_w'$, for $w = 1, 2$, and $\mathbf{r}_t = (1/\sigma)\mathbf{r}_t'$, for $t = 1, 2, 3$, for some positive scalar σ, if recovery is to be unique.

The equality of quantum-catch data in two such scenes can be expressed generally, using Equation 11, as the system of equations

$$\sum_{i=1}^{m} \sum_{j=1}^{n} r_{ij}'(\mathbf{B}_j)_{ki} a_{wi}' = \sum_{i=1}^{m} \sum_{j=1}^{n} r_{ij}(\mathbf{B}_j)_{ki} a_{wi} \qquad (14)$$

which holds for $k = 1, \ldots, p$, $t = 1, \ldots, n$, and $w = 1, \ldots, v$.

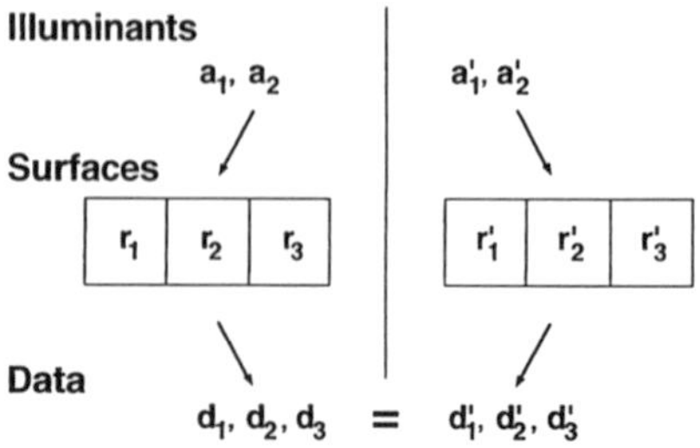

Illuminants

$\mathbf{a}_1, \mathbf{a}_2$ \qquad $\mathbf{a}_1', \mathbf{a}_2'$

Surfaces

| $\mathbf{r}_1$ | $\mathbf{r}_2$ | $\mathbf{r}_3$ | | $\mathbf{r}_1'$ | $\mathbf{r}_2'$ | $\mathbf{r}_3'$ |

Data

$\mathbf{d}_1, \mathbf{d}_2, \mathbf{d}_3$ = $\mathbf{d}_1', \mathbf{d}_2', \mathbf{d}_3'$

FIG. 7.7. Identical quantum-catch data from two different physical situations must imply that the two situations are identical, up to a single unknown scale factor, if recovery is to be unique. See text for details. From D'Zmura and Iverson (1993a). Reprinted by permission.

One can analyze this system case by case, that is, for each choice of problem (p m n v s), and we later describe analytical results of this sort. The system also leads to a model check algorithm that works quite generally to determine whether a particular bilinear model, for a color constancy problem with parameters p, m, n, v, and s, provides unique recovery (D'Zmura & Iverson, 1993a). The model check algorithm is a numerical test of a bilinear model that has been specified using its bilinear model matrix entries. The model check algorithm uses the matrix entries to construct a linear homogeneous system of E equations in U unknowns. The number E of equations and the number U of unknowns are given in terms of binomial coefficients that involve the parameters of the color constancy problem:

$$E = \binom{np - m}{m - v + 1}\binom{m}{m - v + 1} \tag{15}$$

and

$$U = \binom{n^2 + m - v - 1}{m - v + 1} \tag{16}$$

If the $E \times U$ system is of full rank, then the bilinear model provides unique recovery of spectral descriptors, up to a single unknown scaling factor. In using this algorithm, we determine the entries of the $E \times U$ model check matrix, subject this matrix to a singular value decomposition, and then examine the resulting spectrum of eigenvalues. A sharp drop in the sequence of ordered eigenvalues indicates the presence of a nontrivial kernel. Such a model fails the model check. A spectrum without a sharp drop indicates that the model check matrix is of full rank, so that the bilinear model provides unique recovery.

RESULTS FOR TWO-STAGE LINEAR RECOVERY

We used analytic methods and the model check algorithm to test the function of a wide variety of bilinear models for dichromatic, trichromatic, and tetrachromatic color constancy problems (D'Zmura & Iverson, 1993a, 1993b). Figure 7.8 shows results for two-stage linear recovery by dichromatic visual systems ($p = 2$). The layout of this figure is described in the accompanying caption. In brief, there are only two dichromatic problems in which the number of quantum-catch data compare favorably to the number of descriptors to be recovered, using the two-stage algorithm. Each requires at least two views. The first is the problem (p m n v s) = (2 2 2 2 2); the

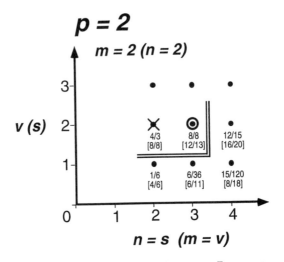

FIG. 7.8. Results for dichromatic visual systems. For two-stage linear recovery, these involve a two-dimensional model of illumination ($p = m = 2$). The horizontal axis marks the dimension n of the reflectance model, which is taken equal to the number s of surfaces, whereas the vertical axis marks the number v of views. The solid lines divide cases that satisfy the necessary condition $svp \geq sn + vm - 1$ (inequality of Equation 12). The number of quantum catch data $Q = svp$ and the number $D = sn + vm$ of spectral descriptors to be recovered are indicated for each problem by the bracketed pair $[Q/D]$ beneath the appropriate point. Points that lie beneath and to the right of the solid lines, where $Q < D - 1$, fail to satisfy the inequality of Equation 12 and so represent problems for which unique recovery is impossible. The lines also divide cases that satisfy the necessary condition for the test provided by the model check algorithm to be performed, namely, that $E \geq U$ (Equations 15 and 16). The pair E/U is shown directly beneath each point. In problems where $m \leq v$, such checks provide necessary and sufficient tests of whether particular bilinear models with the problem's parameters provide perfectly functioning recovery algorithms. By transposition—entailments (d) and (l) of Table 7.2—the result for each problem (p m n v s) also represents the result for the transposed problem (p n m s v), and the transposed parameters are indicated in parentheses at the top of the diagram and along its axes. See text for further discussion. From D'Zmura and Iverson (1993b). Reprinted by permission.

corresponding point on the diagram is marked by an X. Bilinear models for this problem always fail. The second is the problem (2 2 3 2 3), whose corresponding point is marked by a circle, and we have found many bilinear models that work perfectly to recover spectral descriptors in this case. The results show that a dichromatic visual system can use two or more views of three or more surfaces to recover two descriptors per illuminant and three descriptors per surface reflectance.

The failure of spectral recovery for the problem (2 2 2 2 2) can be shown analytically, as described later. The failure is also indicated by the failure of all of the bilinear models that we tested to pass the model check algorithm. Figure 7.9 shows the spectrum of a model check matrix for a particular bilinear model with this problem's parameters, and the precipitous drop between the second and third eigenvalues shows that the model check matrix has a kernel of rank one and thus fails the check. Also pictured is a sample spectrum for the problem (2 2 3 2 3), and the absence of a sharp drop shows that the bilinear model passes the check.

Results for trichromatic visual systems are shown in Fig. 7.10. Figures 7.10A and 7.10B show results for problems that involve a three-dimensional and a two-dimensional model of illumination, respectively ($m = 3$, $m = 2$). In Fig. 7.10A, circles surround each point along the row for three views ($v = 3$, vertical axis), and these indicate that trichromatic visual systems can use three or more views to recover up to eight descriptors ($n = s = 8$, horizontal axis) per surface reflectance function. We used the model check algorithm to check successfully many bilinear models for each of these problems. Several symbols surround points on the row for two views ($v = 2$), and these indicate successful recovery—with some caveats—of up to five descriptors per surface reflectance from two views. We have been able to prove unique recovery only up through three descriptors; the squares around the points for four and five descriptors indicate successful simulations of recovery only. Finally, the point with the triangle on the bottom row, for a single view, indicates successful recovery—with caveats discussed later—in the case (3 3 2 1 2) studied by Maloney and Wandell (1986). In all other problems (below and to the right of the solid line segments), the number of quantum-catch data is too low relative to the number of descriptors to be recovered for unique spectral recovery to be possible. Figure 7.10B indicates that, in all cases where there are sufficiently many quan-

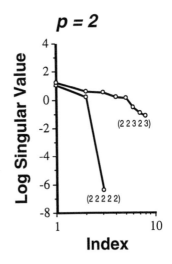

FIG. 7.9. Exemplary spectra for dichromatic problems. Plotted on a log axis are the ordered singular values of the model check matrices for exemplary bilinear models that combine the Smith and Pokorny (1975) protanope, the CIE daylight basis for illumination (Judd, MacAdam, & Wyszecki, 1964; Wyszecki & Stiles, 1982), and the Fourier basis for reflectance (D'Zmura & Lennie, 1986). See text for discussion. From D'Zmura and Iverson (1993b). Reprinted by permission.

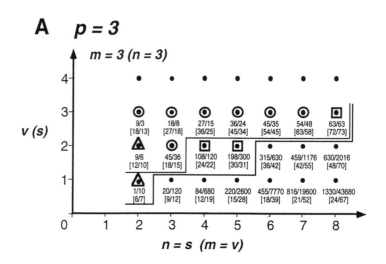

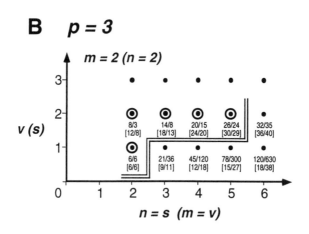

FIG. 7.10. Results for trichromatic visual systems. (A) The case of square bilinear model matrices ($p = m = 3$); (B) the case of rectangular bilinear model matrices ($p = 3$, $m = 2$). The triangles mark problems that are shown by analysis to provide perfectly functioning recovery algorithms. The squares mark problems that are shown by successful simulation of recovery to provide, at worst, imperfect recovery. As in Fig. 7.8, the circles mark problems that are shown by the model check algorithm to support unique recovery. See the caption to Fig. 7.8 and the text for further details. From D'Zmura and Iverson (1993b). Reprinted by permission.

tum-catch data, spectral recovery is possible in both one and two view cases. Complete results for two-stage linear recovery through tetrachromatic systems ($p = 4$) are detailed in our earlier work (D'Zmura & Iverson, 1993a, 1993b).

ANALYSIS OF EIGENSTRUCTURE

The system of Equation 14 expresses the identity of quantum-catch data from two physical situations. If unique recovery is to be possible, then the system must imply that the two situations are identical up to a single unknown factor scale. The gamma matrices

$$\Gamma_{ij} = \mathbf{B}_i^{-1}\mathbf{B}_j \quad \text{for } i,j = 1, \ldots, n \tag{17}$$

arise naturally in manipulating this system. These matrices are labeled with two indices that correspond to dimensions of the surface reflectance model. The right eigenvectors of these matrices lie in the vector space of illuminant descriptors (see Equation 11).

Analysis of gamma matrix eigenstructure provides several results concerning uniqueness (D'Zmura & Iverson, 1993a, 1993b; Iverson & D'Zmura, 1994). The most easily obtained result is that all bilinear models for the color constancy problem ($p\ m\ n\ v\ s$) = (2 2 2 2 2) fail totally to recover descriptors uniquely. For problems that involve a two-dimensional model of reflectance, there is only one independent, nontrivial gamma matrix of matrix size 2×2 (note that $\Gamma_{11} = \Gamma_{22} = \mathbf{I}$ and that $\Gamma_{12} = \Gamma_{21}^{-1}$). The system of Equation 14 leads to an equation in that gamma matrix that shows, by the Cayley–Hamilton theorem (a matrix satisfies its own characteristic equation), that there are an infinite number of different physical situations—not related by a scaling factor—that give rise to the same quantum-catch data.

Analysis of the Maloney and Wandell (1986) problem with parameters ($p\ m\ n\ v\ s$) = (3 3 2 1 2), marked by a triangle in Fig. 7.10A, provides caveats on recovery algorithms with these parameters. There is one independent gamma matrix of size 3×3 for this problem. We find that any vector of illuminant descriptors that lies in a plane spanned by two of the eigenvectors of the gamma matrix will cause recovery to fail. Figure 7.11 illustrates the situation. Figure 7.11A shows three eigenvectors ε_1, ε_2, and ε_3 that, for example's sake, are aligned with the three axes that correspond to individual components of illuminant vectors $\mathbf{a} = [a_1\ a_2\ a_3]^{\mathrm{T}}$. Any illuminant that lies in one of the pictured planes will cause recovery to fail.

Note, however, that not all vectors of illuminant descriptors correspond to physically realizable illuminants. Referring to the top of Fig. 7.4, it is clear that linear combination of basis functions for illumination can pro-

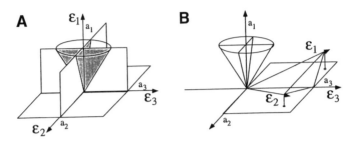

FIG. 7.11. Possible failure of bilinear models with parameters (3 3 2 1 2)
or (3 3 2 2 2). Models with the eigenstructure depicted in panel A fail for
some lights, while those with the eigenstructure depicted in panel B fail
only on physically unrealizable lights. (See text for further discussion.) From
D'Zmura and Iverson (1993b). Reprinted by permission.

duce illuminant functions of wavelength that take on negative values, and
these cannot be realized physically. In Fig. 7.11A, we use the cone to
indicate the set of illuminant vectors that corresponds to physically realizable lights.[3]

Areas of the planes of failure that lie within the cone of physical
realizability are shaded gray in Fig. 7.11A, and it is these physically realizable
illuminants that cause recovery to fail. Yet the planes of failure need not pass
through the cone. As shown in Fig. 7.11B, the three eigenvectors of the
gamma matrix may be positioned in a way that no physically realizable
illuminant causes failure. Numerical examination of physically motivated
bilinear models reveals instances of both situations (D'Zmura & Iverson,
1993b).

Similar reasoning provides caveats for the problem $(p\ m\ n\ v\ s) = (3\ 3$
$2\ 2\ 2)$, which is also marked by a triangle in Fig. 7.10A. Recovery fails if
both illuminants happen to lie within a single plane spanned by a pair of
eigenvectors of the gamma matrix. This progression is broken with the
problem (3 3 2 3 2). It is impossible for three linearly independent vectors
of illuminants to lie in a plane spanned by a pair of eigenvectors, and the
model check algorithm shows that perfect recovery is possible for this
problem.

Further analytic results were developed by Iverson and D'Zmura (1994).
These apply to the problems $(p\ m\ n\ v\ s) = (3\ 3\ 3\ 2\ 3)$ and $(3\ 3\ 3\ 3\ 3)$,
each of which involves a three-dimensional model for reflectance $(n = 3)$.
The bilinear model matrices $(\mathbf{B}_j)_{ki}$ are reorganized to produce modified

---

[3]To understand why we have chosen the cone to represent this set diagrammatically,
consider the three-dimensional Fourier series model of illumination {1, sin, cos}, and the
limits on modulation of descriptors a_2 and a_3 relative to the value of a_1 that are required to
maintain nonnegativity (Brill & Benzschawel, 1985).

bilinear model matrices $(\boldsymbol{\beta}_k)_{ji}$ with identical but reordered entries. The modified gamma matrices differ accordingly:

$$\mathbf{G}_{kk'} = \boldsymbol{\beta}_k \boldsymbol{\beta}_{k'}^{-1} \quad \text{for } k,k' = 1, \ldots, p \tag{18}$$

For a trichromatic visual system there are two independent modified gamma matrices, each of which has matrix size $m \times n$, or 3×3 in the cases of interest.

The intuitive criterion for perfect recovery is that the two modified gamma matrices cannot share an eigenvector. For the problem (3 3 3 3 3), this intuition can be sharpened to provide a first theorem:

Theorem 1. If a nonsingular bilinear model with parameters (3 3 3 3 3) is regular and indecomposable, then it allows perfect recovery. Conversely, a regular, decomposable model is a total failure. (Iverson & D'Zmura, 1994)

By a regular model we mean one in which at least one of the modified gamma matrices has distinct eigenvalues. This condition is met by all physically motivated models that we have examined. By indecomposable, we mean that the two modified gamma matrices cannot be brought simultaneously by a similarity transformation to the form

$$\begin{pmatrix} x & 0 & 0 \\ 0 & x & x \\ 0 & x & x \end{pmatrix}$$

The converse states that a (regular) decomposable model is a total failure: Unique recovery is possible under no circumstances.

The problem $(p\ m\ n\ v\ s) = (3\ 3\ 3\ 2\ 3)$ provides a second theorem (Iverson & D'Zmura, 1994):

Theorem 2. If a nonsingular, regular trichromatic model with parameters (3 3 3 2 3) is irreducible, then it allows perfect recovery. Conversely, a regular, reducible model is, at best, a partial success.

By an irreducible model, we mean one in which the two modified gamma matrices cannot both be brought simultaneously by a similarity transformation into one of the two following forms:

$$\begin{pmatrix} x & x & 0 \\ x & x & 0 \\ x & x & x \end{pmatrix} \quad \text{or} \quad \begin{pmatrix} x & 0 & 0 \\ x & x & x \\ x & x & x \end{pmatrix}$$

A model that is (at best) a partial success, is one in which there are (possibly improper) subspaces of illuminant vectors that cause recovery to fail.

ENTAILMENTS AND ROOTS

Logical entailments between color constancy problems with different parameters are listed in Table 7.2 (D'Zmura & Iverson, 1993a, 1993b). The top set of entailments (Positive) have the form: If unique recovery is possible for the problem with parameters $(p\ m\ n\ v\ s)$, possibly with further conditions on the parameters, then unique recovery is possible for the problem with parameters on the right. For instance, the topmost entailment (a) states that if perfect recovery is possible for a problem with parameters $(p\ m\ n\ v\ s)$, then it is also possible for the problem involving one further class of photoreceptors. This implication is intuitively clear: Adding a further source of information by installing another class of photoreceptors can only help, so that if color constancy is possible with a p-chromatic system it must be possible for a $(p + 1)$-chromatic system. As an example of an entailment with a condition on the parameters, consider entailment (h). This states that if the number s of surfaces exceeds the dimension n of the model for reflectance and unique recovery is possible by a model with parameters $(p\ m\ n\ v\ s)$, then unique recovery is also possible by a model that is presented one fewer surface. The reason is that surfaces in excess of the dimension of the model for reflectance are superfluous: When using an n-dimensional model of reflectance, one can present at most n independent surfaces.

The bottom set of entailments (Negative) in Table 7.2 are the logical negations of the ones listed above them. For instance, the first negative

TABLE 7.2
Entailments

Positive		
	$(p\ m\ n\ v\ s) \Rightarrow (p + 1\ m\ n\ v\ s)$	(a)
	$(p\ m\ n\ v\ s) \Rightarrow (p\ m\ n\ v + 1\ s)$	(b)
	$(p\ m\ n\ v\ s) \Rightarrow (p\ m\ n\ v\ s + 1)$	(c)
	$(p\ m\ n\ v\ s) \Rightarrow (p\ n\ m\ s\ v)$	(d)
$(m > v)$ &	$(p\ m\ n\ v\ s) \Rightarrow (p\ m - 1\ n\ v\ s)$	(e)
$(v > m)$ &	$(p\ m\ n\ v\ s) \Rightarrow (p\ m\ n\ v - 1\ s)$	(f)
$(n > s)$ &	$(p\ m\ n\ v\ s) \Rightarrow (p\ m\ n - 1\ v\ s)$	(g)
$(s > n)$ &	$(p\ m\ n\ v\ s) \Rightarrow (p\ m\ n\ v\ s - 1)$	(h)
Negative		
	$\sim (p\ m\ n\ v\ s) \Rightarrow \sim(p - 1\ m\ n\ v\ s)$	(i)
	$\sim (p\ m\ n\ v\ s) \Rightarrow \sim(p\ m\ n\ v - 1\ s)$	(j)
	$\sim (p\ m\ n\ v\ s) \Rightarrow \sim(p\ m\ n\ v\ s - 1)$	(k)
	$\sim (p\ m\ n\ v\ s) \Rightarrow \sim(p\ n\ m\ s\ v)$	(l)
$(m \geq v)$ &	$\sim (p\ m\ n\ v\ s) \Rightarrow \sim(p\ m + 1\ n\ v\ s)$	(m)
$(v \geq m)$ &	$\sim (p\ m\ n\ v\ s) \Rightarrow \sim(p\ m\ n\ v + 1\ s)$	(n)
$(n \geq s)$ &	$\sim (p\ m\ n\ v\ s) \Rightarrow \sim(p\ m\ n + 1\ v\ s)$	(o)
$(s \geq n)$ &	$\sim (p\ m\ n\ v\ s) \Rightarrow \sim(p\ m\ n\ v\ s + 1)$	(p)

entailment (i) states that if unique recovery is not possible by a p-chromatic system with parameters $(p \ m \ n \ v \ s)$, then it is not possible for a $(p - 1)$-chromatic system with those parameters: The latter system is presented less information.

The entailments naturally lead one to identify root color constancy problems that are not entailed by any other problem. Proving the existence of unique recovery for such a root problem would validate in one fell swoop an entire tree of entailed problems. One root is the problem with parameters $(p \ m \ n \ v \ s) = (3 \ 3 \ 3 \ 2 \ 2)$ examined by Tsukada and Ohta (1990). These authors first conceived of recovering three descriptors per surface reflectance by using information from multiple views. For their problem, the number Q of quantum-catch data is $svp = 12$, and the number D of descriptors to be recovered is $sn + vm = 12$, so that the data-descriptor comparison is favorable, if barely. There is no problem with a favorable comparison of data and descriptors that entails (3 3 3 2 2), so (3 3 3 2 2) is a root. Note, however, that its parameters do not meet the condition $s \geq n$ for two-stage linear recovery. Tsukada and Ohta met with limited success with a nonlinear recovery scheme, and our own examination of this problem shows that there are pathological subspaces in the space of input data that cause nonuniqueness. This root does not provide unique recovery and a tree of entailments. Other root problems remain to be analyzed.

GENERAL LINEAR RECOVERY

Although the root problem $(p \ m \ n \ v \ s) = (3 \ 3 \ 3 \ 2 \ 2)$ does not provide unique recovery, it shows that there are interesting color constancy problems that lie outside the scope of two-stage linear recovery. Recall that two-stage linear recovery depends on the invertibility of the reflectance descriptor matrix and the bilinear model matrices. These invertibilities pose restrictions $s \geq n$ and $p \geq m$, respectively, on the parameters of color constancy problems.

We developed a general linear recovery algorithm that avoids the inversion of bilinear model matrices (D'Zmura & Iverson, 1994). Referring to Equation 11, the algorithm works by:

1. Applying the inverse of the $s \times n$ matrix of reflectance descriptors formed by r_{ij} on the left to separate reflectance from illuminant descriptors.
2. Subtracting the products of bilinear model matrices and illuminant descriptors from both sides to provide a single, linear homogeneous system.

3. Using a singular value decomposition to solve for the illuminant and (inverted) reflectance descriptors.

The first step is like that of the two-stage algorithm and leads to a single restriction $s \geq n$.

This algorithm can be applied to all problems that are amenable to two-stage linear recovery. Yet the scope is more general; general linear recovery also works in situations in which both the dimensions of the illumination and reflectance models may exceed the number of photoreceptoral types. This generality provides, for a p-chromatic system, an infinity of color constancy problems to which the general linear recovery algorithm may be applied.

Figure 7.12 shows some results concerning unique recovery by dichromatic visual systems ($p = 2$) for cases in which both the dimensions of the illumination and reflectance models exceed the number of photoreceptoral types. Figure 7.12A shows results with a three-dimensional model of illumination; there are exactly three problems for which the number of quantum-catch data compare favorably to the number of descriptors to be recovered. A model check algorithm, modified to treat the cases in which both $p < m$ and $p < n$ (D'Zmura & Iverson, 1994), shows that unique recovery is possible for the problems (2 3 2 3 2) and (2 3 4 3 4), marked by circles. Model checks fail for the problem (2 3 3 3 3), marked by an X, and analysis shows that unique recovery is never possible in this situation. Figure 7.12B shows similar results for a triple of problems that involve four-dimensional models of illumination. One naturally wonders whether this pattern of results, found at illumination model dimensions $m = 3$ and $m = 4$, continues at higher dimensions $m \geq 5$.

The model check algorithm for cases in which both $p > m$ and $p > n$, which are accessible only to general linear recovery, comes in two varieties. The model check is simple and straightforward in cases where the number v of views matches the dimension m of the model for illumination. The model check matrix passes this check if it has a kernel of dimension one (this differs from the earlier model check). The model check algorithm is far more complex in cases where fewer views are provided ($v < m$) and leads to prohibitively large systems of equations in most cases of interest.

Examples of the enormous sizes of model check systems are found in Fig. 7.13, which shows results for trichromatic visual systems ($p = 3$). We have used the (simple) model check algorithm in cases where $v = m$ to show that unique recovery is possible in a variety of circumstances (top rows of circled points). Yet certain interesting problems, in cases where $v < m$, remain untouched because the model check algorithm is unwieldy. For instance, the problem (p m n v s) = (3 4 4 2 4) in Fig. 7.13A has a model check system of 6,636 equations in 4,552 unknowns. The problem

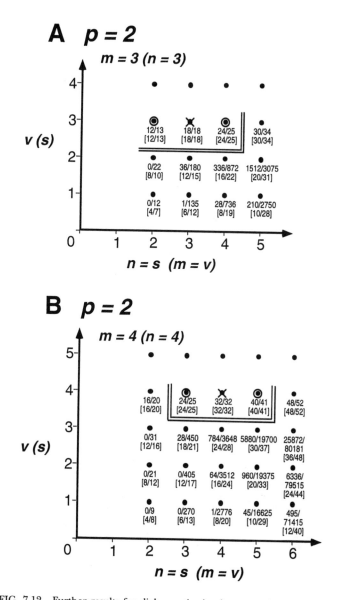

FIG. 7.12. Further results for dichromatic visual systems. (A) The case in which the illumination model has dimension three ($p = 2$, $m = 3$); (B) the case in which the model has dimension four ($p = 2$, $m = 4$). The format is like that used in Fig. 7.8. From D'Zmura and Iverson (1994). Reprinted by permission.

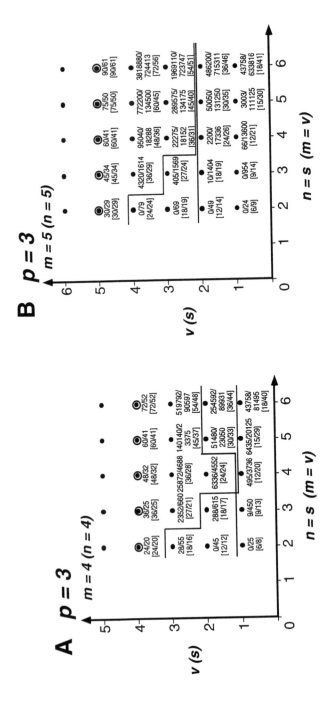

FIG. 7.13. Further results for trichromatic visual systems. (A) The case in which the illumination model has dimension four ($p = 3$, $m = 4$); (B) the case in which the model has dimension five ($p = 3$, $m = 5$). The format is like that used in Fig. 7.8. From D'Zmura and Iverson (1994). Reprinted by permission.

126

(3 4 4 3 4) at the point just above, with one more view, involves a model check matrix of size 25,872 × 4,688. Specifying these systems numerically and determining their rank is beyond our current means.

INFINITE CHAINS OF RECOVERY ALGORITHMS

We naturally wondered whether the pattern of positive results found for cases in which the number v of views equals the dimension m of the illumination model ($v = m$) is altered at higher values of m. One can readily show that there are infinite chains of color constancy problems for which the number of quantum-catch data compare favorably to the number of unknown descriptors to be recovered. One such chain is (3 c c c c), $c \geq 2$, as shown by substituting its parameters into the inequality of Equation 12.

We further investigated this chain by performing model checks using numerically specified bilinear models for $3 \leq c \leq 31$, for odd values of c. The upper bound 31 for c arises from our numerical representation of functions of visible wavelength; these are represented by 31-dimensional vectors with entries that sample the interval 400–700 nm at every 10 nm. Figure 7.14 shows the spectra of the exemplary model check matrices for problems with parameters (p m n v s) = (3 c c c c), running from (3 3 3 3 3) at the bottom to (3 31 31 31 31) at the top. Each matrix has a kernel of dimension one, so that the corresponding bilinear model passes the model check.[4]

This numerical evidence led us to prove that a trichromatic visual system can recover arbitrarily high numbers of descriptors per illuminant and reflectance, when provided adequate information. The proof constructs bilinear models for the color constancy problem (3 c c c c), for arbitrarily high c, that provide unique recovery (D'Zmura & Iverson, 1994).

By entailment (a) of Table 7.2, namely, (p m n v s) $\Rightarrow$ (p + 1 m n v s), this result for trichromatic systems implies that unique recovery is possible for all problems of the form (p c c c c), $p \geq 3$, $c \geq 2$. This shows that polychromatic visual systems can determine spectral descriptions of arbitrarily high dimension when provided adequate information. Of course, this result should not be taken to mean that an arbitrary polychromatic visual system has an infinite "bilinear capacity." Yet numerical tests of empirically motivated trichromatic visual systems (e.g., ones with the Smith and Pokorny, 1975, sensitivities) at high values of c are successful, which suggests that these systems have a very high capacity for recovering spectral descriptions.

Further numerical evidence, obtained from model checks at high values of c, suggests that there is an infinity of (infinite) chains of problems for

---

[4]Recall that this one-dimensional kernel criterion for a successful model check, in cases where $p < m$ and $p < n$, differs from the full-rank criterion in cases where $p \geq m$.

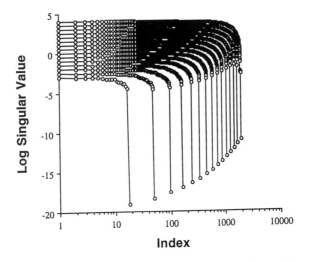

FIG. 7.14. Spectra of model check matrices for exemplary trichromatic bilinear models with parameters $(3\ c\ c\ c\ c)$, for $3 \le c \le 31$, c odd. Plotted on a log axis are the ordered singular values of the model check matrices for the exemplary models. We scaled the spectra to stagger the maximal singular values along the vertical axis at half log unit intervals. Each matrix has a kernel of dimension one and so passes the necessary and sufficient model check. See the text for further discussion. From D'Zmura and Iverson (1994). Reprinted by permission.

which unique recovery is possible, including the problems $(p\ c\ c + 1\ c\ c + 1)$, $p \ge 2$, $c \ge 3$, the problems $(p\ c\ c + 2\ c\ c + 2)$, $p \ge 3$, $c \ge 3$, the problems $(p\ c\ c + 3\ c\ c + 3)$, $p \ge 3$, $c \ge 3$, and so forth.

DISCUSSION

There are two natural types of color constancy problem to consider. The first involves two views of a set of surfaces. These arise in cases where the illumination of a set of surfaces changes. This change can occur in time, so that two different illuminants shine on a set of surfaces, one after the other. This type of change was used by Land (1983, 1986) in his demonstrations of human color constancy. Note also that a change in illumination can also occur across space, as in the common situation where outdoor surfaces, partially in shadow, are lit simultaneously by bluish skylight and by the yellowish light from the solar disk. Careful measurements of light-source spectra by Brown (1994) reveals that there is considerable spatial inhomogeneity in the illumination of natural scenes, and such spatial change can provide multiple views of surfaces.

The other natural class of problems involves a single view of a set of surfaces (Maloney & Wandell, 1986). The fact that a trichromatic visual system of the bilinear form considered here cannot recover more than two reflectance descriptors is, of course, a disappointment, for it is widely thought that our visual system is sensitive to at least three degrees of freedom in surface reflectance functions.

We discussed two recovery algorithms in this article that are applicable to the two classes of problem. Both are linear and work by singular value decomposition. We have also developed a least-squares, nonlinear recovery scheme that suffers no restriction on parameters other than the basic inequality (Equation 12) relating data and unknowns (D'Zmura & Iverson, 1993c).

Several open problems of a theoretical sort remain. For example, proof (or disproof) of unique recovery for the infinite chains, other than for (p c c c), remains to be accomplished. Second, analysis of various nonlinear problems met when $s \leq n$, like the root problem (3 3 3 2 2) of Tsukada and Ohta (1990), remains largely undone. A third and broader problem is the extension of this work with bilinear models to multilinear models; both recovery algorithms and the analysis of uniqueness must be developed.

Another open problem concerns equivalence classes of bilinear models. We define two bilinear models for some particular color constancy problem to be equivalent if (a) their models for reflectance are related by an invertible linear transformation, (b) their models for illumination are related by an invertible linear transformation, or (c) their photoreceptoral spectral sensitivities are related by an invertible linear transformation. There is no substantial difference between two bilinear models that are related in one or more of these ways. The conjecture that there is a single equivalence class of models that provide unique recovery for a given problem is known to be false. This fact raises an open problem, namely, to classify models into equivalence classes.

ACKNOWLEDGMENTS

This work was supported by National Eye Institute grant EY10014 to M. D'Zmura and by National Science Foundation grant DIR-9014278 to the Institute for Mathematical Behavioral Sciences, R. D. Luce, Director.

REFERENCES

Beck, J. (1972). *Surface color perception.* Ithaca, NY: Cornell University Press.
Bennett, B. M., Hoffman, D. D., Nicola, J. E., & Prakash, C. (1989). Structure from two orthographic views of rigid motion. *Journal of the Optical Society of America A, 6,* 1052–1069.

Brainard, D. H., & Freeman, W. T. (1994). Bayesian method for recovering surface and illuminant properties from photosensor responses. *Proceedings of the SPIE Symposium on Human Vision, Visual Processing, and Digital Display V, 2179*, 364–376.

Brainard, D. H., & Wandell, B. A. (1986). An analysis of the retinex theory of color vision. *Journal of the Optical Society of America A, 3*, 1651–1661.

Brill, M. H. (1978). A device performing illuminant-invariant assessment of chromatic relations. *Journal of Theoretical Biology, 71*, 473–478.

Brill, M. H. (1979). Further features of the illuminant-invariant trichromatic photosensor. *Journal of Theoretical Biology, 78*, 305–308.

Brill, M. H., & Benzschawel, T. (1985). Remarks on signal-processing explanations of the trichromacy of vision. *Journal of the Optical Society of America A, 2*, 1794–1796.

Brown, R. O. (1994). The world is not grey. *Investigative Ophthalmology and Visual Science, 35*(Suppl.), 2165.

Buchsbaum, G. (1980). A spatial processor model for object colour perception. *Journal of the Franklin Institute, 310*, 1–26.

Burnham, R. W., Evans, R. M., & Newhall, S. M. (1957). Prediction of color appearance with different adaptation illuminations. *Journal of the Optical Society of America, 47*, 35–42.

Cohen, J. (1964). Dependency of the spectral reflectance curves of the Munsell color chips. *Psychonomic Sciences, 1*, 369–370.

Craven, B. J., & Foster, D. H. (1992). An operational approach to colour constancy. *Vision Research, 32*, 1359–1366.

Curcio, C. A., Sloan, K. R., Jr., Packer, O., Hendrickson, A. E., & Kalina, R. E. (1987). Distribution of cones in human and monkey retina: Individual variability and radial asymmetry. *Science, 236*, 579–582.

Curcio, C. A., Sloan, K. R., Kalina, R. E., & Hendrickson, A. E. (1990). Human photoreceptor topography. *Journal of Comparative Neurology, 292*, 497–523.

Drew, M. S., & Funt, B. V. (1992). Variational approach to interreflection in color images. *Journal of the Optical Society of America A, 9*, 1255–1265.

D'Zmura, M. (1992). Color constancy: Surface color from changing illumination. *Journal of the Optical Society of America A, 9*, 490–493.

D'Zmura, M., & Iverson, G. (1993a). Color constancy. I. Basic theory of two-stage linear recovery of spectral descriptions for lights and surfaces. *Journal of the Optical Society of America A, 10*, 2148–2165.

D'Zmura, M., & Iverson, G. (1993b). Color constancy. II. Results for two-stage linear recovery of spectral descriptions for lights and surfaces. *Journal of the Optical Society of America A, 10*, 2166–2180.

D'Zmura, M., & Iverson, G. (1993c). Color constancy: Feasibility and recovery. *Investigative Ophthalmology and Visual Science, 34*(Suppl.), 748.

D'Zmura, M., & Iverson, G. (1994). Color constancy. III. General linear recovery of spectral descriptions for lights and surfaces. *Journal of the Optical Society of America A, 11*, 2389–2400.

D'Zmura, M., Iverson, G., & Singer, B. (1995). Probabilistic color constancy. In R. D. Luce, M. D'Zmura, D. D. Hoffman, G. Iverson, & K. Romney (Eds.), *Geometric representations of perceptual phenomena: Articles in honor of Tarow Indow's 70th birthday* (pp. 187–202). Mahwah, NJ: Lawrence Erlbaum Associates.

D'Zmura, M., & Lennie, P. (1986). Mechanisms of color constancy. *Journal of the Optical Society of America A, 3*, 1662–1672.

D'Zmura, M., & Mangalick, A. (1994). Detection of contrary chromatic change. *Journal of the Optical Society of America A, 11*, 543–546.

Foster, D. H., Craven, B. J., & Sale, E. R. H. (1992). Immediate colour constancy. *Ophthalmological and Physiological Optics, 12*, 157–160.

Gelb, A. (1929). Die Farbenkonstanz der Sehdinge. In A. Bethe (Ed.), *Handbuch der normalen und pathologischen Physiologie* (Vol. XII, pp. 594–678). Berlin: Springer.

Grzywacz, N. M., & Hildreth, E. C. (1987). Incremental rigidity scheme for recovering structure from motion: Position-based versus velocity-based formulations. *Journal of the Optical Society of America A, 4,* 503–518.

Helson, H. (1938). Fundamental problems in color vision. I. The principle governing changes in hue, saturation and lightness of non-selective samples in chromatic illumination. *Journal of Experimental Psychology, 23,* 439–476.

Helson, H., Judd, D. B., & Warren, M. H. (1952). Object-color changes from daylight to incandescent filament illumination. *Illumination Engineering, 47,* 221–232.

Hoffman, D. D., & Flinchbaugh, B. E. (1982). The interpretation of biological motion. *Biological Cybernetics, 42,* 195–204.

Indow, T. (1988). Multidimensional studies of Munsell color solid. *Psychological Review, 95,* 456–470.

Iverson, G., & D'Zmura, M. (1994). Criteria for color constancy in trichromatic bilinear models. *Journal of the Optical Society of America A, 11,* 1970–1975.

Judd, D. B. (1940). Hue saturation and lightness of surface colors with chromatic illumination. *Journal of the Optical Society of America, 30,* 2–32.

Judd, D. B., MacAdam, D. L., & Wyszecki, G. (1964). Spectral distribution of typical daylight as a function of correlated color temperature. *Journal of the Optical Society of America, 54,* 1031–1040.

Katz, D. (1935). *The world of color* (R. B. MacLeod & C. W. Fox, Trans.). London: Kegan Paul, Trench, Trubner.

Land, E. H. (1983). Recent advances in retinex theory and some implications for cortical computations: Color vision and the natural image. *Proceedings of the National Academy of Sciences USA, 80,* 5163–5169.

Land, E. H. (1986). Recent advances in retinex theory. *Vision Research, 26,* 7–21.

Lee, H.-C. (1986). A method for computing the scene illuminant from specular highlights. *Journal of the Optical Society of America A, 3,* 1694–1699.

Lennie, P., & D'Zmura, M. (1988). Mechanisms of color vision. *Critical Reviews in Neurobiology, 3,* 333–400.

Maloney, L. T. (1985). *Computational approaches to color constancy* (Rep. No. 1985-01). Stanford, CA: Stanford Applied Psychology Laboratory.

Maloney, L. T., & Wandell, B. A. (1986). Color constancy: A method for recovering surface spectral reflectance. *Journal of the Optical Society of America A, 3,* 29–33.

Newhall, S. M., Nickerson, D., & Judd, D. B. (1943). Final report of the OSA subcommittee on spacing of the Munsell colors. *Journal of the Optical Society of America, 33,* 385–418.

Østerberg, G. (1935). Topography of the layer of rods and cones in the human retina. *Acta Ophthalmology (Suppl. 6),* 1–103.

Parkkinen, J. P. S., Hallikainen, J., & Jaaskelainen, T. (1989). Characteristic spectra of Munsell colors. *Journal of the Optical Society of America A, 6,* 318–322.

Sällström, P. (1973). *Colour and physics: Some remarks concerning the physical aspects of human colour vision* (Rep. No. 73-09). Stockholm: University of Stockholm Institute of Physics.

Smith, V. C., & Pokorny, J. (1975). Spectral sensitivity of the foveal cone photopigments between 400 and 500 nm. *Vision Research, 15,* 161–171.

Trussell, H. J., & Vrhel, M. J. (1991). Estimation of illumination for color correction. *1991 International Conference on Acoustics, Speech & Signal Processing* (pp. 2513–2516). Piscataway, NJ: IEEE Conference Publishing.

Tsukada, M., & Ohta, Y. (1990). An approach to color constancy using multiple images. *Proceedings of the Third International Conference on Computer Vision, 3,* 385–393.

Ullman, S. (1979a). The interpretation of structure from motion. *Proceedings of the Royal Society of London B, 203,* 405–426.

Ullman, S. (1979b). *The interpretation of visual motion.* Cambridge, MA: MIT Press.

von Kries, J. (1905). Influence of adaptation on the effects produced by luminous stimuli. *Handbuch der Physiologie des Menschen, 3*, 109–282.

Williams, D. R. (1985). Aliasing in human foveal vision. *Vision Research, 25*, 195–205.

Williams, D. R. (1988). Topography of the foveal cone mosaic in the living human eye. *Vision Research, 28*, 433–454.

Wyszecki, G., & Stiles, W. S. (1982). *Color science. Concepts and methods, Quantitative data and formulas* (2nd ed.). New York: Wiley.

Knowledge Representation

Chapter 8

Computing the Intersection of Knowledge Spaces Using Only Their Bases

Cornelia E. Dowling
Cord Hockemeyer
Technische Universität Carolo-Wilhelmina,
Braunschweig, Germany

Procedures for the adaptive assessment of students' knowledge are useful tools for supplementing computer-aided instruction and everyday school classes. An adaptive assessment system requires a large pool of items from the field of knowledge under consideration. These items are, for example, descriptions of skills or examination questions. For each individual student, a small number of questions are selected from this large item pool and sequentially presented to the student. With each new question, the student's answers to all previous questions are considered, and the questions are increasingly adapted to the student's individual knowledge. Such an adaptive procedure is controlled by prerequisite relationships between the items. Prerequisite relationships are obtained by querying experts with the help of a computerized procedure (Dowling, 1993; Koppen, 1993). The following example illustrates a set of items and their prerequisite relationships.

Example 1. Dowling (1991) determined prerequisite relationships among 28 skills required for using the CAD system AutoCAD.[1] As an example we list 5 of these 28 skills:

a. Being able to use the function CIRCLE

b. Being able to use the function ARC

---

[1]AutoCAD is a trademark of AutoDesk.

    c. Being able to use the function RING

    d. Being able to use the function ELLIPSE

    e. Being able to use the function LINE

For these items, one expert determined the prerequisite relationships shown in Fig. 8.1. These prerequisite relationships are illustrated by an and–or graph that corresponds to the following set of assertions accepted by the expert.

1. If a student has mastered item *d*, then he or she will also have mastered item *a*.

2. If a student has mastered item *d*, then he or she will also have mastered item *b* or *c* (or both).

3. If a student has mastered item *b*, then he or she will also have mastered item *a*.

4. If a student has mastered item *a*, then he or she will also have mastered item *e*.

5. If a student has mastered item *e*, then he or she will also have mastered item *a*.

A *knowledge state* is a subset of the complete set of items that does not contradict these prerequisite relationships.

Example 2. Let Q be the set of items $\{a, b, c, d, e\}$ from Example 1. The set $\{b, c, e\}$, for example, is not a knowledge state because it contains b but not a, and thus contradicts the accepted assertion 3. For this example, the set of all knowledge states is the set $\mathcal{K} = \{\emptyset, \{c\}, \{a, e\}, \{a, b, e\}, \{a, c, e\}, \{a, b, c, e\}, \{a, c, d, e\}, \{a, b, d, e\}, Q\}$.

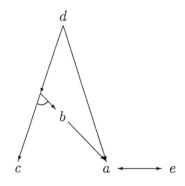

FIG. 8.1. Prerequisite relationships between the items *a, b, c, d,* and *e.*

The set of knowledge states in this example contains the empty set $\emptyset$, the set Q itself, and has the property that it is closed under union. A family $\mathcal{K}$ of subsets of the set Q with these properties is called a *knowledge space* (Doignon & Falmagne, 1985). Knowledge spaces are structures for representing prerequisite relationships. A compressed way of storing prerequisite relationships is to store just the *basis* of a knowledge space. A basis consists of those elements of the knowledge space that cannot be obtained as the union of other members of the space. The basis $\mathcal{B}$ of a knowledge space is its smallest subset of states from which the complete space can be reconstructed by its closure under union. For knowledge spaces on a finite item set such a basis always exists. The closure under union of a family $\mathcal{F}$ of sets is written as $\mathcal{F}^\cup$. A knowledge space $\mathcal{K}$ can therefore be regarded as the closure under union $\mathcal{B}^\cup$ of its basis $\mathcal{B}$.

Example 3.   The basis of the knowledge space in Example 2 is the family $\mathcal{B} = \{\{c\}, \{a, e\}, \{a, b, e\}, \{a, c, d, e\}, \{a, b, d, e\}\}$.

Knowledge spaces or their bases can be derived from the judgment of experts concerning prerequisite relationships among the items. In practice, however, we are confronted with the problem that different experts have different experiences, and therefore yield different knowledge spaces. Dowling (1994) suggested using for the adaptive assessment only those prerequisite relationships on which the different experts agree. These common prerequisite relationships are represented by the closure under union of the union $(\cup_{i=1}^n \mathcal{K}_i)^\cup$ of the knowledge spaces $\mathcal{K}_i$ from the different experts, where n is the number of experts (Dowling, 1994).

Conversely, the intersection of the knowledge spaces $\mathcal{K}_i$, $\cap_{i=1}^n \mathcal{K}_i$, represents the set of prerequisite relationships that have been accepted by at least one of the experts.

The knowledge space $(\cup_{i=1}^n \mathcal{K}_i)^\cup$ is, however, often too large for an efficient adaptive assessment, because too many prerequisite relationships are discarded. It might, therefore, be useful not only to consider the prerequisite relationships on which all experts agree, but to use the prerequisite relationships on which the majority of the experts agree. More precisely, we intend to determine the knowledge space $\mathcal{K}^M$ representing prerequisite relationships on which m out of n experts agree, for a constant number m. This knowledge space is computed as

$$\mathcal{K}^M = \cap \left\{ (\cup_{i \in I} \mathcal{K}_i)^\cup \mid I \subseteq \{1, \ldots, n\} \text{ and } |I| = m \right\} \qquad (1)$$

In practice, we are confronted with the problem that the intermediary knowledge spaces $(\cup_{i \in I} \mathcal{K}_i)^\cup$ are extremely large. As a rule, the computation of $(\cup_{i \in I} \mathcal{K}_i)^\cup$ is either costly, or it cannot be finished in feasible time; examples can be found in the final section.

In this chapter, we suggest a procedure for computing the knowledge space $\mathcal{K}^M$ that avoids the intermediary computation of the knowledge spaces $(\cup_{i \in I} \mathcal{K}_i)^{\cup}$ altogether. To compute $\mathcal{K}^M$ we use only the bases of the intermediary knowledge spaces, and not the knowledge spaces themselves.

In the next section we introduce the previous results required to understand the new intersection procedure; in the section that follows, we describe the main results of this chapter, and in the fourth section we prove the theorems from the third section.

PREVIOUS RESULTS

Doignon and Falmagne (1985) suggested a convenient structure for representing and–or graphs, which we define next.

Definition 1. Let Q be a finite set, and let $\tilde{\mathcal{F}}$ be the set of all families $\mathcal{F}$ of subsets of Q with the property that, for each $\mathcal{F} \in \tilde{\mathcal{F}}$, and all $q \in Q$, there exists a subset $X \in \mathcal{F}$ with $q \in X$. For a family $\mathcal{F} \in \tilde{\mathcal{F}}$, we call a set $X \in \mathcal{F}$ *minimal* for q if $q \in X$, and there is no $Y \in \mathcal{F}$ with $q \in Y \subset X$.

A *surmise system* σ is a mapping from Q to $\tilde{\mathcal{F}} \backslash \{\emptyset\}$ that assigns to each $q \in Q$ a family of subsets of Q, called the *clauses* for q. Let $\tilde{\sigma}$ be the set of all surmise systems on Q.

Define a mapping $s : \tilde{\mathcal{F}} \to \tilde{\sigma}$ by setting for all $q \in Q$, $C \in s(\mathcal{F})(q)$ if and only if C is minimal for q in $\mathcal{F}$, and define a mapping $k : \tilde{\sigma} \to \tilde{\mathcal{F}}$ by requiring for any $X \subseteq Q$, that $X \in k(\sigma)$ if and only if for any $q \in X$, there exists $C \in \sigma(q)$, such that $C \subseteq X$.

A surmise system $\sigma \in \tilde{\sigma}$ is called *space-like* if the following three axioms are satisfied for all $q \in Q$, and $C, C' \in \sigma(q)$.

[R] If $C \in \sigma(q)$, then $q \in C$.

[T] For all $q' \in C$, there exists a $C'' \in \sigma(q')$ such that $C'' \subseteq C$.

[I] If $C \subseteq C'$ or $C' \subseteq C$, then $C = C'$.

Doignon and Falmagne (1985) showed that the mappings s and k just defined establish a Galois connection between the families of subsets of Q and the surmise systems on Q. Theorem 1 follows from this fact.

Theorem 1 (Doignon & Falmagne, 1985). The pair of mappings (k, s) from the preceding definition induces a one-to-one correspondence between the knowledge spaces on the set Q and the space-like surmise systems on that set. For each family $\mathcal{F} \in \tilde{\mathcal{F}}$ of sets, the surmise system $s(\mathcal{F})$ is a space-like surmise system, and, for a surmise system $\sigma \in \tilde{\sigma}$, the family $k(\sigma)$ of subsets is a knowledge space. The combined correspondence $(k \circ s)$

maps a family $\mathcal{F}$ into the smallest knowledge space containing $\mathcal{F}$. Conversely, the map $(s \circ k)$ assigns to σ a space-like surmise system.

The space-like surmise system $(s \circ k)(\sigma)$ is the smallest space-like surmise system larger than or equal to σ with respect to an ordering relation that will be introduced in the fourth section.

Example 4. The following is one surmise system that represents the and–or graph from Fig. 8.1:

$$a \mapsto \sigma(a) = \{\{e\}\}$$
$$b \mapsto \sigma(b) = \{\{a\}\}$$
$$c \mapsto \sigma(c) = \{\emptyset\}$$
$$d \mapsto \sigma(d) = \{\{a, c\}, \{a, b\}\}$$
$$e \mapsto \sigma(e) = \{\{a\}\}$$

The space-like surmise system $(s \circ k)(\sigma)$ is:

$$a \mapsto \sigma(a) = \{\{a, e\}\}$$
$$b \mapsto \sigma(b) = \{\{a, b, e\}\}$$
$$c \mapsto \sigma(c) = \{\{c\}\}$$
$$d \mapsto \sigma(d) = \{\{a, c, d, e\}, \{a, b, d, e\}\}$$
$$e \mapsto \sigma(e) = \{\{a, e\}\}$$

Note that the space-like surmise system $(s \circ k)(\sigma)$ fulfills the axioms [R], [T], and [I] from Definition 1. Note also that the union $\cup_{q \in Q} \sigma(q)$ = $\{\{c\}, \{a, e\}, \{a, b, e\}, \{a, c, d, e\}, \{a, b, d, e\}\}$ is equal to the basis $\mathcal{B}$ displayed in Example 3.

From this example, we see that each clause $C \in \sigma(q)$ in a space-like surmise system is equal to a state minimal for q in the corresponding knowledge space.

MAIN RESULTS

The new procedure for computing "majority spaces" requires an algorithm for computing the basis of the intersecting space $\cap_{j=1}^{l} \mathcal{K}_j$ from the bases of the knowledge spaces $\mathcal{K}_j$, where l corresponds to their number. Such a procedure is developed in this section. It consists of two parts:

- In the first part, a surmise system τ is computed from the l bases $\mathcal{B}_j$ of the knowledge spaces $\mathcal{K}_j$, which can be assigned to the intersecting knowledge space by the map k from Definition 1.
- In the second part, we compute the space-like surmise system $(s \circ k)(\tau)$, so that the axioms [R], [T], and [I] are fulfilled.

Theorem 2 contains the results for the first part just mentioned. It shows that the knowledge space derived from the surmise system τ is indeed equal to the intersection of the knowledge spaces $\mathcal{K}_j$.

Theorem 2. For $j = 1, \ldots, l$, let σ_j be surmise systems on Q and let $\mathcal{K}_j$ be the corresponding knowledge spaces, that is, $\mathcal{K}_j = k(\sigma_j)$. If τ is the surmise system defined by setting

$$\tau(q) = \left\{ \bigcup_{j=1}^{l} C_j \mid C_j \in \sigma_j(q) \right\} \tag{2}$$

then we obtain

$$k(\tau) = \bigcap_{j=1}^{l} \mathcal{K}_j \tag{3}$$

In the following theorem we describe an algorithm that constructs, for a given surmise system τ, the space-like surmise system $(s \circ k)(\tau)$ that represents the same knowledge space as τ, because the same knowledge space $\mathcal{K}$ is assigned to both surmise systems by the mapping k from Definition 1.

Theorem 3. Let Q be a finite set, let τ be a surmise system on Q, and let $\mathcal{K} = k(\tau)$ be the knowledge space assigned to τ by the map k. The following algorithm constructs the space-like surmise system $(s \circ k)(\tau)$.

for all $q \in Q$ **do**
  for all $C \in \tau(q)$ **do**
    if $q \notin C$ **then** replace $C \in \tau(q)$ by $(C \cup \{q\})$; **fi**
  od
od
restrict $\tau(q)$ to its minimal elements;
while (for some $q \in Q$, $C \in \tau(q)$, $q' \in C$: $C' \in \tau(q') \Rightarrow C' \notin C$) **do**
  replace $C \in \tau(q)$ by the set $\{C \cup C' : C' \in \tau(q')\}$;
  restrict $\tau(q)$ to its minimal elements;
od

PROOFS OF THEOREMS 2 AND 3

The proofs of these theorems are based on results by Doignon and Falmagne (1985), which were partially introduced in the second section.

   Definition 2 (Doignon & Falmagne, 1985). Let $\tilde{\sigma}$ be the set of all surmise systems on a finite set Q. For any σ, $\sigma' \in \tilde{\sigma}$, we define a relation $\sqsubseteq$ by setting $\sigma' \sqsubseteq \sigma$ if, for all $q \in Q$ and $C \in \sigma(q)$, there exists a $C' \in \sigma'(q)$ such that $C' \subseteq C$.

   Doignon and Falmagne have pointed out that the relation $\sqsubseteq$ is a quasi order on $\tilde{\sigma}$; that is, it is reflexive and transitive (but not generally antisymmetric). This quasi order $\sqsubseteq$ induces an equivalence relation $\approx$ on $\tilde{\sigma}$. For any surmise systems $\sigma, \sigma' \in \tilde{\sigma}$, we write $\sigma \sqsubset \sigma'$ if and only if $\sigma \sqsubseteq \sigma'$ and $\sigma \neq \sigma'$.

   Theorem 4. (Doignon & Falmagne, 1985). Let $\tilde{\mathcal{F}}$ be the family of sets, $\tilde{\sigma}$ the set of all surmise systems, and (s, k) the pair of mappings defined in Definition 1. The pair (s, k) is a Galois connection between $\tilde{\mathcal{F}}$ and $\tilde{\sigma}$, and therefore the following four conditions are fulfilled for any $\sigma, \sigma' \in \tilde{\sigma}$, and for any $\mathcal{F}, \mathcal{F}' \in \tilde{\mathcal{F}}$.

1. If $\mathcal{F} \subseteq \mathcal{F}'$, then $s(\mathcal{F}) \sqsupseteq s(\mathcal{F}')$.
2. If $\sigma \sqsubseteq \sigma'$, then $k(\sigma) \supseteq k(\sigma')$.
3. $\mathcal{F} \subseteq (k \circ s)(\mathcal{F})$.
4. $\sigma \sqsubseteq (s \circ k)(\sigma)$.

   Proof of Theorem 2. We first prove $k(\tau) \subseteq \cap_{j=1}^{l} \mathcal{K}_j$ for knowledge spaces $\mathcal{K}_j = k(\tau_j)$, the surmise system τ, and the map k from Definition 1. From the definition of the relation $\sqsubseteq$, and from the definition of τ and σ_j in Theorem 2, it follows that $\sigma_j \sqsubseteq \tau$. With axiom 2 in Theorem 4 we obtain $k(\tau) \subseteq k(\sigma_j)$, for all $j = 1, \ldots, l$, and therefore the result follows.

   We now prove $\cap_{j=1}^{l} \mathcal{K}_j \subseteq k(\tau)$. Let X be an element of the intersection $\cap_{j=1}^{l} \mathcal{K}_j$; this intersection $\cap_{j=1}^{l} \mathcal{K}_j$ is not empty because at least the empty set and the set Q itself are elements of each of the knowledge spaces $\mathcal{K}_j$. Using Definition 1 of the map s, it follows that for each item $q \in X$, there exists a clause $C_j \in \sigma_j(q)$ with $C_j \subseteq X$. Therefore the union $\cup_{j=1}^{l} C_j$ is also a subset of X. Using the definition of τ in the theorem, we obtain that this set is $\cup_{j=1}^{l} C_j \in \tau(q)$. Thus, for each $q \in X$, we have a clause $\cup_{j=1}^{l} C_j \in \tau(q)$ for which $\cup_{j=1}^{l} C_j \subseteq X$. From the definition of k it follows that $X \in k(\tau)$.

   Proof of Theorem 3. The proof consists of two main parts: We have to prove that the algorithm terminates, and that the resulting surmise system satisfies the properties [R], [T], [I], and [K] given next (see also Definition 1):

[R] For all $q \in Q$, if $C \in \tau(q)$, then $q \in C$.

[T] For all $q \in Q$, $C \in \tau(q)$, and $q' \in C$, there exists a $C' \in \tau(q')$ such that $C' \subseteq C$.

[I] For all $q \in Q$, and for all C, $C' \in \tau(q)$, if $C \subseteq C'$, then $C = C'$.

[K] For all $K \in \mathcal{K}$ and $q \in K$, there exists a $C \in \tau(q)$ such that $C \subseteq K$.

The termination of this algorithm is guaranteed by the finiteness of Q, because in any pass through the **while** loop, by the choice of q, C, and q', all replacement sets $C \cup C'$ are strict supersets of C.

The surmise system τ clearly satisfies the property [R] as soon as the two nested **for** loops are terminated. It also satisfies property [K], because passes through the **for** loops cannot invalidate this property. It is easy to see that the following restriction statement does not destroy these properties [R] and [K].

The properties [R] and [K] are also invariants of the **while** loop; that is, a pass through the loop cannot invalidate them. The second statement within the **while** loop ensures that, at the end of the loop, the surmise system τ satisfies property [I].

After termination of the **while** loop the control condition in the **while** statement must be false. Because its negation is precisely property [T], all four properties are satisfied after termination of the algorithm.

APPLICATIONS

In one project, three teachers were queried on prerequisite relationships between 48 elementary reading and writing abilities (Dowling, 1991). The three experts' judgments were represented as the knowledge spaces $\mathcal{K}_1$, $\mathcal{K}_2$, and $\mathcal{K}_3$, and their majority space was computed as

$$\mathcal{K}^M = (\mathcal{K}_1 \cup \mathcal{K}_2)^\cup \cap (\mathcal{K}_1 \cup \mathcal{K}_3)^\cup \cap (\mathcal{K}_2 \cup \mathcal{K}_3)^\cup$$

Table 8.1 shows the size of the intermediary spaces $\mathcal{K}_{ij} = (\mathcal{K}_i \cup \mathcal{K}_j)^\cup$, for $1 \leq i < j \leq 3$, the size of the majority space $\mathcal{K}^M$, and the size of the bases corresponding to these knowledge spaces. This table shows the computing times for the two different procedures. The first is an algorithm that computes the majority space from the intermediary spaces $\mathcal{K}_{ij}$. The second procedure uses only the bases of these knowledge spaces, and the "intersection algorithm" given in the third section.

In a second project, six tutors experienced in training students to use the CAD system AutoCAD were queried on prerequisite relationships among 28 abilities required to use this system (Dowling, 1991). The procedure suggested in the third section was used to compute the majority

TABLE 8.1
Computation Times for Computing the Majority
Space on Reading and Writing Abilities

Procedure	$|\mathcal{K}_{1,2}|$	$|\mathcal{K}_{1,3}|$	$|\mathcal{K}_{2,3}|$	$|\mathcal{K}^M|$	Time (min:sec)
Space	22,773	13,718	14,893	63	3:38.81
Basis	264	221	236	30	0:03.12

space representing prerequisite relationships on which four out of six experts agree. The computing time required was 9.48 sec. The size of the intermediary knowledge spaces, however, varied between 621,458 and 2,640,583 knowledge states. Computing the first of the 14 intersections of the intermediary knowledge spaces would have lasted more than 20 hr on a PC 486. We therefore refrained from completing this computation with the space-based procedure.

In a third project, the intermediary knowledge spaces were so large that they could not be generated at all with the resources available (256 MB RAM). The majority space for three experts was, however, generated with the basis-based procedure in 12.87 sec. In this latter project, three teachers were queried on prerequisite relationships among items from the field of fractions (Baumunk & Dowling, 1997).

ACKNOWLEDGMENT

We thank an unknown referee for the careful review of this chapter, which helped to considerably shorten Theorem 3 and its proof.

REFERENCES

Baumunk, K., & Dowling, C. (1997). Validity of spaces for assessing knowledge about fractions. *Journal of Mathematical Psychology, 41*, 99–105.

Doignon, J.-P., & Falmagne, J.-C. (1985). Spaces for the assessment of knowledge. *International Journal of Man-Machine Studies, 23*, 175–196.

Dowling, C. (1991). *Constructing knowledge structures from the judgements of experts.* Braunschweig, Germany: Habilitationsschrift, Technische Universität Carolo-Wilhelmina.

Dowling, C. (1993). Applying the basis of a knowledge space for controlling the questioning of an expert. *Journal of Mathematical Psychology, 37*, 21–48.

Dowling, C. (1994). Integrating different knowledge spaces. In G. H. Fisher & D. Laming (Eds.), *Contributions to mathematical psychology* (pp. 149–158). New York: Springer-Verlag.

Koppen, M. (1993). Extracting human expertise for constructing knowledge spaces: An algorithm. *Journal of Mathematical Psychology, 37*, 1–20.

Chapter 9

Meshing Knowledge Structures

Jean-Claude Falmagne
University of California, Irvine

Jean-Paul Doignon
Université Libre de Bruxelles

Consider a body of information in which knowledge can be assessed by asking solely binary questions—that is, a response to a question or item is only coded as correct or false. In such a case, it makes sense to represent the knowledge state of an individual by the set of all mastered items (i.e., all those items to which the individual is capable of reliably providing correct responses).[1] The collection of all such knowledge states is called the knowledge structure. This approach to knowledge representation was conceived by Doignon and Falmagne (1985) for the design of efficient procedures for the assessment of knowledge, where "assessing knowledge" means uncovering the actual knowledge state of some individual, and "efficient" means that knowledge can be uncovered by testing only a small subset of items. These procedures are not described here (see Falmagne & Doignon, 1988a, 1988b).

To build a knowledge structure, the practitioner can rely either on experts' judgments or on an empirical investigation involving statistical testing. In the first method, the so-called QUERY procedure can be used (Kambouri, Koppen, Villano, & Falmagne, 1993; Koppen & Doignon, 1990; for a different technique, but similar in spirit, see Müller, 1989). The second method is exemplified in Villano (1991). These two methods should be regarded as complementary to each other. However, for somewhat

---

[1]In this chapter we do not consider the issues related to the errors of various kinds that can plague the data. Probabilistic theories are discussed in Falmagne (1989, 1993, 1994).

technical reasons, statistical methods can be used only for a rather small number of items, typically much smaller than the actual size of the set of items of interest. This naturally leads to the question of how to combine different knowledge structures on distinct, possibly overlapping sets. In this chapter we investigate some properties of such a combination of different knowledge structures.

Particular attention is paid to the transfer of combinatorial properties from the pieces to be aggregated, onto the resulting structure.

BACKGROUND

This section provides formal definitions of basic technical terms (for further details and extensive motivation, see, e.g., Doignon & Falmagne, 1985; Falmagne & Doignon, 1988b; or Falmagne, Koppen, Villano, Doignon, & Johannesen, 1990).

Definition 1. A *knowledge structure* $(X, \mathcal{K})$ consists of a nonempty set X of *questions* or *items*, together with a family $\mathcal{K}$ of subsets of X, called the *knowledge states*; we assume that $\mathcal{K}$ contains both X and the empty set $\emptyset$. The set X is called the *domain* of the structure. In this chapter we only consider structures with finite domains.

For any knowledge structure $(X, \mathcal{K})$, the domain X is determined by the family $\mathcal{K}$. Accordingly, we sometimes refer to $\mathcal{K}$ as the knowledge structure. The special case in which two distinct items may never belong to exactly the same knowledge states is worthy of attention and deserves a name.

Definition 2. A structure $(X, \mathcal{K})$ is *discriminative* when for any two distinct questions x and y from X, there exists at least one knowledge state that contains either x or y, but not both.

Some discriminative knowledge structures can be represented by partially ordered sets. They are characterized as being closed under intersection and union (i.e., both the union and the intersection of any subfamily of knowledge states are again a knowledge state). This result is due to Birkhoff (1937). The generalization mentioned next appears in Doignon and Falmagne (1985). It involves the concept of surmise systems, which includes partial orders as a special case. An essential feature of these systems is that a set of prerequisites for a given item may not be unique. In other words, from the mastery of one item, the assessor can only infer the mastery of at least one set of prerequisite items among several possible ones. By comparison, to any item in a partially ordered set is associated exactly one subset of prerequisite items. The knowledge structures derived from surmise systems are closed under union (but not necessarily under intersection), and the converse also holds. These structures play a fundamental role in our theory.

Definition 3. A *knowledge space* is a knowledge structure $(X, \mathcal{K})$ such that the family $\mathcal{K}$ is stable under union.

In the assessment procedure proposed by Falmagne and Doignon (1988b), a computer routine sequentially searches a knowledge structure $\mathcal{K}$ in order to isolate, by gradual elimination, the knowledge state in $\mathcal{K}$ which is most representative of the individual under examination. In the ultimate phase of the search, the procedure moves from one element of $\mathcal{K}$ to another by adding or removing one question. To ensure success in all cases, the repetition of these small steps must enable the procedure to visit the entire structure if necessary. This success is guaranteed by an axiom on the knowledge structure $\mathcal{K}$ that we formulate in Definition 4.

We denote by $|K|$ the cardinality of set K, and by $K \Delta L$ the symmetric difference of sets K and L, that is $K \Delta L = (K \backslash L) \cup (L \backslash K)$.

Definition 4. A knowledge structure $(X, \mathcal{K})$ is *well graded* when for any two distinct states K, L there exists some sequence of states

$$K = K_0, K_1, \ldots, K_m = L \tag{1}$$

such that for $j = 0, 1, \ldots, m - 1$,

$$|K_j \Delta K_{j+1}| = 1$$

and

$$|K \Delta L| > |K_{j+1} \Delta L| \tag{2}$$

The structure $(X, \mathcal{K})$ is *1-connected* if the same condition holds, but without requiring Inequality 2.

Even for a space, 1-connectedness is not equivalent to wellgradedness. Here is an easier formulation of wellgradedness for knowledge spaces.

Proposition 5. A knowledge space $(X, \mathcal{K})$ is well graded if and only if each of its states K belongs to some sequence of states

$$\emptyset = K_0, K_1, \ldots, K_m = X$$

such that for $i = 0, 1, \ldots, m - 1$:

$$K_i \subset K_{i+1} \quad \text{and} \quad |K_{i+1} \backslash K_i| = 1$$

A sequence as in Proposition 5 is called a *gradation*. For later use, we give a new characterization of wellgradedness of knowledge structures.

Proposition 6. A knowledge structure $(X, \mathcal{K})$ is well graded if and only if for any two of its states K and K' there exist a positive integer m and some sequence of states

$$K = K_0, K_1, \ldots, K_m = K'$$

such that for $i = 0, 1, \ldots, m - 1$:

$$|K_i \, \Delta \, K_{i+1}| = 1 \quad \text{and} \quad K_i \cap K' \subseteq K_{i+1} \subseteq K_i \cup K'$$

Proof. 1. Necessity. By definition of wellgradedness of the knowledge structure $(X, \mathcal{K})$, given any two states K, K', there exists some sequence of states

$$K = K_0, K_1, \ldots, K_m = K'$$

such that for $i = 0, 1, \ldots, m - 1$:

$$|K_j \, \Delta \, K_{j+1}| = 1 \quad \text{and} \quad |K \, \Delta \, K'| > |K_{j+1} \, \Delta \, K'|$$

By applying this same definition to the states K_1 and K', and then to the states K_2 (just produced) and K', and so on, there will finally result a similar sequence for which the following also holds:

$$|K_j \, \Delta \, K'| = m - j$$

Using this fact together with $|K_j \, \Delta \, K_{j+1}| = 1$, it can be inductively proven for the new sequence that $K_i \cap K' \subseteq K_{i+1} \subseteq K_i \cup K'$.

2. Sufficiency. Notice that the sequence mentioned in the proposition automatically satisfies $|K_i \, \Delta \, K'| > |K_{i+1} \, \Delta \, K'|$ for all $i = 0, 1, \ldots, m - 1$, and can thus be used to check wellgradedness.

TRACES AND MESHABILITY

Before combining two knowledge structures into a larger one, we indicate how to "induce" a structure on a subset of questions.

Definition 7. Let $\mathcal{K}$ be a knowledge structure on a set X, and let $Y \subseteq X$. A set $F \subseteq Y$ will be called the *trace* on Y of a state $K \in \mathcal{K}$ if $F = K \cap Y$. More generally, the collection

$$\mathcal{K}|_Y = \{F \subseteq Y | F = K \cap Y \text{ for some } K \in \mathcal{K}\}$$

is called the *trace* of $\mathcal{K}$ on Y.

Clearly, the trace of a knowledge structure is a knowledge structure. The same "hereditary" property also holds for various related concepts, such as knowledge space, 1-connected knowledge structure, and well-graded knowledge structure. For the last concept, an easy proof of this hereditary property is built on the characterization of wellgradedness given in Proposition 6.

Proposition 8. Let $(X, \mathcal{K})$ be a knowledge structure and $Y \subseteq X$. If $\mathcal{K}$ is well graded, so is the trace $\mathcal{K}|_Y$.

Proof. Take any two distinct states F and F' in $\mathcal{K}|_Y$. They are the traces of some states K and K' from $\mathcal{K}$. It suffices to notice that the traces of a sequence from K to K' as in Proposition 6 will give (after removal of repetitions) the required sequence from F to F' in the trace.

Definition 9. The knowledge structure $(X, \mathcal{K})$ is called a *mesh* of the knowledge structures $(Y, \mathcal{F})$ and $(Z, \mathcal{G})$ if

(1) $X = Y \cup Z$.

(2) $\mathcal{F}$ and $\mathcal{G}$ are the traces of $\mathcal{K}$ on X and Y, respectively.

Two knowledge structures may have more than one mesh (see Example 15), or no mesh at all (see the next example). Two knowledge structures having a (unique) mesh are called *(uniquely) meshable.*

Example 10. Suppose that $(\{1, 2, 3, 4\}, \mathcal{K})$ is a mesh of the two knowledge structures

$$\mathcal{F} = \{\emptyset, \{1\}, \{1, 2\}, \{1, 2, 3\}\} \qquad \mathcal{G} = \{\emptyset, \{3\}, \{2, 3\}, \{2, 3, 4\}\}$$

Then $\mathcal{K}$ has a state K such that $K \cap \{2, 3, 4\} = \{3\} \in \mathcal{G}$. Thus, either $K = \{1, 3\}$ or $K = \{3\}$, and because in either case $K \subseteq \{1, 2, 3\}$, either $\{1, 3\}$ or $\{3\}$ must be a state of $\mathcal{F}$, which is a contradiction. Thus, $\mathcal{F}$ and $\mathcal{G}$ have no mesh.

Example 11. Sometimes, however, two knowledge structures are uniquely meshable. Take for instance the knowledge structures

$$\mathcal{F} = \{\emptyset, \{1\}, \{1, 2\}\} \qquad \mathcal{G} = \{\emptyset, \{2\}, \{2, 3\}\}$$

It is easy to see that they have the unique mesh

$$\mathcal{K} = \{\emptyset, \{1\}, \{1, 2\}, \{1, 2, 3\}\}$$

(All the nonempty states of $\mathcal{K}$ have to contain 1, and if a state contains j, it has to contain any $i < j$). Notice that in this example the mesh $\mathcal{K}$ does not include the union of the two component knowledge structures $\mathcal{F}$ and $\mathcal{G}$, because $\{2, 3\} \notin \mathcal{K}$.

We first investigate conditions under which a mesh exists.

Definition 12. A knowledge structure $(Y, \mathcal{F})$ is said to be *compatible* with a knowledge structure $(Z, \mathcal{G})$ if, for any $F \in \mathcal{F}$, the intersection $F \cap Z$ is the trace on Y of some state of $\mathcal{G}$. When two knowledge structures are compatible with each other, we simply say that they are *compatible*.

In other words, $(Y, \mathcal{F})$ and $(Z, \mathcal{G})$ are compatible if and only if $\mathcal{F}|_{Y \cap Z} = \mathcal{G}|_{Y \cap Z}$.

Proposition 13. Two knowledge structures are meshable if and only if they are compatible.

Proof. Let $(Y \cup Z, \mathcal{K})$ be a mesh of the two knowledge structures $(Y, \mathcal{F})$ and $(Z, \mathcal{G})$, and suppose that $F \in \mathcal{F}$. By the definition of a mesh, there is $K \in \mathcal{K}$ such that $K \cap Y = F$. Thus, $K \cap Z \in \mathcal{G}$ and $(K \cap Z) \cap Y = F \cap Z$. Hence $(Y, \mathcal{F})$ is compatible with $(Z, \mathcal{G})$. The other case follows by symmetry.

Conversely, suppose that $(Y, \mathcal{F})$ and $(Z, \mathcal{G})$ are compatible. Define

$$\mathcal{K} = \{K \subseteq Y \cup Z | K \cap Y \in \mathcal{F}, K \cap Z \in \mathcal{G}\}$$

Clearly, $(Y \cup Z, \mathcal{K})$ is a knowledge structure. For any $F \in \mathcal{F}$, we have $F \cap Z = G \cap Y$ for some $G \in \mathcal{G}$. Setting $K = F \cup G$, we obtain $K \cap Y = F$ and $K \cap Z = G$, yielding $K \in \mathcal{K}$. Thus $\mathcal{F} \subseteq \mathcal{K}|_Y$. By the definition of $\mathcal{K}$, the reverse inclusion is trivial, so $\mathcal{F} = \mathcal{K}|_Y$. Again, the other case results from symmetry. We conclude that $\mathcal{K}$ is a mesh of $\mathcal{F}$ and $\mathcal{G}$.

The construction of the mesh used in this proof is of interest and deserves a new notation.

THE MESHING OPERATOR

Definition 14. Let $(Y, \mathcal{F})$ and $(Z, \mathcal{G})$ be two compatible knowledge structures. We define a knowledge structure $(Y \cup Z, \mathcal{F} \divideontimes \mathcal{G})$ by the equation

$$\mathcal{F} \divideontimes \mathcal{G} = \{K \subseteq Y \cup Z | K \cap Y \in \mathcal{F}, K \cap Z \in \mathcal{G}\}$$

Obviously, $\mathcal{F} \star \mathcal{G} = \mathcal{G} \star \mathcal{F}$. Note that if $F \in \mathcal{F}$ and $F \subseteq Y \backslash Z$, then $F \in \mathcal{F} \star \mathcal{G}$. A corresponding property holds of course for the knowledge structure $\mathcal{G}$. The mesh defined by this equation is called the *maximal mesh* of $\mathcal{F}$ and $\mathcal{G}$, and $\star$ is referred to as the *maximal meshing operator*. Indeed, we have $\mathcal{K} \subseteq \mathcal{F} \star \mathcal{G}$ for any mesh $\mathcal{K}$ of $\mathcal{F}$ and $\mathcal{G}$.

An equivalent definition of the maximal mesh is as follows:

$$\mathcal{F} \star \mathcal{G} = \{F \cup G \,|\, F \in \mathcal{F},\, G \in \mathcal{G} \text{ and } F \cap Z = G \cap Y\}$$

In some cases, the maximal meshing operator provides only one of several possible meshes.

Example 15. The two knowledge structures

$$\mathcal{L} = \{\emptyset, \{1\}, \{2\}, \{1, 2\}\} \qquad \mathcal{L}' = \{\emptyset, \{2\}, \{2, 3\}\}$$

are compatible, and we have

$$\mathcal{L} \star \mathcal{L}' = \{\emptyset, \{1\}, \{2\}, \{1, 2\}, \{2, 3\}, \{1, 2, 3\}\}$$

But

$$\mathcal{K} = \{\emptyset, \{1\}, \{2\}, \{1, 2\}, \{1, 2, 3\}\}$$

is also a mesh.

Proposition 16. If $\mathcal{F}$ and $\mathcal{G}$ are compatible knowledge structures, then $\mathcal{F} \star \mathcal{G}$ is a space (respectively discriminative space) if and only if both $\mathcal{F}$ and $\mathcal{G}$ are spaces (respectively discriminative spaces).

We omit the straightforward proof, and consider wellgradedness. From Proposition 8, we obtain immediately Proposition 17.

Proposition 17. If $\mathcal{F}$ and $\mathcal{G}$ are compatible knowledge structures, and $\mathcal{F} \star \mathcal{G}$ is well graded, then $\mathcal{F}$ and $\mathcal{G}$ are both well graded.

Proof. This is a direct result of Proposition 8.

The maximal mesh of well-graded knowledge structures, or even spaces, is not necessarily well graded, however. The counterexample that follows establishes this fact.

Example 18. Consider the two well-graded knowledge spaces

$$\mathcal{F} = \{\emptyset, \{1\}, \{2\}, \{1, 2\}, \{1, 3\}, \{2, 3\}, \{1, 2, 3\}\}$$

and

$$\mathcal{G} = \{\emptyset, \{3\}, \{4\}, \{2, 3\}, \{2, 4\}, \{3, 4\}, \{2, 3, 4\}\}$$

which are compatible. Their maximal mesh (necessarily a space)

$$\mathcal{F} \maltese \mathcal{G} = \{\emptyset, \{1\}, \{4\}, \{1, 3\}, \{1, 4\}, \{2, 3\}, \{2, 4\}, \{1, 2, 3\}, \{2, 3, 4\},$$
$$\{1, 2, 4\}, \{1, 3, 4\}, \{1, 2, 3, 4\}\}$$

is not well graded because it contains $\{2,3\}$ but neither $\{2\}$ nor $\{3\}$.

A sufficient condition for wellgradedness is contained in the next definition.

Definition 19. A mesh $\mathcal{K}$ of two knowledge structures $\mathcal{F}$ and $\mathcal{G}$ is called *inclusive* if $F \cup G \in \mathcal{K}$ for any $F \in \mathcal{F}$ and $G \in \mathcal{G}$.

Proposition 20. Consider the following three conditions on two knowledge structures $(Y, \mathcal{F})$ and $(Z, \mathcal{G})$:

1. $\mathcal{F}$ and $\mathcal{G}$ admit some inclusive mesh.
2. $\mathcal{F} \maltese \mathcal{G}$ is inclusive.
3. $(\forall F \in \mathcal{F}, F \cap Z \in \mathcal{G})$ and $(\forall G \in \mathcal{G}, G \cap Y \in \mathcal{F})$.

Then $(1) \Leftrightarrow (2) \Rightarrow (3)$. Moreover, if $\mathcal{F}$ and $\mathcal{G}$ are spaces, then $(2) \Leftrightarrow (3)$.

Proof. Left to the reader.

Example 21. To show that condition 3 in Proposition 20 does not imply condition 2, consider $\mathbb{R}^3$ and the family $\mathcal{F}$ (respectively $\mathcal{G}$) of all the convex subsets of the plane $x = 0$ (respectively $y = 0$). An example with finite domains is also easily constructed. Still in $\mathbb{R}^3$, take $Y = \{(0, 1, 0), (0, 0, 0), (0, 0, 1), (0, 0, 2)\}$ and $Z = \{(1, 0, 0), (0, 0, 0), (0, 0, 1), (0, 0, 2)\}$, with the states being the traces of the convex sets on Y and Z respectively. The maximal mesh $\mathcal{F} \maltese \mathcal{G}$ is not inclusive because $\{(0, 1, 0), (0, 0, 2)\} \in \mathcal{F}$ and $\{(0, 0, 0)\} \in \mathcal{G}$ but the union of these two states is not in $\mathcal{F} \maltese \mathcal{G}$.

Proposition 22. If the maximal mesh $\mathcal{F} \maltese \mathcal{G}$ of two knowledge structures $\mathcal{F}$ and $\mathcal{G}$ is inclusive, then $\mathcal{F} \cup \mathcal{G} \subseteq \mathcal{F} \maltese \mathcal{G}$. When $\mathcal{F}$ and $\mathcal{G}$ are spaces, $\mathcal{F} \cup \mathcal{G} \subseteq \mathcal{F} \maltese \mathcal{G}$ implies that $\mathcal{F} \maltese \mathcal{G}$ is inclusive.

We omit the proof. Example 21 shows that we cannot replace "spaces" by "structures" in Proposition 22.

Proposition 23. If the maximal mesh of two well-graded knowledge structures is inclusive, then it is necessarily well graded.

Example 11 shows that the inclusiveness condition is not necessary for two well-graded knowledge structures (or even spaces) to have a maximal mesh that is also well graded.

Proof. Let $(Y, \mathcal{F})$ and $(Z, \mathcal{G})$ be two well-graded knowledge structures, and suppose that $\mathcal{F} \ast \mathcal{G}$ is inclusive. To prove that $\mathcal{F} \ast \mathcal{G}$ is well graded, we use Proposition 6. Take any $K, K' \in \mathcal{F} \ast \mathcal{G}$. As $K \cap Y$ and $K' \cap Y$ are two states of the well-graded knowledge structure $\mathcal{F}$, there exist a positive integer m and some sequence of states in $\mathcal{F}$

$$K \cap Y = Y_0, Y_1, \ldots, Y_m = K' \cap Y$$

such that for $i = 0, 1, \ldots, m - 1$:

$$|Y_i \Delta Y_{i+1}| = 1 \quad \text{and} \quad Y_i \cap K' \subseteq Y_{i+1} \subseteq Y_i \cup K'$$

Similarly, there exist a positive integer n and some sequence of states in $\mathcal{G}$

$$K \cap Z = Z_0, Z_1, \ldots, Z_n = K' \cap Z$$

such that for $j = 0, 1, \ldots, n - 1$:

$$|Z_j \Delta Z_{j+1}| = 1 \quad \text{and} \quad Z_j \cap K' \subseteq Z_{j+1} \subseteq Z_j \cup K'$$

We then form the sequence

$$X_0 = Y_0 \cup (K \cap Z), X_1 = Y_1 \cup (K \cap Z), \ldots,$$
$$X_m = Y_m \cup (K \cap Z) = (K' \cap Y) \cup Z_0, X_{m+1} = (K' \cap Y) \cup Z_1,$$
$$X_{m+2} = (K' \cap Y) \cup Z_2, \ldots, X_{m+n} = (K' \cap Y) \cup Z_n$$

Clearly, $X_0 = K$ and $X_{m+n} = K'$. Because $\mathcal{F} \ast \mathcal{G}$ is inclusive, we also have $X_k \in \mathcal{F} \ast \mathcal{G}$, for $k = 0, 1, \ldots, m + n$. On the other hand, for $i = 0, 1, \ldots, m - 1$:

$$\begin{aligned}
X_i \cap K' &= (Y_i \cup (K \cap Z)) \cap K' \\
&\subseteq (Y_i \cap K') \cup (K \cap Z) \\
&\subseteq Y_{i+1} \cup (K \cap Z) \\
&= X_{i+1}
\end{aligned}$$

and

$$\begin{aligned}
X_{i+1} &= Y_{i+1} \cup (K \cap Z) \\
&\subseteq Y_i \cup K' \cup (K \cap Z) \\
&= X_i \cup K'
\end{aligned}$$

In a similar way, one proves for $j = m, m + 1, \ldots, m + n - 1$:

$$X_j \cap K' \subseteq X_{j+1} \subseteq X_j \cup K'$$

Finally, it is easy to show that $|X_i \, \Delta \, X_{i+1}|$ equals 0 or 1. Thus, after deletion of repeated subsets in the sequence X_i, we obtain a sequence as in Proposition 6.

We next indicate a simple result, which is very useful from the point of view of practical applications.

Proposition 24. Suppose that $(\mathcal{F}, \mathcal{G})$, $(\mathcal{F} \bigstar \mathcal{G}, \mathcal{K})$, $(\mathcal{G}, \mathcal{K})$ and $(\mathcal{F}, \mathcal{G} \bigstar \mathcal{K})$ are four pairs of compatible knowledge structures. Then, necessarily,

$$(\mathcal{F} \bigstar \mathcal{G}) \bigstar \mathcal{K} = \mathcal{F} \bigstar (\mathcal{G} \bigstar \mathcal{K})$$

Proof. Let X, Y, and Z be the domains of $\mathcal{K}$, $\mathcal{F}$, and $\mathcal{G}$, respectively. The result follows immediately from the following string of equivalences:

$K \in (\mathcal{F} \bigstar \mathcal{G}) \bigstar \mathcal{K}$
   $\Leftrightarrow K \cap (Y \cup Z) \in \mathcal{F} \bigstar \mathcal{G}$ and $K \cap X \in \mathcal{K}$
   $\Leftrightarrow K \cap (Y \cup Z) \cap Y \in \mathcal{F}$ and $K \cap (Y \cup Z) \cap Z \in \mathcal{G}$ and $K \cap X \in \mathcal{K}$
   $\Leftrightarrow K \cap (Y \in \mathcal{F}$ and $K \cap Z \in \mathcal{G}$ and $K \cap X \in \mathcal{K}$

ACKNOWLEDGMENT

This work was supported by NSF grant SPR-9307423 to J.-C. Falmagne at University of California, Irvine (School of Social Sciences).

REFERENCES

Birkhoff, G. (1937). Rings of sets. *Duke Mathematical Journal, 3*, 443–454.
Doignon, J.-P., & Falmagne, J.-C. (1985). Spaces for the assessment of knowledge. *International Journal of Man-Machine Studies, 23*, 175–196.
Falmagne, J.-C. (1989). A latent trait theory via stochastic learning theory for a knowledge space. *Psychometrika, 53*, 283–303.
Falmagne, J.-C. (1993). Stochastic learning paths in a knowledge structure. *Journal of Mathematical Psychology, 37*, 489–512.
Falmagne, J.-C. (1994). Finite Markov learning models for knowledge structures. In G. Fischer & D. Laming (Eds.), *Contributions to mathematical psychology, psychometrics, and methodology* (pp. 75–89). New York: Springer-Verlag.
Falmagne, J.-C., & Doignon, J.-P. (1988a). A class of stochastic procedures for the assessment of knowledge. *British Journal of Mathematical and Statistical Psychology, 41*, 1–23.

Falmagne, J.-C., & Doignon, J.-P. (1988b). A Markovian procedure for assessing the state of a system. *Journal of Mathematical Psychology, 32*, 232–258.

Falmagne, J.-C., Koppen, M., Villano, M., Doignon, J.-P., & Johannesen, L. (1990). Introduction to knowledge spaces: How to build, test, and search them. *Psychological Review, 97*, 201–224.

Kambouri, M., Koppen, M., Villano, M., & Falmagne, J.-C. (1993). Knowledge assessment: Tapping human expertise by the QUERY routine. *International Journal of Human-Computer Studies, 40*, 119–151.

Koppen, M., & Doignon, J.-P. (1990). How to build a knowledge space by querying an expert. *Journal of Mathematical Psychology, 34*, 311–331.

Müller, C. E. (1989). A procedure for facilitating an expert's judgments on a set of rules. In E. Roskam (Ed.), *Mathematical psychology in progress* (pp. 157–170). Berlin: Springer-Verlag.

Villano, M. (1991). *Computerized knowledge assessment: Building the knowledge structure and calibrating the assessment routine* (Doctoral dissertation, New York University, New York). *Dissertation Abstracts International, 552*, 12B.

Chapter 10

An Application of a Stochastic Knowledge Structure Model

Kamakshi Lakshminarayan
Honeywell Technology Center

Frank Gilson
University of California, Irvine

Much of psychometric testing theory has followed in the tradition of Lord and Novick (1974). The initial motivation for the research reported in this chapter was to analyze the performance of a stochastic knowledge structure model (Falmagne, 1989) on data previously analyzed with the normal ogive model. The normal ogive model is unidimensional along one latent ability, and is intended to model performance on items that measure complex, continuously distributed abilities. The knowledge structure model, like other latent class models, assumes discrete dichotomously measured abilities and is better suited to model items testing curricular mastery, rather than general ability (see Molenaar, 1981). The analysis presented in this chapter demonstrates that even though the above is generally true, the performance of the stochastic knowledge structure model is comparable to that of the normal ogive model even on items measuring continuously distributed abilities.

The data analyzed in our source paper (Bock & Lieberman, 1970)[1], and again in this chapter consist of the response patterns of 1,000 subjects to five items from each of two sections of a Law School Admissions Test (LSAT). The five items from section 6 are Figure Classification items and the five items from section 7 are items on Debate.[2] Each item is in the five-alternative multiple-choice format. The response patterns are of the

---

[1]See also Haertel (1990).

[2]We tried, without success, to determine the actual test questions involved.

form $\mathbf{R} = (R_1, R_2, R_3, R_4, R_5)$, where $R_i = 0$ represents an incorrect answer to item i and $R_i = 1$ represents a correct answer to that item.

In Bock and Lieberman (1970) the normal ogive model was used to analyze the data. There are two kinds of parameters for that model: those characterizing test item difficulty and discriminating power, and those characterizing the latent ability of each subject. These parameters were estimated in Bock and Lieberman by maximum likelihood. A test of goodness of fit was also provided.

The stochastic knowledge structure model (SKSM) used in this chapter is of a different spirit than the great body of standard psychometric testing theory. The essential concept of knowledge structure theory is that of a knowledge state. The *knowledge state* of a subject is a particular subset of questions or problems, from some domain, that the subject is capable of solving correctly. This is usually taken to be with respect to a certain field of possible questions such as high school mathematics or, in our case, the LSAT.

Rather than representing the ability of a subject to answer a test item by a latent ability parameter as the normal ogive model does, the SKSM used here assumes that a subject is in a particular knowledge state that either does or does not contain the test item in question.

Another important concept is that knowledge states can be thought of as being placed along learning paths, called *gradations* in the knowledge structure. Thus, a student might originally be incapable of solving any questions in the domain (in the empty knowledge state) and then, by learning the answer to one question at a time, moves along a gradation until he or she is capable of answering all questions in the domain. The speed of this learning process is represented in the SKSM by a learning rate parameter. For an introduction to knowledge structure theory, readers are referred to Falmagne, Koppen, Villano, Doignon, and Johannesen (1990). The analysis reported in this chapter involves the subjects being tested only once, and so the SKSM is not being used to model learning as such. An application where students are tested more than once is described in Lakshminarayan (1996).

The normal ogive model integrates with respect to ability to determine the unconditional probabilities of patterns of responses, weighting via the distribution of ability in the population. The SKSM essentially integrates with respect to all knowledge states within the knowledge structure, weighting via the distribution of knowledge states in the population.

The normal ogive model fits the section 6 data well. It also fits the section 7 data, but not as well. Bock and Lieberman (1970) considered the items of section 6 of the LSAT data to be more interrelated (homogeneous) than the items of section 7. Bock and Lieberman attributed the observation that the model fits worse on section 7 data to the unidimensional nature of the normal ogive model.

Briefly, the analysis of the SKSM will proceed by randomly dividing each section's set of 1,000 response patterns into two sets of 500. One such set is used to develop the knowledge structure and parameters. The other set for each section is used to test the fit of that structure. Both sets of 500 response patterns are also analyzed with the normal ogive model in order to compare the fit of the two models.

NORMAL OGIVE MODEL

Bock and Lieberman (1970) described the normal ogive model in depth. We repeat the essential material here.

In the normal ogive model the response of a subject to a particular item, say item j, is determined by the subject's "response strength" toward that item. The *response strength* is represented by a random variable, Y_j. If $Y_j = y_j > \gamma_j$, where γ_j is the response threshold (item difficulty) for item j, then a correct response to item j is observed. Otherwise, an incorrect response is observed.

The response strength Y_j has the following distribution:

$$Y_j = \alpha_j \Theta + \sqrt{(1 - \alpha_j^2)} \, E$$

where Θ is the *latent ability* of a subject, a random variable that is distributed normally with mean 0 and variance 1 in the population of subjects. The error term E is also a random variable that is distributed normally with mean 0 and variance 1 in the population of responses. The error term E is independent of Θ. The term α_j is the reliability index, or item–trait correlation for item j with $-1 \leq \alpha_j \leq 1$.

A correct response is represented by $R_j = 1$. An incorrect response is represented by $R_j = 0$.

The conditional (on latent ability) probability of a correct response is thus:

$$\Pr(R_j = 1 \mid \Theta = \theta) = \Pr(Y_j > \gamma_j \mid \Theta = \theta)$$

$$= \Pr(\alpha_j \theta + \sqrt{(1 - \alpha_j^2)} \, E > \gamma_j)$$

$$= \Pr\left(E > \frac{\gamma_j - \alpha_j \theta}{\sqrt{(1 - \alpha_j^2)}} \right)$$

$$= 1 - \Phi\left(\frac{\gamma_j - \alpha_j \theta}{\sqrt{(1 - \alpha_j^2)}} \right)$$

where Φ is the distribution function of the standard normal.

The conditional probability of an incorrect response is thus:

$$\Pr(R_j = 0 \mid \Theta = \theta) = \Phi\left(\frac{\gamma_j - \alpha_j\theta}{\sqrt{(1 - \alpha_j^2)}}\right)$$

Conditioned on the latent ability, Θ, the responses to items $1, \ldots, n$ ($n = 5$ in the case of the LSAT data) are independent:

$$\Pr(\mathbf{R} = R_1, R_2, \ldots, R_n \mid \Theta = \theta) = \prod_{i=1}^{n} \Pr(R_i \mid \Theta = \theta)$$

The unconditional probability of a pattern of responses is then:

$$\Pr(\mathbf{R} = R_1, R_2, \ldots, R_n) = \int_{-\infty}^{\infty} \prod_{i=1}^{n} \Pr(R_i \mid \Theta = \theta)\phi(\theta) \, d\theta \tag{1}$$

where $\phi(\theta)$ is the standard normal density at the point θ.

In the actual analysis of the LSAT data in Bock and Lieberman (1970), frequencies of response patterns to the items in each section were used to compute the maximum likelihood estimates of the item parameters for each section. For the section 6 analysis the chi-square statistic reported was 21.28 with 21 degrees of freedom, which is a good fit ($.40 < p < .50$). For the section 7 analysis the chi-square statistic reported was 31.59 with 21 degrees of freedom, which is not as good a fit ($.05 < p < .10$). Bock and Lieberman (1970) stated that this may be the case because the items of section 7 (debate) are more heterogeneous in content than the items of section 6 (figure classification), thus violating the unidimensional character of the normal ogive model.

STOCHASTIC KNOWLEDGE STRUCTURE MODEL

The SKSM used in our analysis of the LSAT response pattern data is that developed in Falmagne (1989). We now summarize the essential character of this model.

Recall again the concept of a knowledge state. The knowledge state of a subject is the particular subset of a set of questions or problems (from a domain) that the subject is capable of solving. A *knowledge structure* with respect to that set of questions would be some collection of knowledge states including the empty state $\emptyset$ and the set of all questions Q.

An example of a knowledge structure is shown in Fig. 10.1. This structure has nine states and three gradations.

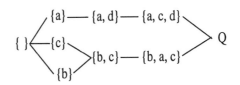

FIG. 10.1. Sample knowledge
structure.

In general, a hypothesized knowledge structure must be verified experimentally. Because a data set of response patterns from a population will be noisy, any deterministic model would be inappropriate. A probabilistic model, specifying the probabilities of all 2^m response patterns, with $m = |Q|$ being the number of items, is necessary.

With $\mathbf{R}$ representing a pattern of responses, the key equation is

$$\Pr(\mathbf{R}) = \sum_{K \in K} \Pr(\mathbf{R}|K) \Pr(K)$$

Thus, the assumptions of the model must specify, for each pattern $\mathbf{R}$ and each state K, the probability $\Pr(K)$ of state K in the population and the conditional probability $\Pr(\mathbf{R}|K)$ of observing $\mathbf{R}$ given K.

Let us first consider the conditional probabilities $\Pr(\mathbf{R}|K)$ of the patterns of responses, given the states. Any pattern $\mathbf{R}$ of responses is a 0–1 vector with m components, where 0 and 1 represent incorrect and correct responses, respectively. In specifying the conditional probabilities $\Pr(\mathbf{R}|K)$, conditional to the knowledge state of the subject, responses to problems are independent. Any correlation between responses is completely explained by the states.

Two parameters are associated with each item. We write β_i for the probability of a "careless error" to problem i $(0 \leq \beta_i < 1)$. So, even if item i belongs to a subject's state, there is the probability β_i that the subject will make an error when responding. We write η_i for the probability of a "guess" $(0 \leq \eta_i < 1)$. When an item i is not in a subject's state, there is the probability η_i that the subject will guess the correct answer.

Using the response pattern $\mathbf{R} = (1, 0, 1, 1, 0)$ and the state $K = \{1, 2, 3\}$ we can see that

$$\mathrm{PR}(\mathbf{R} = (1, 0, 1, 1, 0)|K = \{1, 2, 3\}) = (1 - \beta_1)\beta_2(1 - \beta_3)\eta_4(1 - \eta_5)$$

The product on the right illustrates the conditional independence of the responses. One can see that because the state of the subject contains item 1 and the subject responded correctly to that item, the correct term in the right hand product to represent this is $1 - \beta_1$, the probability of not making a careless error. The other terms are similar.

Now we must consider the specification of the probabilities $\Pr(K)$ of all the states. There are potentially many ways this may be done. Several alternatives are discussed later. In order to properly develop the SKSM used in this chapter, some additional concepts are necessary.

First, a gradation must be properly specified. A gradation consists of a chain of states, beginning with the empty state $\emptyset$ and finishing with the full set of questions Q, and where each state is the previous state incremented by one item. In the knowledge structures considered here, all states are contained on at least one gradation.

In general, we specify the existence of a probability distribution on the set of all gradations, which defines, along with additional features and parameters, a probability distribution on $\mathcal{K}$, the collection of states.

The subject begins the learning process in state $\emptyset$, knowing nothing. A gradation, π, is then chosen with some probability, p_π. So,

$$\sum_{\pi \in G} p_\pi = 1$$

where G denotes the set of all gradations. The notation, $\pi(1)$, $\pi(2)$, ... represents the successive problems mastered along gradation π.

It is reasonable to assume that the time required to master the first problem depends on the difficulty of that problem and the learning rate of the subject. This can be formalized as a random variable, denoted by $\mathbf{T}_{\pi(1),\lambda}$, where λ is a positive number representing the subject's learning rate and $\pi(1)$ denotes the first problem encountered along gradation π.

Having mastered that first problem, the subject is in state $\{\pi(1)\}$ and begins to master problem $\pi(2)$, the next one along the gradation. That will take random time $\mathbf{T}_{\pi(2),\lambda}$. More generally, the time required to master the first j items along gradation π is given by the sum

$$\mathbf{T}_{\pi,j,\lambda} = \mathbf{T}_{\pi(1),\lambda} + \mathbf{T}_{\pi(2),\lambda} + \cdots + \mathbf{T}_{\pi(j),\lambda}$$

Note that the learning rate is assumed to be constant for a given subject.

The probability that, at time τ, a subject with learning rate λ has mastered all the items in the state $\{\pi(1), \ldots, \pi(j)\}$ (and possibly other items), is

$$\Pr(\mathbf{T}_{\pi(1),\lambda} + \cdots + \mathbf{T}_{\pi(j),\lambda} \leq \tau) = \Pr(\mathbf{T}_{\pi,j,\lambda} \leq \tau)$$

For $0 < j < m = |Q|$, the probability that at time τ this subject is exactly in state $\{\pi(1), \ldots, \pi(j)\}$ is

$$\Pr[\{\mathbf{T}_{\pi,j,\lambda} \leq \tau\} - \{\mathbf{T}_{\pi,j+1,\lambda} \leq \tau\}] = \Pr(\mathbf{T}_{\pi,j,\lambda} \leq \tau) - \Pr(\mathbf{T}_{\pi,j+1,\lambda} \leq \tau)$$

where the minus sign in the left member denotes the set difference between the event that the subject has mastered at least the first j items in gradation

π and the event that this subject has mastered at least $j + 1$ items in that gradation.

More work is still necessary to obtain a specific prediction for the probability $\Pr(K)$. This probability will vary with the time τ of the test. We also assume that the learning rate has a distribution in the population. This is formalized by a continuous random variable $\mathbf{L}$, with density function f. The quantity λ is a particular value of $\mathbf{L}$, and $f(\lambda)$ is the density of that value. A random variable $\mathbf{G}$ is introduced for the gradation. So, $\mathbf{G} = \pi$ denotes the event that a subject is following gradation π. It is assumed that the random variables $\mathbf{L}$ and $\mathbf{G}$ are independent, that is,

$$\Pr(\mathbf{L} \leq \lambda, \mathbf{G} = \pi) = \Pr(\mathbf{L} \leq \lambda) \Pr(\mathbf{G} = \pi) = \Pr(\mathbf{L} \leq \lambda)p_\pi$$

Finally, K_τ represents the state of the subject at time τ, and $G(K)$ the set of all gradations passing through state K. Notice, we have for $j < 0$,

$$K = \{\pi(1), \ldots, \pi(j)\} \text{ if and only if } |K| = j \text{ and } \pi \in G(K)$$

We must now compute the probability that a randomly chosen subject is in state K at time τ. This can be obtained as an average over all learning rates λ and all gradations π. Formally,

$$\Pr(K_\tau = K) = \int_0^\infty \sum_{\pi \in G(K)} \Pr(K_\tau = K \mid \mathbf{L} = \lambda, \mathbf{G} = \pi)p_\pi f(\lambda) \, d\lambda$$

We assume the density f vanishes with $\lambda < 0$.

When $|K| = j$, with $0 < j < m$,

$$\Pr(K_\tau = K) = \int_0^\infty \sum_{\pi \in G(K)} \Pr(K_\tau = \{\pi(1), ..., \pi(j)\} \mid \mathbf{L} = \lambda, \mathbf{G} = \pi)p_\pi f(\lambda) \, d\lambda$$

$$= \int_0^\infty \sum_{\pi \in G(K)} \Pr[(\sum_{i=1}^{j} \mathbf{T}_{\pi(i),\lambda} \leq \tau) - (\sum_{i=1}^{j+1} \mathbf{T}_{\pi(i),\lambda} \leq \tau)]p_\pi f(\lambda) \, d\lambda \qquad (2)$$

$$= \int_0^\infty \sum_{\pi \in G(K)} [\Pr(\mathbf{T}_{\pi(j),\lambda} \leq \tau) - \Pr(\mathbf{T}_{\pi,j+1,\lambda} \leq \tau)]p_\pi f(\lambda) \, d\lambda$$

Similar results hold with $K = \emptyset$ and $K = Q$.

We now specify the parametric assumptions of the model. It is assumed that the random variables $\mathbf{T}_{i,\lambda}$ are independent and have the general gamma distribution, with parameters γ_i and λ, where γ_i is a measure of the difficulty of item i. It follows that the total time $\mathbf{T}_{\pi,j,\lambda}$ required for a subject with learning rate λ to master the first j problems in gradation π is also distributed as a general gamma, with parameters

$$\gamma_{\pi,j} = \sum_{i=1}^{j} \gamma_{\pi(i)}$$

and λ. The distribution of the random variable **L**, specifying the distribution of learning rate in the population, is distributed as a general gamma, with parameters $\alpha > 0$ and $\xi > 0$. Specifically,

$$f(\lambda) = \begin{cases} \dfrac{\xi^\alpha}{\Gamma(\alpha)}\lambda^{\alpha-1}e^{-\xi\lambda} & \text{for } \lambda > 0 \\ 0 & \text{for } \lambda \le 0 \end{cases} \tag{3}$$

Equation 2 can be evaluated by routine integration, leading to simple and explicit expressions in terms of the *incomplete beta function ratio*, which has this form:

$$I_\theta(x, y) = \frac{1}{B(x, y)} \int_0^\theta t^{x-1}(1 - t)^{y-1}\, dt$$

Here $p, q > 0$, $0 < \theta < 1$, and B is the *beta function*. More details about the beta function and the incomplete beta function can be found in Johnson and Kotz (1970). The next three results are derived in section 6 of Falmagne (1989). For $|K| = j$, $0 < j < m$,

$$\Pr(K_\tau = K) = \sum_{\pi \in Q(K)} [I_{\frac{\tau}{\tau+\xi}}(\gamma_{\pi,j}, \alpha) - I_{\frac{\tau}{\tau+\xi}}(\gamma_{\pi,j+1}, \alpha)]\, p_\pi$$

and

$$\Pr(K_\tau = Q) = [I_{\frac{\tau}{\tau+\xi}}(\gamma_Q, \alpha)$$

where γ_Q is defined by $\gamma_Q = \gamma_{\pi,m}$, for any gradation π. The final case is obtained from

$$\Pr(K_\tau = \emptyset) = 1 - \sum_{\pi \in G} [I_{\frac{\tau}{\tau+\xi}}(\gamma_{\pi,1}, \alpha) - I_{\frac{\tau}{\tau+\xi}}(\gamma_{\pi,2}, \alpha)]\, p_\pi$$

This represents the probability that a randomly chosen student has not learned the first item along the path he might be on. This model differs from standard psychometric models in several ways. The "latent structure" is not an ability or abilities but a knowledge structure designed to capture the cognitive organization of the material being analyzed. Knowledge states in a knowledge structure are potentially "reachable" in more than one way (via more than one gradation).

Parameters of the SKSM

The following are the parameters of the SKSM that are either directly or indirectly estimated from the data.

1. The parameters specifying the probability distribution over the set of all learning paths in the structure. If there are x paths, then there are $x - 1$ parameters that specify path probabilities.

2. The parameters α and ξ, which govern distribution of student learning rates in the population. The mean of the learning rate distribution given in Equation 3 is α/ξ, and the variance is α/ξ^2. High estimated values of ξ would indicate that the population mean for the learning rate is low, and that the variance is also low. High estimated values of α would indicate that the mean and variance of the learning rate distribution were high.

3. The "time" of testing of the students, τ. The parameter α is estimated directly from the data. The parameters ξ and τ will be estimated together as $\theta = \tau/(\tau + \xi)$.

4. The item difficulties. An item i is associated with a difficulty γ_i. The function that governs the student's transition from knowledge state to knowledge state along the path he or she is following is a function of the student's learning rate and these item difficulties. These parameters, along with the time of testing, interact with each other when the model is used to fit data. For instance, if a large percentage of students tested yield response patterns with few items correct, and very few students get more than one or two items correct, the model will try to fit the data by

a. Assigning high item difficulties.
b. Assigning low learning rates to students, and hence the estimated value for the mean of the learning rate will be small.
c. Estimating θ to be low.

In fact, the model will use a weighted combination of these three, depending on other features of the data. One of the assumptions of the SKSM is that all students tested are assumed to have spent the same time τ, learning the content of the material being tested. This may not be a reasonable assumption. In the application discussed in this chapter, the model is applied to data from aptitude testing and performs well in spite of this strong assumption. This is probably due to the fact that students are not "taught" aptitude and it is not a general part of any curriculum. If the material being tested were strongly tied to curriculum this assumption would cause problems in data fitting. This is supported empirically in Lakshminarayan (1996), where students are tested on concepts relating to high-school geometry.

5. The relationship between the student's knowledge state and his or her response. An item i will be associated with a careless error probability β_i and a guessing probability η_i.

PROCEDURE OF SKSM ANALYSIS

The procedure followed for the two sections (6 and 7) was the same. The respective sets of 1,000 response patterns were randomly split into two groups of 500 response patterns. One group of 500 was used to develop the knowledge structure and parameters in question, and the resultant knowledge structure and parameter values were tested on the remaining group of 500 response patterns for that section. In other words, one half of the data (dirty data) was used to develop and test various knowledge structures until one that fit the data was found. The chi-square approximation to the likelihood ratio statistic was used as a measure of model fit. The search for structures was stopped as soon as a structure that fit the dirty data at $p \geq .05$ was obtained. For each structure, parameter estimation was done by iterative maximization of the log-likelihood function that follows, using the optimization routine Praxis, due to Gegenfurtner (1992):

$$\log \prod_{R \subset Q} \Pr(\mathcal{R} = R)^{N(R)} \tag{4}$$

$N(R)$ stands for the number of subjects with response pattern R.[3]

A best guess as to the initial form of the knowledge structure was arrived at by starting with a space containing six states on one gradation. Response patterns were arranged into sets of patterns with the same number of questions answered correctly (0, 1, 2, 3, 4, or 5). A state was considered to be in the initial knowledge space if the corresponding response pattern had the highest observed frequency within its set.

The items are represented in the knowledge structures by letters of the alphabet. In section 6 items 1–5 are represented by a, b, c, d, e. The initial knowledge structure for section 6 is depicted in Fig. 10.2, with state Q in the figure being {a, b, c, d, e}. This six-state structure has one gradation, a–e–d–b–c.

---

[3]The response pattern R can also unambiguously be denoted by the subset of Q it corresponds to. For instance let $Q = \{a, b, c, d, e\}$. Then the response $R = \{b, c, e\}$, conveys the same meaning as response pattern $R = 01101$.

$$\{\;\}—\{a\}—\{a,e\}—\{a,d,e\}——\{a,b,d,e\}—Q$$

FIG. 10.2. Section 6, six states, one gradation.

The guessing parameters (η_i, $i = 1, \ldots, 5$) were all fixed at $\frac{1}{5}$. This was reasonable due to the fact that each of the five test items was multiple choice with five alternatives. The careless error parameters (β_i, $i = 1, \ldots, 5$) and the item difficulty parameters (γ_i, $i = 1, \ldots, 5$) were allowed to vary in the analysis on the initial 500 patterns.

Each initial knowledge structure was tested on the first group of 500 response patterns. If a fit was not achieved, states were added to the knowledge structure whose frequencies of occurrence were significantly underestimated. When a fit was achieved, parameters were fixed and that structure was tested on the second group of 500 response patterns.

The final knowledge space for section 6 is depicted in Fig. 10.2 and is the same as the initial knowledge structure. Because it fitted to the initial set of 500 response patterns from section 6, it was not necessary to add states. The chi-square statistic for the final knowledge structure on the section 6 data was 28.898 with 31 degrees of freedom ($.5 < p < .75$). All cells had nonzero expected counts and there was no grouping of response categories.

In section 7 items 1–5 are represented by f, g, h, j, k. The initial knowledge structure for section 7 is depicted in Fig. 10.3, with state Q in the figure being {f, g, h, j, k}. This six-state structure has one gradation, k–f–h–g–j.

The guessing parameters were fixed as just given. The item difficulty parameters and the careless error parameters were allowed to vary in the analysis of the initial 500 patterns.

The section 7 data proved to be more complicated. This was anticipated because these items were more heterogeneous than those in section 6, and we did not expect a single gradation model to fit the data easily. The initial section 7 structure did not fit the first set of 500 response patterns. The states {g}, {g,k}, and {f,g,k} had significantly underestimated frequencies of occurrence. They were added to the structure. All possible gradations that could pass through the new structure were added. This added to the initial gradation k–f–h–g–j, gradations k–g–f–h–j, k–f–g–h–j, and g–k–f–h–j. This resulted in the structure shown in Fig. 10.4.

This structure also did not fit the data. However, two of the gradations had near zero estimated probability. These two gradations, k–g–f–h–j and

$$\{\;\}—\{k\}—\{f,k\}—\{f,h,k\}——\{f,g,h,k\}—Q$$

FIG. 10.3. Section 7, six states, one gradation.

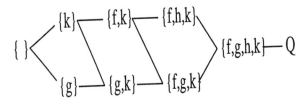

FIG. 10.4. Section 7, nine states, four gradations.

k–f–g–h–j, were dropped. In addition, the states {h,k} and {g,h,k} were added in the same manner, resulting in gradations k–f–h–g–j, g–k–f–h–j, k–h–f–g–j, and k–h–g–f–j. The gradation g–k–h–f–j was not added because the state {g,k}, which already occurred in other gradations, was being overestimated. The knowledge structure containing these states and gradations is in Fig. 10.5.

Again, a fit was not achieved. The states {f}, {f,j}, {f,j,k}, and {f,g,j,k} were added along with the gradation f–j–k–g–h. This resulted in the knowledge structure shown in Fig. 10.6.

This structure fit the initial 500 response patterns for section 7. The estimated parameter values and the probabilities of the gradations from this initial analysis were fixed and the chi-square statistic was predicted for the remaining 500 response patterns. A fit was achieved, with a chi-square statistic of 18.719 with 31 degrees of freedom $(.9 < p)$. Once again all cells had nonzero expected counts and there was no grouping of response categories.

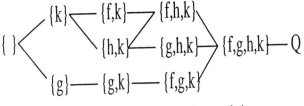

FIG. 10.5. Section 7, 11 states, four gradations.

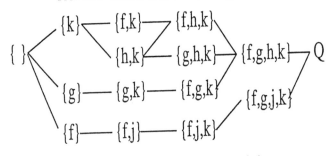

FIG. 10.6. Section 7, 15 states, five gradations.

TABLE 10.1
Sections 6 and 7 Estimated Parameter Values

Parameters	Section 6	Parameters	Section 7
γ_e	1.0413	γ_k	1.4402
γ_d	0.5000	γ_j	0.9328
γ_c	0.5000	γ_h	1.2678
γ_b	3.5058	γ_g	0.5000
γ_a	2.7587	γ_f	0.5163
β_e	0.1131	β_k	0.1210
β_d	0.2230	β_j	0.1702
β_c	0.3855	β_h	0.0179
β_b	0.2080	β_g	0.2131
β_a	0.0703	β_f	0.0915
α	4.2225	α	48.6148
θ	0.7870	θ	0.0864

The estimated item difficulty, careless error, and α, θ parameters for sections 6 and 7 are in Table 10.1. Recall that $\theta = \tau/(\tau + \xi)$. The estimated gradation probabilities are in Table 10.2. The estimated response pattern counts can be found for section 6 in Table 10.3 and for section 7 in Table 10.4.

A drawback of simultaneously determining the knowledge structure while estimating parameters of a particular model based on knowledge structures is that if the data fits poorly the cause for the poor fit may be due to two different reasons, which may not be easy to tease apart. One reason for a poor fit could be that the right knowledge structure was not found, and another reason could be that the model was inappropriate for the data. One way around this is to test every possible knowledge structure. This, however, is not a feasible enterprise in terms of computational resources required. The application discussed in this chapter is unusual (as

TABLE 10.2
Sections 6 and 7 Estimated Gradation Probabilities

Section 6	
a–e–d–b–c	1.0000
Section 7	
k–h–f–g–j	0.0133
f–j–k–g–h	0.2277
g–k–f–h–j	0.1771
k–f–h–g–j	0.3331
k–h–g–f–j	0.2488

TABLE 10.3
LSAT Observed and Expected Response Pattern Counts

	Response Pattern Item	Section 6		
Index	1 2 3 4 5	Observed	Ogive Expected	SKSM Expected
1	0 0 0 0 0	1	1.293	2.552
2	0 0 0 0 1	3	3.183	1.765
3	0 0 0 1 0	1	1.558	1.050
4	0 0 0 1 1	4	5.279	3.671
5	0 0 1 0 0	0	0.332	0.717
6	0 0 1 0 1	1	1.353	1.061
7	0 0 1 1 0	2	0.634	0.536
8	0 0 1 1 1	2	3.130	3.063
9	0 1 0 0 0	0	0.833	0.859
10	0 1 0 0 1	5	3.217	2.171
11	0 1 0 1 0	0	1.517	1.027
12	0 1 0 1 1	8	7.181	6.910
13	0 1 1 0 0	0	0.412	0.515
14	0 1 1 0 1	1	2.249	2.900
15	0 1 1 1 0	1	1.015	1.299
16	0 1 1 1 1	7	6.756	9.895
17	1 0 0 0 0	5	4.682	5.445
18	1 0 0 0 1	14	17.989	16.275
19	1 0 0 1 0	7	8.472	6.814
20	1 0 0 1 1	37	40.552	46.810
21	1 0 1 0 0	3	2.308	2.406
22	1 0 1 0 1	13	12.854	12.262
23	1 0 1 1 0	6	5.780	5.325
24	1 0 1 1 1	43	39.579	40.091
25	1 1 0 0 0	7	5.397	4.281
26	1 1 0 0 1	28	28.943	26.954
27	1 1 0 1 0	12	13.073	11.818
28	1 1 0 1 1	85	86.783	90.994
29	1 1 1 0 0	5	4.348	5.049
30	1 1 1 0 1	28	33.567	37.929
31	1 1 1 1 0	14	14.337	16.740
32	1 1 1 1 1	157	141.393	130.816
Total		500		

compared to other knowledge space theory applications) in that the items were not known. When items are known they can be used to determine the knowledge structure by conceptual analysis and the data is only used to prune the structure instead of being used to determine it by fitting procedures. (See, e.g., Lakshminarayan, 1996, for an application where conceptual analysis is used.)

TABLE 10.4
LSAT Observed and Expected Response Pattern Counts

Index	Response Pattern Item 1 2 3 4 5	Section 7 Observed	Ogive Expected	SKSM Expected
1	0 0 0 0 0	6	5.111	4.910
2	0 0 0 0 1	10	8.641	9.834
3	0 0 0 1 0	0	2.268	1.873
4	0 0 0 1 1	4	5.256	3.277
5	0 0 1 0 0	1	2.553	2.269
6	0 0 1 0 1	10	7.998	10.024
7	0 0 1 1 0	1	2.169	1.221
8	0 0 1 1 1	9	8.395	6.288
9	0 1 0 0 0	5	1.897	3.063
10	0 1 0 0 1	2	5.003	5.231
11	0 1 0 1 0	2	1.352	1.088
12	0 1 0 1 1	3	4.386	2.681
13	0 1 1 0 0	4	2.436	2.382
14	0 1 1 0 1	11	10.643	13.047
15	0 1 1 1 0	4	2.889	2.495
16	0 1 1 1 1	14	15.992	16.817
17	1 0 0 0 0	4	6.015	5.271
18	1 0 0 0 1	19	14.991	16.240
19	1 0 0 1 0	6	4.039	7.727
20	1 0 0 1 1	17	12.594	12.185
21	1 0 1 0 0	7	6.897	4.707
22	1 0 1 0 1	25	29.234	28.680
23	1 0 1 1 0	8	7.937	7.671
24	1 0 1 1 1	45	42.812	44.734
25	1 1 0 0 0	3	4.027	2.999
26	1 1 0 0 1	12	14.073	13.628
27	1 1 0 1 0	4	3.829	3.950
28	1 1 0 1 1	17	16.487	17.041
29	1 1 1 0 0	9	10.645	9.461
30	1 1 1 0 1	68	67.104	66.679
31	1 1 1 1 0	16	17.925	21.231
32	1 1 1 1 1	154	154.411	151.295
Total		500		

REANALYSIS OF NORMAL OGIVE MODEL

In order to provide a basis for comparison of fit between the SKSM and the normal ogive model, we ran the normal ogive model on the initial 500 response patterns belonging to sections 6 and 7 that were used in the SKSM analysis to determine parameter values. These values were then fixed

TABLE 10.5
LSAT Estimated Item Parameters

Items	Item Difficulty, γ		Reliability Index, α	
	[BL]	Re-An.	[BL]	Re-An.
Section 6				
1	1.4329	1.4141	.3856	.3831
2	.5505	.5332	.3976	.4265
3	.1332	.1012	.4732	.4688
4	.7159	.6897	.3749	.2896
5	1.1264	1.1217	.3377	.3050
Section 7				
1	.9462	.9451	.4887	.4779
2	.4073	.4323	.5436	.5400
3	.7451	.7787	.7022	.6887
4	.2683	.2688	.4196	.3887
5	1.0069	0.9832	.3805	.3601

Note. [BL], Bock and Lieberman (1970); Re-An., reanalysis.

for a prediction of the chi-square statistic using the final sets of 500 response patterns from sections 6 and 7 used in the SKSM analysis.

The procedure used to reproduce the analysis differs from that in Bock and Lieberman (1970) by the numerical means used to approximate the definite integral in Equation 1 (which has no closed form). Bock and Lieberman (1970) used Gauss–Hermite quadrature in their numerical analysis. We used a standard polynomial approximation to the normal integral (Johnson & Kotz, 1970, p. 55).

The C version of the Praxis computer program (Gegenfurtner, 1992) was used to maximize log-likelihood. The goodness of fit statistic was based on the chi-square approximation of the likelihood ratio statistic in the same manner as Bock and Lieberman (1970). Estimated response pattern counts can be found for section 6 in Table 10.3 and for section 7 in Table 10.4. Estimated item parameters can be found in Table 10.5.

The section 6 reanalysis fits with a chi-square statistic of 15.897914 (31 df, $.95 < p$). The section 7 reanalysis obtains a chi-square statistic of 20.719056 (31 df, $.8 < p$). In both cases, all cells had nonzero expected counts and there was no grouping of response categories.

CONCLUSION

To summarize, the SKSM and the normal ogive model perform well in predicting the clean data for both sections. The normal ogive model does better on section 6 data as compared to the SKSM. On section 7 data, both models seem to perform equally well. The fit of the SKSM on section 6 data, which was worse than that of the normal ogive model, is probably due to the fact that the items of the LSAT are designed to measure aptitude or general ability, rather than specific skills. The items constituting such tests are designed such that the principle of local independence holds. In other words, the probability of a correct response on any given item would ideally be independent of the probability of a correct response on any other item of the test, conditioned on the level of the latent trait. Due to this, all response patterns tend to be populated. The normal ogive model and other IRT models are appropriate tools for describing the data from tests consisting of such items. The SKSM, on the other hand, is designed for application domains with highly organized or curricular material. Except for the effects of error parameters, the observed patterns of item responses will correspond to underlying knowledge states. Tests where almost all response patterns occur fairly frequently will require large numbers of knowledge states and learning paths. This leads to models having a large number of parameters, and corresponding high variability of the statistical inference of the model's parameters.

The fit of the SKSM to section 7 data indicates that the latent class models may perform well even for items measuring continuously distributed traits. Haertel (1990) also reports the same conclusion and compares the performance of latent class, latent trait, and multiple factor models on the same data set analyzed in this chapter.

ACKNOWLEDGMENTS

This work was supported by National Science Foundation grant IRI 8919068 to Jean-Claude Falmagne at the University of California, Irvine. The authors thank the UCI office of academic computing for use of the Convex C240 in performing the analyses reported in this chapter.

REFERENCES

Bock, R. D., & Lieberman, M. (1970). Fitting a response model for n dichotomously scored items. *Psychometrika, 35*, 179–197.

Falmagne, J.-C. (1989). A latent trait theory via a stochastic learning theory for a knowledge space. *Psychometrika, 54*, 283–303.

Falmagne, J.-C., Koppen, M., Villano, M., Doignon, J.-P., & Johannesen, L. (1990). Introduction to knowledge spaces: How to build, test, and search them. *Psychological Review, 97*, 201–224.

Gegenfurtner, K. (1992). Praxis: Brent's algorithm for function minimization. *Behavior Research Methods, Instruments and Computers, 24*(4), 560–564.

Haertel, E. H. (1990). Continuous and discrete latent structure models for item response data. *Psychometrika, 55,* 477–494.

Johnson, N. L., & Kotz, S. (1970). *Distributions in statistics. Continuous univariate distributions, 2.* New York: Houghton Mifflin.

Lakshminarayan, K. (1996). *A hybrid latent trait and latent class model of learning—Theoretical details and empirical application* (Tech. Rep. No. MBS 96-07). University of California, Irvine.

Lord, F. M., & Novick, M. R. (1974). *Statistical theories of mental test scores* (2nd ed.). Reading, MA: Addison-Wesley.

Molenaar, I. W. (1981). On Wilcox's latent structure model for guessing. *British Journal of Mathematical and Statistical Psychology, 34,* 224–228.

Building a Knowledge Space Via Boolean Analysis of Co-Occurrence Data

Peter Theuns
Vrije Universiteit Brussel

In general, Boolean analysis is presented as a method for 0/1-data analysis that has a greater scope than Guttman analysis (Flament, 1976; Theuns, 1989, 1992, 1994; Van Buggenhaut & Degreef, 1987). The output of a Boolean analysis is an implication scheme; this is a graph consisting of responses to binary items (vertices) and implication relations between these responses (edges). Until now approaches inspired by Flament (1976) resulted in one or more implication schemes that comply with some optimality criterion. Restrictions to implication schemes with regard to theoretical constraints on implications have not been dealt with systematically. Several approaches to approximation of implication schemes concentrated on the global fit of implication schemes to the data (Flament, 1976; Theuns, 1992). Methods have been introduced that optimize the trade-off between the simplicity of implication schemes and their quality of fit (Theuns, 1989, 1992, 1994; Van Buggenhaut, 1987; Van Buggenhaut & Degreef, 1987).

In some areas of research where basic assumptions similar to those in Boolean analysis apply, empirical implication schemes may be rejected because of logical or theoretical considerations. An example is found in the field of knowledge spaces (Degreef, Doignon, Ducamp, & Falmagne, 1986; Doignon & Falmagne, 1985, 1987, 1988; Falmagne & Doignon, 1988a, 1988b; Falmagne, Doignon, Koppen, Villano, & Johannesen, 1990; Koppen, 1989). For important results on knowledge spaces parallels can be drawn with the theory of Boolean analysis. Doignon and Falmagne (1985, p. 188) mentioned "that the existence of a surmise system corresponding to a knowledge space can be inferred from some work by Flament (1976). These results, however, were formulated in a context and using a terminology very different from ours." To our knowledge this inference, which could establish the link between both fields of research, was never made completely explicit. This is the main purpose here.

RESPONSE PATTERNS

In the following, *items* stand for questions or problems that are grouped in a *test*, which could be a questionnaire, a psychological test, and so on. Responses are rated correct/incorrect. Thus, a *response* is a specific value assigned to an item. Responses are obtained from *subjects* (persons, students, etc.).

More formally: Let X be a (finite, linearly ordered) set of items x for which a binary response is possible ($x = 1$ or 0). The number of items is denoted by n (that is, $|X| = n$). The responses, given by each of the N subjects (N is the *sample size*), are gathered into an ordered n-tuple r, called a response *pattern*. The set of all theoretically possible patterns is denoted by R (R corresponds one-to-one with 2^X). Clearly, R contains 2^n patterns. A pattern r can either be denoted as an ordered set of responses or as an ordered enumeration of binary response values. For example, let $X = \{a,b,c\}$. One instance of r may be $\{a = 0, b = 1, c = 1\}$, denoted in short by $a'bc$ or equivalently 011. Clearly,

$$R = \{abc, abc', ab'c, ab'c', a'bc, a'bc', a'b'c, a'b'c'\}$$

which is equivalent to:

$$R = \{111, 110, 101, 100, 011, 010, 001, 000\}$$

A *subpattern* p of a pattern r is an ordered subset of r that is either denoted as a set containing a selection of responses in r or, again, as an ordered enumeration of binary response values in which responses to neglected items are replaced by an "x." Thus, assuming $X = \{a,b,c\}$, the subpattern $\{a = 1, c = 0\}$ is denoted either ac' or 1x0 (in the latter notation "x" replaces the neglected response to item b). For example, the subpattern $p_1 = 1x1$ is a subpattern of patterns 111 and 101, while $p_2 = 1xx$ is a subpattern of 111, 110, 101, and 100. The number of responses in a subpattern is called the *length* of that subpattern and is denoted by k. If all responses of a subpattern p_2 are present in a (sub)pattern p_1 then p_1 is said to *include* p_2. This latter case is denoted $p_2 \subseteq p_1$. In the case p_2 also contains strictly fewer responses than p_1, then p_2 is *strictly included* in p_1, which is denoted $p_2 \subset p_1$.

A subpattern p with length k is included in 2^{n-k} patterns in R. The set of these patterns is called the *extension* of p, denoted $\varepsilon(p)$. So,

$$\varepsilon(p) = \{r \in R \mid p \subseteq r\}.$$

Assuming $X = \{a,b,c\}$, and $R = \{abc, a'bc, ab'c, abc', a'b'c, a'bc', ab'c', a'b'c'\}$, we have for $p = a'c$: $\varepsilon(p) = \{a'bc, a'b'c\}$. Also, $\varepsilon(b') = \{ab'c, a'b'c, ab'c', a'b'c'\}$ and $\varepsilon(abc) = \{abc\}$.

The definition of extension need not be limited to single subpatterns. The extension of a set of subpatterns can be considered as well by taking the union of the extensions of the individual subpatterns. For example,

$$\varepsilon(\{b', a'c\}) = \{ab'c, a'b'c, ab'c', a'b'c', a'bc\}$$

The inverse relation of extension is related to the canonical projection π of a set of patterns. For a set Q of patterns the *canonical projection*, denoted $\pi(Q)$, is defined as the set of subpatterns p for which the extension of p is a subset of Q:

Let Q be a set of patterns; then the canonical projection π of Q is given by:

$$\pi(Q) = \{p: \varepsilon(p) \subseteq Q\}$$

Remark that $Q \subseteq \pi(Q)$ and $\varepsilon(\pi(Q)) = Q$.
Consider the following (special) examples:

Let $A = \{ab'c, a'b'c, ab'c', a'b'c'\}$. Then

$$\pi(A) = \{b', b'c, b'c', ab', a'b', ab'c, a'b'c, ab'c', a'b'c'\}$$

Clearly $\varepsilon(p) \subseteq A$ for all $p \in \pi(A)$ and also $\varepsilon(\pi(A)) = A$.

Let $B = \{a'bc, a'b'c\}$. Then

$$\pi(B) = \{a'c, a'bc, a'b'c\}$$

and again $\varepsilon(p) \subseteq B$ for all $p \in \pi(B)$ and $\varepsilon(\pi(B)) = B$.

Let $C = \{a'b'c\}$. Then

$$\pi(C) = \{a'b'c\}$$

A subpattern $p \in \pi(Q)$ is called *minimal* iff there is no q strictly contained in p such that $q \in \pi(Q)$.

In the preceding examples the first subpattern in every canonical projection is minimal as it does not contain any shorter subpattern in the canonical projection. The minimal subpatterns in these examples are: b' in $\pi(A)$, $a'c$ in $\pi(B)$, and $a'b'c$ in $\pi(C)$.

In the particular cases of each of the former examples it is observed that there is exactly one minimal subpattern. Moreover, the extension of each of the minimal subpatterns in the canonical projections (respectively b', $d'c$, and $d'b'c$) equals the complete projected set: $\varepsilon(b') = A$, $\varepsilon(d'c) = B$, and $\varepsilon(d'b'c) = C$. Therefore these minimal subpatterns are said to *cover* the projected sets (b' covers A, $d'c$ covers B, and $d'b'c$ covers C). Clearly, as shown in the following, a set of patterns generally contains more than one minimal subpattern.

Consider $D = \{ab'c, d'b'c, ab'c', d'b'c', d'bc\}$ $(D = A \cup B)$; then

$$\pi(D) = \{b', b'c, b'c', ab', d'b', d'c, ab'c, d'b'c, ab'c', d'b'c', d'bc\}$$

The minimal subpatterns in $\pi(D)$ are b' and $d'c$. In this case it is clear that none of these solely covers D. At least one pattern in D is missing from each of the extensions of b' and $d'c$ alone. However, the extension of the set consisting of all minimal subpatterns in the canonical projection does cover the entire projected set. For D we have $\varepsilon(\{b', d'c\}) = D$. Obviously, this is a general property.

Definition 1. Let $Q \subseteq R$ be a set of patterns. The *minimal canonical projection* of Q, denoted by $\pi_{min}(Q)$, is the set of minimal subpatterns in $\pi(Q)$.

Thus defined, for a set of patterns $Q \subseteq R$, the minimal canonical projection of Q consists of the minimal (with respect to inclusion) subpatterns in $\pi(Q)$ which are included only in (some) patterns in Q, and in none of the patterns in $R \backslash Q$.

Property. Any set of patterns Q is covered by its minimal canonical projection: $\varepsilon(\pi_{min}(Q)) = Q$.

The minimal canonical projection of a set of patterns is a central notion in Boolean analysis.

A full discussion of the Boolean algebraic parallels to the former terminology can be found in Theuns (1992). Here we concentrate on the analysis of data rather than going further into mathematical details.

BOOLEAN ANALYSIS, A SET THEORETIC APPROACH

Submitting a test to a group of subjects results in a *protocol* $\mathbf{P} = \{(r, f): r \in R \text{ and } f \in F\}$, which is the set of pairs consisting of patterns and their corresponding frequencies. The frequency of a single pattern is denoted by f, the set of observed frequencies by F.[1] According to the pattern frequencies, R is partitioned into a set R^* of *real patterns* or *observed patterns*[2] ($f > 0$) on the one hand and a set $R°$ of *zero patterns* ($f = 0$) on the other:

$$R^* = \{r \in R: f > 0\}$$
$$R° = \{r \in R: f = 0\} \tag{1}$$
$$\text{and clearly } R^* \cup R° = R, \; R^* \cap R° = \emptyset.$$

In Boolean analysis, the actual frequencies of patterns in R^* are only of secondary importance. Pattern frequencies are considered only to determine the dichotomy of R into R^* and $R°$.

The goal of Boolean analysis is to represent R^* as a family of (comprehensive) implications between responses, instead of enumerating its patterns. The implications are the basis for interpretation and reporting of results. These implications are inferred from the minimal canonical projection of $R°$.

Implications

Consider $\pi_{min}(R°)$, the minimal canonical projection of $R°$. We refer to the subpatterns in $\pi_{min}(R°)$ with the term *PCU*, which is short for *projection canonique ultime* (French for *ultimate canonical projection*), a notion that was introduced by Flament (1976) in a somewhat more general meaning.[3] A related term introduced by Flament is a *PC* (*projection canonique*), which stands for any element in the canonical projection of a set of patterns.

Here the notion PC is, in parallel with the notion PCU, restricted to elements in the canonical projection of $R°$. Obviously, the set of PCUs is a subset of the set of PC. The term *PCU* is used for single elements of $\pi_{min}(R°)$, and PCUs is the plural. PCUs are the minimal (by inclusion) subpatterns in $R°$ that have their extension entirely in $R°$. Let p be any PCU; then $\varepsilon(p) \subseteq R°$. Clearly, p contains a configuration of responses that has never been observed: All patterns containing p are elements of $R°$, the set of unobserved or zero patterns. In the following, the *complete set of PCUs*, denoted by P, refers to $\pi_{min}(R°)$, the set of minimal subpatterns in $\pi(R°)$.

---

[1]In special cases the "frequency" may very well be a binary variable when a pattern is either observed, or not.

[2]At this point the set of observed patterns (i.e., patterns with $f > 0$) is considered the same as the set of real patterns. Further on in the chapter a distinction is made.

[3]Flament used the term *PCU* for subpatterns in any minimal canonical projection. Here this notion is restricted to elements in the minimal canonical projection of the set of neglected patterns, $R°$.

Now suppose $X = \{a,b,c,d,e\}$, and let $p = ab'ce$ be a PCU. Clearly, $ab'ce$ never occurred in the observed or real patterns. Consequently, if a sub-pattern of p, say ac, does occur in some patterns in R^* (and it necessarily does[4]), then at least one of the other responses in p appears complemented in the patterns in R^*: We say ac *implies b or e'*. Now every other subpattern of p will result in another *implication*.

For example,

a	implies	b or c' or e'
$b'c$	implies	d' or e'
ace	implies	b

and so on. In the following, these implications are denoted

$$a \;\rightarrow b \oplus c' \oplus e'$$
$$b'c \rightarrow d' \oplus e'$$
$$ace \rightarrow b$$

and so on. As PCUs are actually subpatterns, all notions that have been introduced for subpatterns apply to PCUs as well. Thus, for example, the length of a PCU still is denoted k.

The number of (equivalent) implications that are generated by a PCU depends on its length. This is the result of the following construction rule for implications.

Construction Rule. Let p be a PCU and let $q \subset p$ (q is strictly contained in p). Then all implications defined by p are built according to:

$$q \rightarrow \text{(Boolean sum of complemented responses in } p \backslash q)$$

It can easily be seen that PCUs with length $= 2$ result in the most explicit implications, for example, $a \rightarrow b$. In general, implications yield a very straightforward interpretation: Every subject who gives all the responses on the left side of the implication gives at least one of the responses on the right side as well. Thus the interpretation is fully subject oriented, and implications are quite an attractive result of data analysis. Ultimately, the goal of Boolean analysis is to represent the data as a single structured family of implications.

Flament (1976) proved a number of properties of implications. We mention only that implications are reflexive, antisymmetric, and transitive.

---

[4]The subpattern ac certainly occurs in some patterns in R^*, else ac, instead of $ab'ce$, would have been PCU.

Implication Schemes

A number of equivalent implications correspond with every PCU. Given any PCU these implications can easily be obtained according to the construction rule. Inversely, given any implication, the corresponding PCUs can be reconstructed as the subpattern consisting of the responses on the left side of the implication plus the inverted responses on the right side; for example, the PCU corresponding with the implication $ad' \to b \oplus c'$ is $ab'cd'$. Moreover, the entire set $R°$ can be reconstructed as the extension of the complete[5] set of PCUs.

Because of the one-to-one correspondences between any PCU and a family of equivalent implications on the one hand, and any complete set of PCUs and $R°$ on the other, and the fact that R^* can always be recovered from $R°$ according to Equation 1, we end up with a system in which one-to-one correspondences exist between a family of (equivalent) sets of implications, a complete set of PCUs, and the set $R°$ (and R^*).

The very straightforward interpretation of implications makes it attractive to represent a set of data as a family of implications. In such a representation, the selected implications (one for each PCU) are *chained* as much as possible; that is, implications are represented in a single scheme, such that every response (or Boolean sum or product of responses) figures at most once in the scheme, and the right side of some implications may be taken as the left side for one or more others. For example:

Let $P = \{ab', ac', ad', ae', bc', bd', be', ce', de'\}$ be a complete set of PCUs. For each PCU in P one implication is selected:

$$\begin{array}{ccc}
a \to b & a \to c & a \to d \\
a \to e & b \to c & b \to d \\
b \to e & c \to e & d \to e
\end{array}$$

The implications can be joined into one comprehensive *implication scheme*:

In this implication scheme the right side of, for example, $a \to b$ serves as the left side for $b \to c$ and $b \to d$. Four implications, namely, $b \to e$, $a \to c$, $a \to d$, and $a \to e$, are not represented explicitly, but can be inferred

---

[5]There may exist $A \subset \{PCU\}$ for which $\varepsilon(A) = R°$.

from the scheme by transitivity. Instead of this scheme, another, equivalent, implication scheme could have been drawn:

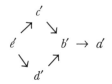

Other schemes, combining implications represented in either one of the former implication schemes, can be drawn as well.

The fit of an implication scheme to a set of data is expressed by a number, called the *sample fit*, which is defined to be the ratio of the sum of real pattern frequencies (N^* = sum of frequencies of patterns in R^*) and N.[6] Thus,

$$\text{Sample fit} = \frac{N^*}{N}$$

KNOWLEDGE SPACES, A BRIEF INTRODUCTION

In the theory of knowledge spaces a body of knowledge is conceptualized as a set of notions, the mastery of which can be assessed with questions or problems.

A person's *knowledge state* is the subset of notions this person has mastered (problems he or she can solve). Basic in the theory of knowledge spaces is that a person can accumulate knowledge by "adding" other subsets of notions to his or her present state. Doignon and Falmagne (1985) give the following definition of a knowledge space.

Definitions. A *knowledge structure* is a pair $(X, \mathbf{K})$ consisting of a set X of problems, and a family $\mathbf{K}$ of subsets of X called knowledge states. For any problem $x \in X$, the set of problems that belong to exactly the same states as x is called a *notion*. A knowledge structure is said to be *discriminating* iff each of its notions contains exactly one problem.

Note that it is possible to consider any equivalence class of problems (any notion) as a single element and derive a knowledge structure on these notions, rather than on the individual problems. This reduced knowledge structure becomes discriminating by definition. Therefore, in the

---

[6]According to Equation 1 the sample fit necessarily equals 1; however, dichotomization methods (like the one introduced in this chapter) alter the definition of R^*, resulting in a lower sample fit.

following we can restrict ourselves to discriminating knowledge structures without any loss of generality.

A knowledge structure is said to be *well graded*[7] if any state K in **K** can be achieved along a *gradation*, or a sequence of successive states $K' = \varnothing$, $K_1, K_2, K_3, \ldots, K_n = K$, where every next state K_i equals the former state K_{i-1}, augmented by exactly one notion. Thus, any state can be achieved by adding notions one by one, proceeding along a *learning path*.

A knowledge structure is called a *knowledge space* if the following two conditions are satisfied:

1. The set X and the empty set $\varnothing$ are states.
2. Every union of states is a state.

A knowledge space is said to be *quasi-ordinal* iff

3. Every intersection of states is a state.

At this point a theorem of Birkhoff (1937) is useful:

Theorem 1. For any set X, the property

$$x S y \text{ iff } (y \in K \text{ implies } x \in K \text{ for all } K \in \mathbf{K})$$

defines a one-to-one correspondence between the set of all quasi-orders S on X and the set of all families K of subsets on X that are closed under union and intersection.

This quasi-order S is called the *surmise relation* of **K** because $x S y$ may be interpreted as "if a subject masters y, it may be surmised that this same subject masters x."

According to Theorem 1 a knowledge structure is fully characterized by its surmise relation only if it is closed under both union and intersection. An important result of the Birkhoff theorem is that any discriminating knowledge structure that is closed under union and intersection is well graded (Doignon & Falmagne, 1985).

BOOLEAN ANALYSIS VERSUS KNOWLEDGE SPACES

From the preceding definition of a knowledge space it may be clear that a number of notions concerning knowledge spaces are quite closely related

---

[7]This definition, formulated by Koppen (1989), is not exactly the same as the original introduced by Falmagne and Doignon (1988b).

TABLE 11.1
Overview of Some Corresponding Notions in Boolean
Analysis and the Theory of Knowledge Spaces

	Boolean Analysis		Knowledge Spaces
x	item	x	problem
X	{items}	X	{problems}
R^*	{real patterns}	$\mathbf{K}$	knowledge structure
$p \in R^*$	real pattern	$K \in \mathbf{K}$	knowledge state
R°	{zero patterns}	$2^X \setminus \mathbf{K}$	{nonstates}
$x \to y$	x implies y	ySx	y can be surmised from x

Note. In the theory of knowledge spaces a state is denoted as a set of mastered notions, whereas in Boolean analysis nonmastered notions are denoted as complemented generators in a pattern. So, for $X = \{a,b,c,d\}$ the state $\varnothing$ corresponds to the pattern $a'b'c'd$, ac corresponds to $ab'cd'$, and so on.

to notions introduced in Boolean analysis by Flament (1976). Other notions in the theory of knowledge spaces can be traced back to notions in Boolean analysis to which some complementary conditions have been imposed.

The correspondence between some notions in Boolean analysis and knowledge spaces is given in Table 11.1.

In the theory of knowledge spaces, the surmise relation ySx indicates that mastery of problem y can be surmised from mastery of problem x. Thus, all subjects who produce a correct answer to x produce a correct answer to y. In Boolean analysis this case would result in a PCU xy' (there is no subject capable of solving x who is not capable of solving y), and consequently the implication $x \to y$ is found. For a generalization to the correspondence between a surmise mapping (Doignon & Falmagne, 1985) and PCUs with lengths exceeding 2, the interested reader is referred to Theuns (1992). A more detailed study of the correspondences in Table 11.1 is the subject of some of the following paragraphs.

Although it can be read from the table that surmise relations and surmise mappings can be interpreted as implications in Boolean analysis, it must be stressed that surmise relations and surmise mappings are special instances of implications. Boolean analysis covers relations between responses that can be either positive or negative, whereas in the theory of knowledge spaces only relations between positive responses (mastery of problems) are considered. Although in Boolean analysis implications like $x' \to y$ and $x \to y'$ can be obtained, the former would not make sense in the theory of knowledge spaces: One cannot surmise mastery of one item from incapability of solving the other, nor could mastery of one item imply incapability of solving the other. It appears that the notion of a surmise relation is narrower than the notion of an implication. The relation between both notions is the subject of Proposition 1.

Proposition 1. Let S be a surmise relation, and p a PCU with length = 2, containing responses to items x and y. The implication corresponding to p is equivalent to ySx or xSy in S iff

$$p = xy' \quad \text{or} \quad p = x'y$$

The correspondence is given by:

PCU		Implication		Surmise Relation
xy'	$\Leftrightarrow$	$x \rightarrow y$	$\Leftrightarrow$	ySx
$x'y$	$\Leftrightarrow$	$y \rightarrow x$	$\Leftrightarrow$	xSy

The proof is the immediate consequence of the definitions of an implication in Boolean analysis and a surmise relation in the theory of knowledge spaces respectively.

Corollary. There is a one-to-one correspondence between the family of surmise relations and the family of complete sets of PCUs with length 2, consisting of one positive and one negative response.

Proof. This correspondence is an immediate consequence of Proposition 1.

Now that we have an explicit link between surmise relations and a restricted class of PCUs, theorems proved in the context of knowledge spaces can be reformulated in terms of Boolean analysis. In order to develop a dichotomization method[8] for Boolean analysis, two propositions prove useful as follows.

Proposition 2. Let $P = \{xy' \mid xy' \text{ is PCU}\}$ be any complete set of PCUs, each with length = 2, consisting of one positive and one negative response. According to the properties of implications, P defines a quasi-order relation on the pairs (x, y).

There is a one-to-one correspondence between the family of all possible sets P and the family of all knowledge structures that are closed under both union and intersection.

Proof. This proposition is no more than a reformulation of the Birkhoff theorem 1.1 in terms of Boolean analysis.

---

[8] A method to determine the partition of R (into R^* and R°) other than the method solely based on the frequency of patterns.

Proposition 3. Let $P = \{xy' \mid xy'$ is PCU$\}$ be a complete set of PCUs consisting of one positive and one negative response, such that $xy' \in P \Rightarrow x'y \notin P$. Then P corresponds with a knowledge structure **K** that is closed under both union and intersection (**K** is a discriminating quasi-ordinal knowledge space).

Proof. According to Proposition 2, closure under union and intersection holds true, and thus only wellgradedness needs to be proved. A result by Koppen (1989) on the one-to-one correspondence between surmise mappings and knowledge spaces shows that for surmise mappings in general the following equivalence holds true:

A surmise mapping σ is *exclusive* in the sense that $x \neq y$ implies $\sigma(x) \cap \sigma(y) = \varnothing \Leftrightarrow \mathbf{K}_\sigma$ is well graded.

Here $\sigma(x) = \{C:\ C$ is a *clause* for $x\}$, a clause for x being a set of prerequisites for x. According to Koppen (1989), the relation between the surmise mapping σ and the surmise relation S of a knowledge space **K** is given by $S(x) = \cap\sigma(x)$.

In our case for surmise relations $S(x) = \{z \in X\colon xSz\}$ and $S(y) = \{z \in X\colon ySz\}$, the equivalence just given becomes:

$$x \neq y \text{ implies } S(x) \neq S(y) \quad \Leftrightarrow \quad \mathbf{K}_\sigma \text{ is well graded.}$$

The left side of this equivalence is to be proved. Now suppose $x \neq y$, and yet $S(x) = S(y) = \{x, y, z_1, \ldots, z_k\}$. According to Proposition 1 we have:

$$S(x) = \{x, y, z_1, \ldots, z_k\} \Leftrightarrow \{xy', xz'_1, \ldots, xz'_k\} \subseteq P$$

and also

$$S(y) = \{x, y, z_1, \ldots, z_k\} \Leftrightarrow \{x'y, yz'_1, \ldots, yz'_k\} \subseteq P$$

However, these PCUs yield (among others) the implications $x \rightarrow y$ and $y \rightarrow x$, and thus $x = y$. This result conflicts with the previous assumption $x \neq y$. It follows that $x \neq y$ implies $S(x) \neq S(y)$. So, $\mathbf{K}_\sigma$ is well graded.

A DICHOTOMIZATION METHOD FOR BUILDING A KNOWLEDGE SPACE

Several approaches to building a knowledge space exist. One method is described in Falmagne et al. (1990). In their approach a knowledge space is built according to judgments made by specialists (e.g., teachers), concerning the interdependence of responses to questions asked of their students. Basically, in this approach it is assumed that specialists have, in their minds, some implicit knowledge space concerning their field of expertise. This idea comes from the observation that when specialists are encouraged to assess a person's knowledge in their field of expertise "efficiently" (e.g., with a time limit), these experts will ask questions that are more or less "difficult" depending on the quality of the examinee's responses to previous questions. The ability to select questions in accordance with previous responses is assumed to depend on the implicit knowledge space, which, however, need not be directly accessible for questioning. Therefore, instead of asking specialists (directly) for judgments on the plausibility of all possible states (which would not be realistic, especially if the number of concerned problems is large), in order to reconstruct their implicit knowledge space, they are asked to make judgments concerning the interrelations between problems. To this end specialists are asked questions like (see, e.g., Falmagne et al., 1990):

> Suppose that a student under examination has just provided wrong responses to problems $x_1, \ldots, x_n$. Is it practically certain that this student will then also fail problem y? We assume that careless errors and lucky guesses are excluded.

From the resulting data, which are obtained from a number of specialists, one or more knowledge spaces can be built according to methods introduced by Koppen and Doignon (1990) and by Dowling (1994). Afterward the resulting spaces are tested against the actual responses of subjects to the problems. This final test then allows one to accept or reject one or more of the retained knowledge spaces or models. One major problem with this approach is that knowledge spaces obtained from different experts may differ significantly (Villano, 1991).

Another approach to building a knowledge space would act on a set of data. However, such an approach immediately causes another major problem. Because the number of possible knowledge states equals 2^n (with n the number of notions), most methods for building a knowledge space from empirical data are restricted to a rather small number of notions; for example, 10 notions already allow for 1,024 possible knowledge states. Obviously this requires that data be collected from a very large sample. As a result, the use of data-analytic techniques may become quite cumbersome.

However, a dichotomization method such as those developed in the context of Boolean analysis may become a useful tool for building knowledge spaces. Such a method will allow one to build a knowledge space from empirical data, the result of which can be compared with the results obtained from, for example, querying experts. The purpose of a specially designed dichotomization method is to assign observed knowledge states (patterns) immediately to a knowledge space (R^*), yet respecting the definition of a knowledge space. A Boolean analysis of the patterns (states) in the obtained knowledge space then will yield an implication scheme that matches the surmise relation corresponding with the knowledge space.

Proposition 3 can serve as a criterion to accept or reject PCUs that emerge in the Boolean analysis of data. Our goal is to select according to a set of observed data (subsets of X) a family $\mathbf{K}$ of subsets of X, which (a) fits the observed data (has sample fit higher than some preset value) and (b) is well graded and closed under both intersection and union.

According to Proposition 3, all sets $\mathbf{K}$ obtained by allowing only PCUs with length = 2, consisting of only one positive and one negative response, and having no pairs of PCUs of the form xy' and $x'y$ are closed under union and intersection. This leads to the following method to determine R^* and $R°$:

- All length-2 subpatterns are listed with their corresponding frequencies.
- Out of these, only subpatterns consisting of one positive and one negative response are considered for declaration as PCUs.
- These subpatterns are ordered according to their frequencies.
- Subpatterns (consisting of one positive and one negative response) with the lowest frequencies are *declared PCUs* one by one and are gathered in a set P' (note that at this point the set of PCUs is denoted P', not P; the latter will denote the complete set of PCUs later on).

According to Proposition 3, any set P' of such declared PCUs, provided that $xy' \in P'$ implies $x'y \notin P'$, results in a quasi-ordinal knowledge space $\mathbf{K} = 2^X \backslash \varepsilon(P')$.

Until this point, however, P' remains a mainly arbitrary set of subpatterns. Obviously, we need a criterion to set the dichotomization threshold—that is, where to stop adding declared PCUs to P'. The theory of knowledge spaces provides such criterion: A knowledge structure can be well graded only if all items (problems) cover distinct notions (i.e., the structure is discriminating). Therefore, as before and without loss of generality, it will a priori be assumed that all equivalence classes of items consist of exactly one item[9] and thus the knowledge structure is supposed to be discriminating. This assumption allows the introduction of the following *dichotomization criterion*:

All length-2 subpatterns of the form xy' are assigned in order of increasing frequency to the set of declared PCUs, called P', until the next subpattern xy' corresponds to a subpattern $x'y$ that is already in P'.

There is still one possible problem that needs some attention here: violations of transitivity. Let $xy' \in P'$ and $yz' \in P'$; then (a) $x'z$ cannot be

---

[9]Clearly, if some notions are being covered by more than one item, then prior to the Boolean analysis scores to these items need be combined to one score for the concerned notion.

assigned to P', and instead (b) xz' must be assigned to P'. It can easily be shown that (a) is always fulfilled; however, (b) is not.

Let $X = \{a, b, c, \ldots, n\}$. The following subpatterns and frequencies can be observed:

Pattern	Frequency	Pattern	Frequency
abc	α	$a'bc$	τ
abc'	β	$a'bc'$	ε
$ab'c$	γ	$a'b'c$	ψ
$ab'c'$	δ	$a'b'c'$	ζ

Now assume (a) does not hold and let ab', bc', and $a'c$ be declared PCUs. This situation would imply:

$$\begin{cases} (\gamma + \delta) < (\tau + \varepsilon) \\ (\beta + \varepsilon) < (\gamma + \psi), \text{ and thus } (\beta + \gamma + \delta + \tau + \varepsilon + \psi) < (\beta + \gamma + \delta + \tau + \varepsilon + \psi) \\ (\tau + \psi) < (\beta + \delta) \end{cases}$$

Obviously this cannot be true and necessarily (a) is fulfilled.
However, (b) requires:

$$\begin{cases} (\gamma + \delta) < (\tau + \varepsilon) \\ (\beta + \varepsilon) < (\gamma + \psi) \end{cases} \text{ implies } (\beta + \delta) \leq (\gamma + \delta) \text{ or } (\beta + \delta) \leq (\beta + \varepsilon)$$

and thus

$$(\beta \leq \gamma) \text{ or } (\delta \leq \varepsilon)$$

Clearly, this implication need not be true.

It follows that the preceding dichotomization criterion results in a set P' of declared PCUs that may be incomplete. Although no strict violations of transitivity will occur, some PCUs that would yield the (expected) transitive implications may be missing. Therefore, in order to determine the complete set P of PCUs some calculations are required. The complete set of PCUs, P, equals the minimal canonical projection of the extension of the set of declared PCUs, P':

$$P = \pi_{\min}(\varepsilon(P'))$$

A classical result shows that the minimal canonical projection of any set $R°$ (here $\varepsilon(P')$) yields transitive implications (see, e.g., Flament, 1976). The preceding method does not indicate how to process length-2 subpatterns of the form xy or $x'y'$ with low frequencies (eventually lower than the frequency of some declared PCU). In our opinion, patterns that contain such low-frequency subpatterns had better not be considered neglectable. In any case, subpatterns of the kind xy or $x'y'$, whatever their frequency, cannot be declared PCUs because the corresponding implications make no sense. Moreover, the resulting knowledge structure is not a space. Consequently, considering these kinds of subpatterns in determining a dichotomization threshold requires lowering the threshold until no such subpattern occurs in a declared zero cell. Obviously this may result in a very low threshold with a low number of PCUs (even 0). Thus, the number of states in the knowledge space may get extremely high. Also, as a consequence, the resulting implication scheme will consist of few implications. Bearing in mind that the final goal of building a knowledge space is to develop an efficient assessment procedure, this result is very undesirable. The fewer are the implications (which is the result of fewer PCUs), the fewer responses can be inferred (surmised) from some observed response(s) and thus, the less efficient the eventual assessment procedure can be.

Clearly, the cost of not assigning some low-frequency patterns (or states) to the knowledge space may become very high. Therefore, in this context, only xy' subpatterns are considered potential PCUs. All other subpatterns are considered nonzero, whatever their frequency. Clearly this may cause some patterns with frequencies below the frequency of some error patterns to show up in the resulting knowledge space. In the following section, an example of this approach is presented.

EXAMPLE

The data that are analyzed next are based on the June 1987 New York State Regents Competency Test in Mathematics (RCT). The RCT is a 60-item test consisting of 20 open-ended and 40 multiple-choice problems covering basic topics in high-school mathematics. Every year over 100,000 students take such a test, because it is a minimal requirement for graduation from high school in New York State. The data treated here consist of 6 of the 20 open-ended questions that were all filled out by 60,000 students, drawn at random from a sample of 67,204 students. A thorough analysis of these data can be found in Villano (1991). In order to allow a future comparison of results obtained with the present method and the results obtained by Villano, the same six items that were analyzed by the latter author are analyzed here. The items $a–f$ correspond to items 1, 5, 10, 14, 16, and 20 in the June 1987 RCT exam. The questions are presented in Fig. 11.1.

Villano selected these items because they cover a broad range of item difficulties. For the items $a–f$, the proportions of correct answers are 0.90, 0.79, 0.56, 0.64, 0.47, and 0.47, respectively. Responses of the 60,000 students were coded correct (1) or wrong (0). The obtained data are presented in Table 11.2.

a) Add:　　　　 546 　　　　　　　1248 　　　　　　+　　 26	d) Divide:　$6.8\overline{)7.48}$
b) Multiply:　　 507 　　　　　　× 　56	e) A class of 117 students is planning a bus trip. What is the least number of busses that must be reserved if each bus carries a maximum of 47 passengers?
c) Subtract:　 1.25 from 4.5.	f) In a triangle ABC, the measure of angle A is 30° and the measure of angle B is 50°. What is the number of degrees in the measure of angle C?

FIG. 11.1. Items *a* to *f* (problems 1, 5, 10, 14, 16, and 20 from the June 1987 RCT exam).

Only subpatterns with length 2 which consist of one positive and one negative response are considered as potential PCUs. These are listed in Table 11.3. Out of these subpatterns a maximal subset P' of subpatterns are declared PCUs, as described earlier. First, the subpattern with the lowest frequency (0xxxx1) is assigned to P'. Then the subpattern with the next lowest frequency (0xxx1x) is assigned to P', and so on until the next subpattern to be assigned to P' would cause the equivalence of two notions in the knowledge space (if a subpattern $xy' \in P'$ then $x'y$ cannot be assigned to

TABLE 11.2
Response Patterns Obtained From 60,000
Students for Items *a–f* on RCT

Pattern	Frequency	Pattern	Frequency	Pattern	Frequency	Pattern	Frequency
000000	884	010000	523	100000	2,676	110000	3,262
000001	81	010001	148	100001	437	110001	1,086
000010	184	010010	222	100010	969	110010	1,883
000011	55	010011	127	100011	330	110011	1,035
000100	169	010100	370	100100	930	110100	2,985
000101	69	010101	199	100101	458	110101	2,007
000110	80	010110	222	100110	571	110110	1,999
000111	47	010111	162	100111	389	110111	1,973
001000	93	011000	187	101000	433	111000	1,680
001001	30	011001	124	101001	258	111001	1,221
001010	43	011010	123	101010	291	111010	1,294
001011	30	011011	135	101011	263	111011	1,557
001100	91	011100	361	101100	672	111100	3,946
001101	62	011101	396	101101	635	111101	5,253
001110	46	011110	301	101110	507	111110	3,636
001111	92	011111	528	101111	782	111111	8,398

TABLE 11.3
Subpatterns With Length = 2 Containing One 1 and One 0

Subpattern	Frequency	Subpattern	Frequency	Subpattern	Frequency
1xxx0x	27,939	x1x0xx	14,607	xxx0x1	6,917
1xxxx0	27,734	xx1xx0	13,704	x0x1xx	5,600
x1xx0x	23,748	xx01xx	12,630	x0xx1x	4,679
x1xxx0	22,994	xxxx01	12,464	x01xxx	4,328
1x0xxx	22,990	xxxx10	12,371	01xxxx	4,128
1xx0xx	18,675	10xxxx	10,601	x0xxx1	4,018
xxx10x	18,603	xx0x1x	10,248	0xx1xx	3,195
x10xxx	18,203	xx0xx1	8,603	0x1xxx	2,642
xxx1x0	16,886	xxx01x	8,541	0xxx1x	2,397
xx1x0x	15,442	xx10xx	7,762	0xxxx1	2,285

P' as this would cause $x = y$). In the example a maximal P' is obtained if in Table 11.3 all of the subpatterns with frequency $\leq 10,248$ are assigned to P':

$$P' = \{xx0x1x, xx0xx1, xxx01x, xx10xx, xxx0x1, x0x1xx, x0xx1x,$$
$$x01xxx, 01xxxx, x0xxx1, 0xx1xx, 0x1xxx, 0xxx1x, 0xxxx1\}$$

The subpatterns in P' are declared PCUs, which results in the following implications:

$$
\begin{array}{ccc}
e \rightarrow c & d \rightarrow b & d \rightarrow a \\
f \rightarrow c & e \rightarrow b & c \rightarrow a \\
e \rightarrow d & c \rightarrow b & e \rightarrow a \\
c \rightarrow d & b \rightarrow a & f \rightarrow a \\
f \rightarrow d & f \rightarrow b &
\end{array}
$$

Apparently, all transitive implications are present, indicating that in this case P' is equal to the complete set of PCUs ($P = \pi_{min}(\varepsilon(P')) = P'$). Increasing the dichotomization threshold further would result in $\{10xxxx\} \in P'$, which conflicts with $\{01xxxx\} \in P'$ because this would imply equivalency of a and b, which cannot be, because nonequivalence of notions is assumed a priori. The (quasi-ordinal) knowledge space $\mathbf{K}$ equals $2^X \setminus \varepsilon(P)$:

$$\mathbf{K} = \{111111, 111101, 111110, 111100, 110100, 110000, 100000, 000000\}$$

The following implication scheme (which corresponds with the surmise relation) is found (sample fit = 51.73%):

$$
\begin{array}{c}
e \searrow \\
\quad\quad c \rightarrow d \rightarrow b \rightarrow a \\
f \nearrow
\end{array}
$$

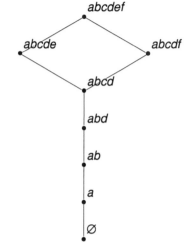

FIG. 11.2. A graph representation of the quasi-ordinal knowledge space obtained for the RCT data, items *a–f*, according to the dichotomization method for building a knowledge space.

This scheme corresponds with the quasi-ordinal knowledge space presented in Fig. 11.2. It also corresponds with the following surmise relation:

$$Sa = \{a\}$$
$$Sb = \{ab\}$$
$$Sc = \{abcd\}$$
$$Sd = \{abd\}$$
$$Se = \{abcde\}$$
$$Sf = \{abcdf\}$$

Clearly, **K** is well graded and closed under union and intersection. Apparently this dichotomization method allows one to build a quasi-ordinal knowledge space quite easily. Comparing the obtained space with the 40-states space obtained by Villano (1991) shows that there are important correspondences. Obviously, a thorough comparison of the obtained results still must be made.[10] The only purpose of the present analysis, however, is to demonstrate that a Boolean approach to building a knowledge space may be valuable.

An important argument for the use of the Boolean approach, introduced earlier, is that it can be used to build knowledge structures covering a relatively large number of notions. For illustration, an analysis was carried out for all 20 open-ended RCT items. Clearly, one should not expect very

---

[10]Such thorough comparison would, for instance, imply that estimated probabilities be calculated for the presented model as well. This is not done here as this would require first a probabilistic model to be introduced. As our concern is with dichotomization methods, such full treatment therefore is estimated to be beyond the scope of this work.

much from such analysis; although a sample of 60,000 students may be found quite large, this number is very low compared to the 1,048,576 (= 2^{20}) possible patterns. Consequently, the knowledge space built on these data may not be very reliable. However, the introduced method allows one to build it without much difficulty. The obtained knowledge space, which is closed under union and intersection, contains over 2,000 knowledge states and accommodates the responses obtained from 19,384 students (sample fit = 32.31%). Because the number of states is so high, no attempt is made here to represent these in a picture, nor do we give the list of retained states. The implication scheme (which gives the surmise relation) proves to be much more compact and is given instead:[11]

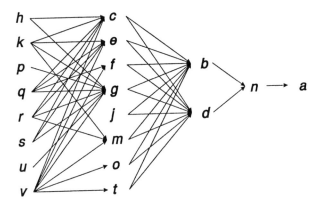

Obviously, this implication scheme remains readable. However, as this may be due to the "small" sample size, compared to the number of possible knowledge states, no further inferences are made from this example. Still it demonstrates the feasibility of such analysis.

Apart from the preceding considerations concerning sample size and sample fit, the major shortcoming of this approach may be more fundamental. The presented dichotomization method allows only one set of prerequisites for every item. In order to loosen this constraint, an approach needs to be developed that allows PCUs with lengths exceeding 2, and that would yet result in a knowledge space (eventually not closed for intersection).

One could hope that the theory of knowledge spaces holds the key to a generalization of the dichotomization method presented here to a method covering PCUs with lengths ≥ 2. However, this is true only to some extent. The major problem, which is not solved yet, is that the theory of knowledge spaces does not provide a criterion for the number of sets of

---

[11]In this implication scheme items 1–20 are labeled *a, b, c, d, e, f, g, h, j, k, m, n, o, p, q, r, s, t, u, v*, respectively.

prerequisites to be allowed for every single problem. In other words, although a proposition has been formulated by Theuns (1992) that indicates the constraints on the PCUs in *P* in this more general case, no indication is given of the maximal length of PCUs to be accepted. As a result an eventual dichotomization method from Boolean analysis depends on arbitrary criteria for setting the dichotomization threshold.

CONCLUSIONS

Boolean analysis can be applied to build a quasi-ordinal knowledge space with the presented method. An interesting result is that the theory of knowledge spaces provides a number of constraints to the data-analytical method so that calculations are very much simplified when compared to other applications of Boolean analysis. The presented method requires no more than a two-way cross-tabulation. Consequently, even very large data sets covering many items and subjects can be processed without much difficulty.

Obviously, building a knowledge space on more than, say, 10 items can be done, but still this would require a very large data set. Probably this is one of the major difficulties of applying the method. Also, the presented method does not give probabilities for the knowledge states. Those must still be estimated according to some other method.

Future research should concentrate on the generalization of the approach to knowledge spaces that are not closed for intersection. For this purpose, the number of prerequisite sets for different problems will need to be determined. Probably this is where expert knowledge must be introduced for building a knowledge space.

REFERENCES

Birkhoff, G. (1937). Rings of sets. *Duke Mathematical Journal, 3*, 443–454.

Degreef, E., Doignon, J.-P., Ducamp, A., & Falmagne, J.-C. (1986). Languages for the assessment of knowledge. *Journal of Mathematical Psychology, 30*, 243–256.

Doignon, J.-P., & Falmagne, J.-C. (1985). Spaces for the assessment of knowledge. *International Journal of Man-Machine Studies, 23*, 175–196.

Doignon, J.-P., & Falmagne, J.-C. (1987). Knowledge assessment: A set-theoretic framework. In B. Ganter, R. Wille, & K. E. Wolff (Eds.), *Beiträge zur Begriffsanalyse* [Contributions to the analysis of concepts] (pp. 129–140). Zürich: Bibliographisches Institut & Brockhaus.

Doignon, J.-P., & Falmagne, J.-C. (1988). Parametrization of knowledge structures. *Discrete Applied Mathematics, 21*, 87–100.

Dowling, C. (1994, July). *Integrating different knowledge spaces.* In G. H. Fischer & D. Laming (Eds.), Contributions to mathematical psychology, psychometrics, and methodology (pp. 149–158). New York: Springer-Verlag.

Falmagne, J.-C., & Doignon, J.-P. (1988a). A class of stochastic procedures for the assessment of knowledge. *British Journal of Mathematical and Statistical Psychology, 41*, 1–23.

Falmagne, J.-C., & Doignon, J.-P. (1988b). A Markovian procedure for assessing the state of a system. *Journal of Mathematical Psychology, 32*, 232–258.

Falmagne, J.-C., Doignon, J.-P., Koppen, M., Villano, M., & Johannesen, L. (1990). Introduction to knowledge spaces: How to build, test, and search them. *Psychological Review, 97*(2), 201–224.

Flament, C. (1976). *L'analyse booléenne de questionnaire* [Boolean analysis of questionnaires]. Paris: Mouton.

Koppen, M. (1989). *Ordinal data analysis: Biorder representation and knowledge spaces.* Unpublished doctoral dissertation, Katholieke Universiteit Nijmegen, Nijmegen, The Netherlands.

Koppen, M., & Doignon, J.-P. (1990). How to build a knowledge space by querying an expert. *Journal of Mathematical Psychology, 34*(3), 311–331.

Theuns, P. (1989). Predicting an optimal threshold in Boolean analysis of questionnaires. In E. E. Roskam (Ed.), *Mathematical psychology in progress* (pp. 329–343). Berlin: Springer-Verlag.

Theuns, P. (1992). *Dichotomization methods in Boolean analysis of co-occurrence data: Applications in psychopathology, organizational psychology, socio-economic research and knowledge theory.* Unpublished doctoral dissertation, Vrije Universiteit Brussel, Brussels.

Theuns, P. (1994). A dichotomisation method for Boolean analysis of quantifiable co-occurrence data. In G. H. Fischer & D. Laming (Eds.), *Contributions to mathematical psychology, psychometrics, and methodology* (pp. 389–402). New York: Springer Verlag.

Van Buggenhaut, J. (1987). Questionnaires booléens: Schémas d'implications et degrés de cohesion [Boolean questionnaires, implication schemes, and degress of cohesion]. *Mathématiques et Sciences Humaines, 98*, 9–20.

Van Buggenhaut, J., & Degreef, E. (1987). On dichotomization methods in Boolean analysis of questionnaires. In E. E. Roskam & R. Suck (Eds.), *Progress in mathematical psychology—1* (pp. 447–453). Amsterdam: North-Holland.

Villano, M. (1991). *Computerized knowledge assessment: Building the knowledge structure and calibrating the assessment routine.* Unpublished doctoral dissertation, New York University, New York.

Learning Models

Multinomial Models for Measuring Storage and Retrieval Processes in Paired Associate Learning

Jeffrey N. Rouder
William H. Batchelder
University of California, Irvine

This chapter defines and analyzes a new family of multinomial processing tree models for an experimental paradigm frequently used in memory research. The paradigm involves a paired-associate learning phase, where subjects study a list of A–B items and subsequently they receive two successive memory tests. First, they receive a free-recall test, and subjects attempt to recall all the A and B items. Then, some time after completing the free-recall task, subjects receive a cued-recall task, in which they attempt to recall each B item when given a suitable cue, such as the corresponding A item or a category label for the B item. Hereafter we refer to the paradigm as free-then-cued recall.

The free-then-cued-recall paradigm is derived from a between-subjects paradigm originally employed by Tulving and Pearlstone (1966), where one group of subjects performed the free-recall task, and the other group of subjects performed the cued-recall task. The cued-recall and free-recall performances were considered proxy measures of item "accessibility" and item "availability," respectively. The paradigm has been used by a number of researchers, such as Drachman and Leavitt (1972), Hirshman (1988), Hirshman, Welley, and Palij (1989), Hultsch (1975), Pra Baldi, de Beni, Cornoldi, and Cavedon (1985), and Thomson and Tulving (1970), because it provides information about the separate contributions of storage and retrieval processes in paired-associate learning. The cued-recall test is presumably less demanding on retrieval processes than the free-recall test. In fact, some researchers (e.g., Drachman & Leavitt, 1972) have operationally defined that if an experimental factor affects free-recall performance without, at the same time, affecting cued-recall performance, then it is a factor that affects retrieval rather than storage processes. We return to the issue of separately measuring storage and retrieval processes in the paradigm later.

Recently, Riefer and Rouder (1992) developed a multinomial processing tree model for the paradigm, and they applied it to data to try to sort out the relative roles of storage and retrieval processes in the so-called bizarreness effect or bizarre-imagery effect. The bizarreness effect refers to the increased memorability of bizarre items, such as "The dog rode the bicycle down the street," compared to that of common items, such as "The dog chased the bicycle down the street." Based on the model, Riefer and Rouder concluded that the bizarreness effect, when it occurred, was primarily due to a retrieval advantage for bizarre items. This conclusion was consistent with retrieval-based theories of the effect (e.g., Einstein, McDaniel, & Lackey, 1989; Hirshman et al., 1989) and inconsistent with storage-based explanations of the effect (e.g., Merry, 1980; Wollen & Cox, 1981).

The free-then-cued paradigm involves two aspects that are interesting from a statistical modeling standpoint. First, the fact that there are two successive memory tests on the same item strongly introduces the possibility of correlated performance due to individual differences in memory parameters. Multinomial processing tree models generally are used to analyze aggregate data that assume that subject-item responses are independent and identically distributed over categories, with no parameter variations. Often statistical analysis, such as in Riefer and Batchelder (1991), shows that a particular multinomial model is robust under violations of parameter invariance. In the free-then-cued paradigm, this strategy may not be sufficient. In fact, there is an active and heated controversy concerning the logic of making inferences from paradigms involving successive memory tests, such as in Hintzman (1993), Flexser and Tulving (1993), and Riefer and Batchelder (1995). For example, Hintzman (1980; Hintzman & Hartry, 1990) argued that all such paradigms provide uninterpretable data because of the possibility of spurious correlations between successive tests due to the heterogeneous populations of subjects and items. On the other hand, some theorists use data from paradigms that employ successive memory tests to infer separate memory systems (cf. Hayman & Tulving, 1989).

A second statistically interesting aspect of the free-then-cued paradigm is that it frequently involves some sparse data categories. For example, one of the response categories involves correct free recall of both the A and B terms followed by incorrect recall of B given A as a cue. This category is needed for the family of models proposed; however, usually data events of this type occur infrequently. For example, in the experiments analyzed by Riefer and Rouder (1992), a data event occurred in this category only about 1% of the time, and it did not even occur at all in some conditions. Because most of the multinomial processing tree models are analyzed with classical asymptotic methods (e.g., Batchelder, 1991; Batchelder & Riefer, 1990; Hu & Batchelder, 1994; Riefer & Batchelder, 1988, 1991), the existence of categories with sparse frequencies necessarily poses a problem, and these problems require special considerations in model analysis.

This chapter is organized into seven main sections. The following two sections describe the development of a general multinomial model of the free-then-cued paradigm. In the fourth section we specialize the general model into a family of related models by making different psychologically motivated parameter restrictions. In the fifth section we discuss the statistical properties of different members of this family, and concentrate on issues of sparse categories and individual differences on correlated memory tests. In the sixth section, we analyze the bizarre imagery data from Riefer and Rouder (1992) with several members of the model family.

Finally, in the conclusion we return to a discussion of the traditional practice of inferring storage and retrieval effects directly from performance data.

DATA REPRESENTATION

The data come from both a free-recall task and a cued-recall task. A subject's performance on the cued-recall task can be scored as correct or incorrect; however, the result of the free-recall task can be scored in several ways. For our purposes, free recall for a given A–B pair is classified into the number of items (two, one, zero) that are correctly recalled. The combination of the three free-recall possibilities and the two cued-recall possibilities yields six separate events on each word pair: E_1, both items freely recalled, correct cued recall; E_2, exactly one item freely recalled, correct cued recall; E_3, neither item freely recalled, correct cued recall; E_4, both items freely recalled, incorrect cued recall; E_5, exactly one item freely recalled, incorrect cued recall; E_6, neither item freely recalled, incorrect cued recall. The six data categories yield five degrees of freedom to work with.

There is an inherent trade-off when defining a partition of data events for a multinomial model. A coarse partition with few categories typically yields large event frequencies in each of the categories, yet it affords few degrees of freedom, therefore limiting the number of possible parameters in the model. On the other hand, if the partition is too fine, categories may have small frequencies, and parameter estimators may be unstable due to sparse categories. Furthermore, the additional parameters needed to model these sparse categories may not measure anything of theoretical interest. Our data partition represents a compromise in regard to these extremes. A coarser partition can be constructed by classifying test performance into the four categories of a 2 × 2 table defined by correct or incorrect on free recall and cued recall, respectively. This partition yields only three degrees of freedom, and might not lend itself to a model with sufficient psychological flexibility. On the other hand, a finer partition can be created by differentiating between recalling the A item and the B item when only one item is recalled. This partition would yield eight data events with an increasing chance of sparse frequency counts, especially in the singleton recall categories. Such a partition would have the advantage that processes relating the probability of recall to order of study can be modeled (e.g., singleton recall of the A item may be modeled differently from that of the B item).

At this point, we introduce some notation. Let N_i be the frequency of event E_i, and let N be the total number of item pairs, $N = \Sigma_{i=1}^{6} N_i$. Let P_i be the proportion of events in the ith category, where $P_i = N_i/N$, and let $p_i = \Pr(E_i)$ be the underlying true probability of E_i.

DEVELOPMENT OF THE MULTINOMIAL MODEL FAMILY

In this section, we adopt the strategy in Batchelder and Riefer (1990) by "overparameterizing" a general model and then considering various psychologically plausible submodels. Our most general model assumes that a subject's performance is a function of six all-or-none cognitive processes as follows.

Associative Storage. Associative storage occurs when an adequate representation of the A item, B item, and their association is formed during study and maintained until the free-recall memory task. Let these processes occur with probability a, $0 \leq a \leq 1$.

Associative Retrieval. Associative retrieval results in correct free-recall performance on both the A and B items. Associative retrieval is contingent on successful associative storage, and occurs with probability r, $0 \leq r \leq 1$. Associative retrieval can occur in different ways, and these ways are not differentiated by the model. For example, the subject may not be able to retrieve the entire association at first, but only a singleton. This singleton might act as a self-generated cue, which then triggers the retrieval the other item through the association. Such singleton-linked retrieval is also considered associative retrieval as the recall of both pair members is mediated by the association.

Stored Singleton Retrieval. It is conceivable that a subject can store an item pair, and yet the members of the pair may be only retrievable as singletons, without retrieval of the association. This occurs for each pair member as a conditionally independent event with identical probability s, $0 \le s \le 1$; that is, singleton retrieval is conditionally independent on one of the associative retrieval routes not occurring.

Failure to Recall Stored Associations. It is both necessary and sufficient for correct cued-recall performance that an item pair be in storage at the time of the cued-recall task. However, there may be a substantial time delay between the free-recall and cued-recall tests, resulting in forgetting. The model allows this "forgetting process" to depend on whether or not successful retrieval of the pair occurred during free recall. The probability of forgetting conditioned on a retrieval success during free recall is f_1, and on retrieval failure during free recall is f_2, $0 \le f_1, f_2 \le 1$.

Recall of Nonassociated Item Pairs. If associative storage of a pair does not occur, it is still possible that the subject stores and retrieves the A and B items as conditionally independent events. Let u be this conditional probability of storing and retrieving an item, $0 \le u \le 1$.

Riefer and Batchelder (1988) and Hu and Batchelder (1994) showed that it is often convenient to express a multinomial model in the form of a general processing tree (GPT). Figure 12.1 presents the tree diagram for the current model. The tree has 11 branches corresponding to the 11 separate processing sequences implied by the assumptions of the model. These branches are aggregated in to the six observable E_i categories. The probabilities of an event being in various empirical data categories can be derived from Fig. 12.1 and they are presented in Equations 1a–1f.

$$p_1 = ar(1 - f_1) + a(1 - r)s^2(1 - f_2) \tag{1a}$$
$$p_2 = 2a(1 - r)s(1 - s)(1 - f_2) \tag{1b}$$
$$p_3 = a(1 - r)(1 - s)^2(1 - f_2) \tag{1c}$$
$$p_4 = ar f_1 + a(1 - r)s^2 f_2 + (1 - a)u^2 \tag{1d}$$
$$p_5 = 2a(1 - r)s(1 - s)f_2 + 2(1 - a)u(1 - u) \tag{1e}$$
$$p_6 = a(1 - r)(1 - s)^2 f_2 + (1 - a)(1 - u)^2 \tag{1f}$$

There are many psychological assumptions embedded in the model that deserve further elaboration. First, the processes occur serially, and in a definite order corresponding to the order of the subtasks in the paradigm, namely, list study, free recall, and cued recall. Only on successful storage of the association can associative retrieval or cued recall be successful.

Successful storage, although necessary for correct performance on the cued recall, is not sufficient to guarantee correct cued-recall performance.

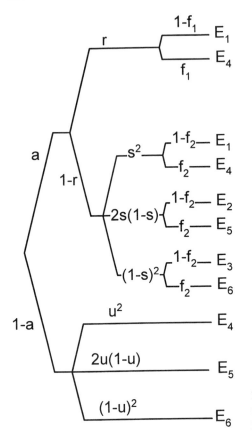

FIG. 12.1. General multinomial model for the free-then-cued-recall paradigm.

The subject may encounter poststorage forgetting that leaves the stored encoding unavailable. We would expect that this is unlikely when there is a short time delay between the end of the free-recall task and the beginning of the cued-recall task. However, forgetting may become significant with delayed cued recall. The probability of poststorage forgetting may differ according to free-recall performance. In particular, we expect memory encodings that afford successful retrieval to be more resistant to this forgetting, that is, $f_1 \leq f_2$. The use of the forgetting parameters is also designed to model the possible interference effects of the free-recall test on the subsequent cued-recall test. Finally, the model treats both the stimulus and response terms as equivalent, conditionally independent events when associative storage or retrieval fails. These assumptions are convenient approximations and are similar to ones found in Batchelder and Riefer's (1986) pair clustering model.

Riefer and Rouder (1992) also presented a multinomial model for measuring storage and retrieval in the free-then-cued-recall paradigm. Their model is not a submodel of the general model presented here. There are two important differences between the model in Fig. 12.1 and the Riefer–Rouder model. Riefer and Rouder assumed that the probability of performing singleton processes are mutually exclusive rather than independent. Should a subject successfully perform a singleton process on an A item, he or she cannot do so on the B item, and vice versa. Jones (1987) had an interesting discussion comparing the independence and mutually exclusive assumptions in modeling cognitive processes. In most applications, there are only slight differences between the singleton independence assumption and the Riefer–Rouder singleton assumption because the singleton parameters are usually quite small. The other major difference between the current model and the Riefer–Rouder model involves parameter restrictions. In order to obtain a four-parameter, testable model, Riefer and Rouder assumed that singleton recall occurs with identical probability whether or not associative storage occurs. We believe there are other more psychologically plausible assumptions reflected in the current model family that can be used to obtain testable submodels.

THE FAMILY OF MODELS

The model in Fig. 12.1 has six parameters that we denote by

$$\theta = \langle a, r, f_1, f_2, s, u \rangle \in \Omega_6 = [0,1]^6 \tag{2}$$

where Ω_6 is the parameter space of the model. Then the event probabilities p_i of Equation 1 can be viewed as functions, $p_i(\theta)$, from Ω_6 into $[0,1]$, $i = 1, 2, \ldots, 6$. Because the data have five degrees of freedom, the general model in Equation 1 is *nonidentifiable*. An identifiable model has at most one parameter vector consistent with any pattern of event probabilities; that is, $p_i(\theta) = p_i(\theta')$, for all $i = 1, \ldots, 6$, implies $\theta = \theta'$. Identifiability is a useful property of a multinomial model if it is to be used as a measurement tool, because otherwise measurement scales for the parameters must be established (e.g., Crowther, Batchelder, & Hu, 1995), and these generally involve trade-offs among the parameters. Thus, in order to use the model in Fig. 12.1, we must make at least one simplifying assumption. Three psychologically plausible possibilities follow.

Assumption 1. The memory trace of the association is equally susceptible to poststorage forgetting, regardless of the success or failure of retrieval. This assumption is embodied by setting $f_1 = f_2 = f$.

Assumption 2. Retrieval of an association on free recall sufficiently strengthens the trace such that it is immune to forgetting for cued recall. This assumption is represented by setting $f_1 = 0$. This version of the model does allow the possibility of cued-recall failure with the parameter f_2, if the associative retrieval fails to occur on free recall.

Assumption 3. A–B pairs are stored only as associative units, and not as singletons. The parameter u is set to zero, and thus the failure to associatively store the item pair, with probability $1 - a$, necessarily leads to an E_6 event.

The six-parameter general model can be restricted by any one of the three assumptions into five-parameter models denoted by M_{5a}, M_{5b}, and M_{5c}, by assumptions 1, 2, and 3, respectively. These and other submodels are depicted in Fig. 12.2. It is possible to implement any two of the three assumptions, producing a model with only four parameters. The resulting three submodels are denoted M_{4a}, M_{4b}, and M_{4c} in Fig. 12.2. When all three assumptions are imposed simultaneously, we produce a three-parameter model, namely, M_3, which can be further reduced into just a two-parameter model, M_2, by setting s, the singleton parameter, equal to zero.

Figure 12.2 shows the nesting relationships among all nine models. The vertical dimension of the graph represents a trade-off between psychological flexibility and statistical tractability. The general model, M_6, is the most flexible, yet it is not identifiable. The five-parameter models are less flexible but, as we show, they all exhibit identifiability. The four-parameter models are even less flexible; however, they are not only identifiable, but also testable in the sense that they could be rejected on the basis of asymptotic goodness-of-fit tests (e.g., Reed & Cressie, 1988).

The two- and three-parameter models may be psychologically implausible, but they are statistically simple. In the conclusion, we show that this two-parameter model is one interpretation of the conventional method described in the introduction of using free-recall and cued-recall performance to separately measure storage and retrieval, and therefore is useful as a means of evaluating the conventional method. Unlike the other models, the two- and three-parameter models require a coarser event partition. For example, M_3 in Fig. 12.2 implies that events E_4 and E_5 cannot occur. The five- and four-parameter models form the set of six models that may be suitable for measurement purposes, so we focus on these models for the remainder of the chapter. The model equations for these six models can be found in the Appendix.

STATISTICAL INFERENCE

Riefer and Batchelder (1988, 1991) described methods for statistical inference for multinomial models like those in Fig. 12.2. Their approach was based on the likelihood function, and in subsequent papers by

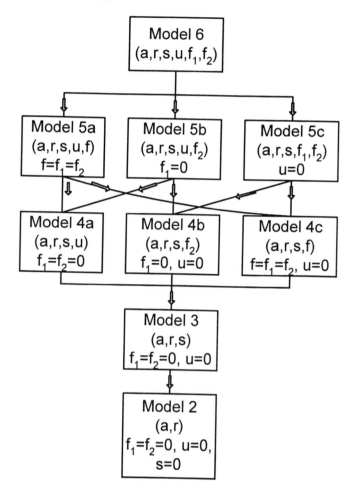

FIG. 12.2. The family of nested multinomial models of the general multinomial model. Lower models are nested in models above them and connected by lines. The arrows point from parent models to nested submodels.

Batchelder (1991) and Hu and Batchelder (1994), a more general approach based on the Reed and Cressie (1988) family of goodness-of-fit measures was described. Hu and Batchelder (1994) described parameter estimation, goodness-of-fit, and hypothesis testing using the EM (expectancy maximization) algorithm described in Dempster, Laird, and Rubin (1977), and they generalized it to the Reed and Cressie family. Hu[1] (1991)

---

[1]The latest version can be obtained by writing to Dr. Xiangen Hu, Department of Psychology, University of Memphis, Memphis, TN 38152. Alternatively, the program is available through a website at http://irvin.psyc.memphis.edu/gpt/.

is a software package that can be used to carry out inference for multinomial processing tree models like those in Fig. 12.2.

Closed-form maximum likelihood estimators (MLEs) for models M_{5a}, M_{5b}, M_{5c}, and M_{4a} are presented in Appendix A. The estimators are MLEs only if the observable $\langle P_i \rangle^6_{i=1}$ satisfy certain inequality restrictions; otherwise the EM algorithm in Hu and Batchelder (1994) can be used to obtain the MLEs. It is easy to detect implicitly when the inequality constraints do not hold, because in that case one or more parameter estimates based on the formulas will fall outside of [0,1]. Unfortunately, we cannot provide an explicit characterization of these inequality constraints for all models. Appendix A does provide them for models M_{4a} and M_{5c}, however. One advantage of closed-form MLEs as provided in the Appendix is that they generally facilitate the inferential analysis of the models with respect to such issues as individual parameter variation and sparse frequencies. In this section we concentrate on results derived from those closed-formed estimators. A more complete analysis would require the repeated use of iterative algorithms to assess the inference properties of the models for data that violate the inequality constraints.

In the remaining subsections of this section, we consider several issues of inference particular to the models of Fig. 12.2. However, before doing this, we discuss in more detail the inequality restrictions, which will be helpful in addressing the more substantive statistical issues.

Constraints on Explicit MLE Expressions

In GPT models, explicit expressions for MLEs are almost always accompanied by inequality constraints among the observed category proportions (e.g., Batchelder & Riefer, 1986, 1990). Using the notation in Riefer and Batchelder (1988), the parameter space of the general model, Ω_6, can be subscripted to indicate the parameter space of a particular model. For example,

$$\Omega_{5a} = \{\langle a,\ r,\ f,\ f,\ s,\ u\rangle \mid 0 \le a,\ r,\ f,\ s,\ u,\ \le 1\} \subseteq \Omega_6$$

We denote the simplex of all possible probability distributions over J category events as $G_J = \{\langle p_i \rangle^J_{i=1} \mid \Sigma^J_{i=1}\ p_i = 1,\ p_i \ge 0\}$. The parameter space for a given model induces restrictions on G_J, and we denote the set of all possible probability distributions consistent with Ω as Ω^*. For example,

$$\Omega^*_{5a} = \{\langle p_i(\theta)\rangle^6_{i=1} \mid \theta \in \Omega_{5a}\} \subseteq G_6$$

In the case of the five-parameter models in Fig. 12.2, closed-form MLEs can be obtained by solving the $p_i(\theta)$ equations directly because the models are *saturated*, that is, five parameters for five degrees of freedom. Appendix A provides these solutions. They can be used to yield MLEs only when they result in estimates of each parameter in [0,1]. However, when one or more of the estimates fall outside of [0,1], it means that the observed P_i's do not satisfy certain constraints. Because the models are saturated, these constraints are violated for an observation $\langle P_i \rangle_{i=1}^6$ iff

$$\langle P_i \rangle_{i=1}^6 \in G_6 - \Omega_{5x}^* \tag{3}$$

where x is a, b, or c. Equation 8, in Appendix A, provides an explicit characterization of one of the constraints implicit in the equations for model M_{5c}; however, we were unable to obtain an explicit characterization of the constraints for models M_{5a} and M_{5b}.

The constraints for model M_{5c} are quite severe and are frequently violated in data. For example, Table 12.1 shows 10 data sets that have been obtained in our laboratory using the free-then-cued-recall paradigm. As can be seen, only 3 of the 10 sets satisfy Equation 8.

We studied the constraints in models M_{5a} and M_{5b} by Monte Carlo techniques. We used parameter values that reflected those that fit our laboratory data such as in Table 12.1. Frequently, MLEs using the EM algorithm on real data yield values of $\hat{a}$ and $\hat{r}$ far away from the boundaries of [0,1], but the other parameters, s, u, f_1, and f_2, are sometimes estimated at values near zero. We simulated samples as small as $N = 100$, which corresponds to a small experiment, and as large as $N = 1,000$, which corresponds to an extremely large experiment (a typical experiment has 20 subjects yielding 10 counts in a condition for a total of 200 counts per condition). The values of the storage and retrieval parameters were varied independently from 0.30 to 0.85, each in three increments. This yielded nine

TABLE 12.1
Empirical Model-Based Statistics

N_1	N_2	N_3	N_4	N_5	N_6	Satisfy Equation 8
93	14	37	0	10	44	Yes
80	5	71	2	7	33	No
86	14	36	1	11	44	Yes
83	7	47	2	11	42	No
103	2	46	0	7	22	No
80	0	65	3	9	23	No
61	4	81	0	11	107	No
36	7	43	1	19	156	Yes
120	3	145	1	3	25	No
138	5	87	2	9	56	No

Note. N_1 = both items freely recalled, correct cued recall; N_2 = exactly one item freely recalled, correct cued recall; N_3 = neither item freely recalled, correct cued recall; N_4 = both items freely recalled, incorrect cued recall; N_5 = exactly one item freely recalled, incorrect cued recall; N_6 = neither item freely recalled, incorrect cued recall.

conditions for each model, and 100,000 simulations were performed for each condition.

To simulate M_{5a}, the values of the other three parameters were set at $s = 0.05$, $u = 0.10$, and $f = 0.01$, and these values were chosen because they are representative of parameters estimated by this model with the data in Table 12.1. Table 12.2 provides the percentage of times the constraints implicit in the GPT equations (Equation 5 in Appendix A) were violated for various sample sizes.

The result of the simulations is that many observations violate the constraints, even in samples as large as 1,000 items. As the underlying parameter values are valid (e.g., within [0,1]), these violations are generated solely by the variability of the multinomial process. The vast majority of these violations occur because in the model M_{5a} the explicit estimators given in the Appendix map observations into a vector with $0 \leq \hat{a}, \hat{r}, \hat{s}, \hat{u} \leq 1$ and $\hat{f} < 0$, and the percentage of observations for $N = 100$ that were violations with this property are shown in the last column of Table 12.2.

The explicit parameter estimators are derived from calculus-based maximization techniques that do not constrain the parameters into [0,1]. As the true value of f is quite low (0.01), and the explicit estimator $\hat{f}$ is unconstrained on the real numbers, it is not surprising that many observations map into $\hat{f} < 0$, resulting in violations. The predominance of this violation does not indicate a discordance between model and data (clearly there is none, as the data were generated with the model). Instead it indicates that the analytic calculus methods used to obtain the parameter estimators do not incorporate an important inequality constraint among the true underlying model probabilities. These difficulties are easily avoided by using a constrained iterative search method, such as the EM algorithm.

TABLE 12.2
Constraint Violations for Model M_{5a}

True Values		Percentage of Constraint Violations			
a	r	$N = 1,000$	$N = 200$	$N = 100$	$N = 100$ and $\hat{f} < 0$
0.30	0.30	40.74	50.55	54.36	54.36
0.30	0.55	32.27	46.19	51.21	51.21
0.30	0.85	23.40	41.76	48.64	47.76
0.55	0.30	28.66	44.50	57.27	57.27
0.55	0.55	15.39	36.57	50.61	50.61
0.55	0.85	06.77	28.81	43.72	43.68
0.85	0.30	10.87	45.81	67.12	66.55
0.85	0.55	02.36	30.84	54.50	53.84
0.85	0.85	00.33	18.95	42.81	41.87

Note. a = probability of associative storage and r = probability of associative retrieval. In all simulations the nuisance parameters were $s = 0.05$, $u = 0.10$, and $f = 0.01$.

TABLE 12.3
Constraint Violations for Model M_{5b}

True Values		Percentage of Constraint Violations		
a	r	$N = 1,000$	$N = 200$	$N = 100$
0.30	0.30	11.39	30.92	37.53
0.30	0.55	21.43	37.51	42.42
0.30	0.85	39.41	46.98	52.10
0.55	0.30	00.94	15.97	25.56
0.55	0.55	04.98	24.78	33.27
0.55	0.85	27.58	41.64	46.44
0.85	0.30	00.04	07.92	18.83
0.85	0.55	00.29	12.98	24.54
0.85	0.85	09.50	31.22	40.63

Note. a = probability of associative storage and r = probability of associative retrieval. In all simulations the nuisance parameters were $s = 0.05$, $u = 0.10$, and $f = 0.01$.

To simulate M_{5b} (Table 12.3), the values of the other three parameters were set at $s = 0.03$, $u = 0.30$, and $f = 0.40$, and these values were chosen because they are representative of parameters estimated by this model with the data in Table 12.1. Again, the result of this simulation is that there is a large percentage of constraint violations, albeit somewhat less than for model M_{5b} or M_{5c}. Again, the conclusion reached is that this model entails underlying constraints on model probabilities, and these constraints are not accounted for in the explicit estimators in the Appendix.

It is easy to derive explicit expressions for the inequality constraints on the model probabilities for M_{4a}, and these are in Equation 10. The major consequence of these constraints is that P_2 cannot be too big as compared to P_1 and P_3. As P_1, P_3, and P_6 are usually sizable, these constraints have never been violated in our laboratory data sets.

Identifiability

As noted before, a model is identifiable if $p(\theta) = p(\theta')$ implies $\theta = \theta'$, for all $\theta, \theta' \in \Omega$. In general, identifiability is a property of the model equations and not of the estimators. It is fairly easy to show identifiability for models M_{5b} and M_{5c}, and the proof is in Appendix B. Because the three- and four-parameter models are nested submodels of either M_{5b} or M_{5c}, the identifiability of M_{5b} and M_{5c} implies the identifiability of the three- and four-parameter models.

Unfortunately, the algebra involved in showing the identifiability for model M_{5a} proved intractable. As an alternative, we show "simulated identifiability." Parameters in Ω_{5a} are randomly sampled from a uniform distribution and model probabilities are generated by Equation 5 (in Appendix A). These model probabilities are within Ω_{5a}^*, and therefore obey the inequality constraints. Using the explicit expression for the MLEs, we recover two parameter estimate vectors (one from each root). If there are any probability vectors that give rise to two distinct parameter vectors, both of which are in Ω_{5a}, then the model has failed simulated identifiability. We simulated models M_{5a} over a billion times and found no probability vectors that violated simulated identifiability for this model. Of course this does not prove identifiability, but may be an adequate substitute for an analytic result at least for practical purposes.

Parameter Sensitivity to Low-Frequency Events

The data event E_4, in which the subject correctly recalls both the stimulus and response term in free recall, yet misses the cued recall, has occurred infrequently in the data sets we have seen. In conventional memory theory, an E_4 event is theoretically troubling, as it implies the retrieval of an item that has not been stored. All six models contain processes that account for E_4 events. However, unless the time interval between the two memory tests is large, one would expect observations in E_4 to be sparse.

When a category has at most a few observations, it is well known that asymptotic statistics may not be appropriate (e.g., Reed & Cressie, 1988). The problem is compounded when a category has zero frequency, and in such cases one can use pseudo-Bayesian procedures to analyze the data (e.g., Bishop, Fineberg, & Holland, 1975). For the current models the problem of concern is the effect on the parameter estimates of sparse categories like E_4. In the multinomial distributions the ratio of variance to mean of a category count is $1 - p_i$. As the frequency of E_4 events is typically quite low (less than 1% of the total observations), we expect that they exhibit a large variance to mean ratio. In all the models, the processes that produce E_4 events are not directly related to storage and retrieval processes. Therefore, it is desirable that the storage and retrieval parameter estimators, $(\hat{a}, \hat{r})$, are relatively unaffected by fluctuations in the estimator of p_4.

One method of assessing the dependence of storage and retrieval parameter estimators on variability in the estimator of p_4 is straightforward, namely, to compute the partial derivative of each parameter estimator with respect to P_4. Of course, such a method is only feasible when the MLE is expressed explicitly. For example, the following equations are the derivatives for model M_{4a}. It is most convenient to express each P_i as N_i/N and differentiate with respect to N_4, where N is the total number of item pairs. In this case the N_i, $i \neq 4$, are not directly functions of N_4, but N is.

$$\frac{\partial \hat{a}}{\partial N_4} = -\frac{N_1 + N_2 + N_3}{N^2} \tag{4a}$$

$$\frac{\partial \hat{r}}{\partial N_4} = 0 \tag{4b}$$

$$\frac{\partial \hat{s}}{\partial N_4} = 0 \tag{4c}$$

$$\frac{\partial \hat{u}}{\partial N_4} = \frac{N_5 + 2N_6}{2(N_4 + N_5 + N_6)^2} \tag{4d}$$

Equations 4a–4b show that the storage estimator, $\hat{a}$, mildly decreases with N_4, and the retrieval estimator, $\hat{r}$, has no dependence on N_4. This is encouraging because it shows that the accuracy of estimation of these parameters is not severely affected by the value of N_4, the usually sparse category.

The preceding differentiation method can be applied to any of the explicit parameter estimators in the Appendix, but the implications of the derivatives are only meaningful for those $\langle P_i \rangle_{i=1}^6$ that do not violate the previously discussed inequality constraints. The algebra produced by this differentiation is formidable in models M_{5a} and M_{5b}, so we do not include it. Instead, we performed computer simulations by systematically varying the value of N_4 from 0 counts to 10 counts while holding all other data frequencies constant. This, of course, varies the value of N. Although the N_i statistics are integer valued in empirical settings, this is not necessary for simulations. The model equations remain valid for real-valued N_i's. In the following simulations, the value of N_i is varied in increments of 0.1.

We noted the following three properties of the data in Table 12.1 in choosing frequency counts for the other five categories:

1. E_1, E_3, and E_6 are the only categories which receive more than 10% of the counts.
2. The actual percentage of counts in E_1, E_3, and E_6 varies substantially from experiment to experiment.
3. The counts in E_5 are positively correlated to those in E_6.

We chose a set of nine observations that roughly approximate these three properties. Figures 12.3 and 12.4, each composed of nine panels, show the result of varying N_4 on the parameter estimators for models M_{5a} and M_{5b}, respectively, for these nine observations. The category frequencies for the nine observations are reported as a six-tuple at either the top left-hand corner (Fig. 12.3) or the bottom center (Fig. 12.4), where the asterisk

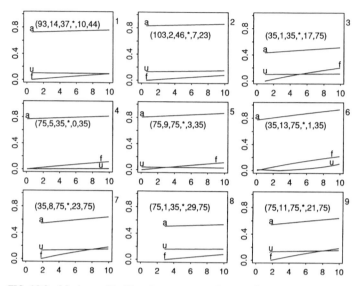

FIG. 12.3.   Maximum likelihood parameter estimates of parameters a, f, and u as a function of N_4 for model M_{5a} for nine selected observations. The frequency counts for each observation is the six-tuple in the top left corner of each panel, where the asterisk denotes the variable N_4 frequency. The plotted parameter estimates are derived by inserting the six-tuple observation into the explicit estimators in the Appendix. The intervals in which no parameter estimates are reported correspond to observations that violate the model constraints.

denotes the variable N_4 frequency. We calculated parameter estimates using the explicit expressions for the MLEs.

In both figures there are panels in which, at some values of N_4, no parameter estimates are plotted; for example, panels 5 and 6 of Fig. 12.4 contain large intervals of values of N_4 in which there are no reported parameter estimates. This is because the observation violated the inequality constraints and such parameter estimates are not MLEs. A more thorough analysis of the effects of N_4 on the parameter estimates would require using the EM algorithm or some other iterative search.

The results of the simulations are quite encouraging for model M_{5a}. Note that $\hat{r}$ and $\hat{s}$ are not functions of N_4 or N (this can be confirmed from inspection of the closed-form parameter estimators of $\hat{r}$ and $\hat{s}$ in the Appendix). There are observations that violate the constraints, but they occur only when N_4 is near zero (e.g., the bottom row of panels), indicating that the constraint violation has to do with small p_4. In all panels, where it is defined, the storage parameter changes slowly, and approximately linearly with N_4. The greatest change in $\hat{a}$ is in panel 6, with a slope of 0.016 per count of N_4.

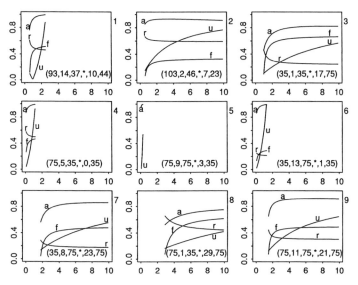

FIG. 12.4. Maximum likelihood parameter estimates of parameters a, r, f, and u as a function of N_4 for model M_{5b} for nine selected observation. Figure 12.4 is analogous to Fig. 12.3 with the exception that the observation six-tuple is reported in the bottom portion of each panel.

The results of simulations for model M_{5b} in Fig. 12.4 show that the inequality constraints for the nine selected observations are much more severe than in model M_{5a}. All nine panels contain observations that violate the inequality constraints. Unlike the simulations of model M_{5a}, the values of N_4 that violate the constraints are not confined to near zero values. For example, in panel 5 the observations violate the constraints for all $N_4 \leq$ 10 except the interval $0.1 \leq N_4 \leq 0.3$. Even for observations in which the explicit parameter estimators were MLEs, the dependence of the parameters on N_4 was both severe and highly nonlinear for small values of N_4. However, in several panels, the parameter estimators $\hat{a}$ and $\hat{r}$ show an approximate invariance to the value of N_4 if N_4 is sufficiently large (usually greater than 6). It may be that model M_{5b} is best suited for observations in which E_4 is not such a sparse event.

Individual Differences

A strong assumption of GPT models is that the observations on each item pair are independent and identically distributed (iid) over the categories. In practice, researchers often pool data across several subjects to increase the stability of the parameter estimators. If subjects have individual differences in their underlying parameters, the observations will not be iid. Violations of these statistical assumptions through individual differences may introduce systematic biases and inflate confidence intervals. These effects are easily studied with the explicit MLE expressions. Without the expressions, evaluating assumption violations would involve repeated use of an iterative search algorithm. Both methods are illustrated in Riefer and Batchelder (1991).

We studied the effect of individual differences on model M_{4a}, the model that has the mild inequality constraints as shown in Equations 10a–10c. To simulate individual differences, we varied θ, and hence $\langle p_i(\theta)\rangle_{i=1}^{6}$, for each item pair. This simulates the case where the performance on each item is governed by a different parameter vector. The simulations were similar to those at the beginning of this section, except all the underlying parameter values that generate the observations were sampled from uniform distributions. Let $\mathbf{x} \sim U(m, d)$ denote a random variable $\mathbf{x}$ distributed uniformly on the open interval $(m - d, m + d)$, $d > 0$. Then, for a given condition, the parameters were distributed as $\mathbf{a} \sim U(m_a, 0.15)$, $\mathbf{r} \sim U(m_r, 0.15)$, $\mathbf{u} \sim U(0.10, 0.10)$, and $\mathbf{s} \sim U(0.05, 0.05)$. We believe that these distributions introduce quite a lot of parameter variation and offer a good check on robustness. The values of m_a and m_r, the mean value of the storage and retrieval parameters, respectively, were each varied from 0.35 to 0.85 in three increments as shown in Table 12.4, yielding nine conditions, and 100,000 observations were generated for each condition.

As individual differences are a violation of the model assumptions, it would be desirable if the analysis of data were robust under this violation. One way to assess this is to examine the goodness-of-fit measure. Riefer and Batchelder (1988) and, more recently, Batchelder (1991) discussed the log-likelihood statistic, G^2, as a suitable measure of model fit. For a

TABLE 12.4
Goodness-of-Fit for Model M_{4a} With Individual Differences

True Values		Percentage of Observations With $G^2 \geq 3.84146$			
m_a	m_r	$N = 5,000$	$N = 1,000$	$N = 200$	$N = 100$
0.30	0.30	54.63	15.32	6.94	4.54
0.30	0.55	54.52	15.52	7.07	4.39
0.30	0.85	54.73	15.30	7.02	4.45
0.55	0.30	38.60	12.00	5.12	3.91
0.55	0.55	38.64	11.84	5.01	3.89
0.55	0.85	38.50	11.90	5.22	3.82
0.85	0.30	16.22	7.53	3.34	2.61
0.85	0.55	16.38	7.33	3.26	2.66
0.85	0.85	16.20	7.43	3.36	2.67

Note. m_a = mean of the distribution of storage parameters and m_r = mean of the distribution of retrieval parameters. In all simulations the nuisance parameters were $s = 0.05$, $u = 0.10$, and $f = 0.01$.

four-parameter model, G^2 is asymptotically distributed as chi-squared with one degree of freedom. Table 12.4 shows the percentage of trials in which G^2 was not less than 3.84146, the value at which a model is rejected with $p < .05$. If the model were true, then each entry should be about 5.00%.

From the results in Table 12.4, it is very difficult to reject the model on the basis of individual differences when the observations are in the range of several hundred counts, as the probabilities of rejection are still a few one-hundredths from the asymptotic chi-squared values. This shows that the model is robust for such typical experimental sample sizes under the conditions of the simulation.

We also looked at the parameter estimates generated in the simulation. Even though the simulated data were produced in violation of the model's assumption, the estimated parameter values did not exhibit any marked bias. The worst cases are for the simulations where the observations are from 100 item pairs, and the following summarizes those results. The means of the storage and retrieval estimates vary from the means of the corresponding underlying distribution by no more than 0.003. The standard deviations of the storage estimators are less than 0.05 for all conditions. The standard deviations of the retrieval estimator are dependent on the value of a. This is not unexpected, as an attempt at retrieval is contingent on successful storage. If an item is not stored, then it can provide no information about the probability of retrieval. The standard deviation of the retrieval estimators is somewhat high for small a, about 0.09, and decreases to 0.03 for larger a. Overall, the fact that parameter estimators are robust in the presence of individual parameter variation is quite encouraging for users of model M_{4a}. In the analysis we have not studied all the models for robustness; however, the methodology for doing this should be clear from this study of model M_{4a}.

BIZARRE IMAGERY: AN EMPIRICAL EXAMPLE

In this section, we use experimental data to compare the performances of the multinomial models. Riefer and Rouder (1992) collected data in the free-then-cued-recall paradigm to assess the storage-retrieval basis of the bizarre imagery effect. Although early research indicated that bizarre imagery is no more memorable than common imagery (e.g., Bergfeld, Choat, & Kroll, 1982; Cox & Wollen, 1981; Wollen, Weber, & Lowery, 1972), more recent research (e.g., Einstein et al., 1989; Hirshman et al., 1989; Riefer & Rouder, 1992) has shown that, under certain conditions, bizarre imagery can have a reliable and beneficial effect on recall. Current theories center on either a retrieval-based explanation of the phenomenon, such as the assumption that the distinctiveness of bizarre images leaves them less susceptible to interference (e.g., Einstein et al., 1989; McDaniel & Einstein, 1991), or storage-based explanations, such as the assumption that bizarre items demand more attention, leaving them better encoded (e.g., Merry, 1980; Wollen & Cox, 1981).

Riefer and Rouder (1992) collected data from 95 subjects using the free-then-cued paradigm in a mixed list design. They asked subjects to form images of presented sentences that related two concrete nouns either in an ordinary manner or in a bizarre manner. An example of an ordinary relationship between the nouns is, "The minister read the bible." An example of a bizarre relationship between the nouns is, "The minister ate the bible." We concentrate on Riefer and Rouder's Experiment 3, as their restricted model did not fit the data. Riefer and Rouder found a significant advantage for bizarre imagery in free recall only ($p < .05$) with univariate t-tests across sentences. The category N_i statistics and empirical statistics are shown in Table 12.5.

Parameter estimates for the five-parameter models are shown in Table 12.6. Model M_{4a} is the only four-parameter model that provides an acceptable fit with the log-likelihood statistic, and the parameter estimators for this model are provided in Table 12.6. Models M_{4b} and M_{4c} do not fit the data, with G^2 exceeding 80 in each condition for each model ($p < .01$), and are dropped from the analysis.

Hypothesis testing on parameters in the two different conditions is done through the log-likelihood framework (as described in Riefer & Batchelder, 1988). The results from all four models are similar. Subjects significantly retrieve more item pairs in the bizarre condition than in the common condition, although there is no significant difference in the storage of item pairs across conditions. The values of the singleton parameters, $\hat{s}$ and $\hat{u}$, which represent the probability of recalling words without retrieving (or storing and retrieving) the association, is relatively low with the exception of the analysis of the common condition with model M_{5b}. According to the models, processing of the word pairs occurs much more often as a whole unit, rather than as a singleton. The value of $\hat{f_1}$ and $\hat{f_2}$, the prob-

TABLE 12.5
Category Count and Empirical Statistics
for Riefer and Rouder's Experiment 3

Condition	N_1	N_2	N_3	N_4	N_5	N_6	Free Recall	Cued Recall
Bizarre	103	2	46	0	7	22	0.62	0.84
Common	80	0	65	3	9	23	0.51	0.81

Note. N_1 = both items freely recalled, correct cued recall; N_2 = exactly one item freely recalled, correct cued recall; N_3 = neither item freely recalled, correct cued recall; N_4 = both items freely recalled, incorrect cued recall; N_5 = exactly one item freely recalled, incorrect cued recall; N_6 = neither item freely recalled, incorrect cued recall.

TABLE 12.6
Parameter Estimates and Fits

Condition	$\hat{a}$	$\hat{r}$	$\hat{s}$	$\hat{u}$	$\hat{f}$	$\hat{f_1}$	$\hat{f_2}$	G_z
M_{5a}								
Bizarre	0.830	0.675[‡]	0.031	0.149	0.003	—	—	—
Common	0.824	0.547[‡]	0.008	0.189	0.034	—	—	—
M_{5b}								
Bizarre	0.880	0.635[†]	0.031	0.211	—	—	0.162	—
Common	0.894	0.517[†]	0.008	0.451	—	—	0.152	—
M_{5c}								
Bizarre	1.000	0.636	0.103	—	—	0.047	0.148	—
Common	1.000	0.518	0.076	—	—	0.009	0.152	—
M_{4a}								
Bizarre	0.828	0.675[‡]	0.031	0.156	—	—	—	0.200
Common	0.796	0.547[‡]	0.008	0.237	—	—	—	1.765

Note. The EM algorithm was used to obtain the estimates and fits. Hu's software package (1991) increases the frequency of each data category by one when there are categories with no counts. This occurs for both conditions, and hence, the estimates and fits for all six models in both conditions are based on these increased frequencies.
[†]$p < .10.$
[‡]$p < .05.$

abilities of forgetting, are also small. Furthermore, $\hat{f_1} < \hat{f_2}$, indicating that successful retrieval leaves the memory representation more immune to forgetting. The results concerning storage and retrieval match those of Riefer and Rouder (1992), which is not surprising as the measurement models employed are similar when singleton recall rates are low. The multinomial model analyses concur with the conclusions drawn from more conventional analyses (Einstein et al., 1989; Hirshman et al., 1989) that the mnemonic advantage of bizarre imagery is due to the increased retrievability of bizarre imagery over that of common imagery.

It is fortunate that although the four applicable models yield different numerical estimates for storage and retrieval, they each produce the same pattern of results. This indicates that for these observations, the pattern of results is not highly dependent on the particulars of modeling the nuisance processes (singleton storage, forgetting).

This lack of dependence of the results on the modeling of nuisance processes may not be true for other data sets. One method of assessing whether two models might yield a similar pattern of results is to examine the covariation of the parameters across models. For example, consider two observations from different experimental conditions and two different models. If the first model yields a higher value for storage in the first condition than the second condition, it is desirable that the second model also do so.

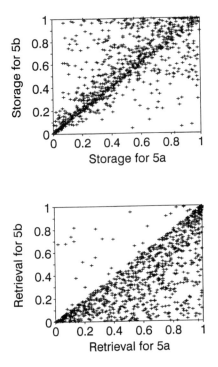

FIG. 12.5. Scatter plots of parameter estimates. The top panel plots the storage estimates of model M_{5b} versus those of model M_{5a}. The bottom panel plots the retrieval estimates of model M_{5b} versus those of model M_{5a}.

To evaluate the covariation of the parameters between models M_{5a} and M_{5b}, we used the explicit expressions in Appendix A to generate scatter plots of parameter estimates by randomly sampling 1,000 parameter vectors (with uniform probability) from $\Omega_{5a}^{*} \cap \Omega_{5b}^{*}$. The first panel of Fig. 12.5 shows the relationship between storage estimates for the two models, and there is a positive correlation ($R^2 = 0.58$). The second panel shows the relationship between retrieval estimators, and although there is a positive correlation ($R^2 = 0.52$), the plot is more indicative of an entailment relation where the retrieval estimates for M_{5b} are an upper bound for those of M_{5a}. Although this is interesting, it raises the possibility that an empirical manipulation may increase retrieval when analyzed with M_{5b} but not when analyzed with M_{5a}.

When multinomial models disagree about the locus of empirical effects, one or more models can be discarded by performing empirical benchmarks, where manipulations thought to affect only one of the processes can be executed. For example, manipulating the duration of the study time per item should have its primary effects on storage, and not on retrieval. Likewise, manipulations that occur during recall, such as changing the physical environment between study and recall, are assumed to affect only retrieval. Varying the delay between the free-recall task and the cued recall is assumed to affect only forgetting.

CONCLUSION

In this chapter we developed a family of multinomial models for the measurement of storage and retrieval processes with the free-then-cued-recall paradigm. By deriving the explicit expressions for the MLEs, we were able to explore a number of issues related to statistical inference, including parameter sensitivity to sparse frequency events and parameter variation from individual differences. Model M_{4a} is a four-parameter, testable and identifiable model in which the parameter estimators are robust to individual differences and categories with sparse frequencies. Furthermore, the model fit most of the empirical data sets generated in our laboratory. Model M_{4a} is obtained by allowing no forgetting, that is, $f = f_1 = f_2 = 0$, and this is a reasonable assumption given that in most of our laboratory applications the cued-recall task immediately followed the free-recall task. Finally, we also analyzed the other two bizarre imagery experiments from Riefer and Rouder (1992) and found that model M_{4a} fits those data sets. The G^2 values for both models for the four experimental conditions (two per experiment) can be found in Table 12.7. Model M_{4a} has a smaller G^2 value for all four conditions than Riefer and Rouder's four-parameter model.

Although it is common to contrast performance on separate memory tasks as measures of different memory processes, major criticisms of this method center around the implied independence of the memory tasks. We believe the multinomial models are one way of explicitly modeling the dependence of separate task performance scores on common underlying processes, especially when coupled with robustness analyses for individual parameter variability. We conclude with a simple illustration of how treating empirical measures as statistically independent random variables can lead to false conclusions.

Let's assume that subjects produce data according to model M_2 of Fig. 12.2. Because subjects have neither forgetting nor singleton processes, they produce only three of the six events: E_1, E_3, and E_6. The probability of correct free recall is just ar and the probability of correct cued recall is just a.

Let's assume that a phenomenon only affects retrieval, and conditions in which the phenomenon is manipulated result only in retrieval differ-

TABLE 12.7
$G^2(1)$ Statistics for Riefer and Rouder's Experiments 1 and 2

Condition	Riefer and Rouder's Model	Model M_{4a}
Experiment 1		
Bizarre	1.19	1.02
Common	3.19	2.33
Experiment 2		
Bizarre	0.92	0.10
Common	1.17	1.06

ences. Clearly, only free-recall performance would be affected. However, if the manipulation should affect both storage and retrieval, the situation becomes more complex.

To investigate this, we assign to two hypothetical groups both storage and retrieval parameters, a_1, a_2, r_1, and r_2, respectively, and memory performance scores, cue_1, cue_2, $free_1$, and $free_2$, respectively. Furthermore, we label the groups such that $cue_1 > cue_2$, which implies $a_1 > a_2$. There are three possible relations between the free-recall performance measures: (a) $free_1 > free_2$, which implies $a_1 r_2 > a_2 r_2$; (b) $free_1 = free_2$, which implies $a_1 r_1 = a_2 r_2$; or (c) $free_1 < free_2$, which implies $a_1 r_1 < a_2 r_2$. If either the second or third relation holds, $a_1 > a_2$ implies that $r_1 < r_2$. However, if the first relationship holds, the contrast of free and cued recall is unable to determine the ordering relationship between r_1 and r_2.

The following example, which is due to Riefer and Rouder (1992), demonstrates how this ambiguity can lead to false conclusions when contrasting free-recall and cued-recall measures with an analysis of variance (ANOVA). Suppose that the first group had parameters $\{a_1 = 0.7, r_1 = 0.7\}$ and the second group had parameters $\{a_2 = 0.3, r_2 = 0.3\}$. If model M_2 were used to produce the data, the performance scores for both groups would be $free_1 = 0.49$, $cue_1 = 0.7$, $free_2 = 0.09$, and $cue_2 = 0.3$. An ANOVA of these performance data yields a main effect for type of test and group, but no interaction. A traditional interpretation of this lack of interaction would be that the performance score differences are storage based, because retrieval differences would be manifested differently in the cued-recall task (where retrieval differences are downplayed) than in the free-recall task. In the context of model M_2, such an interpretation is wrong, as the storage parameter difference is as large as the retrieval parameter difference, namely, 0.40.

APPENDIX A: MODELS AND THEIR ESTIMATORS

Model 5a is obtained by assuming that forgetting is not contingent on retrieval. Therefore $f = f_1 = f_2$, and this substitution yields the following empirical probabilities:

$$p_1 = ar(1 - f) + a(1 - r)s^2(1 - f) \tag{5a}$$
$$p_2 = 2a(1 - r)s(1 - s)(1 - f) \tag{5b}$$
$$p_3 = a(1 - r)(1 - s)^2(1 - f) \tag{5c}$$
$$p_4 = arf + a(1 - r)s^2 f + (1 - a)u^2 \tag{5d}$$
$$p_5 = 2a(1 - r)s(1 - s)f + 2(1 - a)u(1 - u) \tag{5e}$$
$$p_6 = a(1 - r)s(1 - s)^2 f + (1 - a)(1 - u)^2. \tag{5f}$$

The system of equations is nonlinear and may yield nonunique solutions for the parameter vector $\theta_{5a} = (a, r, f, s, u)$. If the equation yields one or more solutions within $[0,1]^5$, then these solutions are the maximum likelihood estimators of the parameters. The following are the analytic expressions for the solutions of this system for θ_{5a}.

$$\hat{s} = \frac{P_2}{2P_3 + P_2}$$

$$\hat{r} = \frac{P_1 - \hat{s}^2(P_1 + P_2 + P_3)}{(P_1 + P_2 + P_3)(1 - \hat{s}^2)}$$

$$\hat{a} = \frac{-c_1 \pm \sqrt{c_1^2 - 4c_2c_0}}{2c_2}$$

$$\hat{f} = \frac{\hat{a} - (P_1 + P_2 + P_3)}{\hat{a}}$$

$$\hat{u} = \sqrt{\frac{P_4 - \hat{a}\hat{f}\hat{r} - \hat{a}(1 - \hat{r})\hat{f}\hat{s}^2}{1 - \hat{a}}}$$

where

$$c_2 = -4(1 - \hat{r})\hat{r}(1 - \hat{s})^2$$
$$c_1 = 4[P_6 + (1 - \hat{r})(1 - \hat{s})^2(P_1 + P_2 + P_3) + (1 - \hat{r})(1 - \hat{s})(1 - \hat{s} - b)]$$
$$c_0 = b^2 - 4[P_6 + (1 - \hat{r})(1 - \hat{s})^2(P_1 + P_2 + P_3)]$$
$$b = P_5 + 2P_6 + 2(1 - \hat{r})(1 - \hat{s})(P_1 + P_2 + P_3)$$

Model $5b$ is obtained by assuming that a successful retrieval enhances the trace such that it is immune to forgetting. Therefore $f_1 = 0$, and this substitution yields the following empirical probabilities:

$$p_1 = ar + a(1 - r)s^2(1 - f_2) \tag{6a}$$
$$p_2 = 2a(1 - r)s(1 - s)(1 - f_2) \tag{6b}$$
$$p_3 = a(1 - r)(1 - s)^2(1 - f_2) \tag{6c}$$
$$p_4 = a(1 - r)s^2 f_2 + (1 - a)u^2 \tag{6d}$$
$$p_5 = 2a(1 - r)s(1 - s)f_2 + 2(1 - a)u(1 - u) \tag{6e}$$
$$p_6 = a(1 - r)(1 - s)^2 f_2 + (1 - a)(1 - u)^2 \tag{6f}$$

Parameter estimation is carried in the same fashion as model $5a$ and the estimators are:

$$\hat{s} = \frac{P_2}{2P_3 + P_2}$$

$$\hat{f}_2 = \frac{-c_1 \pm \sqrt{c_1^2 - 4c_2c_0}}{2c_2}$$

$$\hat{a} = P_1 + P_2 + P_3 + \frac{P_3\hat{f}_2}{(1 - \hat{f}_2)(1 - \hat{s})^2}$$

$$\hat{r} = 1 - \frac{P_3}{\hat{a}(1 - \hat{f_2})(1 - \hat{s})^2}$$

$$\hat{u} = \sqrt{\frac{P_4 - \hat{a}(1 - \hat{r})\hat{s}^2\,\hat{f_2}}{1 - \hat{a}}}$$

where

$$c_2 = (b + 2P_3)^2 - 4[zP_6(1 - \hat{s})^2 + P_6P_3 + P_3z(1 - \hat{s})^2 + P_3]$$
$$c_1 = 4[2zP_6(1 - \hat{s})^2 + P_6P_3 + P_3z(1 - \hat{s})^2] - 2b(b + P_3)$$
$$c_0 = b^2 - 4zP_6(1 - \hat{s})^2$$
$$b = (1 - \hat{s})(P_5 + 2P_6)$$
$$z = P_4 + P_5 + P_6$$

Model $5c$ is obtained by assuming that the word pair is remembered only as a whole, and it is not possible to store just stimulus or response as singletons. Therefore, $u = 0$, and the probabilities of the empirical data categories are:

$$p_1 = ar(1 - f_1) + a(1 - r)s^2(1 - f_2) \tag{7a}$$
$$p_2 = 2a(1 - r)s(1 - s)(1 - f_2) \tag{7b}$$
$$p_3 = a(1 - r)(1 - s)^2(1 - f_2) \tag{7c}$$
$$p_4 = ar f_1 + a(1 - r)s^2 f_2 \tag{7d}$$
$$p_5 = 2a(1 - r)s(1 - s)f_2 \tag{7e}$$
$$p_6 = a(1 - r)(1 - s)^2 f_2 + (1 - a) \tag{7f}$$

Parameter estimation is carried out in the same fashion as model $5a$ and the estimators are:

$$\hat{s} = \frac{P_2}{2P_3 + P_2}$$

$$\hat{f_2} = \frac{P_5}{P_2 + P_5}$$

$$\hat{r} = 1 - \frac{P_3}{P_3\hat{f_2} + (1 - P_6)(1 - \hat{f_2})(1 - \hat{s})^2}$$

$$\hat{a} = \frac{P_3}{(1 - \hat{r})(1 - \hat{s})^2(1 - \hat{f_2})}$$

$$\hat{f_1} = \frac{P_4 - \hat{a}\hat{f_2}\hat{s}^2(1 - \hat{r})}{\hat{a}\hat{r}}$$

Because the algebra is relatively simple, it is possible to obtain a closed-form restriction on the data space. The resulting restriction is

$$P_5 \leq \frac{4P_3P_2P_6}{(P_2 + 2P_3)^2} \tag{8}$$

This restriction is substantial as data obtained from the paradigm frequently violate it.

Model 4a is obtained by assuming that postretrieval forgetting is not possible. Therefore $f_1 = f_2 = 0$, and the probabilities of the empirical data categories are:

$$p_1 = ar + a(1 - r)s^2 \tag{9a}$$
$$p_2 = 2a(1 - r)s(1 - s) \tag{9b}$$
$$p_3 = a(1 - r)(1 - s)^2 \tag{9c}$$
$$p_4 = (1 - a)u^2 \tag{9d}$$
$$p_5 = 2(1 - a)u(1 - u) \tag{9e}$$
$$p_6 = (1 - a)(1 - u)^2 \tag{9f}$$

Closed-form maximum likelihood estimators are easily obtained for model 4a using calculus methods (Hogg & Craig, 1978).

$$\hat{a} = P_1 + P_2 + P_3$$

$$\hat{s} = \frac{P_2}{P_2 + 2P_3}$$

$$\hat{r} = \frac{P_1}{P_1 + P_2 + P_3} - \left(\frac{P_2 + P_3}{P_1 + P_2 + P_3}\right)\left(\frac{\hat{s}^2}{1 - \hat{s}^2}\right)$$

$$\hat{u} = \frac{P_5 + 2P_4}{2(P_4 + P_5 + P_6)}$$

From these estimators, it is straightforward to derive space restrictions on the data. The following is a complete list of such restrictions:

$$P_3 > 0 \tag{10a}$$
$$P_4 + P_5 + P_6 > 0 \tag{10b}$$
$$P_1 \leq \frac{P_2^2(P_2 + P_3)}{4P_3^2} \tag{10c}$$

These restrictions are rather mild because in data it usually happens that P_1 and P_3 are substantially larger than P_2.

Model 4b is obtained by simultaneously assuming that the word pair is remembered only as a whole (no singleton storage) and that retrieval enhances the memory trace such that forgetting is impossible. Therefore, $u = 0$ and $f_1 = 0$, and the probabilities of the empirical data categories are:

$$p_1 = ar + a(11a)(1 - r)s^2(1 - f_2) \tag{11a}$$
$$p_2 = 2a(1 - r)s(1 - s)(1 - f_2) \tag{11b}$$
$$p_3 = a(1 - r)(1 - s)^2(1 - f_2) \tag{11c}$$
$$p_4 = a(1 - r)s^2 f_2 \tag{11d}$$
$$p_5 = 2a(1 - r)s(1 - s)f_2 \tag{11e}$$
$$p_6 = a(1 - r)(1 - s)^2 f_2 + (1 - a) \tag{11f}$$

Model 4c is obtained by simultaneously assuming that the word pair is remembered only as a whole (no singleton storage), and that forgetting is independent of retrieval. Therefore, $u = 0$ and $f = f_1 = f_2$, and the probabilities of the empirical data categories are:

$$p_1 = ar(1 - f) + a(1 - r)s^2(1 - f) \tag{12a}$$
$$p_2 = 2a(1 - r)s(1 - s)(1 - f) \tag{12b}$$
$$p_3 = a(1 - r)(1 - s)^2(1 - f) \tag{12c}$$
$$p_4 = arf + a(1 - r)s^2 f \tag{12d}$$
$$p_5 = 2a(1 - r)s(1 - s)f \tag{12e}$$
$$p_6 = a(1 - r)(1 - s)^2 f + (1 - a) \tag{12f}$$

APPENDIX B: IDENTIFIABILITY

To show identifiability, we show that if two parameter vectors, $\omega = \langle a, r, s, u, f_1, f_2 \rangle$, $\omega' = \langle a', r', s', u', f_1', f_2' \rangle \in \Omega_x$, generate identical event probabilities p, then $\omega = \omega'$, where x is a particular model.

For model M_{5b}, we start with the hypothesis

$$ar + a(1 - r)s^2(1 - f_2) = a'r' + a'(1 - r')s'^2(1 - f_2') \tag{13a}$$
$$a(1 - r)s(1 - s)(1 - f_2) = a'(1 - r')s'(1 - s')(1 - f_2') \tag{13b}$$
$$a(1 - r)(1 - s)^2(1 - f_2) = a'(1 - r')(1 - s')^2(1 - f_2') \tag{13c}$$
$$a(1 - r)s^2 f_2 + (1 - a)u^2 = a'(1 - r')s'^2 f_2' + (1 - a')u'^2 \tag{13d}$$
$$a(1 - r)s(1 - s)f_2 + (1 - a)u(1 - u) =$$
$$\quad a'(1 - r')s'(1 - s')f_2' + (1 - a')u'(1 - u') \tag{13e}$$
$$a(1 - r)(1 - s)^2 f_2 + (1 - a)(1 - u)^2 =$$
$$\quad a'(1 - r')(1 - s')^2 f_2' + (1 - a')(1 - u')^2 \tag{13f}$$

Dividing Equation 13b by Equation 13c yields $s = s'$. Summing Equations 13d, 13e, and 13f and rearranging yields

$$(1 - r)f_2 = a'(1 - r')f_2' + a - a' \tag{14}$$

Substituting this and $s' = s$ into Equations 13d and 13e, and solving for a, respectively yields

$$a = \frac{u'^2 - u^2}{s^2 - u^2} + a' \qquad s \neq u \tag{15a}$$

$$a = \frac{u'(1 - u') - u(1 - u)}{s(1 - s) - u(1 - u)} + a' \qquad s \neq u \tag{15b}$$

Solving these two equations for a yields

$$(u' - u)[s(u' + u) - uu' - s^2] = 0$$

which implies either $u' - u = 0$ or $u = s$ or $u' = s$. Equation 15a is not valid for $u = s$, and substituting $u' = s$ yields $a = 1 + a'$, which implies that $\omega \wedge \omega' \notin \Omega_{5b}$. Therefore $u = u'$, and, by Equation 15a, $a = a'$. Should $u = s$, Equation 14 can be substituted in Equations 13d, 13e, and 13f. The resulting equations can be solved for a', under the constraint $s' \neq u'$.

Summing Equations 13a, 13b, and 13c yields

$$ar + a(1 - r)(1 - f_2) = a'r' + a'(1 - r')(1 - f_2') \tag{16}$$

Substituting $s' = s$ into Equation 13b yields

$$a(1 - r)(1 - f_2) = a'(1 - r')(1 - f_2')$$

Substituting this into Equation 16 yields $ar = a'r'$, which implies $r = r'$, and, by Equation 16, $f = f'$. Thus model M_{5b} is identifiable.

For model M_{5c}, we start with, by hypothesis,

$$ar(1 - f_1) + a(1 - r)s^2(1 - f_2) = a'r'(1 - f_1') + a'(1 - r')s'^2(1 - f_2') \tag{17a}$$
$$a(1 - r)s(1 - s)(1 - f_2) = a'(1 - r')s'(1 - s')(1 - f_2') \tag{17b}$$
$$a(1 - r)(1 - s)^2(1 - f_2) = a'(1 - r')(1 - s')^2(1 - f_2') \tag{17c}$$
$$arf_1 + a(1 - r)s^2 f_2 = a'r'f_1' + a'(1 - r')s'^2f_2' \tag{17d}$$
$$a(1 - r)s(1 - s)f_2 = a'(1 - r')s'(1 - s')f_2' \tag{17e}$$
$$a(1 - r)(1 - s)^2f_2 + (1 - a) = a'(1 - r')(1 - s')^2f_2' + (1 - a'). \tag{17f}$$

Dividing Equation 17b by Equation 17c yields $s = s'$. Dividing Equation 17b by Equation 17e yields $f_2 = f_2'$. Substituting these into Equation 17c implies $a(1 - r) = a'(1 - r')$. Substituting all three equalities into Equation 17f yields

$$a'(1 - r')(1 - s)^2f_2 + (1 - a) = a'(1 - r')(1 - s)^2f_2' + (1 - a')'$$

which implies $a = a'$ and $r = r'$. By Equation 17a, $f_1 = f_1'$. Thus, model M_{5c} is identifiable.

ACKNOWLEDGMENTS

The authors acknowledge the helpful comments of an anonymous reviewer. Also, we acknowledge support to J. Rouder of National Science Foundation training grant DBS-9614278 to the Institute of Mathematical Behavioral Sciences, University of California, Irvine, and National Science Foundation grant SBR-9309667 to W. Batchelder and D. Riefer.

REFERENCES

Batchelder, W. H. (1991). Getting wise about minimum distance measures [Review of *Goodness-of-fit statistics for discrete multivariate data* by T. R. C. Reed and N. A. C. Cressie]. *Journal of Mathematical Psychology, 35,* 267–273.

Batchelder, W. H., & Riefer, D. M. (1986). The statistical analysis of a model for storage and retrieval processes in human memory. *British Journal of Mathematical and Statistical Psychology, 39,* 129–149.

Batchelder, W. H., & Riefer, D. M. (1990). Multinomial processing models of source monitoring. *Psychological Review, 97,* 548–564.

Bergfeld, V. A., Choate, L. S., & Kroll, N. E. A. (1982). The effect of bizarre imagery on memory as a function of delay: Reconfirmation of interaction effect. *Journal of Mental Imagery, 6,* 141–158.

Bishop, Y. M. M., Fineberg, S. E., & Holland, P. W. (1975). *Discrete multivariate analysis: Theory and practice.* Cambridge, MA: MIT Press.

Cox, S. D., & Wollen, K. A. (1981). Bizarreness and recall. *Bulletin of the Psychonomic Society, 18,* 244–245.

Crowther, C. S., Batchelder, W. H., & Hu, X. (1995). A measurement-theoretic analysis of the fuzzy logic model of perception. *Psychological Review, 102,* 396–408.

Dempster, A. P., Laird, N. M., & Rubin, D. B. (1977). Maximum likelihood from incomplete data via the EM algorithm. *Journal of the Royal Statistical Society, Series B, 39,* 1–38.

Drachman, D. A., & Leavitt, J. (1972). Memory impairment in the aged: Storage versus retrieval deficit. *Journal of Experimental Psychology, 93,* 302–308.

Einstein, G. O., McDaniel, M. A., & Lackey, S. (1989). Bizarre imagery, interference, and distinctiveness. *Journal of Experimental Psychology: Learning, Memory, & Cognition, 15,* 137–146.

Flexser, A. J., & Tulving, E. (1993). Recognition failure constraints and the average maximum. *Psychological Review, 100,* 149–153.

Hayman, C. A. G., & Tulving, E. (1989). Contingent disassociation between recognition and fragment completion: The method of triangulation. *Journal of Experimental Psychology: Learning, Memory, & Cognition, 15,* 228–240.

Hintzman, D. L. (1980). Simpson's paradox and the analysis of memory retrieval. *Psychological Review, 87,* 398–410.

Hintzman, D. L. (1993). On variability, Simpson's paradox, and the relation between recognition and recall: Reply to Tulving and Flexser. *Psychological Review, 100,* 143–148.

Hintzman, D. L., & Hartry, A. L. (1990). Item effects in recognition and fragment completion: Category relations vary for different subsets of words. *Journal of Experimental Psychology: Learning, Memory, & Cognition, 16,* 955–969.

Hirshman, E. (1988). The expectation-violation effect: Paradoxical effects of semantic relatedness. *Journal of Memory and Language, 27,* 40–58.

Hirshman, E., Whelley, M. M., & Palij, M. (1989). An investigation of paradoxical memory effects. *Journal of Memory and Language, 28,* 594–609.

Hogg, R. V., & Craig, A. T. (1978). *Introduction to mathematical statistics.* New York: Macmillan.

Hu, X. (1991). *General program for processing tree models (Version 1.0).* Irvine: University of California.

Hu, X., & Batchelder, W. H. (1994). The statistical analysis of general processing tree models with the EM algorithm. *Psychometrica, 59,* 21–47.

Hultsch, D. F. (1975). Adult age differences in retrieval: Trace-dependent and cue-dependent forgetting. *Developmental Psychology, 1,* 197–201.

Jones, G. V. (1987). Independence and exclusivity amone processes: Implications for the structure of recall. *Psychological Review, 94,* 229–235.

McDaniel, M. A., & Einstein, G. O. (1986). Bizarre imagery as an effective memory aid: The importance of distinctiveness. *Journal of Experimental Psychology: Learning, Memory, & Cognition, 12,* 54–65.

McDaniel, M. A., & Einstein, G. O. (1991). Bizarre imagery: Mnemonic benefits and theoretical implications. In R. H. Logie & M. Denis (Eds.), *Mental images in human cognition* (pp. 183–192). New York: Elsevier.

Merry, R. (1980). Image bizarreness in incidental learning. *Psychological Reports, 46,* 427–430.

Pra Baldi, A., de Beni, R., Cornoldi, C., & Cavedon, A. (1985). Some conditions of the occurrence of the bizarreness effect in recall. *British Journal of Psychology, 76,* 427–436.

Reed, T. R. C., & Cressie, N. A. C. (1988). *Goodness-of-fit statistics for discrete multivariate data.* New York: Springer-Verlag.

Riefer, D. M., & Batchelder, W. H. (1988). Multinomial modeling and the measure of cognitive processes. *Psychological Review, 95,* 318–339.

Riefer, D. M., & Batchelder, W. H. (1991). Statistical inference for multinomial processing tree models. In J.-P. Doignon & J.-C. Flamagne (Eds.), *Mathematical psychology: Current developments* (pp. 313–335). New York: Springer-Verlag.

Riefer, D. M., & Batchelder, W. H. (1995). A multinomial modeling analysis of the recognition-failure paradigm. *Memory & Cognition, 23,* 611–630.

Riefer, D. M., & Rouder, J. N. (1992). A multinomial modeling analysis of the mnemonic benefits of bizarre imagery. *Memory & Cognition, 20,* 601–611.

Thomson, D. L., & Tulving, E. (1970). Associative encoding and retrieval: Weak and strong cues. *Journal of Experimental Psychology, 86,* 255–262.

Tulving, E., & Pearlstone, Z. (1966). Availability versus accessibility of information in memory for words. *Journal of Verbal Learning & Verbal Behavior, 5,* 381–391.

Wollen, K. A., & Cox, S. D. (1981). Sentence cueing and the effect of bizarre imagery. *Journal of Experimental Psychology: Human Learning & Memory, 7,* 386–392.

Wollen, S. B., Weber, A., & Lowery, H. D. (1972). Bizarreness versus interaction of mental images as a determinant of learning. *Cognitive Psychology, 3,* 518–523.

Chapter 13

Concept Learning Rates and Transfer Performance of Several Multivariate Neural Network Models

Patrick Suppes
Lin Liang
Stanford University

The purpose of this chapter is to present results for several related learning models, which may be useful both in machine learning and in the analysis of human learning. One motivation has been our desire to develop efficient and powerful methods of concept learning to use in our work on machine learning of natural language (Suppes, Böttner, & Liang, 1995; Suppes, Liang, & Böttner, 1992). In this earlier work, concepts were assumed known and the learning concentrated on language. It is obviously important to combine both concept and language learning for many kinds of situations. In unpublished research we have already used the learning models proposed here in the early stages of robotic concept and language learning.

The models proposed are compared in two major ways: their comparative rates of concept learning, and their comparative transfer performance when the learning of one concept is followed by another. The several models are compared on six sets of data.

1. The well-known Edgar Anderson data on three species of iris. Four measurements are provided on each sample. The data were first made a prominent subject of statistical analysis by Fisher (1936).
2. Measurement data on genuine and forged Swiss bank notes (Flury & Riedwyl, 1988).
3. Measurement data on three species of beetles (Lubischew, 1962).
4. Randomly generated data on an artificial, but interesting, problem of classification. It is that of distinguishing when an observation,

consisting of two "features," the x- and y-coordinates of a point in the plane, lies in a circle of radius r, or in the region bound by this circle and a circle of radius r', with $r' > r$.

5. The classical problem of learning the binary sentential connective exclusive or, usually written XOR.

6. Transfer data from experiments reported in Suppes (1965) on young children learning identity and equipollence of sets.

The first section that follows presents the six models and related theory, beginning with a multivariate normal learning model. The second section introduces a model for comparatively evaluating the performance of the several learning models. The third presents and analyzes the learning results for the several models of data sets 1–5 just described. The fourth section is devoted to problems of transfer, and in particular to data set 6. The final section compares the models and results to a variety of other models discussed in the literature.

SIX ALTERNATIVE LEARNING MODELS

Why so many models? The large number is a reflection of our conviction that we are still a considerable distance from understanding in any very deep way which learning models are most appropriate for which situation. We are especially skeptical of there being one universally best choice. On the other hand, all six of the models are, broadly speaking, neural network models for learning concepts, or, in an equivalent statistical language, learning classifications based on input vectors of feature data.

Thus each model has feature inputs $x_1, \ldots, x_h$, where each feature x_i may be numerical or only binary. The number g of outputs or classification responses is always taken to be finite. Moreover, the learning is always supervised, with the unique correct response being used to update each model after each trial.

Model I: Multivariate Normal Model

The basic assumption of this model is that the features of instances of a concept have a multivariate normal distribution. Surprisingly, this widely used statistical model has been little studied as a learning model, and its learning rate has not been compared to that of alternatives.

First, we make the Bayesian assumption of a prior distribution $\pi = \pi_1$, $\ldots, \pi_g$ on the classification responses assigning an object with the features $\mathbf{x} = (x_1, \ldots, x_h)$ to one of the classes or groups.

To obtain the posterior probability of each class $1, \ldots, g$, we use a uniform prior as a special case of a Dirichilet prior and then compute a Dirichilet-like posterior probability $p_{j,n}$ with parameters α and β for class j on trial n as

$$p_{j,n} = (n_j + \alpha\beta^n) / (\sum_{j=1}^{g} n_j + g\alpha\beta^n) \qquad (1)$$

where $\alpha > 1$ and $0 < \beta < 1$, n_j is the number of members of class j observed through trial n, and so in our setup $\sum n_j = n$. For a general prior π, Equation 1 becomes

$$p_{j,n} = (n_j + \pi_j\alpha\beta^n) / (\sum_{j=1}^{g} n_j + \alpha\beta^n) \qquad (2)$$

Second, we assume that on trial n the group-conditional distribution $f_{j,n}$ of any object, that is, feature vector $\mathbf{x}$, is given by

$$f_{j,n}(\mathbf{x}; \mathbf{m_{j,n}}, \Sigma_{j,n}) = (2\pi)^{-h/2} |\Sigma_{j,n}|^{-\frac{1}{2}} \exp\left\{ -\frac{1}{2}(\mathbf{x} - \mathbf{m_{j,n}})' \Sigma_{j,n}^{-1}(\mathbf{x} - \mathbf{m_{j,n}}) \right\} \qquad (3)$$

where $\mathbf{m_{j,n}}$ is the vector of conditional feature means for category response j at the beginning of trial n, $\Sigma_{j,n}$ is the corresponding feature covariance matrix for category j and trial n, $\mathbf{x}'$ is the transpose of vector $\mathbf{x}$, and h is the number of features (McLachlan, 1992, p. 53). The recursive learning rules for updating on each trial the vector of sample means $\mathbf{m_j}$ and the sample covariance matrix $\mathbf{s_j}$ are the following:

Incremental Computation of Mean. The number m_{ij} is the sample mean of feature x_i for category j. It is unchanged when a category is not the correct response. Incremental computation of m_{ij} [a connection from the feature i to the category j at the $(n + 1)$th step] is as follows. According to the definition we have

$$m_{ij,n+1} = \frac{\sum_{k=1}^{n+1} \delta_{j,k} x_{i,k}}{\sum_{k=1}^{n+1} \delta_{j,k}}$$

$$= \frac{\delta_{j,n+1} x_{i,n+1} + \sum_{k=1}^{n} \delta_{j,k} x_{i,k}}{\sum_{k=1}^{n+1} \delta_{j,k}} \qquad (4)$$

Using the same definition, we also have

$$m_{ij,n} = \frac{\displaystyle\sum_{k=1}^{n} \delta_{j,k} x_{i,k}}{\displaystyle\sum_{k=1}^{n} \delta_{j,k}} \tag{5}$$

Substituting Equation 5 into Equation 4, we find

$$m_{i,j,n+1} = \frac{\delta_{j,n+1} x_{i,n+1} + \displaystyle\sum_{k=1}^{n} \delta_{j,k} m_{ij,n}}{\displaystyle\sum_{k=1}^{n+1} \delta_{j,k}} \tag{6}$$

where $\delta_{j,n}$ denotes that at the nth trial, if the correct response is category j, $\delta_{j,n}$ is 1, and if the correct response is not category j, $\delta_{j,n}$ is zero. (Note that the correct response does not depend on the actual response, but is just the correct classification.)

Incremental Computation of Variance. The variance computations on trial $n + 1$ are also conditioned to the correct response and the incremental computation of variance from a feature i to a category j.

$$V_{ij,n+1} = \frac{\displaystyle\sum_{k=1}^{n+1} \delta_{j,k}(x_{i,k} - m_{ij,n+1})^2}{\displaystyle\sum_{k=1}^{n+1} \delta_{j,k} - 1}$$

$$= \frac{\displaystyle\sum_{k=1}^{n+1} (\delta_{j,k} x_{i,k}^2 - 2\delta_{j,k} x_{i,k} m_{ij,n+1} + \delta_{j,k} m_{ij,n+1}^2)}{\displaystyle\sum_{k=1}^{n+1} \delta_{j,k} - 1}$$

$$= \frac{\displaystyle\sum_{k=1}^{n+1} \delta_{j,k} x_{i,k}^2 - 2 m_{ij,n+1} \displaystyle\sum_{k=1}^{n+1} \delta_{j,k} x_{i,k} + \displaystyle\sum_{k=1}^{n+1} \delta_{j,k} m_{ij,n+1}^2}{\displaystyle\sum_{k=1}^{n+1} \delta_{j,k} - 1}$$

$$= \frac{\sum_{k=1}^{n+1} \delta_{j,k} x_{i,k}^2 - \sum_{k=1}^{n+1} \delta_{j,k} m_{ij,n+1}^2}{\sum_{k=1}^{n+1} \delta_{j,k} - 1} \tag{7}$$

Using the same procedure, we can have

$$V_{ij,n} = \frac{\sum_{k=1}^{n} \delta_{j,k} x_{i,k}^2 - \sum_{k=1}^{n} \delta_{j,k} m_{ij,n}^2}{\sum_{k=1}^{n} \delta_{j,k} - 1} \tag{8}$$

Substituting Equation 8 into Equation 7, we have

$$V_{ij,n+1} = \frac{\delta_{j,n+1} x_{i,n+1}^2 + (\sum_{k=1}^{n} \delta_{j,k} - 1) V_{ij,n} + \sum_{k=1}^{n} \delta_{j,k} m_{ij,n}^2 - \sum_{k=1}^{n+1} \delta_{j,k} m_{ij,n+1}^2}{\sum_{k=1}^{n+1} \delta_{j,k} - 1} \tag{9}$$

In order to do the incremental computation of variance, we need current values and mean values, previous mean values, and previous variances. In Model I, separate computation of the variance is made redundant by the covariance computation, but not in other models, which is why we have shown the recursion here.

Incremental Computation of Covariance. Covariance computations for trial $n + 1$ are also conditioned to the correct response and the incremental computation of covariance from a feature i to a category j.

$$S_{il,j,n+1} = \frac{\sum_{k=1}^{n+1} \delta_{j,k} (x_{i,k} - m_{ij,n+1})(x_{l,k} - m_{lj,n+1})}{\sum_{k=1}^{n+1} \delta_{j,k} - 1}$$

$$= \frac{\sum_{k=1}^{n+1} \delta_{j,k}(x_{i,k}x_{l,k} - x_{i,k}m_{lj,n+1} - x_{l,k}m_{ij,n+1} + m_{ij,n+1}m_{lj,n+1})}{\sum_{k=1}^{n+1} \delta_{j,k} - 1}$$

$$= \frac{\sum_{k=1}^{n+1} \delta_{j,k}x_{i,k}x_{l,k} - \sum_{k=1}^{n+1} \delta_{j,k}m_{ij,n+1}m_{lj,n+1}}{\sum_{k=1}^{n+1} \delta_{j,k} - 1}$$

$$= \frac{\delta_{j,k}x_{i,n+1}x_{l,n+1} + \sum_{k=1}^{n} \delta_{j,k}x_{i,k}x_{l,k} - \sum_{k=1}^{n+1} \delta_{j,k}m_{ij,n+1}m_{lj,n+1}}{\sum_{k=1}^{n+1} \delta_{j,k} - 1} \tag{10}$$

Using the same procedure, we have

$$S_{il,j,n} = \frac{\sum_{k=1}^{n} \delta_{j,k}x_{i,k}x_{l,k} - \sum_{k=1}^{n} \delta_{j,k}m_{ij,n}m_{lj,n}}{\sum_{k=1}^{n} \delta_{j,k} - 1} \tag{11}$$

Substituting Equation 11 into Equation 10, we have

$$S_{il,j,n+1} = \frac{\delta_{j,k}x_{i,n+1}x_{l,n+1} + (\sum_{k=1}^{n} \delta_{j,k} - 1)S_{il,j,n} + \sum_{k=1}^{n} \delta_{j,k}m_{ij,n}m_{lj,n} - \sum_{k=1}^{n+1} \delta_{j,k}m_{ij,n+1}m_{lj,n+1}}{\sum_{k=1}^{n+1} \delta_{j,k} - 1} \tag{12}$$

Of course, when $i = l$, $S_{il,j,n+1} = V_{ij,n+1}$, as given by Equation 9. We show in Fig. 13.1 a simple network for the case of just three features and two responses. The pairs of sample means and variances are the weights of the nodes connecting features x_1, x_2, and x_3 to responses R_1 and R_2. The sample covariances are the weights connecting pairs of features to the responses.

Let p_j denote the prior posterior probability for the group G_j, $j = 1, \ldots,$ g, as defined in Equation 1 and $f_{j,n}$ the group-conditional distribution as

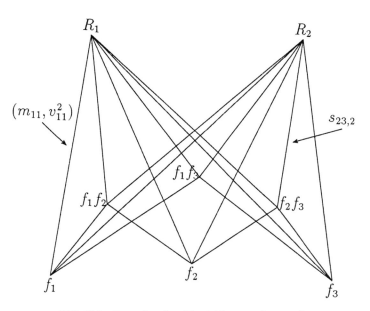

FIG. 13.1. Example of multivariable normal network.

defined in Equation 3. We then use a log ratio to compute the posterior probability of the category given the data. In fact, it is convenient to compute the log.

$$\eta_j = \log(p_j) + \log(|\Sigma_j|^{-\frac{1}{2}} \exp\{-\frac{1}{2}(\mathbf{x} - \mathbf{m_j})'\Sigma_j^{-1}(\mathbf{x} - \mathbf{m_j})\}$$
$$= \log(p_j) - \frac{1}{2}\log(|\Sigma_j|) - \frac{1}{2}(\mathbf{x} - \mathbf{m_j})'\Sigma_j^{-1}(\mathbf{x} - \mathbf{m_j}) \tag{13}$$

Bayes' rule assigns an object or stimulus with feature vector $\mathbf{x}$ to G_{j^*} if j^* is the j that maximizes, for $1 \leq j \leq g$,

$$(\log(p_j) - \frac{1}{2}\log(|\Sigma_j|) - \frac{1}{2}(\mathbf{x} - \mathbf{m_j})'\Sigma_j^{-1}(\mathbf{x} - \mathbf{m_j}))$$

That is, Bayes's rule selects the category j^* that is most probable, given the feature vector $\mathbf{x}$.

Model II: Multivariate Features Only Model

This model is a special case of the multivariate normal model. Only the conditional means and variances of the features x_i are used in the model. The covariance matrix is not recursively computed and therefore is not used in the decision rule. The recursive computations of the means and variances for each response class are just those already given for Model I.

The most probable category choice (minimum probability of error) decision rule for assigning on trial n an input vector $\mathbf{x}$ of features to a response class reduces to the familiar least-square criterion. Pick the response class j for which

$$\sum_{i=1}^{k} \frac{(x_i - m_{ij,n})^2}{V_{ij,n}}$$

is minimum.

Model III: Multinomial Model, Level 1

Like Model II, this model also considers only the features x_i of an input. In Model III, weights w_{ij} that connect feature x_i to response class j are used. They are modified by a linear learning model, rather than conditional variances as in Model II; the conditional means play a similar role in both models. Initially, for $1 \leq i \leq k$ and $1 \leq j \leq g$, $w_{ij} = 1.0$. The linear learning model is defined as follows. First, we introduce a probabilistic aspect with norm $w_{ij,n} = w_{ij,n} / \Sigma_{i=1}^{k} w_{ij,n}$. Second, if for any feature i and incorrect response j on trial n,

$$(\text{norm } w_{ij,n})(x_i - m_{ij,n})^2 > (\text{norm } w_{ij^*,n})(x_i - m_{ij^*,n})^2 \tag{14}$$

where j^* is the correct response, then

$$\begin{aligned} w_{ij,n+1} &= (1 - \theta)w_{ij,n} \\ w_{ij^*,n+1} &= (1 - \theta)w_{ij^*,n} + \theta \end{aligned} \tag{15}$$

Note that learning affects only the weights satisfying the inequality of Equation 14. Third, if the actual response is correct on trial n, no weights are changed:

$$w_{ij,n+1} = w_{ij,n} \quad \text{for} \quad 1 \leq j \leq g, 1 \leq i \leq k \tag{16}$$

The parameter θ is a learning parameter, $0 \leq \theta \leq 1$, which is set a priori in machine learning, but estimated from data in the case of human learning. The decision rule on trial n for assigning an input vector $\mathbf{x}$ of features to a response class is a weighted least-square criterion. Choose the response class j for which

$$\sum_{i=1}^{k} (\text{norm } w_{ij,n})(x_i - m_{ij,n})^2$$

is minimum. In general the x_i's are quantitative features, normed by their conditional variances in Model II, and now in Model III normed rather by what is roughly speaking their probabilities of being associated with a correct response, that is, norm $w_{ij,n}$.

Models IV–VI: Multinomial Models, Levels 2–4

Models IV–VI have the same structure as Model III, with for Model IV the features x_i replaced by the pairwise products $x_i x_{i'}$. For Model V the features x_i are replaced by the triple products $x_i x_{i'} x_{i''}$. For Model VI the features x_i are replaced by the quadruple products $x_i x_{i'} x_{i''} x_{i'''}$. In each of these three models the conditional means $m_{ij,n}$ of Model III are replaced by the appropriate products of conditional means. Weights are for pairs, triples, or quadruples of features, with, of course, all features in a product distinct.

MODEL EVALUATION

We now introduce a learning model that is itself used to evaluate and predict the behavior of the six models introduced in the first section. Let L be a finite nonempty set of learning models whose comparative performance during the course of learning we want to evaluate. Let the evaluation for each model i be the linear learning model, with learning parameter α independent of i. Thus for any model i in L the recursive role is:

$$q_{i,n+1} = \begin{cases} (1 - \alpha)q_{i,n} + \alpha & \text{if a correct prediction was made by model } i \text{ on trial } n \\ (1 - \alpha)q_{i,n} & \text{otherwise} \end{cases}$$

For the evaluation of a given model, we take the initial probability of a correct response to be the same as that of the model, which will in general be the probability that a random response is correct.

Note that for each model i and trial n, $q_{i,n}$ may be interpreted as the probability of a correct prediction by model i on trial n. This evaluation provides a direct comparison of the different models in L, but in addition it provides a means of smoothing the predictions for a given model i during a single run of a sample of the response categories to be learned. It provides a prediction based on the weighting over recent trials determined by α.

EXPERIMENTAL RESULTS

We begin with the iris data.

Iris Data

In Fig. 13.2 we show the mean learning curve for Model I based on 1,000 statistically independent runs through one cycle of the data of 150 iris specimens. Each run sampled the 150 data vectors randomly without re-placement. The mean learning curve is the probability of a correct response in each block of six trials, averaged over the 1,000 runs. The input vector on each trial consists of four measurements in centimeters: sepal length, sepal width, petal length, and petal width. The three-way classification consists of the three species: *Iris setosa, Iris versicolor,* and *Iris virginica.*

As can be seen from the figure, the multivariate normal learning model did very well, reaching an asymptote of 0.973 for the probability of a correct response, on average, after less than 90 trials. (The learning curve is based on blocks of six trials, so each data point is the relative frequency of 6,000 responses.) In effect, this model correctly classified all but two specimens after trial 90. Also shown in Fig. 13.2 is the evaluation curve for $\alpha = 0.3$. Of course the evaluation is really useful in smoothing the data on individual runs, and cannot hope to be as accurate as possible, that is, identical with the mean learning curve. The next figure illustrates this point.

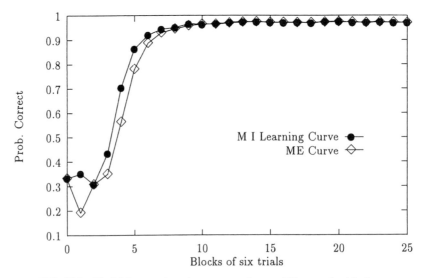

FIG. 13.2. Model I, mean learning curve and mean ME curve for iris data based on 1,000 runs.

In Fig. 13.3, two values of α, 0.1 and 0.3, are used to plot two model evaluation (ME) curves for a single run of Model I. Of course, the larger is α, the better is the fit on average to the individual run, but with $\alpha = 1.0$, we just reproduce by a lag of one trial the individual run and get none of the interesting smoothing effects of the evaluation. On the basis of a great deal of data, but without formal statistical evaluation, we believe $\alpha = 0.3$ is on average near optimal for combining a reasonable degree of smoothing with a reasonable degree of accuracy. How the ME curves smooth an individual learning curve is evident from Fig. 13.3.

In Fig. 13.4 we show, on the basis of 1,000 independent runs—just as in the case of Model I shown in Fig. 13.2—the mean learning curve for Model II, as well as the ME curve based on $\alpha = 0.3$. The results are similar to those for Model I, but not quite as good. The asymptote of the mean learning curve, closely approximated after trial 90, is 0.929.

Similar results are shown for Model III in Fig. 13.5, but the asymptote for the mean learning curve is 0.951, better than Model II but not quite as good as Model I.

In Fig. 13.6 the learning evaluation (ME) curves, with $\alpha = 0.3$, are shown for Models I–III based on the 1,000 independent runs for each model. The most interesting aspect of this figure and others is that it shows that learning is slower for Model I than for either of the other two, even though its asymptotic performance is better. This slowness of learning is not surprising, given the larger number of parameters to be learned from the data. What is surprising is that Model III has a fast rate of learning and also a reasonably good asymptote. Of the three models it is the only one with weights adjusted from trial to trial. In Models I and II all of the parameters are estimated by statistical procedures that are independent of the accuracy of the prediction from trial to trial.

In Fig. 13.7 we show the mean learning curves based on 1,000 independent runs for Models I–VI. With weights based on success or failure

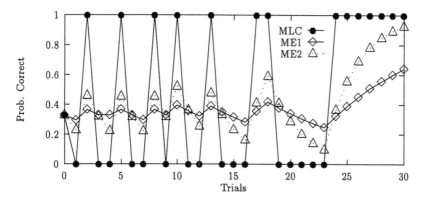

FIG. 13.3. Model I, an individual learning curve and ME curves for two values of α for a single run of iris data (ME1: $\alpha = 0.1$; ME2: $\alpha = 0.3$).

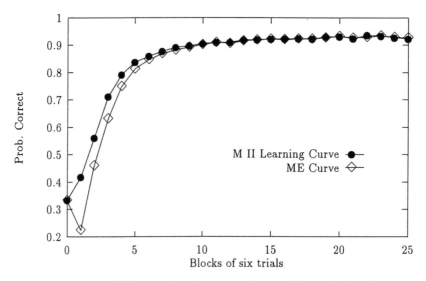

FIG. 13.4.   Model II, mean learning curve and mean ME curve for iris data based on 1,000 runs.

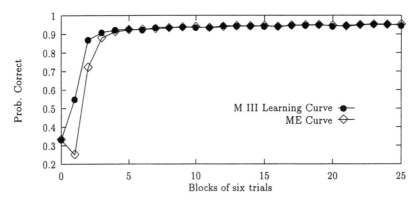

FIG. 13.5.   Model III, mean learning curve and mean ME curve for iris data based on 1,000 runs.

of predictions, Models IV, V, and VI, like Model III, learn faster than Models I and II. These results, and the XOR data, are the only ones we consider for Models IV–VI.

Swiss Bank Note Data

We next consider the Swiss bank note data, consisting of 100 genuine and 100 forged specimens with six measurements on each: length of note, width of margin on the left, width of margin on the right, width of margin

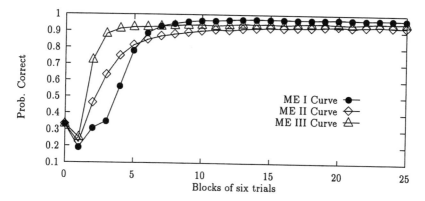

FIG. 13.6. Mean ME curves ($\alpha = 0.3$) of Models I–III for the iris data.

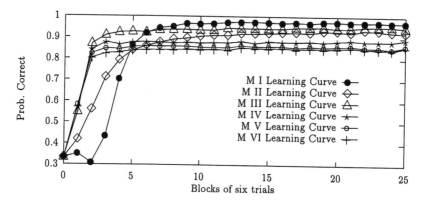

FIG. 13.7. Models I–VI, mean learning curves for iris data.

at bottom, width of margin at top, and length of image diagonal. In Fig. 13.8 we show the mean learning curves for Models I–VI based on 1,000 independent runs. Asymptotically—really by the end of the 200 trials—all the models perform well. However, of comparative importance here is the very fast learning rate of Models III–VI.

Beetle Data

We now turn to the beetle data for three species with 21 specimens of *coleoptera concinna*, 31 specimens of *coleoptera heikertingeri*, and 22 specimens of *coleoptera heptapotamica*. Two measurements were made on each specimen. The measurements are the maximal width of the aedeagus in the forepart (in micrometers) and the front angle of the aedeagus (in units of 7.5 degree). In Fig. 13.9 we show the mean learning curves for Models I–III, based on 1,000 runs. Only the multivariate normal learning model

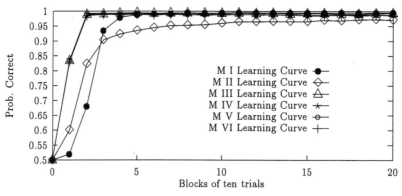

FIG. 13.8. Models I–VI, mean learning curves for bank note data.

comes close to an asymptote of 1. By the end of a run of 72 trials it correctly classified 71 out of 72 specimens. On the other hand, Model III had, as previously, a fast learning rate. The ME curves for the same models shown in Fig. 13.10 are similar in shape to the mean curves shown in Fig. 13.9.

Concentric Circle Data

The concentric circle problem is shown in Fig. 13.11. Response 1 is the correct response for points (x, y) lying in the interior of the inner circle, and response 2 is correct for those in the outer circle but not in the inner circle. The two features are just the x and y coordinates of a point. We

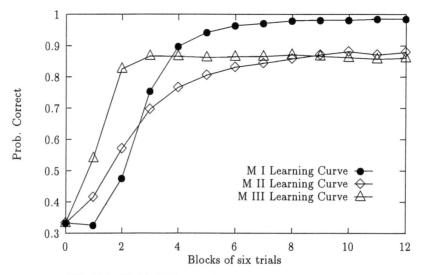

FIG. 13.9. Models I–III, mean learning curves for beetle data.

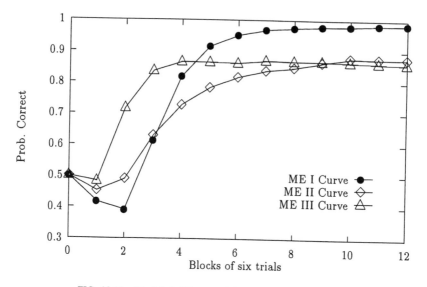

FIG. 13.10. Models I–III, mean ME curves for beetle data.

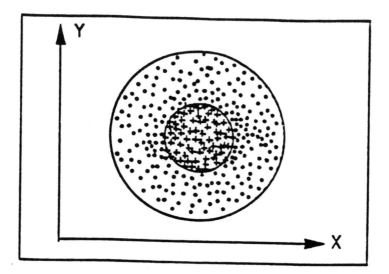

FIG. 13.11. Data points for the problem of two concentric circles.

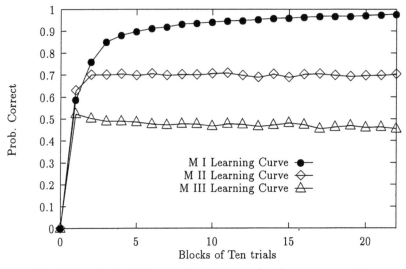

FIG. 13.12. Models I–III, mean learning curve for the concentric circle problem.

ran Models I–III on 1,000 runs of one cycle consisting of 110 feature pairs from the inner circle and 110 from the outer circle lying outside the inner circle. The mean learning curves are shown in Fig. 13.12. Only Model I, the multivariate normal model, did really well. Models II and III performed rather poorly, mainly because the asymptote mean values of the features are the same for both response-conditional distributions. Model III is worse than Model II because no account is taken of the conditional variances, which are different for the two regions.

XOR Data

A classical problem for neural nets is to learn the exclusive or (XOR) sentential connective, which is formally identical to addition mod 2. More explicitly, by the XOR problem, we mean the problem defined by the truth table for XOR. The stimulus inputs are the component truth value pairs, and the correct output is the truth value of the pair for XOR. We take, as in other cases, 1 and −1 for the input values. Ignoring sampling estimates for Model I, then if the probability of each stimulus is 0.5, the variance of the input is 1, and, as is easily computed, the two conditional covariance matrices have the form

$$\begin{pmatrix} 1 & 1 \\ 1 & 1 \end{pmatrix} \quad \begin{pmatrix} 1 & -1 \\ -1 & 1 \end{pmatrix}$$

The first is for truth value 1 and the second for truth value −1. Both matrices are singular. The multivariate normal model fails on this task because the covariance matrix is singular and consequently the posterior probability cannot be computed, because the covariance matrices must be inverted. As is clear from a priori analysis of Models I–III, they cannot solve the problem, and Models V and VI are inapplicable because they require more than two features as input. Model IV, on the other hand, learns in one cycle of four trials, so we do not show a figure for this model. In the language of mathematical learning theory, this is a case of one-trial learning for each pair of feature inputs.

Of interest is a more general model for the two features, f_1 and f_2, namely Model VII, which has in addition to f_1 and f_2 the constructed nodes f_1^2, f_2^2, and $f_1 f_2$. The mean learning curve for 100 runs of two cycles as shown in Fig. 13.13 has one striking characteristic. On the fourth—that is, the last—trial of the first cycle the probability of correct response is zero. The conceptual reason for this, however, has a straightforward explanation. Suppose trial 4 has the presentation of features $(-1, 1)$. Then on the first three trials $(1, 1)$ and $(-1, -1)$ had to be presented. The consequence of this fact is that the conditional mean values of the features for response 1 at the beginning of trial 4 are $f_1 = f_2 = 0$ and $f_1^2 = f_2^2 = f_1 f_2 = 1$. In contrast, for the other conditional distribution, only $(1, -1)$ has been presented and so at the beginning of trial 4 the conditional mean values of the features for response 2 are $f_1 = 1$, $f_2 = f_1 f_3 = -1$, and $f_1^2 = f_2^2 = 1$. Thus, when the least square computation is made for the two possible responses on trial 4, response 2 has a minimum. In particular, it is 6 for

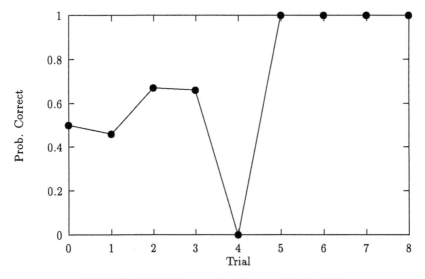

FIG. 13.13. Model IV, mean learning curve for the XOR.

response 1 in contrast to 8 for response 2, when we have ignored the weights in this small number of trials. The analysis is completely similar for presentation of any of the other three feature pairs on trial 4.

ANALYSIS OF TRANSFER

In a great variety of contexts, positive or negative transfer in learning one skill or task after another plays a crucial role in the rate of learning. Problems of transfer are also a way of moving conceptually from a static to a dynamic environment. In spite of a number of claims to the contrary, it is our impression that dynamic environment changes, particularly those involving classical problems of transfer, have as yet been little studied in the literature on neural networks. This is also a problem for standard statistics including Bayesian principles of rationality.

As a setting in which to study transfer, we used the data and analysis of transfer on 24 first-grade children learning for 56 trials equipollence of sets, that is, the concept of sets having the same number of elements, and then learning for 56 trials the concept of identity of sets, as given in Suppes (1965). The sets depicted by the simple stimulus displays had one, two, or three elements. The sets were shown in pairs, and the children were instructed to press one button when the pairs displayed were "the same" and the other button when they were not. In these experiments, no given pair of stimulus displays was repeated. This was done to prevent learning by pure stimulus association.

What we have not yet explained is what features did Model III—the only model studied here—use as input. Of course, we would have liked to model exactly the perceptual features attended to by the children, but we had no possibility of determining with any precision what those features were. Consequently, we devised a set of 12 relatively high-level features that we took as input. Given two sets in the form of $\{f_1, f_2, f_3\}$ and $\{g_1, g_2, g_3\}$, with f_2, f_3, g_2, and g_3 possibly null displays, and $f_i \neq f_j$, $g_i \neq g_j$ for $i \neq j$, our first nine features were: f_1g_1, f_2g_1, f_3g_1, f_1g_2, f_2g_2, f_3g_2, f_1g_3, f_2g_3, and f_3g_3, where

$$f_ig_j = \begin{cases} 1 & \text{if } f_i = g_j \\ -1 & \text{if } f_i \neq g_j \\ 0 & \text{if } f_i \text{ or } g_j \text{ is null} \end{cases}$$

The three other features were at a higher level still, namely, O, $I\bar{O}$, and $E\bar{I}$, where

$$O = \begin{cases} 1 & \text{if the two sets displayed are identical in the sense of ordered sets} \\ -1 & \text{otherwise} \end{cases}$$

$$I\bar{O} = \begin{cases} 1 & \text{if the two sets displayed are identical but not identical in the sense of} \\ & \quad \text{ordered sets} \\ -1 & \text{otherwise} \end{cases}$$

$$E\bar{I} = \begin{cases} 1 & \text{if the two sets displayed are equipollent but not identical} \\ -1 & \text{otherwise} \end{cases}$$

In what follows, we also use the notation O, I, $\bar{O}$, $\bar{I}$, $I\bar{O}$, E, $E\bar{I}$, and $\bar{E}$ for subsequences of trials on which the pair of stimulus displays exemplified one or more of these features.

Models with β-Weighted Means. We found in transfer experiments that the usual Bayesian posterior or maximum likelihood estimates of means, which we computed recursively from trial to trial, is too insensitive to change after a substantial number of trials. (This is a general problem with a static Bayes approach to learning in a changing environment.) The weighting rule is again in terms of a linear model. If response j is the correct response on trial n,

$$m_{ij,n+1} = (1 - \beta)m_{ij,n} + \beta x_{i,n}$$

When this weighted estimate is used, we designate the model with a β. Throughout this section when we refer to Model III, it is really to Model β-III, with $\beta = 0.1$, except in one case noted with $\beta = 0$. In the data analysis that follows, the comparison of the first graders with Model III stops at 56 trials, for that was the number of trials in the experiment with the children. We continued the learning of Model III for another cycle of 56 trials, as can be seen in Figs. 13.14–13.18. The mean curves for Model III shown in these figures are based on 100 runs. As remarked earlier, the first graders data are based on 24 children.

In Fig. 13.14 we show for the first graders and Model III the comparison of learning identity first and learning identity after equipollence. Two aspects of the results are salient. In these mean curves for the first 56 trials, that is, seven blocks of eight trials, the four curves are very similar. The first graders and Model III have almost identical mean performance.

Second, in the overall mean performance there is little evidence of positive or negative transfer for either the first graders or Model III. However, as we examine subconcepts generating subsequences of learning trials, the evidence of positive or negative transfer, depending on the subconcept, becomes quite salient.

There are two natural ways to analyze in further detail the data on transfer. The first and simplest is to divide the pairs of stimulus displays

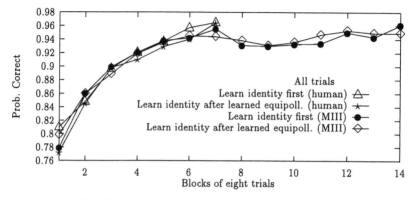

FIG. 13.14. Comparison of transfer curves using all trials.

into two groups: those exemplifying the concept of identity (I) and those not exemplifying it ($\bar{I}$). This analysis is shown in Figs. 13.15–13.18. Included with it are the mean learning curves for 48 other first graders who learned identity of sets first. In Fig. 13.15 we show four curves. Two are for the human, that is, first-grade, students. One curve is for first learning to respond correctly to the pairs of displays that are $\bar{I}$, that is, not identical. The second is the transfer curve, that is, the learning curve of $\bar{I}$ after 56 trials on equipollence. Model β-III, the multinomial learning model with β-weighted means, showed almost the same negative transfer as the first graders, with β = 0.1. Model III, without β-weighted means (i.e., β = 0), is hopelessly slow in learning identity of sets after equipollence, so the results with β = 0 are not shown.

As is clear from Fig. 13.15, the learning on $\bar{I}$ trials of the first graders and Model III were very close in rate in the first part of the experiment, the learning of identity. But Model III was slower than the first graders

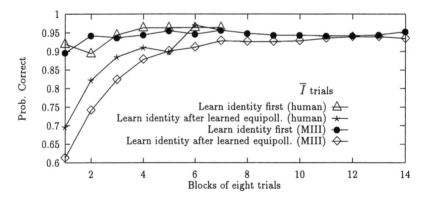

FIG. 13.15. Comparison of transfer curves for concept $\bar{I}$.

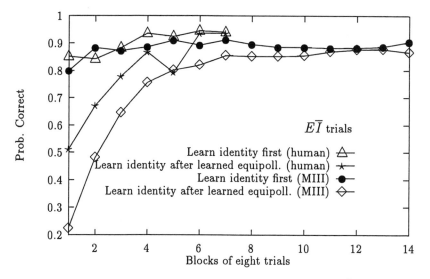

FIG. 13.16. Comparison of transfer curves for concept $E\bar{I}$.

and therefore showed more negative transfer on the $\bar{I}$ trials after first learning equipollence.

This greater negative transfer also holds, as shown in Fig. 13.16, for the $E\bar{I}$ trials, the critical ones to change when learning identity after equipollence.

In Fig. 13.17 we show the I trials before and after transfer, which is positive. We notice at once, from inspection of the graphs, that the rates for Model III and the first graders learning identity first are nearly the same.

In Fig. 13.18 we show the learning of identity on $I\bar{O}$ trials before and after transfer. Now the learning before transfer, that is, the learning of I on $I\bar{O}$ trials initially, is not at approximately the same rate for Model III and the first graders. In this case Model III is faster than the first graders, contrary to the approximately same rate for I trials before transfer, as shown in Fig. 13.17. The explanation is that on O trials, not shown in either figure, I was learned faster by the first graders than by Model III. This is not surprising, because the O trials present the natural concept of identity for children, and Model III does not have their prior experience.

On the other hand, the positive transfer for Model III is greater than for the first graders. This is true for both Figs. 13.17 and 13.18. We emphasize that on I or $I\bar{O}$ trials we expect for both first graders and any reasonable model positive, not negative, transfer. What is interesting is comparison of the amount of positive transfer. The greater positive transfer for Model III arises mainly from complete retention of the earlier learning of the correct responses to $I\bar{O}$ trials when equipollence was the concept being learned. The first graders exhibit less such retention, as is easily seen by comparing the proportion correct on the first block of trials of learning

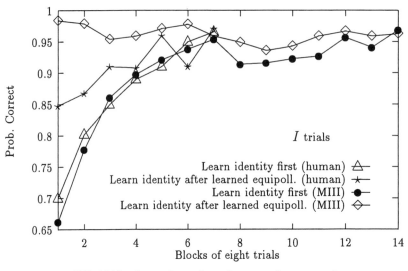

FIG. 13.17. Comparison of transfer curves for concept *I*.

identity of sets after equipollence. This proportion is about 0.97 for Model III and about 0.74 for the first graders.

COMPARISONS OF MODELS

We consider in this final section several other models and the problems they address, and summarize our own analyses.

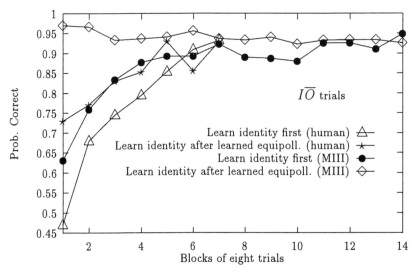

FIG. 13.18. Comparison of transfer curves for concept *IŌ*.

Back-Propagation Models

The kind of probabilistic models we have concentrated on are conceptually related to, but in detail different from, neural net models using a back-propagation algorithm. The general consensus in the literature is pretty much that for the kinds of learning tasks considered here, back-propagation methods are comparatively slow. Using the back-propagation algorithm described in Wasserman (1989, 1993) with two hidden units, we obtained for a single run of $150 \times 20 \times 60 = 180,000$ trials the learning curve for the iris data shown in Fig. 13.19. The comparison with Fig. 13.2 for the multivariate normal model (MI) with one cycle of 150 trials is striking, but in fact the comparison is even more dramatic, for a compatible probability correct was reached by Model I after only 30 trials, and only 20 trials by Model III. Typically, as other investigators have found, and as is the case for the iris data, classification performance of the back-propagation network required a large number of learning trials and the resulting asymptotic performance was no better than Models I and III. This indicates that situations where linear learning methods are superior in performance to back-propagation can occur, and may indeed be common.

After some conversation about the data sets and models in this paper, David Rumelhart agreed to run one of his more powerful back-propagation models on the iris data. Using 10 hidden units, he trained the model on the first 100 iris samples and tested on the last 50. With 1,000 runs of the training data, no mistakes were made on the test data.

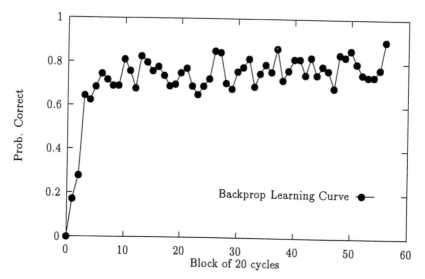

FIG. 13.19. Single run of back-propagation model on iris data for 180,000 trials.

Probability Matching

A principle feature of stochastic learning models developed three to four decades ago is *probability matching.* What is meant by this may be explained by examining some details of the linear model used in Model III for change of weights and the ME model of evaluation. In simplest form, let there be only one input feature, a red light signaling that it is time to make either an R_1 or R_2 response. Because there is only one constant input feature assumed at the beginning, we may ignore it and formulate the model just in terms of responses and reinforcement, E_1 and E_2, that is, information about the correct response. (We limit ourselves here to just two responses.) The linear theory is formulated for the probability of a response on trial $n + 1$, given the entire preceding sequence of responses and reinforcements. For this preceding sequence we use the notation x_n. Thus, x_n is a sequence of length $2n$ with 0s and 1s in the odd positions indicating responses R_1 and R_2, and 1s and 2s in the even positions indicating reinforcing events E_1 and E_2. The axioms of the linear theory are as follows:

Axiom L1. If $E_n = 1$ and $P(x_n) > 0$, then

$$P(R_{n+1} = 1|x_n) = (1 - \theta)P(R_n = 1|x_{n-1}) + \theta$$

Axiom L2. If $E_n = 2$ and $P(x_n) > 0$, then

$$P(R_{n+1} = 1|x_n) = (1 - \theta)P(R_n = 1|x_{n-1})$$

Here, as usual, θ is to be thought of as the learning parameter. We consider what is from a theoretical standpoint one of the simplest cases: noncontingent reinforcement. This case is defined by the condition that the probability of E_1 on any trial is constant and independent of the subject's responses. It is customary in the literature to call this probability π. Thus, $P(E_n = 1) = \pi$, $P(E_n = 2) = 1 - \pi$.

For the noncontingent case, we can derive from L1 and L2 the same asymptotic mean result,

$$\lim_{n \to \infty} P(R_n = 1) = \pi \tag{17}$$

Because π is the asymptotic probability of response R_1, we have probability matching of responses and reenforcements on average. It is clear that Equation 17 is not the prediction of the multivariate normal model (MI), for with the Bayes posterior for the two response classes, asymptotically R_1 would be chosen with probability 1 when $\pi > \frac{1}{2}$. Similar remarks apply to essentially all the models previously discussed, with one exception. In the models with β-weighted means, probability matching will occur with $\beta = 1$. More detailed results can be obtained using the methods developed in Estes and Suppes (1959) for analyzing the detailed properties of the linear model.

Summary of Analysis

The model evaluation methods introduced in the second section are seen to be most useful when applied to single runs of test data. This is particularly evident in the resulting smoothing of the learning to be seen in Fig. 13.3. More work will be required to determine which values of the parameter α are best for what purposes. The value $\alpha = 0.3$ worked rather well in our preliminary investigations.

We considered six data sets and seven models. In Table 13.1 we summarize the results in two ways. We show, for each data set, which model exhibited the fastest learning and which model had the best asymptotic result. In several cases there were ties, so several models are entered in the table.

The most striking fact about the table is that no one of the seven models comes close to being uniformly best. Models I and III were best most often, but their virtues are clearly different. Model I is most often best asymptotically—three out of the six cases. Model III had most often the fastest learning rate, again three out of six cases.

We also note that multinomial models V and VI were not best in any of the 12 categories of Table 13.1.

Actually, the situation is a little more complicated than we have described, because considering the β-weights explicitly increases dramatically the number of models. Moreover, the need for the β-weights is quite clear both conceptually and computationally in the case of the transfer data (Section 4). Because the β-weights fly in the face of much standard statistical practice in estimating parameters, but not in time-series analysis, their

TABLE 13.1
Comparison of Model Performance

Data Set	Fast Learning	Best Asymptotic
Iris	III	I
Bank notes	III, IV	I, III, IV
Beetles	III	I
Circles	I, II	I
XOR	IV, VII	IV, VII
Transfer	β-III	β-III

relevance for parameter estimation in transfer experiments warrants further study.

REFERENCES

Estes, W., & Suppes, P. (1959). Foundations of linear models. In R. Bush & W. Estes (Eds.), *Studies in mathematical learning theory* (pp. 137–179). Stanford: Stanford University Press.

Fisher, R. A. (1936). The use of multiple measurements in taxonomic problems. *Annals of Eugenics, 7,* 179–188.

Flury, B., & Riedwyl, H. (1988). *Multivariate statistics, a practical approach.* London: Chapman and Hall.

Lubischew, A. A. (1962). On the use of discriminant functions in taxonomy. *Biometrics, 18,* 455–477.

McLachlan, G. (1992). *Discriminant analysis and statistical pattern recognition.* New York: Wiley.

Suppes, P. (1965). On the behavioral foundations of mathematical concepts. *Child Development Monograph,* Serial 99, Vol. 30, No. 1.

Suppes, P., Böttner, M., & Liang, L. (1995). Comprehension grammars generated from machine learning of natural languages. *Machine Learning, 19,* 133–152.

Suppes, P., Liang, L., & Böttner, M. (1992). Complexity issues in robotic machine learning of natural language. In L. Lam & V. Naroditsky (Eds.), *Modeling complex phenomena* (pp. 102–127). New York: Springer-Verlag.

Wasserman, P. (1989). *Neural computing, theory and practice.* New York: Van Nostrand Reinhold.

Wasserman, P. (1993). *Advanced methods in neural computing.* New York: Van Nostrand Reinhold.

Cognitive Modeling

Chapter 14

Comparing Parallel and Sequential Multinomial Models of Letter Identification

Vincent Brown
University of Texas at Arlington

THE NEED FOR ATTENTIONAL SELECTION IN SHAPE IDENTIFICATION

A typical visual scene is filled with a variety of perceptual objects that could lead to a variety of responses on the part of an observer. For example, if one's goal is to avoid a collision with the bike crossing the path ahead, the important information to be extracted from the visual scene is the distance of the bike (i.e., its depth) and its velocity. Properties such as the color of the bike and the identity of the rider may be of less importance to the immediate goal of avoiding collision. However, if one has agreed to meet a friend at a certain time and location, and that friend generally travels by bike, then the color of and the identity of the rider of any bike in the general location become more important. Certain perceptual judgments, such as determining the location and velocity of objects, may be carried out quickly and rather automatically by the visual system; that is, certain perceptual judgments seem to occur whether or not the observer is attending to them. Other judgments, such as determining the identity of objects, may not be automatic but may require the concentration of attention to perform.

Identifying an object, which requires detecting invariances in a particular set of spatial relations, as well as a likely complicated set of memory operations, is probably more complex than computating something like the velocity of an object (Marr, 1982). The more complex a computation is, the less likely it is to be performed massively in parallel for all elements in a visual scene. Thus, it seems unlikely that the visual system identifies all objects in a visual scene simultaneously. The function of selecting a subset of sensory input for further processing is one important aspect of the somewhat nebulous concept of attention (e.g., James, 1890/1983; LaBerge, 1990).

The assumed complexity of the shape identification process requires a mechanism that prevents the entire visual scene from being input to the shape identification mechanism at one time. This is necessary regardless of whether one makes the strong assumption that shape identification takes place one object at a time or one makes the weaker assumption simply that shape identification is not a massively parallel process. The study reported here examines the question of whether identifying two separate and distinct letters is a parallel or sequential process.

IDENTIFYING PARALLEL AND SERIAL PROCESSES

The general question of how to determine whether a given perceptual or cognitive process takes place in a parallel or serial fashion has been treated extensively in recent years (see Luce, 1986, chap. 12, and Townsend, 1990, for summaries and reviews; see Townsend & Ashby, 1983, for a comprehensive treatment). The upshot is that distinguishing parallel from serial models can be difficult: It is often the case that for a given experimental paradigm parallel models can mimic serial models, and vice versa. One clear example is the standard single-target visual (or memory) search paradigm, where a linearly increasing response time curve as a function of number of display elements is often taken to signal a serial self-terminating search, when in fact some limited-capacity parallel models produce the same result (Townsend, 1974; Townsend & Ashby, 1983).

Because of the difficulty of determining the nature of the underlying processing from a single set of data, researchers often rely on converging evidence from a number of experiments to make the determination of parallel or serial processing (e.g., Treisman & Souther, 1985). The parallel–serial testing paradigm (PST) described in Townsend and Ashby (1983) (see also Luce, 1986, chap. 12) utilizes the idea of making comparisons across experimental conditions in a more rigorous fashion. In three experimental conditions, observers are asked to respond either to the location, a conjunction, or the disjunction of targets appearing in two possible (spatial or temporal) locations. Under very general distributional assumptions, it can be shown that self-terminating parallel and serial models are always distinguishable at the level of the mean response times obtained from the three conditions (Townsend & Ashby, 1983).

Most of the experimental and theoretical approaches to examining parallel versus serial processing have been based on response-time measures, although a few have been based on accuracy (see Townsend, 1990, for a summary of the major approaches). This chapter employs the approach of multinomial modeling, as detailed by Riefer and Batchelder (1988), to compare accuracy-based parallel and sequential models of letter identification. The main focus of the work is to explore the nature of shape identification, and not to address the general issue of parallel versus serial processing in all domains, although it is hoped that the approach used here, which is preliminary in many respects, will contribute to the body of existing results on the issue.

TESTING FOR PARALLEL OR SEQUENTIAL SHAPE IDENTIFICATION

Consider the following example. An observer is presented with two sufficiently separated letters, one to each side of fixation. A subset of stimuli are designated as targets. Four types of trials can occur: There is no target present, there is one target present on the left, there is one target present on the right, or there are two targets present. The observer is instructed not to respond if no targets are perceived, to respond "left" or "right" if one target is perceived, and to respond "two" if two targets are perceived.

Assume for the purpose of the example that identification is deterministic (the target letter is either identified perfectly or not at all) and the letter detectors on each side of fixation perform identically (the threshold stimulus duration and luminance are the same for both detectors). Both assumptions are overly restrictive, but they allow us to develop some initial intuitions about the experimental paradigm. Relaxing these assumptions leads to the multinomial models presented in the next section.

To continue with the example, let's examine the case when two targets are present. Suppose letter identification is performed spatially in parallel. Then when the observer is able to identify one target, the observer always identifies the other target as well. When the stimulus duration is decreased (or equivalently, when luminance is decreased) so that it is below the threshold for identification, the observer will fail to identify both targets. That is, in the parallel case, the observer would never identify just one of the targets. Intuitively, if letter identification is a sequential process, then when the stimulus duration is sufficiently short, the observer should be unable to process both targets if they are present, but should be able to process one of the targets. That is, at certain durations errors of the type, the response "left" or "right" is made when two targets are present, should increase dramatically (see Fig. 14.1).

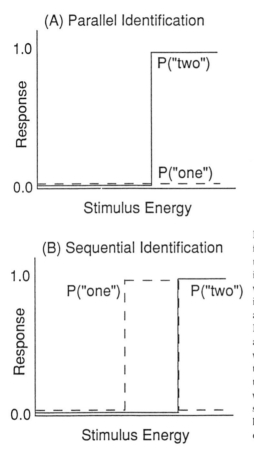

FIG. 14.1. Hypothetical responses for deterministic letter identification. (A) If two target letters are identified in parallel, the observer will always see them both until the identification threshold is reached, and then no stimuli are identified. In the (deterministic) parallel case, a single target is never perceived when two are present. (B) If the target letters are identified sequentially, at some point the observer will not have sufficient time to switch processing to the second letter and will perceive one target even when two are present.

Of course, real-world observers' responses are not deterministic, and processing is not likely to be precisely identical for stimuli at different locations. Thus, more flexible, probabilistic models are needed. These are presented next.

MULTINOMIAL MODELS

In the experimental situation just described, an observer makes one of four separate (mutually exclusive) and exhaustive responses: "none," "left," "right," or "two." The probability of each response should vary as a function of the stimulus parameters (e.g., when two targets are presented the observer should say "two" more often and "none" less often as duration or luminance is increased). A weighted four-sided die (with weights changing as a function of stimulus parameters) would serve as a good model for observers' responses. That is to say, responses follow a multinomial distribution with response probabilities

$$P(\text{"none"}) + P(\text{"left"}) + P(\text{"right"}) + P(\text{"two"}) = 1 \qquad (1)$$

Because we are interested in the accuracy of the observers' responses, we look at responses conditional on how many targets are present in the two-element display, that is, P(response|number of targets presented).

If we assume that the response probabilities are generated by some underlying perceptual process, we should attempt to describe the observed response proportions as a function of the variables representing the underlying process. Suppose each target location is either examined simultaneously by two different letter "detectors" or one at a time by the two detectors. The term *detector* is just an idealization for the purposes of modeling; it is easier to say "detector" than "the process of shape identification applied to location x." Assume the detectors' probabilities of correctly identifying the target when it is present are increasing functions of stimulus luminance, I, and duration, T, $G(I,T)$ for the left detector and $H(I,T)$ for the right detector. We don't know $G(I,T)$ and $H(I,T)$, but assuming that observers' responses are based on the output of the letter detectors, we can describe simple parallel and sequential models for an observer's responses given some $G(I,T)$ and $H(I,T)$.

Two parallel and two sequential models are described next. These four models by no means exhaust the space of all possible parallel and sequential models of the task. However, they are four of the most straightforward parallel and sequential models conceivable, and would therefore seem to be an appropriate starting point. It is more parsimonious to examine simpler models before introducing more complex ones. Furthermore, each model is based on plausible assumptions about the nature of the underlying perceptual processes, as detailed next.

The Simple Parallel Model

If the stimulus letters are processed simultaneously and independently, then $P(2|2)$, the probability that the observer says "two" when two targets are present, is just the probability that both detectors identify a target. $P(L|2)$ and $P(R|2)$ are the probabilities that one detector identifies a target and the other doesn't. $P(0|2)$ is the probability that both detectors fail to identify the targets.

It is straightforward to include parameters for stimulus confusion, that is, the probability that an observer responds as if there were a target in a location where none is present. This occurs when the observer mistakenly sees a nontarget as a target. Let $L(I,T)$ be the probability that a target is mistakenly identified in the left location when the left location contains a nontarget, and $R(I,T)$ be the probability that a target is mistakenly identified in the right location when the right location contains a nontarget. As an example, $P(R|L)$ is the probability that the observer fails to identify the target in the left location and mistakenly identifies a nontarget as a target in the right location. The equations for the simple parallel model are given in Appendix A.

In addition to confusion errors, false positive responses could result from pure guesses by the observer. Thus, the model could also be amended to include parameters for guessing, that is, the probability that the observer makes a particular response when uncertain about the identity of the stimulus. However, the observers in the present experiment were instructed not to guess but to respond only when certain of the identity of the stimulus (i.e., they were to indicate only the number of stimuli they were sure of having seen). As a consequence, the occurrence of false positive responses was low (particularly in the low luminance and/or low duration conditions, where the number of guesses would be expected to be high if observers were not following the "high threshold" instructions). The number of additional parameters required to account for an apparently low number of pure guesses did not seem worth the potential (small) gain in fit, and it seemed reasonable to let the confusion parameters take up the slack.

The relationship between the supposed detection probabilities and the observers' responses are more easily seen graphically as a tree structure (a multinomial tree) (Fig. 14.2). It should be pointed out that although the independence of stimulus detection probabilities is not a necessary condition for parallel processing, this simplifying assumption provides a good starting point. One way of relaxing the assumption of independence is introduced in the second parallel model, the parallel gestalt model.

The Parallel Gestalt Model

If we assume that on some trials the observer "chunks" the two-letter stimulus into a single object, we must make a slight modification to the simple parallel model. A similar "gestalt" assumption was added to the parallel model described in Townsend and Ashby's (1983) version of the PST mentioned earlier. In this case, when the presented stimulus set contained two identical stimuli, they were assumed to be processed as a single unit. In the model presented here, it is assumed that gestalts can be formed from two nonidentical stimuli (as happens in the case of letters making up a word), because identical stimuli are never presented at the same time. We assume that with a certain probability, the stimulus pair is chunked (a gestalt is formed), and as a consequence the observer correctly identifies both items of the pair. Then, with one minus the chunking probability,

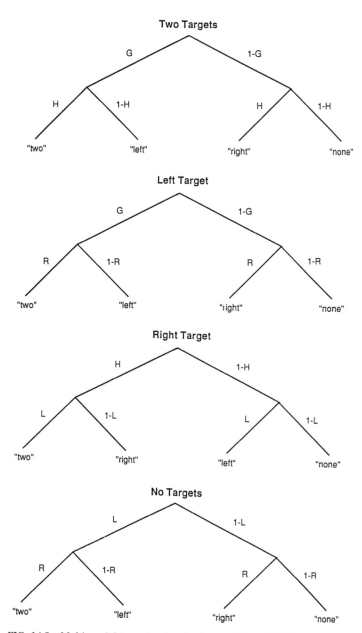

FIG. 14.2. Multinomial trees for the simple parallel model. The top node gives number of targets presented. Branches are labeled with parameters of the model: G is the probability of identifying the left target; H is the probability of identifying the right target; L is the left confusion parameter and R is the right confusion parameter. Terminal nodes are labeled with the response given the path through the tree. Response probabilities can be found by multiplying the parameters along each branch of the path (see Appendix A).

the observer just responds according to the simple parallel model, which assumes independent letter identifications. W_2 is the probability that two targets are chunked and correctly identified. Likewise, W_1 is the probability that a one target/one nontarget display is chunked, and W_0 is the probability that the no-target displays are chunked.

The trees for the parallel gestalt model (see Fig. 14.3) are identical to those for the simple parallel model, with the addition of the W and $(1 - W)$ branches; the simple parallel model simply hangs off the $(1 - W)$ branches. The equations for the parallel gestalt model are given in Appendix B.

The Symmetric Sequential Model

Assume the amount of time an observer has to examine a stimulus representation internally is an increasing function of stimulus energy (duration and luminance) (e.g., Coltheart, 1980; Long, 1980). Suppose an observer engages a strategy of examining one stimulus location for a portion of the available time and then shifts to the second location for the remaining time. The symmetric sequential model assumes that the stimulus examination times do not depend on the success or failure of the identification process. (The second sequential model presented, the ordered sequential model, assumes that shifting processing to the second stimulus takes place only after an identification of the first stimulus has been made.) Let τ represent the time available to the observer and t be the time taken to examine the first stimulus. In general, τ and t are random variables dependent on luminance I and duration T. We let $G_1(I,T)$ and $H_1(I,T)$ be the probabilities that the first target examined is identified and $G_2(I,T)$ and $H_2(I,T)$ be the probabilities that the second target examined is identified. (Again, G and H represent detection probabilities for the left and right stimulus locations, respectively.) The detection probabilities G_1, H_1 and G_2, H_2 summarize the effectiveness (accuracy) of the processes completed during the intervals $(0,t)$ and (t,τ) and do not depend on any specific distributional assumptions about t and τ nor on the nature of the functional relationship between stimulus luminance I, duration T, and the duration of the internal representations t and τ, because the model parameters are estimated separately for each combination of stimulus variables.

$P(2|2)$ is then the probability that the detector at the left location identifies the target in time t and the detector at the right location identifies the target in remaining time $\tau - t$, or the detector at the right location identifies the target in time t and the detector at the left location identifies the target in time $\tau - t$. Next, $P(L|2)$ is the probability that the observer identifies the target at the left location after time t and then fails to identify

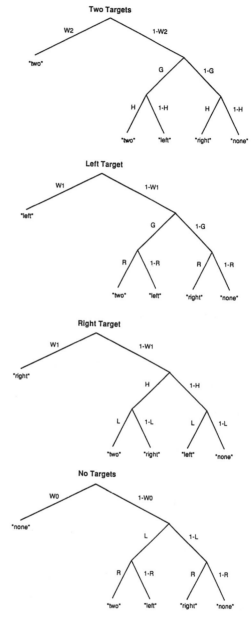

FIG. 14.3. Multinomial trees for the parallel gestalt model. The top node gives number of targets presented. Branches are labeled with parameters of the model: W_2 and W_0 are the probability of chunking both targets or both nontargets, respectively; G is the probability of identifying the left target when the display is not chunked; H is the probability of identifying the right target when the display is not chunked; L is the left confusion parameter and R is the right confusion parameter. Terminal nodes are labeled with the response given the path through the tree. Response probabilities can be found by multiplying the parameters along each branch of the path (see Appendix B).

the target at the right location after time $\tau - t$, or the observer fails to identify the target at the right location after time t and then identifies the target at the left location after time $\tau - t$. Lastly, $P(0|2)$ is the probability that the observer fails to identify the target both at the left location after time t and at the right location after time $\tau - t$, or fails to identify the target both at the right location after time t and at the left location after time $\tau - t$. Let P represent the probability that the observer begins with the left stimulus [the location with detection function $G_1(I,T)$]. The tree for the symmetric sequential model is given in Fig. 14.4 and the equations are given in Appendix C. Note that because what happens during the interval (t,τ) is assumed to be independent of what happens during the interval $(0,t)$, the symmetric sequential model is really just the combination of two simple parallel models.

The Ordered Sequential Model

Suppose that the identification process works in such a way that processing does not proceed to the next item until processing on the first item is complete. Thus, if an observer examines the left item first and successfully identifies it, the observer (or the observer's perceptual system) proceeds to process the next item; if the observer fails to successfully identify the first item examined in the time available, the observer would not examine the second item at all. This strategy makes the detection probabilities for the second item examined clearly contingent on the outcome of processing the first item examined.

The tree for the ordered sequential model is shown in Fig. 14.5 and the equations are presented in Appendix D. One consequence of this model is that the probability of responding "two" when no items are present is zero. Including parameters for guessing would make $P(2|0)$ in general larger than zero, but again observers were instructed not to guess, and in fact false positives were low and $P(2|0)$ in particular was nearly always zero.

EXPERIMENTAL METHODS

This section outlines the experimental design and procedure used to compare the models just described. The idea was to present observers with two stimulus items and ask how many targets were present and in which location. Stimulus duration, luminance, and spatial separation were the experimental variables.

Subjects. Four observers participated in the experiment. Two were paid for their participation (observers 1 and 2); one received course credit in addition to partial payment (observer 3); and one observer (4) was the author.

Apparatus. Stimulus presentation and response measurement were under control of an AST Premium 386/16 computer with VGA graphics capability. Stimuli were displayed on a Relisys RE9513 VGA color monitor. Observers responded by pressing the shift keys of the attached keyboard.

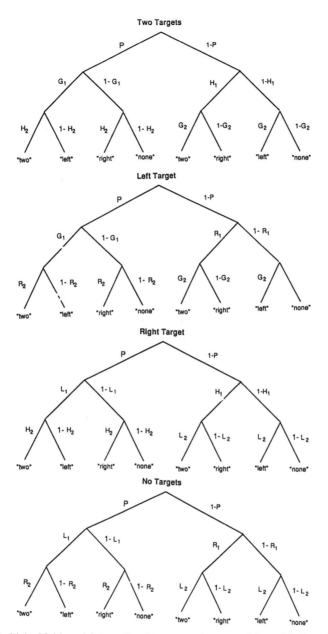

FIG. 14.4. Multinomial trees for the symmetric sequential model. Branches are labeled with parameters of the model: G_1 is the probability of identifying the left target first; H_2 is the probability of identifying the right target second; H_1 is the probability of identifying the right target first; G_2 is the probability of identifying the left target second; L_1 and L_2 are the left confusion parameters and R_1 and R_2 are the right confusion parameters; P is the probability of processing the left target first. Terminal nodes are labeled with the response given the path through the tree. Response probabilities can be found by multiplying the parameters along each branch of the path (see Appendix C).

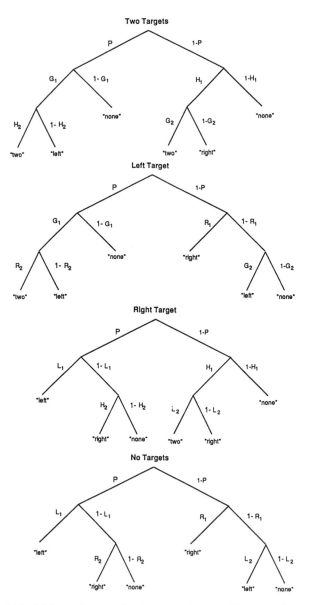

FIG. 14.5. Multinomial trees for the ordered sequential model. Branches are labeled with parameters of the model: G_1 is the probability of identifying the left target first; H_2 is the probability of identifying the right target second; H_1 is the probability of identifying the right target first; G_2 is the probability of identifying the left target second; L_1 and L_2 are the left confusion parameters and R_1 and R_2 are the right confusion parameters; P is the probability of processing the left target first. Terminal nodes are labelled with the response given the path through the tree. Response probabilities can be found by multiplying the parameters along each branch of the path (see Appendix D).

Stimuli and Responses. The stimulus set consisted of the upper case letters B, H, I, O. With the vertical size of the monitor display reduced to its minimum, each character measure approximately 0.28 × 0.20 cm. Observers were seated approximately 50 cm from the monitor, at which distance each character subtended approximately 0.32 degrees of visual angle vertically and 0.23 degrees horizontally. Stimulus letters were displayed two at a time, one on each side of a red fixation dot.

For each observer, two letters were designated as targets, leaving two letters as nontargets. (For observer 1, the target letters were H and O; for observer 2, the targets were B and I; for observer 3, B and H; and for observer 4, H and I.) All possible combinations of targets and nontargets were presented, with each display containing two unique characters (i.e., no display contained two identical characters).

The observers' task was to indicate the number and location of targets perceived in the display. Responses were made by pressing one or both of the shift keys on the computer keyboard. Observers were instructed to respond only on the basis of the number of targets they were certain of having seen.

Experimental Variables. Several aspects of the presentation of the letters were varied. Each observer was presented displays ranging in duration from 17 to 300 msec. Durations of 17, 33, 50, 67, 83, 100, 133, 167, 200, 250, and 300 msec were used. Each observer was presented with three display luminances. The luminances were set separately for each observer. Low, medium, and high luminances in foot-lamberts were, respectively, for each observer: observer 1, 0.046, 0.067, 0.085; observer 2, 0.022, 0.033, 0.067; observer 3, 0.016, 0.022, 0.046; observer 4, 0.046, 0.067, 0.085. The background luminance of the monitor was approximately 0.0037 foot-lamberts. Duration and luminance were varied factorially. Duration was mixed randomly within blocks, whereas luminance was blocked.

The spatial separation of the stimulus letters was also varied. Separations of 0.60 degrees (narrow), 2.1 degrees (medium), and 3.4 degrees (wide) were used. All observers were presented with the medium separation displays. In addition, observer 2 was shown the narrow separation displays, observer 3 the wide separation displays, and observer 4 both the narrow and wide separation displays. To allow the observers to optimize their processing of the displays, stimulus separation was blocked.

Experimental Sessions. Each experimental session consisted of three blocks of 176 trials each. In each session, the observers were presented with all stimulus durations within blocks and with the three luminance levels separately between blocks. Display separation was held constant within a session.

Observer 1 ran 18 sessions of the medium separation condition. Observer 2 ran 18 sessions each of the narrow and medium separation conditions. Observer 3 ran 15 sessions each of the medium and wide separation conditions. Observer 4 ran 24 sessions each of the narrow, medium, and wide separation conditions.

DATA

Response proportion given display type (number of targets) is plotted as a function of stimulus duration with luminance as the parameter for observer 4, who was presented with all three target separations (Fig. 14.6).

Overall, the effects of luminance, duration, and separation are quite clear. The proportion of correct responses, $P(L|L)$, $P(R|R)$, and $P(2|2)$, appears to increase monotonically with luminance and duration and decrease with separation as expected. Confusion errors, which can be inferred from the graphs of $P(0|0)$, seem to increase slightly with duration, and then decrease, presumably as the stimuli become more visible. A similar pattern is seen for $P(L|2)$ and $P(R|2)$, the proportion of times the observer reported seeing just one target of a two-target display.

TESTING AND COMPARING THE MODELS

There are a number of ways to go about assessing whether or not a given model provides an adequate description of a set of data. One sensible approach is to select some probability (such as .05) of the data having resulted as a sample from the probability distribution specified by the model, below which the model is rejected. In the case of the multinomial distribution the likelihood ratio statistic G^2, which has an asymptotic chi-square distribution, is a natural measure of goodness of fit.

Using this approach is problematic in the present situation, however. The experiment consists of a large number of separate conditions, 3 luminances $\times$ 11 durations = 33 conditions. The standard way to summarize the goodness of fit of a model to the entire experiment would be to compare the sum of the goodness of fit measures of each condition with the chi-square value of the desired probability for rejection. This approach unfortunately could easily lead to a situation where a model would be accepted if each condition were examined separately but would be rejected if tested against the combined experiment as a whole. For example the chi-square value with tail probability .05 and 8 degrees of freedom is 15.5 or about twice the number of degrees of freedom, but the chi-square value

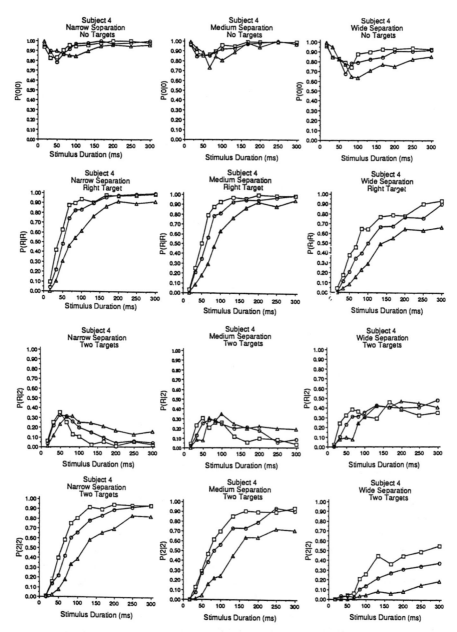

FIG. 14.6. Selected responses as a function of duration with luminance as the parameter for Observer 4. The first row shows the proportion of "no" responses for the No-target condition. The second row shows the proportion of "right" responses for the Right-target condition. The third row shows the proportion of "right" responses for the Two-target condition. The fourth row shows the proportion of "two" responses for the Two-target condition. Squares represent high luminance. Circles represent medium luminance. Triangles represent low luminance.

with tail probability .05 and $33 \times 8 = 264$ degrees of freedom is 303, which is much less than twice the degrees of freedom.

Akaike proposed comparing the obtained goodness-of-fit value with minus twice the expected log-likelihood (Akaike, 1973; Read & Cressie, 1988). For the chi-square distribution (the asymptotic distribution of G^2, which is minus twice the log-likelihood of the multinomial distribution), the expected value is the degrees of freedom. This approach has the desirable property of biasing the goodness-of-fit test toward models with fewer parameters (greater degrees of freedom) (see Read & Cressie, 1988). It also eliminates the discrepancy between examining goodness of fit for individual conditions and the situation as a whole.

The maximum-likelihood parameter estimates for the simple parallel model can be found directly from the trees, because each terminal node constitutes a complete response category. Closed-form solutions for the maximum-likelihood estimates of the other models have not been obtained. A numerical method for estimating the parameters know as the EM (expectancy maximization) algorithm was used (Dempster, Laird, & Rubin, 1977; Hu & Batchelder, 1994). The algorithm is guaranteed to converge to the maximum likelihood solution when it exists.

The Parallel Models

We first look at whether the parallel models may be a reasonable description of the data. Because the parallel models are hierarchically related, we can test whether the more complicated parallel gestalt model obtains a significantly better fit to the data than the more parsimonious simple parallel model.

Table 14.1 gives the values of G^2 for the parallel models for four observers in three stimulus separation conditions. Not every observer ran each condition, so there are just eight conditions in all. Those conditions where the models are not rejected under Akaike's criterion are marked with an asterisk. Next Table 14.1 gives the difference between the goodness of fits to the simple parallel and parallel gestalt models. Those conditions where the parallel gestalt model provides a better fit to the data under Akaike's criterion are marked with a double asterisk.

Under the criterion adopted, neither model appears to fit in all cases. Both parallel models are in fact accepted in the same cases. It is interesting to note that both parallel models fit the data from the two narrow separation conditions and neither parallel model fits the data from the two wide separation conditions. In five of eight conditions the parallel gestalt model is accepted over the simple parallel model, with one condition (subject 4, wide separation) a clear borderline case.

TABLE 14.1
Comparison of Goodness of Fit for the
Simple Parallel and Parallel Gestalt Models

Subject	Separation	Model	df	2df	G^2
1	Medium	Simple parallel	264	528	496.5*
		Parallel gestalt	165	330	247.8*
		Difference	99	198	248.7**
2	Narrow	Simple parallel	264	528	480.4*
		Parallel gestalt	165	330	224.1*
		Difference	99	198	256.3**
2	Medium	Simple parallel	264	528	338.5*
		Parallel gestalt	165	330	210.3*
		Difference	99	198	128.2
3	Medium	Simple parallel	264	528	896.4
		Parallel gestalt	165	330	337.3
		Difference	99	198	558.7**
3	Wide	Simple parallel	264	528	668.8
		Parallel gestalt	165	330	337.6
		Difference	99	198	331.2**
4	Narrow	Simple parallel	264	528	415.2*
		Parallel gestalt	165	330	186.7*
		Difference	99	198	228.5**
4	Medium	Simple parallel	264	528	366.4*
		Parallel gestalt	165	330	213.6*
		Difference	99	198	152.8
4	Wide	Simple parallel	264	528	694.6
		Parallel gestalt	165	330	497.5
		Difference	99	198	197.1

Note. Values of G^2 marked by an asterisk indicate that the model would not be rejected for the condition. Values marked by a double asterisk represent conditions where the parallel gestalt model provides a significantly better fit to the data than the simple parallel model. df, Degrees of freedom.

The Sequential Models

Because the simple parallel model is a submodel of the symmetric sequential model, we can test whether the added complexity of the symmetric sequential model provides a significantly better fit to the data. Because the symmetric sequential model is not identifiable (that is, the nine parameters are not uniquely specified given the data), the value of the parameter P was set to .5 in all cases. Table 14.2 gives the difference in goodness of fits between the simple parallel and symmetric sequential models. Those conditions where the symmetric sequential model provides a significantly better fit to the data than the simple parallel model are marked by a double asterisk.

TABLE 14.2
Comparison of Goodness of Fit Between the
Simple Parallel and the Symmetric Sequential Model

Subject	Separation	Model	df	2df	G^2
1	Medium	Simp–Sym	132	264	149.7
2	Narrow	Simp–Sym	132	264	197.2
2	Medium	Simp–Sym	132	264	97.8
3	Medium	Simp–Sym	132	264	520.9**
3	Wide	Simp–Sym	132	264	356.8**
4	Narrow	Simp–Sym	132	264	118.3
4	Medium	Simp–Sym	132	264	94.0
4	Wide	Simp–Sym	132	264	375.9**

Note. Conditions marked by a double asterisk indicate that the symmetric sequential model provides a better fit to the data than the simple parallel model. Simp, simple parallel model; Sym, symmetric parallel model; df, degrees of freedom.

The additional parameters in the symmetric sequential model do not overall seem to produce a better fit to the data than the simple parallel model. However, it is interesting to note that the symmetric sequential model seems to provide a better fit to both wide separation conditions while providing a better fit to neither narrow separation condition. Recall that both parallel models fit the data from the two narrow separation conditions and neither parallel model fits the data from the two wide separation conditions. Up to this point the parallel gestalt model would seem to provide the best fit to the data.

Because the ordered sequential model is not hierarchically related to the other models, we will assess its goodness of fit directly. A strong prediction of the ordered sequential model is $P(2|0) \equiv 0$, which means that any nonzero values of $P(2|0)$ in the data will prevent the model from fitting. However, because $P(2|0) = 0$ for the vast majority of cases [$P(2|0) = 0$ in 217 out of 251 experimental conditions; overall, $P(2|0) = .002$], we can test the fit of the ordered sequential model by setting all cell counts $N(2|0) = 0$. It can be seen from Table 14.3 that it fits fairly well, about as well as the parallel models.

Unfortunately, because the parallel models are not submodels of the ordered sequential model, we cannot compare them directly. We must resort to other means to compare them, and we will attempt the comparison as follows. Because the parallel gestalt model provides at least as good a fit to the data as the simple parallel model, we compare the parallel gestalt model to the ordered sequential model. Because we know the maximum-likelihood estimates of the parameters of the models, we can generate an estimate of the data that would have been expected if each of the models were true. Then we can attempt to fit each model to the expected

TABLE 14.3
Goodness of Fit of the Ordered Sequential Model

Subject	Separation	Model	df	2df	G^2
1	Medium	Ord Seq	98	196	307.2
2	Narrow	Ord Seq	98	196	226.1
2	Medium	Ord Seq	98	196	187.9*
3	Medium	Ord Seq	98	196	98.7*
3	Wide	Ord Seq	98	196	131.4*
4	Narrow	Ord Seq	98	196	163.6*
4	Medium	Ord Seq	98	196	176.1*
4	Wide	Ord Seq	98	196	255.3

Note. Conditions marked by an asterisk indicate acceptance of the model. Ord Seq, ordered sequential; df, degrees of freedom.

data generated by the other models. (A similar procedure was employed by Townsend & Ashby, 1983, to compare the a priori similarity of their parallel and serial models in the PST paradigm.) If one of the models fits the expected data generated by the other model, we may wish to conclude that our interest in the fact that the model fits the experimental data is somewhat lessened.

The reasoning behind this claim is as follows. The set of parameters of each model will map out a surface in n-dimensional space, where n is the number of possible responses for the given task. Because the dimension of the model subspace is generally less than the dimension of the full response space, the data (which are represented as a single point in response space) will not be likely to fall precisely in the subspace specified by a given model. However, a model is deemed to "fit" the data if the data are sufficiently close to the subspace defined by the model. The best fitting parameters for the model in question give the point in the model subspace that is closest to the data.

In the case of two hierarchically related models, the subspace mapped out by one model (the model with fewer parameters) is in turn a subset of the space mapped out by the other model (the model with more parameters). The data will always fall closer to the model defining the larger subspace (i.e., the model with more parameters), because the larger subspace contains the smaller subspace. However, if the data fall sufficiently close to the model defining the smaller subspace (i.e., the model with fewer parameters), then that model is said to provide the best fit to the data. That is, the least general model that fits the data is deemed to provide a better description of the data; the most unique model that fits the data is in a sense the most informative.

However, when two models are not hierarchically related—that is, when one model's subspace is not a proper subset of the other's—the comparison is not so straightforward. If one model fits the data and the other does not, the decision is clear. However, the data in fact may be "sufficiently close" to both models' subspaces. Consider two nonnested models, A and B, both of which appear to fit a set of data by some standard goodness-of-fit measure. An estimate of the data expected given model A is the point in response space generated by the maximum-likelihood parameters for model A. If model B fits this "data" from model A, and if model A does not fit the data expected given model B, then model B is in a sense more general than model A (less unique), at least locally in the region of the obtained empirical data. Thus, following the principle that the least general model is the most informative, model A would be chosen as providing the best description of the data.

To compare the parallel gestalt model and the ordered sequential model, the maximum-likelihood parameter estimates for each model were entered into the expressions in Appendix B and Appendix D, and each model was fitted to the data thus generated by the other model. It is clear from Table 14.4 that the parallel gestalt model does not fit the data generated by the ordered sequential model, whereas the ordered sequential model does fit the data generated by the parallel gestalt model. It seems

TABLE 14.4
Comparison of the Ordered Sequential and Parallel Gestalt Models

Subject	Separation	Model	df	2df	G^2
1	Medium	Ordered sequential	98	196	245.0
		Parallel gestalt	165	330	2411.5
2	Narrow	Ordered sequential	98	196	162.2*
		Parallel gestalt	165	330	2785.8
2	Medium	Ordered sequential	98	196	84.7*
		Parallel gestalt	165	330	2701.4
3	Medium	Ordered sequential	98	196	105.7*
		Parallel gestalt	165	330	1795.0
3	Wide	Ordered sequential	98	196	68.1*
		Parallel gestalt	165	330	858.4
4	Narrow	Ordered sequential	98	196	118.7*
		Parallel gestalt	165	330	2949.2
4	Medium	Ordered sequential	98	196	121.6*
		Parallel gestalt	165	330	3610.8
4	Wide	Ordered sequential	98	196	111.9*
		Parallel gestalt	165	330	2132.9

Note. This table presents goodness of fit of two models to (hypothetical) data generated by the other model. That is, the fit of the ordered sequential model to (hypothetical) data generated by the parallel gestalt model is evaluated using the obtained maximum-likelihood estimates of the model parameters; likewise, the fit of the parallel gestalt model to (hypothetical) data generated by the ordered sequential model is evaluated. Conditions marked by an asterisk indicate an acceptable fit of the model. df, Degrees of freedom.

a reasonable conclusion that the obtained experimental data are better described by the underlying structure of the parallel gestalt model than by the ordered sequential model.

Comparison of Exponential Versions of the Parallel Models

The models presented here assume that the parameters representing detection probabilities are increasing functions of stimulus energy. One way to test the assumption that the parameters are increasing is to see if the data are still fitted by the model if we force the parameters to follow some increasing function. The exponential distribution function is a reasonable choice, because it incorporates three important characteristics of psychophysical data, namely, a threshold, a variable slope, and an asymptote. Exponential versions of both the simple parallel and parallel gestalt models were fitted to the data. That is, detection parameters (all parameters other than the confusion parameters L and R) were assumed to have the following form:

$$\theta_i(T) = A_i\{1 - \exp[-k_i(T - t_i)]\} \qquad T > t_i,$$
$$= 0 \qquad\qquad\qquad\qquad \text{otherwise} \qquad (2)$$

where θ_i represents G, H from the simple parallel model or G, H, W_0, W_1, W_2 from the parallel gestalt model. The parameter A_i represents the asymptotic (with respect to T) level of performance for a given condition; k_i is the rate of improvement of performance with time (the slope of the exponential function); and t_i is the threshold duration below which the stimuli are assumed to be unidentifiable. The confusion parameters $L(T)$ and $R(T)$ were determined separately for each T, as before. Note that the additional constraints provided by the exponential function increase the degrees of freedom for testing the models. The parameters A, k, and t, along with $L(T)$ and $R(T)$, were found that simultaneously maximized the multinomial likelihood function (i.e., that minimized G^2) for all stimulus durations. The parameters were found using an optimization algorithm called PRAXIS (Gegenfurtner, 1987) based on Brent's modifications of Powell's method for gradient search using conjugate bases (Brent, 1973; Powell, 1964; Press, Flannery, Teukolsky, & Vetterling, 1988).

Earlier we found that both parallel models fit the data fairly well, with the parallel gestalt model fitting better. The values of G^2 for the exponentialized version of the simple parallel and parallel gestalt models are given in Table 14.5. Both models seem to provide an adequate fit to the data (conditions marked by a single asterisk); however, the exponential parallel gestalt model fits in all cases. Furthermore, the exponential parallel gestalt model provides a significantly better fit than the exponential simple parallel

TABLE 14.5
Comparison of Goodness of Fit for Exponential Versions
of the Simple Parallel and Parallel Gestalt Models

Subject	Separation	Model	df	2df	G^2
1	Medium	Simple parallel	312	624	571.6*
		Parallel gestalt	285	570	318.6*
		Difference	27	54	253.0**
2	Narrow	Simple parallel	312	624	545.0*
		Parallel gestalt	285	570	325.7*
		Difference	27	54	219.3**
2	Medium	Simple parallel	312	624	399.7*
		Parallel gestalt	285	570	330.6*
		Difference	27	54	69.1**
3	Medium	Simple parallel	312	624	1000.5
		Parallel gestalt	285	570	457.0*
		Difference	27	54	543.5**
3	Wide	Simple parallel	312	624	855.2
		Parallel gestalt	165	570	426.5*
		Difference	27	54	428.7**
4	Narrow	Simple parallel	312	624	495.7*
		Parallel gestalt	165	570	336.6*
		Difference	27	54	59.1**
4	Medium	Simple parallel	312	624	457.1*
		Parallel gestalt	285	570	306.4*
		Difference	27	54	150.7**
4	Wide	Simple parallel	312	624	780.1
		Parallel gestalt	285	570	569.4*
		Difference	27	54	210.7**

Note. Values of G^2 marked by an asterisk indicate that the model would not be rejected for that condition. Values marked by a double asterisk represent conditions where the parallel gestalt model provides a significantly better fit to the data than the simple parallel model. df, Degrees of freedom.

model in all cases. We should feel confident at this point in concluding that the parallel gestalt model gives the best fit to the data, because it provides a better fit than the simple parallel model and, as argued earlier, better than the sequential parallel model. Furthermore, it is interesting to note that the data of Townsend and Snodgrass (1974) obtained using a version of the PST paradigm were fitted best by the version of the gestalt parallel model described earlier (Townsend & Ashby, 1983).

THE EXPONENTIAL PARALLEL GESTALT MODEL

The exponential curves for $H(T)$ and $W_1(T)$ are plotted in Figs. 14.7 and 14.8 along with the previously determined maximum likelihood estimates of the multinomial parameters. [The chunking parameter $W_1(T)$ was cho-

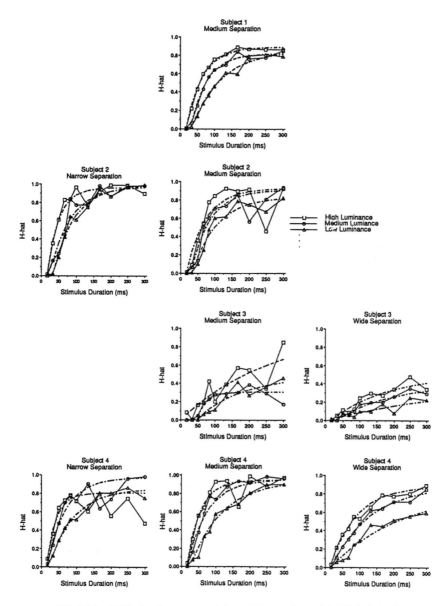

FIG. 14.7. $H(T)$ for the exponential parallel gestalt model (thick dashed lines). The individual parameter estimates from the model given in Appendix B are plotted as shapes for high luminance (squares), medium luminance (circles), and low luminance (triangles).

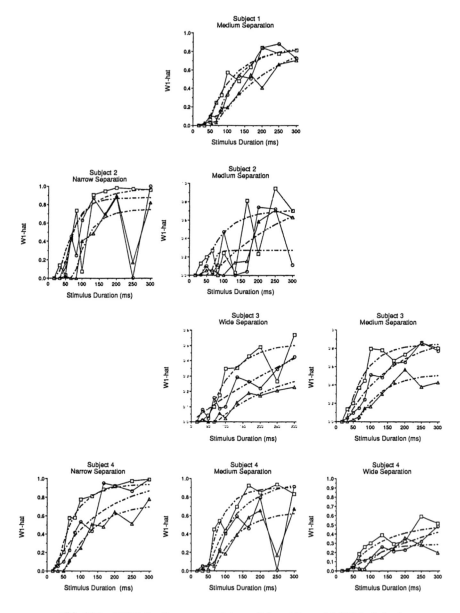

FIG. 14.8. $W_1(T)$ for the exponential parallel gestalt model (thick dashed lines). The individual parameter estimates from the model given in Appendix B are plotted as shapes for high luminance (squares), medium luminance (circles), and low luminance (triangles).

sen for illustration because it was estimated from a greater number of data points than $W_0(T)$ or $W_2(T)$ and so is the most reliably estimated of the three chunking parameters.] The exponential curves correspond to the individual parameter estimates fairly well. The parameters of the exponential curves for G, H, and W_1 are presented in Table 14.6.

TABLE 14.6
Exponential Parameters for G, H, and W_1
of the Parallel Gestalt Model

O	S	A_G			k_G			t_G		
		Exponential Parameters for $G(T)$								
2	N	0.979	0.999	0.938	0.014	0.010	0.027	28.4	16.1	14.8
4	N	0.808	0.957	0.800	0.010	0.018	0.020	29.1	27.8	15.7
1	M	0.840	0.841	0.872	0.010	0.019	0.020	31.2	30.6	25.3
2	M	0.967	0.956	0.975	0.011	0.019	0.019	31.2	27.7	15.6
3	M	0.997	0.628	0.994	0.002	0.005	0.004	30.9	30.4	1.9
4	M	0.819	0.662	0.796	0.010	0.036	0.026	29.3	28.1	15.5
3	W	1.000	0.423	0.554	0.001	0.008	0.009	16.7	33.3	11.5
4	W	0.420	0.532	0.636	0.011	0.013	0.013	26.4	15.3	13.8

O	S	A_H			k_H			t_H		
		Exponential Parameters for $H(T)$								
2	N	0.987	0.969	0.958	0.016	0.017	0.030	32.0	23.4	16.2
4	N	0.846	0.972	0.802	0.014	0.019	0.036	22.0	15.1	13.8
1	M	0.858	0.822	0.891	0.011	0.020	0.020	30.6	28.4	16.3
2	M	0.838	0.909	0.927	0.014	0.018	0.018	32.8	29.5	16.3
3	M	0.479	0.308	0.990	0.008	0.035	0.004	45.7	45.8	0.1
4	M	0.942	0.953	0.948	0.011	0.017	0.025	26.3	16.1	15.3
3	W	0.412	0.392	0.491	0.002	0.007	0.006	2.7	33.6	16.7
4	W	0.817	0.877	0.880	0.005	0.007	0.013	26.3	16.1	15.3

O	S	A_{W_1}			k_{W_1}			t_{W_1}		
		Exponential Parameters for $W_1(T)$								
2	N	0.746	0.875	0.976	0.024	0.030	0.017	77.5	45.7	28.6
4	N	0.732	1.000	0.941	0.012	0.007	0.019	56.9	15.5	29.0
1	M	1.000	0.847	0.847	0.006	0.014	0.013	63.6	62.3	39.8
2	M	0.999	0.269	0.709	0.004	0.099	0.016	66.7	63.6	36.2
3	M	0.519	0.942	0.848	0.014	0.008	0.018	63.5	28.7	29.7
4	M	0.640	0.972	0.903	0.014	0.012	0.023	66.6	47.6	46.9
3	W	0.356	0.973	0.515	0.006	0.002	0.014	76.0	0.4	46.6
4	W	0.285	0.681	0.504	0.025	0.004	0.010	79.2	33.3	33.1

Note. Parameters are listed in order of increasing luminance (low, medium, high). O is for observer (1, 2, 3, or 4); S is for separation: narrow (N), medium (M), or wide (W). A is the asymptote of the exponential; k is the slope; t is the threshold duration.

From the figures and table, we observe a few regularities in the parameter estimates. The parameters for the single-letter detection functions $G(T)$ and $H(T)$ do not appear to differ greatly from each other [$\theta_H(T) > \theta_G(T)$ in 38 of 72 cases], but they are both affected by the experimental conditions.

The thresholds t_G and t_H for the single-letter detection curves clearly decrease with luminance (t_i for high luminance exceeds t_i for low luminance in 15 of 16 conditions). The slope parameters k_G and k_H increase with luminance (k_i for high luminance is greater than k_i for low luminance in 15 of 16 conditions). The changes of the slopes and thresholds indicate the expected improvement in processing with luminance. However, the asymptotes A_G and A_H do not appear to be affected by luminance (A_i for high luminance exceeds A_i for low luminance in only 9 of 16 conditions). This is expected because longer durations are able to compensate for lower luminance levels.

Because not all observers were run at all separations, the effect of separation is assessed by comparing the change in parameters from medium to wide separation for observers 3 and 4. The thresholds do not appear to change with separation (t_i for medium separation is less than t_i for wide separation in just 6 of 12 conditions). However, slopes appear to decrease from medium to wide separation (k_i for medium separation is greater than k_i for wide separation in 8 of 12 conditions), and asymptotes definitely decrease from medium to wide separation (A_i for medium separation exceeds A_i for wide separation in 10 of 12 conditions). This could be due to the reduction in acuity at a separation of over 3 degrees of visual angle.

The chunking function $W_1(T)$ also changes with the stimulus variables. The threshold, t_{W_1}, for chunking decreases with luminance (t_{W_1} for high luminance is less than t_{W_1} for low luminance in 8 of 8 conditions). It is interesting to note that t_{W_1} for chunking appears to be roughly double the values of t_G and t_H for single-letter detection (contingent on the stimulus not being chunked). The mean ratio of t_{W_1} to the mean of t_G and t_H is 2.39. The slope k_{W_1} does not appear to change with luminance, although the estimates fluctuate too much to tell. The asymptote A_{W_1} increases with luminance (in 6 of 8 conditions), indicating that brighter stimuli are more likely to be chunked.

The chunking threshold t_{W_1} does not appear to change with separation (t_{W_1} for medium separation is greater than t_{W_1} for wide separation in 3 of 6 conditions). The slope k_{W_1} does decrease from medium to wide separation (in 5 of 6 conditions). The asymptote A_{W_1} is also seen to decrease from medium to wide separation (in 5 of 6 conditions). Both the decrease in slope and that of the asymptote are indications that more widely separated stimuli are less likely to be chunked.

To sum up then, the single-letter detection parameters indicate an overall improvement in processing as luminance increases, and a decrease with increasing separation, at least from the medium to wide separations used here. Both increasing luminance and decreasing separation seem to increase the likelihood that the letter stimuli are chunked into a single object. We also note that the fact that the parameters of the exponential version of the parallel gestalt model behave reasonably as a function the stimulus variables provides further evidence that the parallel gestalt model gives a reasonable description of the present data.

SUMMARY AND CONCLUSIONS

The approach of this study was to use multinomial models (see Riefer & Batchelder, 1988) of response probabilities from a two-display task to examine the question of whether shape identification is parallel or sequential. The experimental task was as simple as possible in order to minimize the effects of memory load, perceptual processing load, and visual and memory search strategies, and thus concentrate on the process of shape identification itself. Observers were presented two-letter displays. In any presentation, two, the left, the right, or no locations contained a letter designated as a target. The observer was to respond with the number and location of any targets he or she was certain of having seen: "two," "left," "right," or "none." The stimulus letters were presented at a range of durations, luminances, and physical separations.

In the initial analysis, it was found that both parallel models and one of two sequential models fit the data. However, additional analysis showed that the data would not have been likely to fit the parallel gestalt model if it had been generated by the structure assumed for the ordered sequential model, whereas the reverse was not true—the ordered sequential model would fit data generated by the parallel gestalt model. On these considerations, it was concluded that the data was best described by a parallel multinomial model of response probabilities.

There were two parallel models under consideration. The simple parallel model assumed independent probabilities for identifying the target at each location (left or right). The parallel gestalt model assumed that with some probability the observer chunked the display into a single object and identified it as a whole; in the case where the observer failed to chunk the display, the observer was assumed to identify the target letters independently at each location. In the initial analysis the parallel gestalt model seemed to fit slightly better than the simple parallel model.

Next, we examined whether the detection parameters of the parallel models were approximately exponentially increasing functions of display duration. Although the exponentialized versions of both parallel models fit the data to some extent, the exponential parallel gestalt model provided a significantly better fit than the exponential simple parallel model. Thus, we concluded that the data were best described by the parallel gestalt model, which assumes that on some trials the observer chunks the stimulus and processes it as a whole, or, failing that, processes the display items independently in parallel.

The finding that a parallel identification model describes the present data is at variance with the strong assumption that shape identification is a one-at-a-time process. However, the fact that the parallel gestalt model seems to do the best job of fitting the data is consistent with the interpretation that the shape identification mechanism attempts to process input as a whole before it will attempt to process the parts separately (cf. the word superiority effect, e.g., Johnston & McClelland, 1974, and Reicher, 1969, and the object superiority effect, Williams & Weisstein, 1978). Examination of the parameters of the parallel gestalt model also leads to the conclusion that brighter and closer stimuli are more likely to be chunked (identified as a single unit) than dimmer and more separated stimuli.

ACKNOWLEDGMENTS

The author thanks Dr. James Townsend and an anonymous reviewer for helpful comments on earlier drafts of this chapter.

APPENDIX A: THE SIMPLE PARALLEL MODEL

As defined in the text, response proportions are given as P(number of targets seen|number of targets presented). $G(I,T)$ and $H(I,T)$ are the probabilities of a left or right target, respectively, being identified as a function of luminance (I) and stimulus duration (T). $L(I,T)$ and $R(I,T)$ are the confusion parameters for the left and right side, respectively. To simplify the presentation, the arguments I and T are dropped from the notation that follows.

$$P(0 \mid 0) = (1 - L)(1 - R) \tag{A1}$$
$$P(L \mid 0) = L(1 - R) \tag{A2}$$
$$P(R \mid 0) = (1 - L)R \tag{A3}$$
$$P(2 \mid 0) = LR \tag{A4}$$

$$P(0 \mid L) = (1 - G)(1 - R) \tag{A5}$$
$$P(L \mid L) = G(1 - R) \tag{A6}$$
$$P(R \mid L) = (1 - G)R \tag{A7}$$
$$P(2 \mid L) = GR \tag{A8}$$

$$P(0 \mid R) = (1 - H)(1 - L) \tag{A9}$$
$$P(L \mid R) = (1 - H)L \tag{A10}$$
$$P(R \mid R) = H(1 - L) \tag{A11}$$
$$P(2 \mid R) = HL \tag{A12}$$

$$P(0 \mid 2) = (1 - G)(1 - H) \tag{A13}$$
$$P(L \mid 2) = G(1 - H) \tag{A14}$$
$$P(R \mid 2) = (1 - G)H \tag{A15}$$
$$P(2 \mid 2) = GH \tag{A16}$$

APPENDIX B: THE PARALLEL GESTALT MODEL

As defined in the text, response proportions are given as P(number of targets seen|number of targets presented). $W_0(I,T)$, $W_1(I,T)$, and $W_2(I,T)$ are the probabilities that the items in no-, one-, or two-target displays, respectively, are chunked as a single object and correctly identified. $G(I,T)$ and $H(I,T)$ are the probabilities of a left or right target, respectively, being identified as a function of luminance (I) and stimulus duration (T), conditional on not having been chunked. $L(I,T)$ and $R(I,T)$ are the confusion parameters for the left and right side, respectively, conditional on the display not having been chunked. To simplify the presentation, the arguments I and T are dropped from the notation that follows.

$$P(0 \mid 0) = W_0 + (1 - W_0)(1 - L)(1 - R) \tag{B1}$$
$$P(L \mid 0) = (1 - W_0)L(1 - R) \tag{B2}$$
$$P(R \mid 0) = (1 - W_0)(1 - L)R \tag{B3}$$
$$P(2 \mid 0) = (1 - W_0)LR \tag{B4}$$

$$P(0 \mid L) = (1 - W_1)(1 - G)(1 - R) \tag{B5}$$
$$P(L \mid L) = W_1 + (1 - W_1)G(1 - R) \tag{B6}$$
$$P(R \mid L) = (1 - W_1)(1 - G)R \tag{B7}$$
$$P(2 \mid L) = (1 - W_1)GR \tag{B8}$$

$$P(0 \mid R) = (1 - W_1)(1 - H)(1 - L) \tag{B9}$$
$$P(L \mid R) = (1 - W_1)(1 - H)L \tag{B10}$$
$$P(R \mid R) = W_1 + (1 - W_1)H(1 - L) \tag{B11}$$
$$P(2 \mid R) = (1 - W_1)HL \tag{B12}$$

$$P(0 \mid 2) = (1 - W_2)(1 - G)(1 - H) \tag{B13}$$
$$P(L \mid 2) = (1 - W_2)G(1 - H) \tag{B14}$$
$$P(R \mid 2) = (1 - W_2)(1 - G)H \tag{B15}$$
$$P(2 \mid 2) = W_2 + (1 - W_2)GH \tag{B16}$$

APPENDIX C: THE SYMMETRIC SEQUENTIAL MODEL

As defined in the text, response proportions are given as P(number of targets seen|number of targets presented). $G_1(I,T)$, $G_2(I,T)$ and $H_1(I,T)$, $H_2(I,T)$ are the probabilities of a left or right target being identified first or second as a function of luminance (I) and stimulus duration (T). $L_1(I,T)$, $L_2(I,T)$ and $R_1(I,T)$, $R_2(I,T)$ are the probabilities of a left or right non-target being confused with a target as a function of luminance (I) and stimulus duration (T). P is the probability of processing the left stimulus first. To simplify the presentation the arguments I and T are dropped from the notation that follows.

$$P(0 \mid 0) = P(1 - L_1)(1 - R_2) + (1 - P)(1 - R_1)(1 - L_2) \tag{C1}$$
$$P(L \mid 0) = PL_1(1 - R_2) + (1 - P)(1 - R_1)L_2 \tag{C2}$$
$$P(R \mid 0) = P(1 - L_1)R_2 + (1 - P)R_1(1 - L_2) \tag{C3}$$
$$P(2 \mid 0) = PL_1R_2 + (1 - P)R_1L_2 \tag{C4}$$

$$P(0 \mid L) = P(1 - G_1)(1 - R_2) + (1 - P)(1 - R_1)(1 - G_2) \tag{C5}$$
$$P(L \mid L) = PG_1(1 - R_2) + (1 - P)(1 - R_1)G_2 \tag{C6}$$
$$P(R \mid L) = P(1 - G_1)R_2 + (1 - P)R_1(1 - G_2) \tag{C7}$$
$$P(2 \mid L) = PG_1R_2 + (1 - P)R_1G_2 \tag{C8}$$

$$P(0 \mid R) = P(1 - L_1)(1 - H_2) + (1 - P)(1 - H_1)(1 - L_2) \tag{C9}$$
$$P(L \mid R) = PL_1(1 - H_2) + (1 - P)(1 - H_1)L_2 \tag{C10}$$
$$P(R \mid R) = P(1 - L_1)H_2 + (1 - P)H_1(1 - L_2) \tag{C11}$$
$$P(2 \mid R) = PL_1H_2 + (1 - P)H_1L_2 \tag{C12}$$

$$P(0 \mid 2) = P(1 - G_1)(1 - H_2) + (1 - P)(1 - H_1)(1 - G_2) \tag{C13}$$
$$P(L \mid 2) = PG_1(1 - H_2) + (1 - P)(1 - H_1)G_2 \tag{C14}$$
$$P(R \mid 2) = P(1 - G_1)H_2 + (1 - P)H_1(1 - G_2) \tag{C15}$$
$$P(2 \mid 2) = PG_1H_2 + (1 - P)H_1G_2 \tag{C16}$$

APPENDIX D: THE ORDERED SEQUENTIAL MODEL

As defined in the text, response proportions are given as P(number of targets seen|number of targets presented). $G_1(I,T)$, $G_2(I,T)$, and $H_1(I,T)$, $H_2(I,T)$ are the probabilities of a left or right target being identified first or second as a function of luminance (I) and stimulus duration (T). $L_1(I,T)$, $L_2(I,T)$, and $R_1(I,T)$, $R_2(I,T)$ are the probabilities of a left or right nontarget being confused with a target as a function of luminance (I) and stimulus duration (T). The parameters G_2, H_2, L_2, R_2 are contingent on the first target examined having been correctly identified or correctly rejected. P

is the probability of processing the left stimulus first. To simplify the presentation the arguments I and T are dropped from the notation that follows.

$$P(0 \mid 0) = P(1 - L_1)(1 - R_2) + (1 - P)(1 - R_1)(1 - L_2) \tag{D1}$$
$$P(L \mid 0) = PL_1 + (1 - P)(1 - R_1)L_2 \tag{D2}$$
$$P(R \mid 0) = P(1 - L_1)R_2 + (1 - P)R_1 \tag{D3}$$
$$P(2 \mid 0) = 0 \tag{D4}$$

$$P(0 \mid L) = P(1 - G_1) + (1 - P)(1 - R_1)(1 - G_2) \tag{D5}$$
$$P(L \mid L) = PG_1(1 - R_2) + (1 - P)(1 - R_1)G_2 \tag{D6}$$
$$P(R \mid L) = (1 - P)R_1 \tag{D7}$$
$$P(2 \mid L) = PG_1R_2 \tag{D8}$$

$$P(0 \mid R) = P(1 - L_1)(1 - H_2) + (1 - P)(1 - H_1) \tag{D9}$$
$$P(L \mid R) = PL_1 \tag{D10}$$
$$P(R \mid R) = P(1 - L_1)H_2 + (1 - P)H_1(1 - L_2) \tag{D11}$$
$$P(2 \mid R) = (1 - P)H_1L_2 \tag{D12}$$

$$P(0 \mid 2) = P(1 - G_1) + (1 - P)(1 - H_1) \tag{D13}$$
$$P(L \mid 2) = PG_1(1 - H_2) \tag{D14}$$
$$P(R \mid 2) = (1 - P)H_1(1 - G_2) \tag{D15}$$
$$P(2 \mid 2) = PG_1H_2 + (1 - P)H_1G_2 \tag{D16}$$

REFERENCES

Akaike, H. (1973). Information theory and an extension of the maximum likelihood principle. In B. N. Petrov & F. Csaki (Eds.), *2nd International Symposium on Information Theory* (pp. 267–281). Budapest: Akademiai Kiado.

Brent, R. P. (1973). *Algorithms for minimization without derivatives.* Englewood Cliffs, NJ: Prentice-Hall.

Coltheart, M. (1980). Iconic memory and visible persistence. *Perception & Psychophysics, 27,* 183–228.

Dempster, A. P., Laird, N. M., & Rubin, D. B. (1977). Maximum likelihood from incomplete data via the EM algorithm. *Journal of Royal Statistics Society B, 39,* 1–38.

Gegenfurtner, K. (1987). *PRAXIS* [Computer program]. New York: New York University, Department of Psychology.

Hu, X., & Batchelder, W. H. (1994). The statistical analysis of general processing tree models with the EM-algorithm. *Psychometrika, 59,* 21–48.

James, W. (1983). *The principles of psychology.* Cambridge, MA: Harvard University Press. (Original work published 1890)

Johnston, J. C., & McClelland, J. L. (1974). Perception of letters in words: Seek and ye shall not find. *Science, 184,* 1192–1194.

LaBerge, D. (1990). Attention. *Psychological Science, 1,* 156–162.

Long, G. M. (1980). Iconic memory: A review and critique of the study of short-term visual storage. *Psychological Bulletin, 88,* 785–820.

Luce, R. D. (1986). *Response times.* New York: Oxford University Press.

Marr, D. (1982). *Vision.* New York: Freeman.

Powell, M. (1964). An efficient method for finding the minimum of a function in several variables without calculating derivatives. *Computer Journal, 7,* 155–162.

Press, W. H., Flannery, B. P., Teukolsky, S. A., & Vetterling, W. T. (1988). *Numerical recipes in C: The art of scientific computing.* New York: Cambridge University Press.

Read, T. R. C., & Cressie, N. A. C. (1988). *Goodness-of-fit statistics for discrete multivariate data.* New York: Springer-Verlag.

Reicher, G. M. (1969). Perceptual recognition as a function of meaningfulness of stimulus material. *Journal of Experimental Psychology, 81,* 274–280.

Riefer, D. M., & Batchelder, W. H. (1988). Multinomial modeling and the measurement of cognitive processes. *Psychological Review, 95,* 318–339.

Townsend, J. T. (1974). Issues and models concerning the processing of a finite number of inputs. In B. H. Kantowitz (Ed.), *Human information processing: Tutorials in performance and cognition* (pp. 133–168). Hillsdale, NJ: Lawrence Erlbaum Associates.

Townsend, J. T. (1990). Serial vs. parallel processing: Sometimes they look like tweedledum and tweedledee but they can (and should) be distinguished. *Psychological Science, 1,* 46–54.

Townsend, J. T., & Ashby, F. G. (1983). *Stochastic modeling of elementary psychological processes.* Cambridge, England: Cambridge University Press.

Townsend, J. T., & Snodgrass, J. G. (1974, November). *A serial vs. parallel testing paradigm when "same" and "different" comparison rates differ.* Paper presented at the annual meeting of the Psychonomic Society, Boston.

Treisman, A. M., & Souther, J. (1985). Search asymmetry: A diagnostic for preattentive processing of separable features. *Journal of Experimental Psychology: General, 114,* 285–310.

Williams, A., & Weisstein, N. (1978) Line segments are perceived better in a coherent context than alone: An object-line effect in visual perception. *Memory & Cognition, 6,* 85–90.

Chapter 15

Reciprocity as an Interaction Principle

Hubert Feger
Free University of Berlin

Ulrich von Hecker
University of Potsdam

In a simple and elegant design, Flament and Apfelbaum (1966) had group members exchange messages—paper slips, each labeled with just a "+" or "0." The more of the positive messages a group member received, the higher was the person's final evaluation. The participants did not know that different percentages of positive messages were allocated to the four positions in a group (A = 65%, B = 55%, C = 45%, D = 35%). All positive messages were randomly mixed with neutral ones. The authors claim that exchange is governed by mutuality, and that coalitions forming between the group members will be observed. Furthermore, the group structure as revealed by sociometric choices is derived from the exchange process.

An experiment with such a fundamental result seems worth replicating. This chapter reports the analytical problems we encountered in our attempt to replicate these results and to predict the exchange behavior of a group member. Our research is still continuing, and only some preliminary results can be provided.

The replication of this experiment in Berlin added groups without differences in resources. Resource differentiation seems to speed up (but is not a necessary condition for) structuration. Flament and Apfelbaum derived—but only from a global interpretation of their data—that social exchange is guided by a mutuality principle. To test their claim we first had to understand that mutuality can be realized in different ways, and that the analysis needs to be of the behavior of each participant separately. Mutuality can be realized in different ways. We derive the predictions of two principles, "immediate proportional reciprocity" and the "debtor principle," each with two variants. Reciprocity advises sending as many positive messages to a position as this position had given to the sender (a) in the interval before the present one or (b) cumulatively from the beginning of the experiment that passed until the present. The debtor principle additionally takes into account the resources provided by the sender to any position, either during the previous interval or until now. We test whether a group member uses one of these principles.

THE FLAMENT AND APFELBAUM EXPERIMENT

Flament and Apfelbaum (1966) studied the effect of communication on the development of structure in a group. With respect to communication, they were interested in the effect of the contact between two persons created by every communication, and in the effect created by the socio-affective value of every communication. Thus, they were not concerned with the meaning or information content of a message. Experimentally, this abstraction was obtained by having participants exchange slips of paper each labeled only with a "0" or a "+." The participants were instructed that at the end of the experiment they would be evaluated by the number of positive messages, those labeled with a "+," in their possession.

The participants were seated in boxes so that they had no contact with each other except for exchanging messages, which they could do at their own speed. They were free to send a card to any of their fellow participants, but only in the order the cards were given them. They knew—by the color of the messages received—who had been the sender of a specific message. They did not know that the number of positive messages differed among the participants. Calling the four positions A, B, C, and D, the proportions of positive messages—from now on called *resources*—were 65%, 55%, 45%, and 35%. Two hundred well-mixed slips of paper, labeled with either "0" or "+," were provided to each participant. The experiment came to its end when one participant had used all her messages. After the exchange of messages was finished, some sociometric questions were asked to test the predictions on the sociometric structure which the group developed during the interaction process.

As one of their results, Flament and Apfelbaum stated (p. 382):

> At the very beginning of the experiment, each subject divided his "+" messages equally among his three fellow members. . . . During the experimental session, the distribution of "+" messages sent by each subject to his teammates at any time varies proportionally with the distribution of "+" messages most recently received by him.

This paragraph and other parts of their paper imply that Flament and Apfelbaum explain their results by the action of a principle guiding the distribution performed by each individual participant. We are interested in this kind of principle and tried to derive the distributional behavior of the participants from these principles.

THE BERLIN REPLICATION

Flament and Apfelbaum (1966, p. 383) stated that they could not provide a more detailed test of their model because for this purpose it would be necessary "to know exactly the succession of all the exchanges of messages, not just the mean number of messages exchanged over long periods of time." In our Hamburg replications, we tried to obtain this information by using several trained observers to record simultaneously the ongoing process by hand. But we failed; there was simply too much happening within very short periods, and the observers, who were registering the kind and time of messages, interfered with the process. This was, of course, even more pronounced when we increased the number of participants to five.

Therefore, in our Berlin replications, we used a LAN computer network to register all exchanges without interfering with the process itself (see von Hecker, 1991). The 88 participants of the 22 groups of four persons were mostly psychology undergraduates at the Free University of Berlin. Each student was seated in a box and had no contact with the other participants. He or she did not know who was (randomly) assigned to which of the positions. In front of him or her, a PC monitor and keyboard were placed (Fig. 15.1).

von Hecker (1991, p. 13) described the procedure: The screen display was divided into an upper and a lower section. The upper section contained

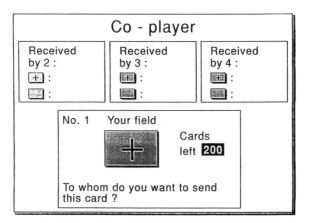

FIG. 15.1. Display for participant 1 on the screen.

three windows, one for each partner. In each window, cards incoming from the respective partner were registered, broken down into pluses and zeros, with the current count always displayed. Partners in each position were identified by numbers ranging from 1 to 4, which showed up in each partner window. One number was assigned for the subject's position, which he or she could see in the lower section of the screen. The number assignment had nothing to do with resource strength, nor with the seating order in the laboratory.

The lower section of the screen contained the position's card stack. At any time, a card was exposed to be used by the person in this position as the next card. This "card" had to be sent off by pressing a numeric key corresponding to the chosen partner's number. Pluses and zeros appeared in a random sequence, which was determined anew for each group and position. Just after each sending reaction, a short interval was provided in which no reaction was accepted. Then the next card appeared. Thus, sending speed could be freely chosen by the subjects, as in the original experiment. Cards had to be sent off one by one, thereby precluding the possibility of aggregating whole sets of cards in one sending act. Neither could any card be arbitrarily chosen from the stack, but the subject could only send the card actually appearing. Sessions lasted for about 11 to 14 min.

In our replication, we extended the Flament and Apfelbaum experiment by introducing what may be called a *control condition*. We studied 10 four-person groups, each with an equal distribution of resources, that is, 50% positive messages for each person. Table 15.1 reports the final distributions of positive messages received for these groups. In all groups, large intra- and interindividual differences occur, but it is not possible to predict who will be rich and who will be poor. In an analysis of variance (with sender–receiver pairs as a repeated measurement factor) the main effects are not significant ($p > 30\%$). However, in a pair of persons, the transaction results are correlated ($r = .69$); that is, either both members of a pair achieve good results, or both are not successful. Thus, differences in resources provided by an external source are not necessary to lead to marked differences in exchange.

Given certain conditions, an unequal distribution of resources will hinder the development of exchange coalitions. Let us assume that each participant can send exactly one positive message at discrete time intervals, and that each participant reacts in a strict "tit for tat" manner, sending a positive message to that partner from whom he or she received a positive message on the previous trial. If he or she received more or less than one positive message on the previous trial, he or she decides at random to whom to send his or her positive message.

Under these conditions, the exchange must converge to two pairs, and all exchange is done exclusively within these two pairs. The convergence

TABLE 15.1
Final Distributions of the Number of Positive Messages
Received for the Groups of the Control Condition

Group	aB	aC	aD	bA	bC	bD	cA	cB	cD	dA	dB	dC
1	22	23	22	30	4	21	35	5	60	29	22	41
2	7	30	29	6	79	15	19	45	21	29	32	31
3	38	16	46	38	30	20	26	29	10	31	14	3
4	12	23	36	9	30	1	26	49	25	46	11	30
5	35	6	59	39	31	29	15	29	7	42	52	6
6	48	19	33	24	25	23	10	5	7	45	33	12
7	17	17	56	7	45	47	6	64	17	25	31	28
8	31	28	30	28	41	21	21	47	32	20	22	31
9	2	32	40	6	34	26	49	46	3	58	41	1
10	35	16	9	54	9	39	18	9	31	12	42	39

Note. aB corresponds to position a as the sender, and B as the receiver.

is delayed by the "random decisions," by error, and if reactions are not immediate but lagged. In the Flament and Apfelbaum design, with different amounts of resources for each of the positions, it is necessary to introduce "0" messages (assumed to be neutral). These messages delay convergence to exchange coalitions and they force memory to play a role: Each subject must consider the behavior of the partners for more than just one of the previous trials. The correlation of transaction results reported earlier for the data in Table 15.1 can be explained by a "tit-for-tat" tendency, distorted by factors delaying convergence.

RESULTS OF FLAMENT AND APFELBAUM
AND OF THE BERLIN REPLICATIONS

This section reports comparisons between the results of Flament and Apfelbaum and results of the Berlin replication. We first test the assumption that participants at the very beginning of the experiment distribute their positive messages equally among the other positions. Then we compare the "theoretical curves" that Flament and Apfelbaum used to describe their results with the general tendencies observed over all groups in the Berlin replication.

At the beginning of the experiment, when consistent and stable information about the sending behavior of the partners is not available, several reaction options exist. In the experimental design used here, a person cannot just wait and see, but has to react. At least two principles can be invoked in this situation. The person may intend to create a uniform distribution when sending positive messages (as quite a few of the participants of our Hamburg replication reportedly did), or the person may react "at random," that is, without paying any attention to his or her own behavior or to the reactions of the partners. In both cases, no information about the behavior of the partners is needed to determine one's own behavior.

Producing a uniform distribution or reacting at random should both lead to statistically equal numbers of positive messages for the three positions available to every sender. The hypothesis of a uniform distribution should be tested for each sender position separately, because the resources are different from the very beginning of the experiment. We determine arbitrarily what the "beginning" means, and select (a) the first 5 trials, and (b) the first 10 trials. A trial in this context corresponds to a person sending a message, either a positive or a neutral one. Table 15.2 reports the frequency distributions (summed over 32 groups) of the positive messages sent, specified for the various sender/receiver combinations, and for the first 5 and 10 trials.

Only one of the eight χ^2 tests is significant with $\alpha < 5\%$; therefore we do not reject the assumption of no preferences for specific positions at the start of the experiment.

There exists a second possibility to test this assumption. One alternative to random behavior and intended equal distribution is early commitment to one (or two) of the other participants, neglecting the others. This should result in "extreme" distributions of the positive messages of a sender over the three receivers. Rather arbitrarily we define the "first part" of the experiment for a particular subject as the time required for that subject to send the first ten positive messages. Then a part of the data is analyzed that differs from the one covered in Table 15.2.

Table 15.3 lists all possible distributions of 10 messages over three positions, with 10,0,0, the most extreme, indicating early and exclusive com-

TABLE 15.2
Testing for Uniform Distributions at the Beginning of the Experiment

First 5 Trials				First 10 Trials			
Combination			χ^2	Combination			χ^2
aB	aC	aD		aB	aC	aD	
17	19	10	2.95	34	36	23	3.16
bA	bC	bD		bA	bC	bD	
23	12	12	5.15	36	30	24	2.40
cA	bC	cD		cA	cB	cD	
14	10	13	0.69	21	22	28	1.20
dA	dB	dC		dA	dB	dC	
5	8	19	10.18	19	19	28	2.44

Note. Because the positive messages were distributed at random, their total number during the first 5 or 10 trials is not fixed.

TABLE 15.3
Testing for Early Commitment

Distribution	p(exp.)	f(exp.)	f(obs.)	χ^2 Component
10 0 0	.045	5.76	2	2.45
9 1 0	.09	11.52	3	6.30
8 2 0	.09	11.52	4	4.91
8 1 1	.045	5.76	2	2.45
7 3 0	.09	11.52	5	3.69
7 2 1	.09	11.52	12	0.02
6 4 0	.09	11.52	6	2.65
6 3 1	.09	11.52	9	0.55
6 2 2	.045	5.76	3	1.32
5 5 0	.045	5.76	3	1.32
5 4 1	.09	11.52	13	0.19
5 3 2	.09	11.52	23	11.44
4 4 2	.045	5.76	18	3.65
4 3 3	.045	5.76	25	15.77

mitment, and 4,3,3, the least extreme, approaching a uniform distribution as close as possible. Then Table 15.3 reports the expected proportions of occurrence if all distributions are assumed equally likely. For example, 10,0,0, and 0,10,0 and 0,0,10 are 3 possibilities of a set of 66 possibilities altogether, leading to $p = 3/66 = .045$ for one 10 and two 0s. A χ^2 test compares this expected distribution with the observed frequencies; also reported are the χ^2 components. The overall χ^2 is 56.71 with df = 13 and $\alpha < .001$. Inspecting the distributions, the result is very clear: There exists no indication of early commitment. The assumption of random behavior or intended equal distributions at the start of the experiment can be maintained.

As their major result, Flament and Apfelbaum reported (in their Fig. 1) the "emission of positive messages" during the four quarters of the experiment. They also idealize these results (in their Fig. 2). Both sets of sender-oriented functions are reproduced in our Fig. 15.2. Note that Flament and Apfelbaum removed level effects created by the differences in the resources of the positions. They achieved this by "taking as our zero point for each subject one-third of the value . . . of the messages sent to all three team-mates during each period" (p. 382). Flament and Apfelbaum provided the following interpretation:

> During the experimental session, the distribution of "+" messages sent by each subject to his team-mates at any one time varies proportionally with the distribution of "+" messages recently received by him.
> To understand the functioning of the proposed mechanism, it must be pointed out that the subject cannot increase at will the total number of his "+" messages; in order to increase the number of "+" messages which he

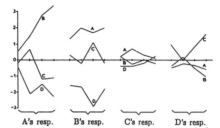

A's resp.   B's resp.   C's resp.   D's resp.

Emissions of positive messages during the four parts of the experiment.

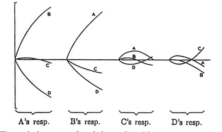

A's resp.   B's resp.   C's resp.   D's resp.

Theoretical curves of emissions of positive messages, compared to the experimental curves of Fig. 1.

FIG. 15.2.   Results of Flament and Apfelbaum (1966).

sends to one of his fellow members, he will have to diminish the number of "+" messages sent to another. Then the following type of relationship occurs: if during the period preceding a given moment subject A received a greatly increased number of "+" messages from subject B, a moderately increased number from subject C, and a slightly increased number from subject D, then subject A will increase his "+" messages to B and decrease them to D, while the number of messages to C will be modified in an intermediate fashion. (p. 382)

No equations are derived, and nothing more than quoted is said about the "theoretical curves."

Although the responses of positions A and B could agree with the predictions derived from the reciprocity principle,[1] the responses of C and D provide some difficulties. Reciprocity does not predict the intersection of any curves, nor does it predict that most curves of C and D have a turning point. But these intersections and turning points were important to Flament and Apfelbaum because they based their interpretation of the development of group structure on these phenomena. On the other hand, the changes in the curves representing the behavior of C and D are small,

---

[1]This principle is introduced in a more formal way in the next section.

and may not be reliable. We therefore provide the results of the Berlin replication in Fig. 15.3.

Comparing the results of the experiments in Aix-en-Provence and in Berlin the general impression might be confusing. We therefore quote the summary given by Flament and Apfelbaum (p. 385) and then translate it into a synopsis (Table 15.4).

(1) A and B favor each other more and more as the experiment proceeds, while they both neglect player D more and more; their attitude toward C

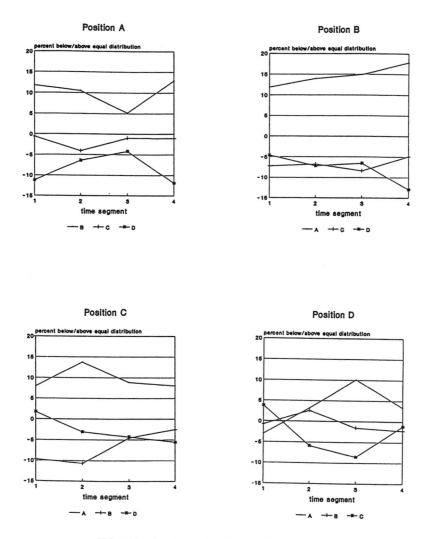

FIG. 15.3. Overall results of the Berlin replication.

TABLE 15.4
Comparison of Predicted and Observed Global Results

Relation	F&A: Change Predicted	F&A: Change Observed	Observed in Berlin
A → B	Increase	Yes	?
B → A	Increase	?	Yes
A → D	Decrease	Yes	?
B → D	Decrease	Yes	?
A → C	Negative end	Yes	No
B → C	Negative end	Yes	No
C → A	Curvilinear	Yes	Yes
C → B	Curvilinear	?	No
C → D	Increase	Yes	Yes
D → A	Curvilinear	?	Yes
D → B	Curvilinear	Yes	Yes
D → C	Increase	Yes	?

is intermediate, but tends to become negative toward the end of the experimental session.

(2) C favors first A and B, and then, faced at the end with the lack of interest which these players show in him, he favors D.

(3) D follows a similar, though more rapid, shift, and he favors C rather early in the session.

In Table 15.4, predicted and observed are the number of positive messages sent during the exchange process; "yes" refers to a correct prediction, "no" to an incorrect one, and "?" indicates an open question. Note that the second column contains our interpretation of the quotation just cited. Furthermore, we here deliberately refrain from all inferential statistics. However, we stress our result that differences within and between groups are very large. From this fact we conclude that it probably is desirable to concentrate the analysis on the single group member.

PRINCIPLES OF EXCHANGE BEHAVIOR
IN INTERACTIONS

Interaction requires at least two partners that, in the course of time, react to the behavior of the other participant(s). The term *behavior* is used here in a very broad sense. It can be analyzed from various perspectives. Flament and Apfelbaum chose to observe the exchange of "messages," and their experimental design was intended to create a situation in which only the value of the messages varies. Every subject has to choose repeatedly to whom he or she will send a message, and this act (so the subject is led to assume) will be evaluated positively by the recipient whenever it is a valued message. At the same time the sender receives valuable messages from the three other partners. How should a person act in this situation to maximize the sum of incoming positive messages?

In the postexperimental interviews of our replication, several participants spontaneously described their behavior by referring to general rules or principles like, "I wanted to keep in contact with everyone" or "After some time, I thought I had to be loyal to GREEN [one of the positions]" or "If somebody stopped sending to me, I tried to revive him." These principles referred to the behavior of the others, relating one's own behavior to that of the others as either "giving more" or "receiving more," with changing bases of comparison. They alluded to one's own expectations of the behavior of the other participants and to one's own attacking and countering tactics.

We now discuss some exchange principles prescribing or predicting one's own behavior toward others that take into account the previous and expected behavior of these others. The principles should state whether or not at a specific trial a sender provides a specific receiver with a small reward. Two principles are given special attention: the reciprocity and the debtor principle. *Reciprocity* describes the intention (or actual behavior) to give as much to a person as one received from this person, relative to what one received from the other persons in the same exchange situation. The *debtor principle* furthermore takes into account how much one has given to the others previously. The way the friendly behavior of the others (as well as one's own) is remembered will be analyzed subject to two assumptions:

1. All is remembered at any time by anyone.
2. There exists an interval of remembered trials, and this interval is equally fixed for all participants and for all phases of the experiment.

The first is called the *cumulative case*, and the second the *fixed-interval case*. Several intermediate variants between the reciprocity and the debtor principle and between the cumulative and the fixed interval case could be constructed and analyzed, but this is not done here.

The behavior of sending positive messages to other participants is conceived to be directed by general distribution principles. It is behavior that increases the resources of other persons. These very persons are—at the same time as the subject—competing for goods, and these goods are available only from others. With respect to a principle, several strategies may exist to achieve the goals implied by the principle. In the highly standardized situation of this experiment, only one kind of information is explicitly provided (on the screen) that might be used to direct one's actions: the number of positive messages received until now from each of the other participants. The number of positive messages sent by oneself on previous trials to those participants is—more or less correctly and completely—remembered. This forms a different, although related, kind of information, also available to the subject.

We do not assume that the distribution principles can always be explicitly stated by every participant at every time. We merely assume that behavior can be described and predicted by these principles. Thus an important decision is: Should the principle be related to the information provided in the messages received from others, and should one use this information instead of or in addition to the information remembered about the messages sent by oneself? If a person either does not notice or chooses to ignore this information, another principle would be to randomly send the messages to all participants. This random principle is not meaningless, especially not during the first trials when reliable and sufficient information on sending and receiving is not available.

Still another principle would be to send the same amount or proportion to every possible receiver, independently from the receiver's sending behavior in the past or at present. This principle of *equality* has explicitly been stated by a few subjects in the postexperimental interviews. It could be recognized in the activities of its proponents by direct attempts to correct any imbalance of scores that might have been created by random fluctuation, temporary inattention, and so forth.

Now let us assume that a participant indeed wants to use the receiving (and sending) information. Then a principle that suggests itself, especially as a strategy to increase one's own score of positive messages received, is *mutuality*: I do to you what you do to me, or "tit for tat." One could, of course, also use this information to apply an inverse strategy: Neglect those who provided benefit. However, no person did anything in this direction, and therefore this line of reasoning is not pursued here.

Reciprocity with a Fixed Interval

One variant of the mutuality principle is to reciprocate what one gets, and to do so in proportion to what one has received in the previous interval. (We perform all our analyses here for a given interval of several trials, and not stepwise trial by trial.) To apply this principle for deriving how many positive messages should be sent within the next following interval we need information on what was received from every other participant during the previous interval. Furthermore, we must know which resources are or will be available to this sender during the next interval. We define the following variables:

$(A \rightarrow B)_2$: number of positive messages to be sent in the next interval from A to B

$(B \rightarrow A)_1$: number of positive messages sent in the previous interval from B to A

$R_{A(2)}$: resources available to A in the next interval: in general, or as actually provided by the random procedure

The reciprocity principle can now be stated as:

$$(A \rightarrow B)_2 = R_{A(2)}(B \rightarrow A)_1 / [(B \rightarrow A)_1 + (C \rightarrow A)_1 + (D \rightarrow A)_1] \quad (1)$$

Thus, the reciprocity principle is defined as a recommendation to send in the next interval to any receiver a certain proportion of all messages available. This proportion is identical to the proportion obtained from the prospective receiver. The proportion is calculated by dividing the number of positive messages received from the position of this receiver by the number of positive messages received from all senders during the previous interval.

To derive the qualitative properties of the functions describing the sending behavior suggested by the reciprocity principle, we start with the assumption that in the first interval every position sends an equal amount of his resources to every possible receiver. This is shown in Table 15.5 for the first interval of 10 trials. Note that with 65% of positive messages available to position A, 6.5 positive messages will on the average be available in the first interval. In the same way, the resources of B, C, and D are found. As a convention for all tables to follow, rows define the sender position whereas columns define the receiver roles of the same participants.

The numbers of positive messages in the cells of any row add up to the resources available during this interval. The column sums show that applying the equality principle leads to a complete reversal of the distribution of resources: At the start, A is the richest position, and at the end, it is the poorest. The generality of this remarkable result is limited, for example, to the kind of resources used here. These resources cannot be saved to be used for oneself; they have to be given away to be useful, like expertise or love, and unlike, for example, food (Feger, 1987).

TABLE 15.5
Equal Distribution of Sending at the Start

	A	B	C	D	Σ
a	—	2.2	2.2	2.2	6.5
b	1.8	—	1.8	1.8	5.5
c	1.5	1.5	—	1.5	4.5
d	1.2	1.2	1.2	—	3.5
Σ	4.5	4.9	5.2	5.5	

Note. Here, as in all tables to follow, rows indicate senders, and columns indicate receivers.

TABLE 15.6
Sending Distributions at the Second Interval, Proportional Reciprocity

	A	B	C	D	Σ
a	—	2.60	2.15	1.76	6.5
b	2.48	—	1.71	1.32	5.5
c	1.89	1.58	—	1.04	4.5
d	1.40	1.16	0.95	—	3.5
Σ	5.77	5.34	4.81	4.12	

In the second interval, A will (again) send 6.5 positive messages. They will be distributed to B, C, and D, according to the proportion received from these senders in the previous interval. That is, A got 1.8 positive messages from B, 1.5 from C, and 1.2 from D. Thus, A received 40% of all his or her positive messages from B, 33% from C, and 27% from D. Accordingly, in the second interval, A should send 2.6 out of his or her 6.5 positive messages to B, 2.15 to C, and 1.76 to D. Table 15.6 gives the derived sending distributions for the entire group.

Note that the rank order of the amounts in the distribution of positive messages received (column sums) is reversed again in the second interval. It now corresponds in rank order to the original distribution of resources provided by the experimenter. Iterating this procedure from one interval to the next, we find for the seventh interval the distributions reported in Table 15.7. In further iterations, these values are stable within rounding errors (the precision here is two decimals)—that is, the distributions converge. One may note:

1. The distribution of resources provided by the experimenter (row sums) is approached by the final distribution of the resources that were collected during all intervals (column sums). The principle of proportional reciprocity is utterly conservative; it stabilizes the distribution of resources.

2. The differences between the number of positive messages sent and received within any pair of participants converges to zero. There is

TABLE 15.7
Sending Distribution at the Seventh Interval, Proportional Reciprocity

	A	B	C	D	Σ
a	—	2.84	2.11	1.55	6.5
b	2.82	—	1.56	1.12	5.5
c	2.10	1.57	—	0.84	4.5
d	1.58	1.09	0.84	—	3.5
Σ	6.50	5.50	4.51	3.51	

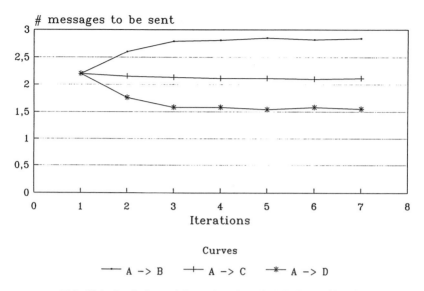

FIG. 15.4. Predictions of the reciprocity principle for position A.

as much giving as there is taking within every pair. The final differences exist between pairs.

Figure 15.4 shows, as derived from the principle of proportional reciprocity, how much A should give to each receiver. The form of the functions is the same for every sender. The range of the numbers to be sent varies, of course, with the differing number of positive messages available to the four positions. Every sender should increase sending (in a negatively accelerated way; see Fig. 15.4) to that position that has the highest resources. The sender should keep his or her sending about equal to the medium resources position, and should (in a negatively accelerated way) diminish sending to the poorest.

Using the same predictions derived from reciprocity, Fig. 15.5 shows for positions A and B how their sending behavior converges. As mentioned before, the differences approach zero in all pairs, whereas the rich aim at a high level and the poor at a low level of exchange.

Cumulative Reciprocity Principle

For the whole course of the experiment, at each particular moment, a participant usually remembers how much he or she received so far from every other person. Furthermore, this information is constantly presented to each participant (see Fig. 15.1). Therefore, reciprocity might not be based only at the time period immediately preceding the instant of sending

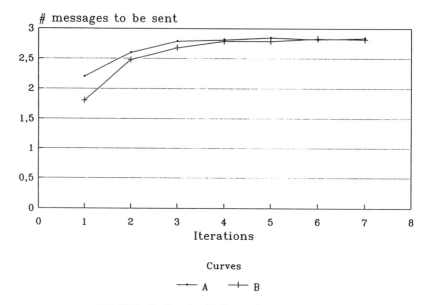

FIG. 15.5. Reciprocity: Exchange between A and B.

but on all positive messages received thus far from every participant. Then a slight modification of the reciprocity definition given earlier in this section is required. $(A \rightarrow B)_n$ and $R_{A(n)}$ (referring to the resources at each sender's disposition in the next interval) remain as defined earlier. $(B \rightarrow A)_1$ is replaced by $(B \rightarrow A)_c$, indicating the cumulative number of positive messages received by A from B during the experiment until the present moment. Thus, the cumulative reciprocity principle corresponds to

$$(A \rightarrow B)_n = R_{A(n)} \frac{(B \rightarrow A)_c}{(B \rightarrow A)_c + (C \rightarrow A)_c + (D \rightarrow A)_c} \tag{2}$$

Theoretical analysis reveals that this principle is equivalent to reciprocity with a fixed interval except for the speed of convergence; with cumulative reciprocity, convergence and the development of differences in behavior toward the various positions are slower. Furthermore, in contrast to reciprocity with a fixed interval, the predicted values change very slowly in later parts of the experiment.

The Debtor Principle

In an exchange relation between persons A and B, either A is debtor and B creditor, or vice versa. We assume that every person tries to be a creditor, or, more generally, person A wants to minimize any negative difference of the type $[(A \rightarrow B) - (B \rightarrow A)]$, with $(A \rightarrow B)$ defined as the number of positive messages sent from A to B (either cumulatively until the time of observation, or in the last interval). Furthermore, we think that A wants to maximize any positive difference of this kind. This is the essence of the debtor principle.

From these assumptions, we derive the general form of the exchange functions. For the first interval, we assume as before that every participant applies equality as his or her distribution principle. Therefore the same result is obtained as reported before in Table 15.5. For the second interval, we calculate for every sender–receiver pair the quotient of the number of positive messages received and the number of positive messages sent, using the values provided by the matrix of the first interval. For A, this leads to:

$$(B \rightarrow A)/(A \rightarrow B) = 1.8/2.2 = 0.82$$
$$(C \rightarrow A)/(A \rightarrow C) = 1.5/2.2 = 0.68$$
$$(D \rightarrow A)/(A \rightarrow D) = 1.2/2.2 = 0.55$$

The larger this quotient, the more pronounced or urgent is the role of the debtor for this sender. Therefore, this sender should send his or her resources (R_A) in proportion to this quotient. Thus, A should send to B:

$$(R_A)0.82/(0.82 + 0.68 + 0.55) = (0.82/2.05)6.5 = 2.6$$

In the same way, we derive for the second interval the matrix given in Table 15.8.

The general form of the debtor principle is:

$$(A \rightarrow B)_2 = R_{A(2)}[a/(a + b + c)] \tag{3}$$

with

$$a = (B \rightarrow A)_1/(A \rightarrow B)_1$$
$$b = (C \rightarrow A)_1/(A \rightarrow C)_1$$
$$c = (D \rightarrow A)_1/(A \rightarrow D)_1$$

TABLE 15.8
Sending Distribution at the Second Interval: Debtor Principle

	A	B	C	D	Σ
a	—	2.60	2.16	1.74	6.5
b	2.46	—	1.68	1.35	5.5
c	1.91	1.56	—	1.04	4.5
d	1.40	1.15	0.96	—	3.5
Σ	5.77	5.31	4.80	4.13	

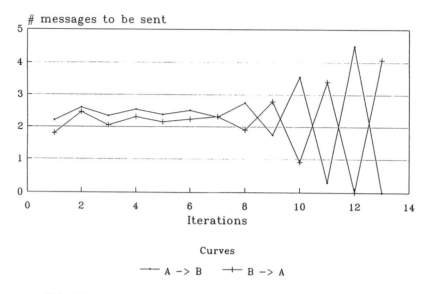

FIG. 15.6. Sending behavior of A to B and B to A as suggested by the debtor principle.

Iterations lead to the curves shown in Fig. 15.6. In this figure, we report the sending behavior of A to B and B to A as derived from the debtor principle. It is representative for most pairs. After some small oscillations in the first six or seven intervals, the oscillations increase dramatically and reach the maxima and minima. That is, the derived advice is to send all resources to one (or two) receivers during the one interval while neglecting the others, but in the next interval to completely reverse this behavior. The debtor principle achieves the stability of an undampened pendulum. This ping-pong game within as well as between the senders leads to large instabilities in the number of positive messages received from one interval to the next.

The Cumulative Debtor Principle

This principle is equivalent with the one for a fixed interval except that the consideration of only one single previous interval is replaced by the total of all previous intervals. The general form is:

$$(A \rightarrow B)_{c+1} = R_{A(c+1)}[a/(a + b + c)] \qquad (4)$$

with $(A \rightarrow B)_{c+1}$ the number of positive messages to be sent from A to B in the next interval, $R_{A(c+1)}$ the number of positive messages available to A in the next interval, and a the ratio of all positive messages received by A from B

TABLE 15.9
Cumulative Debtor Principle, Result of 15th Iteration

	A	B	C	D	Σ
a	—	2.44	2.19	1.87	6.50
b	2.20	—	1.77	1.53	5.50
c	1.74	1.56	—	1.20	4.50
d	1.29	1.17	1.04		3.50
Σ	5.23	5.17	5.00	4.60	20.00

over all intervals until now, to the number of positive messages sent by A to B over all intervals until now; b and c are defined correspondingly.

In the theoretical analysis of this function, we tested 15 iterations (precision: two decimals) and found stable values beginning with the sixth iteration. Although A gains more than B, B more than C, and so on, the differentiation is very slow. For all participants, as Table 15.9 shows, the advice is to send most to A, then to B, C, and least to D. The difference between the number of positive messages sent and received within a pair does not approach zero. In every pair, the member with the higher resources sends more to the other member.

The Mixed Case

Up to this point we have derived two different and contradicting sets of predictions, one from the principle of proportional reciprocity and the other from the debtor principle. If both principles are actually used by participants, then it is likely that within the same group both principles are applied simultaneously. What is the effect? We tested several combinations. In all cases, the general effect of mixing the principles is that oscillations result as in the noncumulative debtor case, perhaps with a slight delay.

TESTING THE RECIPROCITY PRINCIPLE

As stated earlier, the cumulative reciprocity principle can be expressed by Equation 2. When empirically testing this equation, $R_{A(n)}$ (the number of resources available to A during the interval for which the sending behavior of A is predicted) requires some attention. If the interval is assumed to be identical with one trial, $R_{A(n)}$ is either 0 or 1. For 0 the prediction is that A will not send a positive message because none is available. For 1 the value of the quotient in Equation 2 may be interpreted as the probability that the one positive message available will be sent by A to B. Our analysis will be limited to the cases when a positive message is available; otherwise a large number of predicted and observed values equal to 0 is created, inflating any measure of goodness of fit.

To derive the prediction of cumulative reciprocity of the sending behavior of A to B in trial t (written RaB_t), we use the cumulated values (over all previous trials until trial t) of bA_t, written as CbA_t, and so on, to calculate

$$RaB_t = \frac{CbA_t}{CbA_t + CcA_t + CdA_t}$$

Linear regression with RaB_t as predictor and the dichotomous aB_t as criterion (logistic regression did not provide substantially different results) leads to

$$aB_t = 0.18 + 0.52\, Rab_t$$

The results from the regression analysis are:

Source	SS	df	MS
Regression	14.05	2	7.02
Residual	29.49	129	0.23

and $R^2 = .359$. For the corresponding analysis for the fixed-interval case with an interval size of 20 steps, we first determine $IbA_t = CbA_t - CbA_{t-20}$, and so on, and calculate

$$IaB_t = \frac{IbA_t}{IbA_t + IcA_t + IdA_t}$$

as the predictor of the regression analysis with aB_t the criterion as before. The results of this analysis are $aB_t = 0.38 - 0.044\, IaB_t$:

Source	SS	df	MS
Regression	16.66	2	8.33
Residual	29.25	124	0.24

with $R^2 = .364$. Thus, for aB both variants of the reciprocity principle lead to the same result of explaining about 35% of the variability in A's sending behavior toward B. These reciprocity principles take the sending of all participants into account and so consider the merits of one sender relative

TABLE 15.10
Raw Reciprocities (Group I)

aB	.365	bA	.463
aC	.403	cA	.600
aD	.279	dA	.519
bC	.149	cB	.107
bD	.477	dB	.355
cD	.300	dC	.310

to the two other senders. For comparisons, we calculate SBA, the number of positive messages sent from B to A during the last 20 trials, without using any information on the behavior of C or D. SBA is a kind of credit of B with respect to A. We opt for a larger interval here (20 trials) because A might be willing to answer positively but does not have a positive message immediately at hand, or A is unsure to which of two or more creditors he or she should provide a positive message. The regression equation for this "raw" reciprocity is $aB_t = 0.378 - 0.006$ SBA with $R^2 = .365$ and shows the same achievement in prediction as the "relative" reciprocity principles. We calculated the raw reciprocity for all members of this group (see Table 15.10). It explains from 11% to 60% of the sending behavior. We expect a slight correlation of the raw reciprocity values within a pair because reciprocity may be learned.

Although these values of raw reciprocity can be used to evaluate the strength of other interaction principles, Monte Carlo studies could be performed to determine the amount of reciprocity that can be achieved at all, given the conditions of this experiment. With 0 messages present, perfect convergence can not be reached even if all participants would use reciprocity as much as possible.

DISCUSSION

Our replication and theoretical analysis of the Flament and Apfelbaum study motivated us to reconceptualize the process of exchange. (In this chapter, we did not treat the formation of structure within groups; coalition formation is treated by von Hecker, 1991.)

Besides mutuality some other principles seem to be involved, such as a tendency to make sure that contact to none of the partners is completely disrupted. We also recognize repeated attempts—especially by the rich positions that can afford it—to communicate. Partners try this with small bursts of two or three positive messages in immediate succession. Some of our participants spontaneously commented on their purpose for such behavior: to stimulate sending by the receiver of these messages, or to thank that person.

However, we still consider mutuality in one form or another to be the major guiding principle in the exchange process. We had to learn that mutuality can be conceived quite differently, and the consequences for the prediction of behavior are substantial. Let us mention some options available for the measurement of mutuality:

1. If A gives to B, then B should return. Considerations include how much, how soon, what has he or she gained from others, and what has he or she invested into this specific partner, or into all persons in the system? (In our experiment, no qualitative differences exist in the goods exchanged, and thus no equivalence judgements are invoked.)

2. The time perspective is involved in the notion of mutuality in several ways. If B returns immediately, we are very much inclined to attribute this behavior to a mutuality principle. We probably are willing to allow for some delay with this interpretation. However, the longer this delay lasts, the more likely it is that two effects will appear. Either we attribute mutuality to a lesser degree, or something else happens that interferes with our and with the participants' interpretations.

Time is involved in the question of how far forward a participant plans, uses tactics, and how far backward he or she looks for information. The reciprocity as well as the debtor principle could be changed to refer not only to one single previous trial but to the whole cumulative history of the process until the present moment. We assume that the range of consideration into the past and into the future depends on the value of the resources to be exchanged.

Short-term and long time aspects of mutuality may be distinguished. The former need a close inspection of the data, trial by trial, and analysis instruments like the Boolean prediction rules (see Feger, 1994, chap. 8).

We do not use the concept *of trust* in this context. Trust seems to imply and has been operationalized (see Feger, 1979) as offering the opponent an opportunity to inflict harm to oneself. Our design lacks this simultaneous dependency.

3. One should distinguish between mutuality effects in the results, that is, the distribution of the resources at the end of the process, and mutuality as guiding behavior during the process. In both studies, in Aix-en-Provence and Berlin, we find a substantial correlation of the results of the two partners in every pair. But this can be achieved, as the A/D pair demonstrates, in quite different ways. Even within a few trials we may observe A → B, B → A, A → B, B → A; or twice A → B, then twice B → A. Is there more mutuality in the first case; is our everyday conception of mutuality sufficiently precise?

4. Although mutuality is conceived to exist in a social relation between two persons, to study it one has to include at least one third person. In other words, if there are only A and B then neither A nor B has a choice to whom to send. Therefore, some kind of preference must be shown, and this implies a third person.

We are planning several lines to continue our research. First, it seems very desirable to increase the number of messages per subject so that we can observe to which kind of asymptotes, if any, the sending behavior converges. The process should be synchronized by providing the same start and end of a trial to all participants. In another series of experiments, we want to clarify the function of the "0" or "neutral" messages by introducing explicitly negative messages. These messages are planned to reduce the score of positive messages of the receiver, and could speed up the structure-forming processes. To test the generality of our results, we want to increase the number of participants, at least to five, perhaps to even more group members. Because the use of monetary rewards quite often has changed the behavior of persons in similar situations (see several contributions in Criswell, Solomon, & Suppus, 1962, or quite a few experiments in the tradition of prisoner's dilemma games), we want to associate a certain amount of money with every positive message received. We already mentioned that the results might be limited to the kind of resources that are useless if kept to oneself. Therefore, we plan to give to each participant his or her own account into which he or she can pay without risk. So we open for the participant the decision of whether and under which conditions to enter social exchange at all.

To extend our theoretical understanding, the information already available on reaction times will be analyzed. We expect to find shorter reaction times in well established, frequently used exchange relations. Computerized Monte Carlo studies will follow as soon as we have achieved a solid theoretical and empirical basis for them.

SUMMARY

1. Flament and Apfelbaum observed that differences in resource possession lead to group structure in the form of exchange coalitions and hierarchical structure in sociometric choices. We showed that these effects occur even with a uniform distribution of resources. However, knowing the initial distribution of the resources is useful for predicting the final distribution of positive messages received during the experiment.

2. The two tests we performed indicate that participants in the early part of the experiment either react at random or intentionally create a

uniform distribution of the positive messages they send to the other positions. Ordered exchange behavior depends on a certain minimum amount of information about the behavior of the others being available to (almost) all participants.

3. Flament and Apfelbaum analyzed the effects on the aggregated group level. Because of the large interindividual and intergroup differences, we emphazise the analysis of interaction behavior of the individual and of the pair. For this purpose, the major theoretical concept introduced is the distribution principle.

4. We report formal analyses of the reciprocity and the debtor principles. Row reciprocity assumes the return of positive messages to senders without further consideration. Under optimal conditions, it leads within few trials to fixed exchange coalitions. Relative reciprocity uses the information on the amount of positive messages received from the other participants as well. This principle predicts an increasing differentiation between the positions as receivers and no difference in the amount exchanged in the final part of the experiment. The debtor principle further assumes that one's own investments in the other positions should be taken into account. It predicts large oscillations of exchange behavior in later stages of interaction. Our preliminary investigations seem to suggest that the other principles do not explain more of the exchange behavior than raw reciprocity does.

5. The evaluation of our results, and of the results of Flament and Apfelbaum as well, depend on a judgment about how much reciprocity is maximally possible within this experimental design. The existence of "0" messages prevents convergence to fixed exchange coalitions even if every participant would always apply the reciprocity principle.

ACKNOWLEDGMENTS

Thanks are due to an anonymous referee and to the editors for very helpful suggestions.

REFERENCES

Criswell, J. H., Solomon, H., & Suppes, P. (Eds.). (1962). *Mathematical methods in small group processes.* Stanford, CA: Stanford University Press.

Feger, H. (1979). Kooperation und Wettbewerb. In A. Heigl-Evers (Ed.), *Die Psychologie des 20. Jahrhunderts* (Vol. VIII, pp. 290–303). München: Kindler.

Feger, H. (1987). Kommunikationsstrukturen in Kleingruppen. In M. Grewe-Partsch & J. Groebel (Eds.), *Mensch und Medien. Festschrift für Hertha Sturm* (pp. 134–143). München: Saur.

Feger, H. (1994). *Structure analysis for co-occurrence data.* Aachen: Verlag Shaker.

Flament, C., & Apfelbaum, E. (1966). Elementary processes of communication and structuration in a small group. *Journal of Experimental Social Psychology, 2,* 376–386.

von Hecker, U. (1991). *How do exchange relations form? A replication of the Flament and Apfelbaum experiment.* Unpublished manuscript, Department of Psychology, Free University of Berlin.

Chapter 16

Additive Effects of Factors on Reaction Time and Evoked Potentials in Continuous-Flow Models

Richard Schweickert
Jeffrey Mounts
Purdue University

Cognitive scientists often compare the brain with a computer. Early writers (e.g., von Neuman, 1958) emphasized comparisons with both analog and digital computers, but as the use of analog computers declined, so did their role as a metaphor for the mind. Although the biological evidence is congenial to a computer metaphor, it does not exclusively favor digital or analog computing (Miller, 1988). Neurons, for example, produce action potentials to strong stimuli, and graded responses to weak ones, and so appear to have the ability for processing in either mode. Recently, interest in neural networks has led to a renewed interest in analog computing both for computer scientists (Mead, 1989) and psychologists.

It has been easier to use the computer metaphor to guide guesses about human information processing than it has been to find tests of which guesses are correct. Here we continue with a strategy, used by several researchers, of extending methodologies for systems with discrete events to those with continuous flows (McClelland, 1979; Miller, 1988; Schweickert, 1989; Townsend & Ashby, 1983). The issue is part of the larger problem of deciding which kind of computer, if either, is the better metaphor for the mind.

Donders (1868/1969) conceived of mental processing as a series of stages. The first stage began when the stimulus was presented, the second stage began when the first was completed, and so on. Discrete events marked transitions between one stage and another. The time to respond to a stimulus was the sum of the times required to complete the separate stages.

Sternberg (1969) proposed a well-known test for this architecture. If each of two experimental factors selectively influences a different stage, then the combined effect of prolonging the two stages should be the sum of their individual effects. Sternberg's technique, known as the additive factor method, has been widely used (see Luce, 1986, and Townsend & Ashby, 1983, for critiques).

Consider the alternative continuous-flow conception (Eriksen & Schultz, 1977; McClelland, 1979) of a subject pressing a key in response to a stimulus. When the stimulus is presented, signals stream through the neural system of the subject, and activation accrues until the subject's muscle force overcomes the opposing force in the key and a switch is closed, stopping the clock. There are no crucial discrete events except for the stimulus onset and the switch closing. Response time is typically predicted indirectly in continuous-flow models, from the values of a quantity, such as force, changing over time.

ADDITIVE EFFECTS OF FACTORS ON RESPONSE TIMES

Many studies using Sternberg's additive factor method reported additive effects of factors on response times, and these were often implicitly taken to support the existence of stages beginning and ending with discrete events. Later, continuous-flow models in which factors affecting different processes have additive effects on response time were produced (Ashby, 1982; McClelland, 1979; Townsend & Ashby, 1983, pp. 401–409), demonstrating that additive factors do not rule out continuous-flow processing.

Previous examples of continuous-flow models predicting additive effects of factors on response time were constructed to achieve other ends as well. For example, the Townsend and Ashby (1983) linear system model provides for signals persisting in memory. Hence, it is not clear which aspects of the models lead to additivity.

The following continuous-flow model produces additive factors in a simple way. In a *composition-of-functions* system, the activation at a given time t can be written $a(t) = f(g(t))$, where f and g are functions. As an example, the model of Grice, Canham, and Boroughs (1984) is described as a composition-of-function system in Schweickert (1989). The cascade model (Ashby, 1982; McClelland, 1979) is also an example, in that the activation from the last node is a function of time, and the output of this function is the input to a function giving the response-time distribution. (Activation transmitted from node to node in the cascade model does not follow a composition-of-functions model, however.)

Suppose in such a system that the response is made when the activation reaches a criterion c. Further, suppose that one factor changes the function

f, whereas the other factor changes the function g, so that when factor 1 is at level i and factor 2 is at level j, the activation is

$$a_{ij}(t) = f_i(g_j(t))$$

For example, for the activations illustrated in Fig. 16.1

$$g_1(t) = t + 2$$
$$g_2(t) = t$$
$$f_1(x) = 4x$$
$$f_2(x) = 2x$$

Now suppose when the criterion $c = 12$ is reached, the response is completed. Let t_{ij} be the time at which the criterion 12 is reached when the combination of factors is i,j. Then

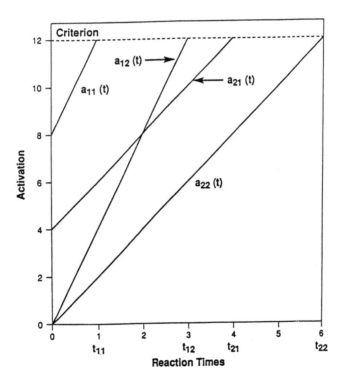

FIG. 16.1. A continuous-flow model with additive effects of factors on response time. Activation increases over time in each condition of a hypothetical 2×2 factorial design, and the response is made when activation reaches the criterion.

$$a_{11}(t_{11}) = 4t_{11} + 8$$
$$a_{12}(t_{12}) = 4t_{12}$$
$$a_{21}(t_{21}) = 2t_{21} + 4$$
$$a_{22}(t_{22}) = 2t_{22}$$

By setting each of the activations to 12, and solving, one finds $t_{11} = 1$, $t_{12} = 3$, $t_{21} = 4$, and $t_{22} = 6$. The factors have additive effects on time, but the time is not divided into separate intervals, so that during each interval one factor alone has an effect.

Additive Factors in Composition-of-Functions Systems

The example just given, as well as others, shows that additive factors can be found with continuous-flow models. Furthermore, it appears that a wide variety of continuous-flow models are capable of producing approximately additive effects of factors (Miller, van der Ham, & Sanders, 1995). The following theorem shows that in composition-of-function models, factors have additive effects on response times only under unusual circumstances— that is, only when for every level j of factor 2, g_j is related to g_1 by a shift, specifically,

$$g_j(t) = g_1(t - t_{1j} + t_{11})$$

The functions do not have to be linear as they were in the earlier example.

Theorem. Suppose f_i and g_j are functions with inverses for $i,j = 1, 2, .$ $. . .$ Suppose when factor 1 is at level i and factor 2 is at level j, the activation at time t is $a_{ij}(t) = f_i(g_j(t))$. Suppose for all combinations of the factor levels i and j, there is a time t at which the activation $a_{ij}(t) = c$. Suppose for any j, if y is in the domain of g_j^{-1} there exist a c and an i such that $f_i^{-1}(c) = y$. Let $t_{ij} = g_j^{-1} f_i^{-1}(c)$ be the response time when factor 1 is at level i and factor 2 is at level j.

Then the factors have additive effects on response time if and only if for every j

$$g_j(t) = g_1(t - t_{1j} + t_{11})$$

for all arguments for which the functions are defined.

Proof. Suppose for all levels i and j,

$$t_{ij} = t_{i1} + t_{1j} - t_{11}$$

Then

$$g_j^{-1}f_i^{-1}(c) = g_1^{-1}f_i^{-1}(c) + t_{1j} - t_{11} \tag{1}$$

For any y in the domain of g_j^{-1} there exist a c and an i such that $f_i^{-1}(c) = y$. Then, from Equation 1, for any y in the domain of g_j^{-1},

$$g_j^{-1}(y) = g_1^{-1}(y) + t_{1j} - t_{11}$$

Now consider any t in the domain of g_j and let $y = g_j(t)$. By the equation just given,

$$g_j^{-1}g_j(t) = g_1^{-1}g_j(t) + t_{1j} - t_{11}$$

and the conclusion follows.

Reversing the argument gives the proof in the other direction.

An equivalent condition follows from Equation 1: For every level j of factor 2, there is a function $h_j(c)$ such that

$$g_j^{-1}f_i^{-1}(c) = g_1^{-1}f_i^{-1}(c) + h_j(c) \tag{2}$$

To see this, for every level j of factor 2, let $h_j(c) = g_j^{-1}f_i^{-1}(c) - g_1^{-1}f_1^{-1}(c) = t_{1j} - t_{11}$.

The conclusion, in brief, is that additive effects of factors on response time are predicted by both discrete-event and continuous-flow models, but additivity is not a general property of continuous-flow models. The linear system predicting additive factors in Townsend and Ashby (1983, p. 407) has a stage-like quality in that the weighting functions become 0 after a time. Roberts and Sternberg (1993, p. 642) conjectured that approximate additivity may occur in the cascade model (Ashby, 1982; McClelland, 1979) when it operates in a stage-like manner, and Miller et al. (1995) noted that reaction times in the cascade model can be approximated by a sum in which each term has a parameter from a different process. The composition-of-functions model just discussed is not stage-like, because there is no point prior to the response at which output from the initial process ceases. However, Equation 2 shows that the outputs must have a special form for additive factors to be predicted. If factors have exactly additive effects on response times, then they can always be represented as selectively influencing discrete serial stages (Dzhafarov & Schweickert, 1995; Schweickert, 1989).

In closing this section, we remark that questions phrased as though the system were exclusively discrete or continuous are oversimplified. Logically, some parts of the system could have discrete-event processing, whereas others have continuous-flow processing (Coles, de Jong, Gehring, & Gratton, 1988). Schweickert, Fisher, and Goldstein (1992) proposed that both processing modes can be represented in precedence networks.

Random Error. For simplicity, we assumed that outputs of processes are represented by real numbers. A generalization to random variables is straightforward, based on Schweickert (1989). Suppose the input to function f includes not only the output of function g, but also noise represented by a random variable N_g, so the output of f is $f[g(t),N_g]$. Likewise, suppose the activation consists of the output of f combined via some function p with yet more noise, this noise represented by a random variable N_f. That is, suppose the activation in condition (i,j) is

$$A_{ij} = p[f_i[g_j(t),N_{gi}],N_{fi}]$$

where the entities with subscripts i or j may change as the corresponding factor levels change.

Although activation is now a random variable, Schweickert (1989) showed that if the functions p and f_i are monotonic in each of their arguments, then there exist new monotonic functions f_i' such that the expected value of A_{ij} can be written.

$$E[A_{ij}] = f_i' g_j(t)$$

Then our results can be reformulated in terms of the expected value of the random variable A_{ij}, because this expected value has the same form as the activation a_{ij} in the earlier equation.

ADDITIVE EFFECTS OF FACTORS ON ACTIVATION

Factorial manipulations may be of more use with continuous-flow models if their effects on activation are considered as well as their effects on response time. The first problem is to define structure in the amorphous continuous flow.

Signal Flowgraphs

Whether or not processes are separated by discrete events, an organizational structure can be constructed from the input–output relations of the processes. This is the basis for a scheme of anatomical divisions of the primate visual system (for a review see Felleman & Van Essen, 1991). From a functional point of view, continuous-flow processing can often be represented in a signal flowgraph (e.g., Robichaud, Boisvert, & Robert, 1962). Consider a subject squeezing a dynamometer with his or her right hand for one response, and with the left for the other. The stimulus, a signal, can be thought of as a quantity varying as a function of time, $s(t)$. The first processes to operate on the signal produce outputs that are functions

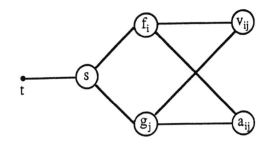

FIG. 16.2. A signal flowgraph. Stimulus *s* varies as a function of time. Each node calculates a function from its input and sends the value to its immediate successors. Subscripts indicate levels for two factors selectively influencing the unordered nodes *f* and *g*. Nodes *v* and *a* are terminal.

of the signal, and perhaps of time as well. Later processes have outputs from certain earlier processes as their inputs, and so on. The measured force, $a(t)$, exerted by a particular hand at time *t* is the output of a terminal function. Figure 16.2 gives an example of a flowgraph. Each node calculates some function of the values input to it from its immediate predecessors. The inputs and outputs may be vectors, although we will consider them as scalars.

Feedback is easily represented in such a system. Note that the only function whose output can be instantaneously fed back as input to itself is the identity. For suppose $y(t)$ is the output of a function h, and is instantly used as one of the inputs of h. Suppose the other inputs of h at time *t* are $x_1(t), \ldots, x_n(t)$. Then

$$y(t) = h(x_1(t), \ldots, x_n(t), y(t))$$

Clearly, h is simply an identity function that associates with every input of its $n + 1$ arguments the value of argument $n + 1$. When there is feedback from a node to itself, we assume it occurs after a temporal delay, unless the node represents an identity function.

Two nodes in a flowgraph without feedback are related in two ways. The output of one may be input to the other, perhaps via intermediate nodes. Then there is a directed path from one to the other, and the arcs are *ordered*. Otherwise, they are called *unordered*.

Suppose *f* and *g* are nodes in the flowgraph, and the function calculated by *f* depends on the level of one experimental factor, whereas that calculated by *g* depends on another. In particular, suppose when the level of the first factor is *i*, the function calculated by the node *f* is f_i, and when the level of the second factor is *j*, the function calculated by the node *g* is g_j. Let $a_{ij}(t)$ be the activation at a terminal node. The activation might be a force or an electrical potential.

Evoked Potentials

An electrode placed on the scalp of a subject will pick up signals by volume conduction from regions in the cortex whose neural geometry is suitable (see, e.g., Coles, Gratton, & Fabiani, 1990). The essential requirement for the geometry is either an open field, that is, a large number of neurons with cell bodies in one part of the region and dendrites aligned roughly in parallel in another part, or the superposition of an open field and another field. With such arrangements, the individual electric fields produced do not cancel at points some distance away (Lorente de No, 1947).

Suppose some regions represented by nodes in the flowgraph have such suitable geometry. If there are several nodes that are generators of electrical potential, the combined potential they produce at an electrode located at a point in space is simply the sum of their separate potentials at that point (e.g., Nunez, 1981). Hence, a linear terminal node in the flowgraph is created at the place where an electrode is placed on the scalp.

The prediction of additivity is straightforward. Suppose several generators contribute to the potential $v(s,t)$ at an electrode located at a site s on the scalp at time t. If the contribution of generator h is denoted $v(h,s,t)$, then

$$v(s,t) = \Sigma v(h,s,t)$$

where the sum is over all contributing generators, h (see, e.g., Mocks, 1988). If there are two experimental factors, one influencing only the contribution due to a generator f and the other influencing only the contribution due to a different generator g, the factors would clearly have additive effects on the potential at every time t. If the voltages in the above equation were random variables, additivity would be predicted for the expected values.

Despite the simplicity of this equation, additive effects of factors on evoked potentials have not been widely sought nor reported. Exceptions include a theoretical paper by Johnson (1993) proposing an additive model for the P300, and a few experiments in the literature, some of which are summarized later. We now discuss some complications that may prevent additive effects from being ubiquitous.

Ordered Versus Unordered Nodes. Suppose two generators f and g are represented as nodes in a flowgraph. Selective influence of the factors seems most likely to hold if the nodes are unordered, so the output of g is not input to f, or vice versa (Fig. 16.2). It is tempting to conclude that additive effects of two factors on potential demonstrate that they selectively influence two unordered nodes. The following counterexample shows this is not the case.

Suppose node g precedes node f, and the output of f at a time t is a function of the output of g at an earlier time $t - \tau$, where the delay τ is the time required to transmit the output from g to f. Suppose the voltage (i.e., the potential) measured at an electrode has contributions from both f and g. For simplicity, suppose the voltage contributed by a node is a constant times the output of the node (cf. Mocks, 1988). When the factor selectively influencing f is at level i and that influencing g is at level j, the combined voltage at time t at the electrode is

$$v_{ij}(t) = ag_j(t) + bf_ig_j(t - \tau_j) + e(t) \tag{3}$$

where a and b are constants and $e(t)$ is the contribution of all the other generators. We suppose the transmission delay τ_j depends on g, but not on f.

If this equation applies, it turns out that in a 2×2 design, the factors will have additive effects on the voltage if there is a constant c such that $f_2(x) = f_1(x) + c$. A comparison with Equation 2 shows this condition to be analogous to the one given there for factors to have additive effects on time.

To see why this condition leads to additivity, note that if the factors have additive effects on the potential v,

$$v_{22}(t) - v_{12}(t) - v_{21}(t) + v_{11}(t) = 0$$

Then

$$f_2g_2(t - \tau_2) = f_1g_2(t - \tau_2) + f_2g_1(t - \tau_1) - f_1g_1(t - \tau_1)$$

If we suppose this equation holds no matter what the value of $g_2(t - \tau_2)$, the condition leading to additivity follows immediately. From the derivation one can see that a necessary and sufficient condition for additivity at time t is a weaker condition in which c depends on time, with $c(t) = f_2g_1(t - \tau_1) - f_1g_1(t - \tau_1)$. The upshot is that factors selectively influencing ordered nodes can indeed have additive effects, but only under special circumstances.

Determining the Order. If Equation 3 holds it is possible in principle, although perhaps not in practice, to determine the order of the two nodes f and g. Suppose at a given electrode site, b has the same value for all levels of both factors, and a is the same for all levels j. Subject to this constraint, the values of a and b may vary from site to site. With a little algebra it can be seen that the ratio

$$\frac{v_{22}(t) - v_{12}(t)}{v_{21}(t) - v_{11}(t)}$$

will be the same at all sites. On the other hand, a similar looking ratio,

$$\frac{v_{22}(t) - v_{21}(t)}{v_{12}(t) - v_{11}(t)}$$

need not be the same for all sites. The difference between the two ratios is in the ordering of the subscripts in certain terms, and this indicates the order in which the nodes f and g occur. In practice, obtaining good statistical estimates of the required ratios would make this procedure difficult to use.

Failures of Additivity. Experimental factors might fail to have additive effects on voltages at electrode sites for two kinds of reasons. The first, of direct interest here, is that the factors do not selectively influence unordered nodes acting simultaneously in time. The second is that nonadditivity may be caused by more subtle electrical effects of one node on another, or on the conducting medium between nodes.

For our purposes, a voltage generator can be approximated as a current dipole. The accuracy of the approximation is not an issue, because an exact expression for the voltage measured at an electrode could always be obtained by adding further terms in a multipole expansion. Our concern is with the form of an individual term in this sum, and the dipole term is a good representative.

A current dipole consists of a current source for a current of I amps and a sink for a current of I amps, with the source and sink separated by a distance d. Consider an electrode at point s located distance r from the midpoint m of the source and sink, so that a straight line from s to m makes an angle θ with the segment joining the source and sink. If r is considerably larger than d, then the voltage produced by the current dipole, measured at point s, is approximately

$$V = Id \cos \theta / 4r^2\pi\sigma \tag{4}$$

where σ is the conductivity (see, e.g., Nunez, 1981, p. 117). There is a term like this for every current dipole entering into the expression for the total voltage at the electrode.

Suppose an experimental factor influences a particular generator, denoted f, by changing the values of parameters in Equation 4 for the term associated with this generator. Suppose another experimental factor influences a different generator, g. What follows is a list of some of the ways the factor influencing generator f might also, in theory, change parameter values in the term associated with generator g. These changes would lead to effects on the voltage produced at the electrode by generator g.

The first consideration is that when the factor changes electrical activity in generator f, it may somehow physically affect synapses in generator g. If such effects are possible, then because dendrites in an open field are aligned, electrical activity in one open field might have a concerted effect on another open field. It is unlikely that the distance r from the generator g to the electrode could be changed significantly, if at all, by activity in generator f. However, a neuron is a fluid-filled bag suspended in another fluid, and as the cell walls are not rigid they may change their location or orientation in space, thus changing (a) the separation d or (b) the orientation θ of the dipole of generator g. (c) The magnitude, I, of the current in generator g might be changed. If such changes were to somehow occur systematically in a large set of neurons, and if they did not cancel each other out, the result of changes in d, θ, or I would be a failure of additivity for the two factors. But if such substantial changes in generator g occur as the level of the factor influencing generator f changes, it seems entirely appropriate to conclude that the generators are ordered in the flowgraph, rather than unordered. Thus even if such effects are possible, they do not seem likely to lead to an erroneous conclusion.

The space between generator g and the electrode is filled with the material of the brain. Theoretically, this material need not follow Ohm's Law (see, e.g., Reitz & Milford, 1960, p. 128) so that the conductivity $\sigma(E)$ may depend on the imposed electric field, E. As this field E depends on the level of the factor influencing generator f, in theory the factor could affect the properties of the medium between the generator g and the electrode, thus leading indirectly to changes in the potential measured at the electrode. However, according to Nunez (1981), "In most physical materials, violations of Ohm's law normally occur only in an environment that would be quite incompatible with living tissue" (p. 65). Practically speaking, then, changes in conductivity are not a serious possibility.

To summarize our discussion of Equation 4 so far, indirect electrical effects do not seem likely to lead to an erroneous interpretation of an interaction. What about indirect effects due to the output of the generators? Generator f sends output information to successor nodes. The potential produced by the successors might depend on this information, which, in turn, might depend on the level of the factor. Generator g might also send output information to these successors. The combined effects of the output information from generators f and g on the potentials produced by the successor nodes may not be additive. Such voltage contributions would be especially damaging if the output of the generators f and g were transmitted almost instantaneously to their immediate successors. This complication is not as easily dismissed as the earlier ones.

Fortunately, not all regions of cortex carrying out processing or transmission of information will produce a potential detectable at the scalp electrode. This loss of the signal from time to time actually produces a benefit for analysis. It implies that when a change in potential is produced at a node, an interval of time may elapse before a successor node produces a consequent change that is detectable at the electrode. An ideal arrangement for finding additive effects of factors on potential would have open fields for the generators selectively influenced by the factors, and closed fields for their immediate successors. This ideal situation may not be necessary to predict additivity, but some assumption about the successor nodes is needed. The following assumption has the advantage of simplicity: If two levels of the factor selectively influencing a node f produce different voltages at an electrode at time t, then there is a time t^* such that for all times t', $t < t' < t^*$, the potentials contributed to the electrode by nodes following f are unaffected by the levels of the factor. These considerations suggest that additive effects of factors on evoked potentials will sometimes be found, but the conditions leading to additivity depend on the input and output arrangements of the nodes.

Applications

In this section we discuss three studies testing additivity. In the first, Hansen and Hillyard (1983) reported a failure of additivity in an examination of auditory selective attention. The event-related potential (ERP) of interest was the N1 component (N1 is a negative deflection in voltage occurring roughly 80–120 msec after the presentation of a tone). A more negative N1 occurs when attention is directed to a tone; the change in magnitude is obtained by subtracting ERPs obtained from unattended stimuli from the ERPs obtained with identical, attended stimuli. This yields the negative difference wave (Nd), also termed the processing negativity, which is believed to be indicative of stimulus processing (Näätänen, 1990).

The stimuli were tone pips created by combining binary values along the dimensions of duration, pitch, and location (defined by interaural intensity). Between subjects, pitch and location values were manipulated to yield different relative discriminabilities. The study tested whether the experimental factors of pitch and location had additive effects. Targets were always defined by a longer duration. In one task, for example, subjects were instructed to count those longer duration tones that were low pitched and presented to the right ear. Nontargets could thus be tones that (a) shared the target's pitch and location, but were of a shorter duration, or (b) shared only the pitch or only the location of the target, or (c) shared neither the pitch nor the location of the target. The presence of the Nd component is assumed to indicate that the tone is being processed as a potential target. Thus, if processing of the tone's pitch and location were independent, with each running to completion, then the ERP contribution associated with each dimension should be additive.

Hansen and Hillyard failed to find additivity on all three of their dependent measures: the voltage amplitude of the negative peak, the mean voltage over 100–700 msec, and the root mean square amplitude over the same interval. Instead, underadditivity was found. They concluded, from these results and others, that the data are consistent with contingent processing of the dimensions of pitch and location; processing proceeds in parallel in both channels until nontarget evidence is found, at which time processing along both channels is terminated.

The second study is by Kounios and Holcomb (1992). The ERP component of interest was a negative deflection that peaks around 400 msec, the N400. This component was described by Kutas and Hillyard (1980), who found that when subjects silently read sentences, some of which ended in a semantically anomalous word, the N400 was more negative in response to the anomalous words. Kounios and Holcomb (1992) displayed sentences such as *No dogs are animals*, and subjects indicated whether the sentences were true or false. To avoid eye movements, the first three words were presented for 550 msec, followed by the predicate word in the same location after a 300-msec delay. Two experimental factors are relevant here:

1. The subject was either related to the predicate, as in the sentence already given, or unrelated, as in *All animals are shirts.*
2. The subject could be the more general word, as in the second example, or the predicate could be the more general word, as in the first example. Sentences in which the subject was more general were labeled *superset*, and the others, *subset*. (These labels are somewhat awkward for the case of unrelated subjects and predicates, which are, in fact, disjoint.)

The measure of N400 magnitude was mean voltage amplitude over the period 300–500 msec. This mean was significantly more negative when the subject and predicate were unrelated, and for superset as opposed to subset sentences. There was no interaction, with the factors demonstrating additive effects throughout the entire waveforms. Kounios and Holcomb explained the additive effects by saying the two factors affect processes that are independent, parallel, and synchronized in some way. (The first two properties predict the additivity. The evidence for synchronization is the presence of an ERP component; unsynchronized activity is generally considered to be too weak to produce prominent effects at the scalp.) In our terminology, we would say the factors selectively influence unordered nodes that operate simultaneously.

Incidentally, the time at which the peak of the N400 occurred was not affected by the two factors. The factors had overadditive effects on response time, and it is not clear how the response-time effects relate to the N400 effects.

In the third study, Holcomb, Kounios, and Andersen (1992; see also Kounios, 1996) used a paradigm similar to that of Kounios and Holcomb described earlier, with sentences presented one word at a time. They examined the P2 component, a positive wave appearing 150 to 300 msec after stimulus presentation. Two factors examined were (a) whether the sentence stem predicted an abstract or concrete final word and (b) whether the final word was actually abstract or concrete. The first factor is based on a property of the context, whereas the second factor is based on a property of the final word in itself. The two factors had additive effects on the P2 amplitude. As in the previous study, the conclusion was that the two factors, concreteness and context, affect independent, parallel, and synchronized processes.

SUMMARY AND CONCLUSIONS

Despite the fact that additive effects of factors on response time are not diagnostic for discrete-event versus continuous-flow processing, when additive effects are found, they tightly constrain the possibilities. If the only fact to be accounted for is the additive effect of factors on reaction time, then the choice between discrete and continuous models can be based on convenience. For most dependent measures other than reaction time, there is little theory about how results of factorial experiments might be used for inferences about cognitive architecture. Evoked potentials are an exception. They are especially promising because voltages due to different generators simply add to produce the net voltage at a point in space.

A Remark on Analog Computation. In the time following Gödel's proof and Turing's work on computational limits, many have speculated that the mind may be capable of computations beyond those possible for a digital computer. One of the latest and most popular proponents of this view is Penrose (1989). Here we simply point out that an analog computer that overcame the problem of errors of measurement in its intermediate results would be more powerful than a digital computer in at least one way: in having an exact representation of real numbers, although the representation might not be symbolic. Machines using real numbers are discussed in Smale (1990). The benefit of using real numbers may not merely be an improvement in the precision of computations, but a dramatic change in what can be computed. Gödel's theorem states that there are undecidable propositions about integers, but the result does not generalize to real numbers (Blum & Smale, 1993; Tarski, 1951). As a consequence, the limitations of analog computers are not necessarily the same as those for digital computers.

It is sometimes overlooked that in quantum mechanics there are situations in which the value of a physical quantity can, in principle, be any positive real number (e.g., Margenau & Murphy, 1950, p. 324). Without being specific about how it is done, many models by cognitive scientists tacitly assume that when percepts are produced, their subjective qualities and quantities are directly related to physical qualities and quantities. If so, it is possible that percepts are sometimes exact representations of real numbers, and analog mental operations on these are computations not possible for a Turing machine.

ACKNOWLEDGMENTS

We thank Bopanna Ballachanda, Michael Coles, Emanuel Donchin, John Kounios, Robert Melara, James T. Townsend, Amy Wohlert, and Noriko Yamagishi for helpful discussions. Any errors of fact or interpretation are the responsibility of the authors. This work was supported by grant 9123865-DBS from the National Science Foundation to the first author.

REFERENCES

Ashby, F. G. (1982). Deriving exact predictions from the cascade model. *Psychological Review, 89,* 599–607.

Blum, L., & Smale, S. (1993). The Gödel incompleteness theorem and decidability over a ring. In M. W. Hirsch, J. E. Marsden, & M. Shub (Eds.), *From topology to computation: Proceedings of the Smalefest* (pp. 321–339). New York: Springer-Verlag.

Coles, M. G. H., Gratton, G., & Fabiani, M. (1990). Event related brain potentials. In J. T. Cacioppo & L. G. Tassinary (Eds.), *Principles of psychophysiology: Physical, social and inferential elements* (pp. 413–455). Cambridge, England: Cambridge University Press.

Coles, M. G. H., de Jong, R., Gehring, W. J., & Gratton, G. (1988, June). Continuous versus discrete information processing: Evidence from movement-related potentials. *Ninth International Conference on Event-Related Potentials of the Brainh (EPIC IX),* Nordwick, the Netherlands.

Donders, F. C. (1969). On the speed of mental processes. Translation by W. G. Koster. In W. G. Koster (Ed.), *Attention and performance II, Acta Psychologica, 30,* 412–431. (Original work published 1868)

Dzhafarov, E. N., & Schweickert, R. (1995). Decomposition of response times: An almost general theory. *Journal of Mathematical Psychology, 39,* 285–314.

Eriksen, C. W., & Schultz, D. W. (1977). Information processing in visual search: A continuous flow conception and experimental results. *Perception & Psychophysics, 25,* 249–263.

Felleman, D. J., & Van Essen, D. C. (1991). Distributed hierarchical processing in the primate cerebral cortex. *Cerebral Cortex, 1,* 1–47.

Grice, G. R., Canham, L., & Boroughs, J. M. (1984). Combination rule for redundant information in reaction time tasks with divided attention. *Perception & Psychophysics, 35,* 451–463.

Hansen, J. C., & Hillyard, S. A. (1983). Selective attention to multidimensional auditory stimuli. *Journal of Experimental Psychology: Human Perception and Performance, 9,* 1–19.

Holcomb, P. J., Kounios, J., & Andersen, J. E. (1992, October). *The N400 reflects differences in the processing of concrete and abstract words in semantically anomalous sentences.* Paper presented at the meeting of the Society for Psychophysiological Research, San Diego.

Johnson, R. (1993). On the neural generators of the P300 component of the event related potential. *Psychophysiology, 30,* 90–97.

Kounios, J. (1996). On the continuity of thought and the representation of knowledge: Behavioral and electrophysiological time-course measures reveal levels of structure in semantic memory. *Psychonomic Bulletin & Review, 3,* 265–286.

Kounios, J., & Holcomb, P. J. (1992). Structure and process in semantic memory: Evidence from event-related brain potentials and reaction times. *Journal of Experimental Psychology: General, 121,* 459–479.

Kutas, M., & Hillyard, S. A. (1980). Reading senseless sentences: Brain potentials reflect semantic incongruity. *Science, 207,* 203–205.

Lorente de No, R. (1947). Action potential of the motoneurons of the hypoglossus nucleus. *Journal of Cellular and Comparative Physiology, 29,* 207–287.

Luce, R. D. (1986). *Response times: Their role in inferring elementary mental organization.* New York: Oxford University Press.

Margenau, H., & Murphy, G. M. (1950). *The mathematics of physics and chemistry.* Toronto: van Nostrand.

McClelland, J. L. (1979). On the time relations of mental processes: An examination of systems of processes in cascade. *Psychological Review, 86,* 287–330.

Mead, C. (1989). *Analog VLSI and neural systems.* Reading, MA: Addison-Wesley.

Miller, J. O. (1988). Discrete and continuous models of human information processing: Theoretical distinctions and empirical results. *Acta Psychologica, 67,* 191–257.

Miller, J. O., van der Ham, F., & Sanders, A. F. (1995). Overlapping stage models and reaction time additivity: Effects of the activation equation. *Acta Psychologica, 90,* 11–28.

Mocks, J. (1988). Decomposing event-related potentials: A new topographic components model. *Biological Psychology, 26,* 199–215.

Näätänen, R. (1990). The role of attention in auditory information as revealed by event-related potentials and other brain measures of cognitive function. *Behavioral and Brain Sciences, 13,* 201–208.

Nunez, P. (1981). *Electrical fields of the brain.* New York: Oxford University Press.

Penrose, R. (1989). *The emperor's new mind: Concerning computers, minds, and the laws of physics.* New York: Penguin.

Reitz, J. R., & Milford, F. J. (1960). *Foundations of electromagnetic theory.* Reading, MA: Addison-Wesley.

Robichaud, L. P. A., Boisvert, M., & Robert, J. (1962). *Signal flow graphs and applications.* Englewood Cliffs, NJ: Prentice-Hall.

Roberts, S., & Sternberg, S. (1993). The meaning of additive reaction time effects: Tests of three alternatives. In D. E. Meyer & S. Kornblum (Eds.), *Attention and performance XIV* (pp. 611–653). Cambridge, MA: MIT Press.

Schweickert, R. (1989). Separable effects of factors on activation functions in discrete and continuous models: d' and evoked potentials. *Psychological Bulletin, 106,* 318–328.

Schweickert, R., Fisher, D. L., & Goldstein, W. (1992). *General latent network theory: Structural and quantitative analysis of networks of cognitive processes* (Tech. Rep. No. 92-1). West Lafayette, IN: Purdue University Mathematical Psychology Program.

Smale, S. (1990). Some remarks on the foundations of numerical analysis. *SIAM Review, 32*, 211–220.

Sternberg, S. (1969). The discovery of processing stages: Extensions of Donders' method. In W. G. Koster (Ed.), *Attention and performance II* (pp. 276–315). Amsterdam: Elsevier-North Holland.

Tarski, A. (1951). *A decision method for elementary algebra and geometry.* San Francisco: University of California Press.

Townsend, J. T., & Ashby, F. G. (1983). *Stochastic modeling of elementary psychological processes.* Cambridge, England: Cambridge University Press.

von Neuman, J. (1958). *The computer and the brain.* New Haven, CT: Yale University Press.

Author Index

Subject Index

A

Accuracy, 255
Activation, 316–324
Additive effect, 311–325
Additive factor method, 312
Analysis of variance, 94, 97
AND–OR-graph, 134,
Assessment of knowledge, 133, 135, 143
Attention, 81, 254
Attitude, 20, 25

B

Back-Propagation Model, 249
Bayes' rule, 233
Beta function, 162
Beta inhibition model, 82–85
Bilinear model, 100, 104–129
    unique recovery, 112–115
Bizarre imagery effect, 196
    empirical example, 213–216
Boolean analysis, 20–30, 173–184,
    191–193
Boolean implication, 21, 177
Boolean minimization, 21, 22
Bourdon test, 87

C

Canonical projection, 175–177
    minimal, 176, 177
Clause, 136, 137
Co-occurrence data, 20, 173
Coefficient of reproducibility, 25, 26
Cohesion, grade of, 24, 27, 29
Color constancy, 99–105, 128, 129
Color discrimination, 53–55

Color space, 53
Communication, 286
Comparison judgment, 48, 49
Compatible vertex ordering, 37
Complex concept, 17–24, 30
Composition-of-functions system,
    312–315
Constant stimuli, method of, 47, 48
Context, 47–51, 62
Continuous flow model, 311–325
Covariance, 231–233

D

Debtor principle, 286, 295, 300–303
    cumulative, 302, 303
Detector, 257
Dichotomization, 23, 27, 30, 183–188,
    190–193
Dichotomization criterion, 186
Dichotomization threshold, 27
Dichromacy, 108, 116, 124
Dimensionality, 18, 19, 28, 29
Discrimination, 48–51
    ellipsoid, 54, 56–61
Distance, 35
    Hausdorff, 43, 44
Distraction, 81, 82
Distribution principle, 287, 289–303

E

Eigenstructure, 119–121
EM algorithm, *see* Expectancy Maximiza-
    tion algorithm
Equilibrium, 84, 85
Error, 18–26, 29
    careless, 159, 165, 167,

335